Annual Cookbook Gives You a Year's Worth of Tasty Recipes—510 in All!

THE BEST RECIPES from *Taste of Home* just kept on coming during 2006. America's #1 food magazine brought you hundreds and hundreds more of the most delicious, family-pleasing recipes…and now they've been conveniently compiled for you here!

This *2007 Taste of Home Annual Recipes* contains every single rave-winning recipe published during the past year, plus 36 "bonus" recipes—510 in all! The collection is brimming with a wide variety of favorite dishes, shared by cooks just like you.

So whether you're fixing supper for your family, serving dinner to a holiday crowd or simply whipping up something for yourself, you'll have plenty of suitable recipes from which to choose. To get you started, take a sneak peek at the winners of our six national recipe contests held last year.

• **Ham It Up.** No bones about it—ham is a natural for any number of occasions, from winter holidays to summer grill-outs. Stuffed Ham with Raisin Sauce (p. 60) took top honors in this hearty recipe contest, while White Cheddar Scalloped Potatoes (p. 46) came in a close second.

• **Marvelous Muffins.** These versatile goodies can be sweet or savory, plain or iced, a breakfast treat or an afternoon snack. From dozens and dozens of entries came first-place winner Berry Cheesecake Muffins (p. 99) and runner-up White Chocolate Macadamia Muffins (p. 96).

• **Ready for Rhubarb.** Things were rosy in our Test Kitchen as the judges sampled cookies, bars, smoothies, chutney and more. In the end, they picked Rhubarb Swirl Cheesecake (p. 142) as the favorite, while Rhubarb Upside-Down Cake (p. 122) was the second-place finisher.

• **Stick to Kabobs.** Want a way to make summer meals extra-special? Kabobs are not only fun and festive, they're delicious, too. Our taste-testing panel was fired up after sampling grand-prize winner Chicken and Asparagus Kabobs (p. 61) and runner-up Spicy Salmon Kabobs (p. 70).

• **Absolutely Apples!** At the core of this recipe contest were bushels of "apeeling" recipes, from classic pies to dessert pizzas. Chunky Apple Cake (p. 133) made the most of this favorite fruit and

received the highest rating…Grilled Apple Tossed Salad (p. 29) was next on the list.

• **Meat Loaf and Meatballs.** Does your mouth water at the mere thought of home-style meat loaf, sliced thick and hot from the oven? You'll want to turn to page 82 to see the grand-prize winner, Taco Meat Loaves. And check out page 41 for the runner-up, Meat Loaf Gyros.

With 510 recipes in this big, colorful cookbook, you won't run out of mouth-watering menu choices any time soon. You're sure to find something special for everyone and every occasion.

SWEET-TART TEMPTATIONS. Rhubarb Swirl Cheesecake (p. 142) won the grand prize and Rhubarb Upside-Down Cake (p. 122) took second place in our national "Ready for Rhubarb" recipe contest.

2007 Taste of Home Annual Recipes

Editor Michelle Bretl
Art Director Emma Acevedo
Executive Editor/Books Heidi Reuter Lloyd
Senior Editor/Books Mark Hagen
Associate Editor Jean Steiner
Layout Designers Kathy Crawford,
Catherine Fletcher, Nancy Novak
Proofreader Linne Bruskewitz
Editorial Assistant Barb Czysz

Taste of Home

Editor Ann Kaiser
Managing Editor Barbara Schuetz
Senior Art Director Sandra L. Ploy
Associate Food Editors
Diane Werner RD, Coleen Martin
Assistant Food Editor Karen Scales
Senior Home Economist Patricia Schmeling
Senior Recipe Editor Sue A. Jurack
Recipe Editors Mary King, Christine Rukavena
Assistant Editor Melissa Phaneuf
Copy Editor S.K. Enk
Editorial Assistant Mary Ann Koebernik
Graphic Art Associate Ellen Lloyd
Test Kitchen Home Economists
Ann Liebergen, Peggy Fleming RD,
Tina Johnson, Marie Parker, Annie Rose,
Wendy Stenman, Amy Welk-Thieding RD;
Contributing: Dot Vartan
Test Kitchen Assistants Rita Krajcir,
Kris Lehman, Sue Megonigle, Megan Taylor
Photographers Rob Hagen (Senior),
Dan Roberts, Jim Wieland
Associate Photographer Lori Foy
Set Stylists Jenny Bradley Vent;
Contributing: Stephanie Marchese, Julie Ferron,
Nancy Seaman, Grace Natoli Sheldon,
Gail Engeldahl; Assistant: Melissa Haberman
Food Stylists Joylyn Trickel (Senior),
Sarah Thompson; Contributing: Diane Armstrong,
Suzanne Breckenridge, Sue Draheim, Mary Franz,
Julie Herzfeldt, Jennifer Janz, Jim Rude;
Assistant: Kate Baumann
Photo Studio Coordinator Suzanne Kern

President Barbara Newton
Senior Vice President, Editor in Chief
Catherine Cassidy
Creative Director Ardyth Cope
Founder Roy Reiman

Taste of Home Books
©2006 Reiman Media Group, Inc.
5400 S. 60th St., Greendale WI 53129

International Standard Book Number: 0-89821-512-9
International Standard Serial Number: 1094-3463

PICTURED AT RIGHT: Clockwise from upper left: Basil Cream Cheese Bruschetta (p. 14), Spicy Barbecued Chicken (p. 75), Peanut Butter Cup Cheesecake (p. 136), Sunrise Slushies (p. 15), Puff Pastry Salmon Bundles (p. 210), Strawberry Spinach Salad (p. 211) and Comforting Broccoli Casserole (p. 210).

Taste of Home 2007 Annual Recipes

PICTURED ON FRONT COVER. Clockwise from upper left: Spiral Ham with Cranberry Glaze (p. 66), Honey-Oat Pan Rolls (p. 224), Grape Broccoli Salad (p. 32) and Cinnamon Apple Cheesecake (p. 144).

PICTURED ON BACK COVER. Sherbet Cream Cake (p. 130).

For additional copies of this book, write *Taste of Home* Books, P.O. Box 908, Greendale WI 53129.

To order by credit card, call toll-free 1-800/344-2560 or visit our Web site at www.reimanpub.com.

Snacks & Beverages

As special party starters or mid-afternoon snacks for the family, these outstanding appetizers and thirst-quenchers will tide everyone over and please their taste buds, too.

BEFORE-DINNER DELIGHTS. Clockwise from upper left: Raspberry Fondue Dip (p. 16), Spicy Shrimp (p. 14), Fried Ham Cubes (p. 12), Rhubarb Cheesecake Smoothies (p. 13) and Ham 'n' Cheese Biscuit Stacks (p. 14).

Spiced Orange Pecans

Prep: 10 min.   **Bake:** 30 min. + cooling

You won't be able to eat just one of these spicy sweet nibblers. They're especially nice to keep on hand during the Christmas season for unexpected company.
—*Ruth Peterson, Jenison, Michigan*

- 2 **egg whites, lightly beaten**
- 3 **tablespoons orange juice**
- 2 **cups pecan halves**
- 1-1/2 **cups confectioners' sugar**
- 2 **tablespoons cornstarch**
- 2 **tablespoons grated orange peel**
- 1 **teaspoon ground cinnamon**
- 3/4 **teaspoon ground cloves**
- 1/4 **teaspoon ground allspice**
- 1/8 **teaspoon salt**

In a large bowl, combine the egg whites and orange juice. Add pecans and toss to coat; drain. In another large bowl, combine the remaining ingredients. Add pecans and toss to coat.

Spread in a single layer in a greased 15-in. x 10-in. x 1-in. baking pan. Bake at 250° for 30-35 minutes or until dry and lightly browned. Cool completely. Store in an airtight container. **Yield:** 5 cups.

Savory Ham Cheesecake

Prep: 35 min.   **Bake:** 1 hour + chilling

My mom was the best cook—everything she made was special. She served this elegant cheesecake as an appetizer on Sunday following a Saturday ham dinner. Now my family loves it, too!   —*Shannon Soper, West Bend, Wisconsin*

- 3 **cups oyster crackers, crushed**
- 1 **cup grated Parmesan cheese**
- 1/3 **cup butter, melted**
FILLING:
- 4 **packages (8 ounces** *each***) cream cheese, softened**
- 4 **eggs, lightly beaten**
- 2 **cups finely chopped fully cooked ham**
- 2 **cups (8 ounces) shredded Swiss cheese**
- 1/3 **cup minced chives**
- 1/4 **cup minced fresh basil**
- 1/4 **teaspoon salt**
- 1/4 **teaspoon white pepper**
Assorted crackers

In a bowl, combine the cracker crumbs, Parmesan cheese and butter. Set aside 1/4 cup for topping. Press remaining crumb mixture onto the bottom and 2 in. up the sides of a greased 9-in. springform pan. Cover and refrigerate for at least 30 minutes.

In a large mixing bowl, beat cream cheese until

Creamy Black Bean Dip

(Pictured above)

Prep: 10 min. + chilling

This appealing Southwestern dip can be prepared well in advance. It goes perfectly with tortilla chips.
—*Ashley Donovan, Glasgow, Kentucky*

☑ **Uses less fat, sugar or salt. Includes Nutrition Facts and Diabetic Exchanges.**

- 2 **packages (8 ounces** *each***) fat-free cream cheese, cubed**
- 1 **can (15 ounces) black beans, rinsed and drained,** *divided*
- 3/4 **cup shredded reduced-fat cheddar cheese**
- 6 **green onions, chopped**
- 1-1/2 **teaspoons ground cumin**
Dash cayenne pepper
TOPPING:
- 1/4 **cup shredded reduced-fat cheddar cheese**
- 2 **tablespoons diced fresh tomato**
- 2 **tablespoons chopped green onion**
Baked tortilla chips

In a food processor, cover and process cream cheese until smooth. Add half of the beans. Cover; pulse until blended. Transfer to a bowl; stir in cheese, onions, cumin, cayenne and remaining beans. Cover; refrigerate 8 hours or overnight.

Just before serving, garnish with the cheese, tomato and onion. Serve with tortilla chips. **Yield:** 3 cups.

Nutrition Facts: 1/4 cup dip equals 95 calories, 3 g fat (2 g saturated fat), 10 mg cholesterol, 335 mg sodium, 8 g carbohydrate, 2 g fiber, 10 g protein. **Diabetic Exchanges:** 1 lean meat, 1/2 starch.

smooth. Add eggs; beat on low speed just until combined (mixture will be thick). Add the ham, Swiss cheese, chives, basil, salt and pepper; beat just until combined. Pour into crust. Sprinkle with reserved crumb mixture.

Place pan on a baking sheet. Bake at 325° for 60-70 minutes or until filling is almost set. Turn oven off. Leave cheesecake in oven with door ajar for 30 minutes. Cool on a wire rack for 10 minutes. Carefully run a knife around edge of pan to loosen; cool 1 hour longer. Refrigerate overnight. Remove sides of pan. Serve chilled or at room temperature with crackers. **Yield:** 24-30 servings.

BLT Dip

Prep/Total Time: 10 min.

This is a quick and easy dip to bring to your next potluck. I serve it with potato chips and always receive lots of compliments. —Cathleen Bushman, Geneva, Illinois

>   1 cup (8 ounces) sour cream
>   1 cup mayonnaise
>   1 cup (4 ounces) shredded cheddar cheese
>   1 cup chopped seeded tomatoes
>   6 bacon strips, cooked and crumbled
>   1 tablespoon chopped green onion, optional
> **Assorted crackers**

In a bowl, combine the sour cream, mayonnaise, cheese, tomatoes and bacon. Refrigerate until serving. Garnish with green onion if desired. Serve with crackers. **Yield:** 3 cups.

Instant Spiced Tea

(Pictured at right)

Prep/Total Time: 10 min.

For a fun holiday hostess gift, pour this festive blend into a decorated 12-ounce jelly jar. The recipe makes enough to fill two jars. —Shirley Heston, Pickerington, Ohio

>   2 cups orange breakfast drink mix
>   1 cup unsweetened instant tea
>   1/3 cup sweetened lemonade drink mix
>   2 tablespoons sugar
>   1 teaspoon ground cinnamon
>   1 teaspoon ground cloves

In a large bowl, combine all of the ingredients. Store in an airtight container.

For one serving: Pour 1 cup boiling water into a mug; stir in 1 tablespoon tea mix until dissolved. **Yield:** 3 cups mix (48 servings).

Roasted Red Pepper Triangles

Prep: 35 min.   **Bake:** 50 min.

Full-flavored meats, cheeses and sweet red peppers top a golden crust in this appetizing recipe. I use marinara sauce for dipping. —Amy Bell, Arlington, Tennessee

>   2 tubes (8 ounces *each*) refrigerated
>   crescent rolls
>   1-1/2 cups finely diced fully cooked ham
>   1 cup (4 ounces) shredded Swiss cheese
>   1 package (3 ounces) sliced pepperoni,
>   chopped
>   8 slices provolone cheese
>   1 jar (12 ounces) roasted sweet red peppers,
>   well drained and cut into thin strips
>   4 eggs
>   1/4 cup grated Parmesan cheese
>   3 teaspoons Italian salad dressing mix

Unroll one tube of crescent dough into a long rectangle; press onto the bottom and 3/4 in. up the sides of a greased 13-in. x 9-in. x 2-in. baking dish. Seal seams and perforations. Top with half of the ham; layer with Swiss cheese, pepperoni, provolone cheese and remaining ham. Top with red peppers.

In a small bowl, whisk the eggs, Parmesan cheese and salad dressing mix; set aside 1/4 cup. Pour remaining egg mixture over peppers. On a lightly floured surface, roll out remaining crescent dough into a 13-in. x 9-in. rectangle; seal seams and perforations. Place over filling; pinch edges to seal. Cover and bake at 350° for 30 minutes. Uncover; brush with reserved egg mixture. Bake 20-25 minutes longer or until crust is golden brown. Cool on a wire rack for 5 minutes. Cut into triangles. Serve warm. **Yield:** 2 dozen.

Ricotta Puffs

(Pictured below)

Prep: 20 min.   **Bake:** 15 min.

Roasted red peppers and ricotta cheese give these pastry puffs delicious flavor, while parsley and oregano add a little spark.   —*Maria Regakis, Somerville, Massachusetts*

- 1 package (17-1/4 ounces) frozen puff pastry, thawed
- 1/2 cup ricotta cheese
- 1/2 cup roasted sweet red peppers, drained and chopped
- 3 tablespoons grated Romano *or* Parmesan cheese, *divided*
- 1 tablespoon minced fresh parsley
- 1 teaspoon dried oregano, crushed
- 1/2 teaspoon pepper
- 1 teaspoon milk

Unfold puff pastry; cut each sheet into nine squares. In a bowl, combine the ricotta, red peppers, 2 tablespoons Romano cheese, parsley, oregano and pepper.

Brush pastry edges with milk; place 2 rounded teaspoons of cheese mixture in the center of each square. Fold edges of pastry over filling, forming a rectangle; seal edges with a fork. Cut slits in pastry; brush with milk. Sprinkle with remaining Romano cheese.

Place on lightly greased baking sheets. Bake at 400° for 15-20 minutes or until golden brown. Remove to a wire rack. Serve warm. Refrigerate leftovers. **Yield:** 1-1/2 dozen.

Shrimp Lover Squares

(Pictured below left)

Prep: 20 min. + chilling

During the holidays, we enjoy having a variety of appetizers as a meal while playing a board game or watching a movie together. This recipe is always on the menu.
—*Ardyce Piehl, Poynette, Wisconsin*

- 1 tube (8 ounces) refrigerated crescent rolls
- 1 package (8 ounces) cream cheese, softened
- 1/4 cup sour cream
- 1/2 teaspoon dill weed
- 1/8 teaspoon salt
- 1/2 cup seafood sauce
- 24 cooked medium shrimp, peeled and deveined
- 1/2 cup chopped green pepper
- 1/3 cup chopped onion
- 1 cup (4 ounces) shredded Monterey Jack cheese

In a greased 13-in. x 9-in. x 2-in. baking dish, unroll the crescent dough into one long rectangle; seal seams and perforations. Bake at 375° for 10-12 minutes or until golden brown. Cool completely on a wire rack.

In a small mixing bowl, beat the cream cheese, sour cream, dill and salt until smooth. Spread over crust. Top with seafood sauce, shrimp, green pepper, onion and cheese. Cover; refrigerate for 1 hour. Cut into squares. **Yield:** 2 dozen.

Cranberry Feta Cheesecake

Prep: 25 min.   **Bake:** 30 min. + chilling

For an elegant appetizer, I turned a cheese spread into a cheesecake by changing the filling with ricotta cheese, cranberry-and-orange sauce and other ingredients.
—*Josephine Piro, Easton, Pennsylvania*

7 crisp sesame breadsticks, crushed (about
   2/3 cup)
3 tablespoons butter, melted
1 cup ricotta cheese
8 ounces crumbled feta cheese
1/2 cup heavy whipping cream
1 tablespoon cornstarch
1 teaspoon prepared horseradish
2 eggs, lightly beaten
1 carton (12 ounces) cranberry-orange sauce
1/2 cup chopped pecans, toasted
1 teaspoon minced fresh thyme
1/2 teaspoon minced fresh rosemary
Assorted crackers

In a bowl, combine the breadstick crumbs and butter. Press onto the bottom and 1 in. up the sides of a greased 9-in. springform pan. Place on a baking sheet. Bake at 350° for 5 minutes. Cool on a wire rack.

In a large mixing bowl, beat the ricotta, feta and cream until smooth. Add the cornstarch and horseradish; mix well. Add eggs; beat on low speed just until combined. Fold in the cranberry-orange sauce, pecans, thyme and rosemary. Spoon into crust. Place pan on a baking sheet.

Bake at 350° for 30-35 minutes or until center is almost set. Cool on a wire rack for 10 minutes. Carefully run a knife around edge of pan to loosen; cool 1 hour longer. Cover and refrigerate overnight. Let cheesecake stand at room temperature 30 minutes before serving. Remove sides of pan. Serve with crackers. **Yield:** 24-30 servings.

Grilled Bacon-Onion Appetizers

Prep: 20 min. + marinating   **Grill:** 10 min.

I'm a father of three girls who loves cooking for the family in my spare time. All of us really like this savory treat.
—Dayton Hulst, Moorhead, Minnesota

2 large sweet onions
12 hickory-smoked bacon strips
1/2 cup packed brown sugar
1/2 cup balsamic vinegar
1/4 cup molasses
2 tablespoons barbecue sauce

Cut each onion into 12 wedges. Cut bacon strips in half widthwise; wrap a piece of bacon around each onion wedge and secure with toothpicks. Place in an ungreased 13-in. x 9-in. x 2-in. dish.

Combine the brown sugar, vinegar, molasses and barbecue sauce; pour 1/2 cup over onions. Cover and refrigerate for 1 hour, turning once. Cover and refrigerate remaining marinade for basting.

Drain and discard marinade. Grill appetizers, covered, over medium heat for 10-15 minutes, turning and basting frequently with reserved marinade. **Yield:** 2 dozen.

Popcorn Jack-o'-Lanterns

(Pictured above)

Prep/Total Time: 30 min.

These pumpkins are always a big hit in the fall. Everyone makes popcorn balls at Christmastime, but it's really fun to make them for other occasions, too. They are so cute!
—Ruth Peterson, Jenison, Michigan

3 quarts popped popcorn
1/4 cup butter, cubed
1 package (10-1/2 ounces) miniature
   marshmallows
1 package (3 ounces) orange gelatin
12 green Dots candies
1 to 2 tablespoons marshmallow creme
Green Fruit by the Foot fruit roll
Black shoestring licorice

Place popcorn in a large bowl. In a large microwave-safe bowl, heat butter and marshmallows on high for 1-1/2 to 2 minutes or until melted; stir in gelatin powder until dissolved. Pour over popcorn and toss to coat.

With lightly buttered hands, quickly shape mixture into twelve 3-in. balls, flattening one side slightly. For stem, insert a green Dot candy at the top of pumpkin, attaching with marshmallow creme. Decorate jack-o'-lantern faces as desired with fruit roll and licorice, attaching with marshmallow creme if necessary. **Yield:** 1 dozen.

Editor's Note: This recipe was tested in a 1,100-watt microwave.

in an airtight container. **Yield:** about 2-1/2 dozen.

Editor's Note: We recommend you test your candy thermometer before each use by bringing water to a boil; thermometer should read 212°. Adjust your recipe temperature up or down based on test. Any remaining caramel mixture may be poured into an 8-in. square pan. Cool to room temperature before cutting into squares and wrapping in waxed paper.

Caramel Pretzel Sticks

(Pictured above)

Prep: 2 hours **Cook:** 35 min.

This treat is always a huge hit at Christmastime parties. People think you spent all day in the kitchen!
—*Mary Brown, Evanston, Wyoming*

- 2 cups sugar
- 1 cup light corn syrup
- 1 cup butter, cubed
- 1 can (14 ounces) sweetened condensed milk
- 1 package (10 ounces) pretzel rods
- 6 to 12 ounces white candy coating
- 6 to 12 ounces milk chocolate candy coating
- 3/4 cup finely chopped walnuts, optional

In a heavy saucepan, combine the sugar, corn syrup and butter. Bring just to a boil over medium heat, stirring constantly. Continue boiling, without stirring, at a moderate-steady rate for 4 minutes. Remove from the heat; stir in milk. Return to the heat. Reduce to medium-low; cook and stir until a candy thermometer reads 245° (firm-ball stage). Keep warm.

Pour 2 cups caramel into a 2-cup glass measuring cup. Quickly dip each pretzel halfway into caramel. Allow excess to drip off. Place on well-buttered baking sheets; let stand until hardened.

In a microwave-safe bowl or measuring cup, melt white candy coating. Dip half of the caramel-coated pretzels into coating. Melt milk chocolate coating; dip remaining pretzels.

Drizzle white-coated pretzels with milk chocolate coating; drizzle milk chocolate-coated pretzels with white coating. Sprinkle with walnuts if desired. Store

Pizza Egg Rolls

Prep: 35 min. + cooling **Cook:** 10 min.

My husband and kids love these nontraditional egg rolls. Their crisp wrappers and flavorful pizza filling make them irresistible. —*Tammy Schill, Omaha, Nebraska*

- 1 pound bulk Italian sausage
- 3/4 cup diced green pepper
- 1 garlic clove, minced
- 1 can (15 ounces) crushed tomatoes
- 1/4 cup tomato paste
- 1/2 teaspoon salt
- 1/2 teaspoon dried oregano
- 1/4 teaspoon sugar
- 1/8 teaspoon dried rosemary, crushed

Dash pepper
- 1 block (8 ounces) part-skim mozzarella cheese, cut into 1/4-inch cubes
- 13 egg roll wrappers
- 1 egg, lightly beaten

Oil for frying

In a large skillet, cook the sausage, green pepper and garlic over medium heat until meat is no longer pink; drain. Stir in the tomatoes, tomato paste and seasonings. Bring to a boil. Reduce heat; cover and simmer for 10 minutes. Uncover and simmer 10 minutes longer. Remove from the heat; cool for 20 minutes. Stir in cheese.

Place 1/3 cup sausage mixture in the center of each egg roll wrapper. Fold bottom corner over filling; fold sides toward center over filling. Brush remaining corner with egg; roll up tightly to seal.

In an electric skillet or a deep-fat fryer, heat 1 in. of oil to 375°. Fry egg rolls in batches for 1-2 minutes on each side or until golden brown. Drain on paper towels. **Yield:** 13 egg rolls.

Cinnamon Mocha Coffee

Prep/Total Time: 20 min.

One snowy day, my neighbor called and invited me over to try a new drink she'd made. It was delicious!
—*Bernice Morris, Marshfield, Missouri*

☑ **Uses less fat, sugar or salt. Includes Nutrition Facts and Diabetic Exchanges.**

1/2 cup ground dark roast coffee
1 tablespoon ground cinnamon
1/4 teaspoon ground nutmeg
5 cups water
1 cup milk
1/3 cup chocolate syrup
1/4 cup packed brown sugar
1 teaspoon vanilla extract
Whipped cream, optional

In a small bowl, combine coffee grounds, cinnamon and nutmeg; pour into a coffee filter of a drip coffeemaker. Add the water; brew according to the manufacturer's directions.

In a large saucepan, combine the milk, chocolate syrup and brown sugar. Cook over low heat until sugar is dissolved, stirring occasionally. Stir in the vanilla and brewed coffee. Ladle into mugs; garnish with whipped cream if desired. **Yield:** 6 servings.

Nutrition Facts: 1 cup (prepared with fat-free milk, sugar-free chocolate syrup and 2 tablespoons Splenda brown sugar blend; calculated without whipped cream) equals 95 calories, trace fat (trace saturated fat), 1 mg cholesterol, 43 mg sodium, 21 g carbohydrate, 1 g fiber, 3 g protein. **Diabetic Exchanges:** 1 starch, 1/2 fruit.

Broiled Buttery Shrimp

Prep/Total Time: 30 min.

These zippy appetizers are always popular on a party buffet table, and they're so easy to prepare. I simply toss the shrimp with a flavored butter mixture, then broil. A little hot pepper sauce gives them a bit of a kick, but you could leave out that ingredient if you prefer.
—Nancy Jernigan, Laurel, Mississippi

1 cup butter, melted
1/2 cup lemon juice
1 tablespoon Worcestershire sauce
1 tablespoon steak sauce
1 teaspoon salt
1/2 teaspoon dried thyme
1/2 teaspoon pepper
1/4 teaspoon hot pepper sauce
1 pound uncooked large shrimp, peeled and deveined

In a large bowl, combine the first eight ingredients; add shrimp and toss to coat. Arrange shrimp in a single layer in a greased 15-in. x 10-in. x 1-in. baking pan. Broil 4-6 in. from the heat for 6-8 minutes or until shrimp turn pink, turning once. **Yield:** 10-12 servings.

Cinnamon Chocolate Nachos

(Pictured below)

Prep: 20 min. **Bake:** 15 min.

This is an unusually "sweet" way to serve nachos. It's the perfect variation for my family and friends who have a sweet tooth. The buttery crisps disappear fast, so be sure to have plenty on hand.   —Kathy Kittell, Lenexa, Kansas

6 flour tortillas (8 inches)
7 tablespoons butter, melted, *divided*
6 tablespoons sugar, *divided*
1/2 teaspoon ground cinnamon
1/2 cup heavy whipping cream
1/3 cup packed brown sugar
1 square (1 ounce) unsweetened chocolate, chopped
1/2 teaspoon vanilla extract
1/2 cup chopped pecans

Brush both sides of tortillas with 4 tablespoons butter. Combine 2 tablespoons sugar and cinnamon; sprinkle over one side of each tortilla. Stack tortillas, sugared side up; cut into 12 wedges. Arrange in a single layer on baking sheets. Bake at 350° for 12-14 minutes or until crisp.

Meanwhile, in a heavy saucepan, combine the cream, brown sugar and remaining butter and sugar. Bring to a boil over medium heat, stirring constantly. Cook and stir for 5 minutes or until slightly thickened. Remove from the heat; stir in chocolate and vanilla. Cool slightly.

Arrange half of the tortilla wedges on a large serving platter. Drizzle with half of the chocolate sauce; sprinkle with half of the pecans. Repeat layers. **Yield:** 12 servings.

Curried Crab Pizza

Prep/Total Time: 30 min.

I've been making this appealing appetizer pizza for years, and it still goes over big at our family get-togethers and potlucks. —Ann Stanton, Treasure Island, Florida

        3/4 cup mayonnaise
          2 teaspoons curry powder
          1 prebaked Italian bread shell crust
            (10 ounces)
          2 cans (6 ounces *each*) lump crabmeat,
            drained
        3/4 cup shredded part-skim mozzarella cheese
        3/4 cup shredded cheddar cheese

In a small bowl, combine the mayonnaise and curry. Spread over crust. Sprinkle with crab and cheeses. Place on a pizza pan or baking sheet. Bake at 350° for 20-25 minutes or until cheese is melted. **Yield:** 8-10 slices.

Nutty Chicken Strips

(Pictured above)

Prep/Total Time: 25 min.

I enjoy cooking for my parents and two brothers, and I usually prepare things that are a little out of the ordinary. These strips, seasoned with curry, are great for a family game night. —Betsy Baertlein, Mazeppa, Minnesota

          1 cup soft bread crumbs
        1/2 cup chopped almonds
          2 tablespoons minced fresh cilantro
      1-1/2 teaspoons curry powder
        1/4 cup all-purpose flour
          1 egg
        1/2 cup milk
      1-1/2 pounds boneless skinless chicken
            breasts, cut into 1-inch strips
        1/4 cup vegetable oil
    YOGURT DIPPING SAUCE:
          1 cup (8 ounces) plain yogurt
          2 tablespoons minced fresh cilantro
          1 tablespoon honey

In a large resealable plastic bag, combine the bread crumbs, almonds, cilantro and curry powder. Place flour in a shallow bowl. In another shallow bowl, beat the egg and milk. Dip the chicken strips in flour, then in the egg mixture. Place the chicken strips in the bag and shake to coat.

In a large skillet, cook chicken in oil for 10-12 minutes or until juices run clear, turning once. Drain on paper towels. In a small bowl, combine the sauce ingredients. Serve with chicken. **Yield:** 6 servings.

Fried Ham Cubes

(Pictured on page 4)

Prep/Total Time: 30 min.

Sometimes I serve these popular snacks with a creamy ranch dip instead of the homemade cheese sauce that the recipe calls for. People are usually surprised at how easy they are to make. —Robin Lott, Avon, New York

          2 eggs
          1 tablespoon milk
      1-1/2 cups dry bread crumbs
        1/2 cup grated Parmesan cheese
          1 tablespoon dried parsley flakes
      1-1/2 pounds boneless fully cooked ham, cut
            into 1-inch cubes
    Oil for frying
    CHEESE DIPPING SAUCE:
          5 ounces process cheese (Velveeta), cubed
        1/4 cup milk
        1/2 cup salsa

In a shallow bowl, beat eggs and milk. In another bowl, combine the bread crumbs, Parmesan cheese and parsley. Dip ham cubes in egg mixture, then roll in crumb mixture.

In an electric skillet, heat 1/4 in. of oil to 375°. Fry ham cubes, a few at a time, for 2 minutes on each side or until golden brown. Drain on paper towels.

In a small saucepan, heat cheese and milk over medium heat for 3-4 minutes or until cheese is melted. Remove from the heat; stir in salsa. Serve with ham cubes. **Yield:** about 3 dozen.

Rhubarb Cheesecake Smoothies

(Pictured on page 4)

Prep: 20 min. + cooling

Cream cheese adds an extra-special touch to this sweet concoction. —*Kathy Specht, Cambria, California*

> 2 **cups diced fresh *or* frozen rhubarb**
> 1/4 **cup water**
> 4 **tablespoons honey, *divided***
> 1-1/2 **cups vanilla ice cream**
> 1 **cup milk**
> 1 **cup frozen sweetened sliced strawberries**
> 2 **packages (3 ounces *each*) cream cheese, cubed**
> 1/2 **cup vanilla yogurt**
> 1/4 **cup confectioners' sugar**
> 5 **ice cubes**

In a large saucepan, bring the rhubarb, water and 2 tablespoons honey to a boil. Reduce heat; cover and simmer for 5-10 minutes or until rhubarb is tender. Remove from the heat; cool to room temperature.

In a blender, combine the ice cream, milk, rhubarb mixture, strawberries, cream cheese, yogurt, confectioners' sugar, ice cubes and remaining honey; cover and process for 1 minute or until smooth. Pour into chilled glasses; serve immediately. **Yield:** 6 servings.

Squash Appetizer Cups

Prep: 35 min. **Bake:** 20 min.

These cheesy bites go fast! If I'm in a hurry, I bake the mixture in a greased 9-in. x 13-in. pan and cut the appetizer into squares. —*Lori Bowes, Waterford, Michigan*

> 1-1/2 **cups shredded zucchini**
> 1-1/2 **cups shredded yellow summer squash**
> 1/2 **cup diced onion**
> 1/4 **cup shredded Parmesan cheese**
> 1/4 **cup shredded Colby cheese**
> 2 **tablespoons minced fresh parsley**
> 1-1/2 **teaspoons minced fresh marjoram *or***
> 1/2 **teaspoon dried marjoram**
> 1 **garlic clove, minced**
> 1 **cup biscuit/baking mix**
> 1/2 **teaspoon seasoned salt**
> **Dash pepper**
> 4 **eggs, lightly beaten**
> 1/2 **cup vegetable oil**

In a large skillet, saute the zucchini and yellow squash over medium heat until reduced to about 1-1/2 cups, about 10 minutes. Transfer to a small bowl. Add the onion, cheeses, parsley, marjoram and garlic.

In a large bowl, combine the biscuit mix, seasoned salt and pepper. Stir in eggs and oil just until combined. Fold in squash mixture.

Fill greased miniature muffin cups three-fourths full. Bake at 350° for 20-25 minutes or until golden brown and a toothpick comes out clean. Cool for 5 minutes before removing from pans to wire racks. Serve warm. Refrigerate leftovers. **Yield:** about 3 dozen.

Striped Chocolate Popcorn

(Pictured below)

Prep: 15 min. + standing

I'd seen chocolate popcorn in a store and thought I'd duplicate that treat in my kitchen. This was the yummy result. —*Mary Schmittinger, Colgate, Wisconsin*

> 12 **cups popped popcorn**
> 2 **cups miniature pretzels**
> 1 **cup pecan halves, toasted**
> 1/4 **cup butter, melted**
> 4 **ounces white candy coating, coarsely chopped**
> 2 **ounces milk chocolate candy coating, coarsely chopped**

In a large bowl, combine the popcorn, pretzels and pecans. Drizzle with butter and toss. Place white candy coating in a microwave-safe bowl. Microwave, uncovered, at 50% power for 2-3 minutes or until melted. Drizzle over popcorn mixture; toss to coat. Spread on foil-lined baking sheets.

In another microwave-safe bowl, heat milk chocolate coating, uncovered, at 50% power for 1-2 minutes. Drizzle over popcorn mixture. Let stand in a cool place until chocolate is set. Store in an airtight container. **Yield:** 17 cups.

Editor's Note: This recipe was tested in a 1,100-watt microwave.

Spicy Shrimp

(Pictured on page 4)

Prep/Total Time: 30 min.

I think this shrimp recipe is unique, and it's really easy to prepare. I like to serve it with corn bread pudding.
—Bob Gebhardt, Wausau, Wisconsin

- 6 bacon strips, diced
- 1 cup butter, cubed
- 2 garlic cloves, minced
- 2 tablespoons seafood seasoning
- 2 tablespoons Dijon mustard
- 1-1/2 teaspoons chili powder
- 1 teaspoon pepper
- 1/2 to 1 teaspoon Louisiana-style hot sauce
- 1/4 teaspoon *each* dried basil, oregano and thyme
- 1-1/2 pounds uncooked shell-on medium shrimp

In a large skillet, cook bacon over medium heat until partially cooked but not crisp; drain. Stir in the butter, garlic, seafood seasoning, mustard, chili powder, pepper, hot sauce, basil, oregano and thyme. Cook over low heat for 5 minutes.

Place the shrimp in an ungreased 13-in. x 9-in. x 2-in. baking dish. Add sauce and stir to coat. Bake, uncovered, at 375° for 20-25 minutes or until shrimp turn pink, stirring twice. **Yield:** 6 servings.

Basil Cream Cheese Bruschetta

(Pictured below)

Prep/Total Time: 20 min.

Instead of olive oil, these savory treats are spread with reduced-fat cream cheese, then topped with tomato, onion and olives. —Michelle Wentz, Ft. Polk, Louisiana

✓ Uses less fat, sugar or salt. Includes Nutrition Facts and Diabetic Exchanges.

- 12 slices French bread (1/2 inch thick)
- 1/2 cup chopped seeded tomato
- 2 tablespoons chopped green onion
- 1 tablespoon chopped ripe olives
- 4 ounces reduced-fat cream cheese
- 1 tablespoon minced fresh basil

Place bread on an ungreased baking sheet. Broil 6-8 in. from the heat for 3-4 minutes or until golden brown. Meanwhile, in a small bowl, combine the tomato, onion and olives; set aside.

Combine cream cheese and basil; spread over the untoasted side of bread. Broil 3 minutes longer or until cheese is melted and edges are golden brown. Top with tomato mixture. Serve warm. **Yield:** 1 dozen.

Nutrition Facts: 1 slice equals 81 calories, 3 g fat (2 g saturated fat), 7 mg cholesterol, 164 mg sodium, 11 g carbohydrate, 1 g fiber, 3 g protein. **Diabetic Exchange:** 1 starch.

Ham 'n' Cheese Biscuit Stacks

(Pictured on page 4)

Prep: 1 hour   **Bake:** 10 min. + cooling

I make these finger sandwiches for holidays and Super Bowl parties, too. —Kelly Williams, La Porte, Indiana

- 2 tubes (12 ounces *each*) refrigerated buttermilk biscuits
- 3/4 cup stone-ground mustard, *divided*
- 1/2 cup butter, softened
- 1/4 cup chopped green onions
- 1/4 cup mayonnaise
- 1/4 cup honey
- 10 thick slices deli ham
- 10 slices Swiss cheese
- 2-1/2 cups shredded romaine
- 40 frilled toothpicks
- 20 pitted ripe olives, drained and patted dry
- 20 pimiento-stuffed olives, drained and patted dry

Cut each biscuit in half, forming half circles. Place 2 in. apart on ungreased baking sheets. Spread each with 1/2 teaspoon mustard. Bake at 400° for 8-10 minutes or until golden brown. Remove from pans to wire racks to cool.

In a small bowl, combine the butter and onions. In another bowl, combine the mayonnaise, honey and remaining mustard. Cut each slice of ham into four rectangles; cut each slice of cheese into four triangles.

Split each biscuit in half; spread bottom halves with butter mixture. Layer one ham piece, one cheese piece and 1 tablespoon romaine on each biscuit bottom. Spread mustard mixture over biscuit tops; place over romaine. Thread toothpicks through olives; insert into stacks. Refrigerate leftovers. **Yield:** 40 appetizers.

Lemon Cream-Stuffed Grapes

Prep: 35 min. + chilling

This is a refreshing snack on a hot summer day. It's simple, plus it offers an alternative to heartier party foods.
—Janis Plourde, Smooth Rock Falls, Ontario

    4 **ounces cream cheese, softened**
    3 **tablespoons confectioners' sugar**
1-1/2 **teaspoons lemon juice**
  1/2 **teaspoon grated lemon peel**
    1 **pound seedless globe grapes, rinsed and**
      patted dry

In a small mixing bowl, beat cream cheese, confectioners' sugar, lemon juice and lemon peel until blended. Cover and refrigerate for 1 hour.

Cut a deep X in the top of each grape to within 1/4 in. of bottom. Carefully spread each grape apart. Transfer cream cheese mixture to a heavy-duty resealable plastic bag; cut a small hole in a corner of bag. Pipe filling into grapes. Refrigerate until serving. **Yield:** 3 dozen.

99 mg sodium, 21 g carbohydrate, 1 g fiber, 1 g protein. **Diabetic Exchanges:** 1/2 fruit, 1/2 fat.

Orange Dip for Fruit

Prep/Total Time: 10 min.

This light and creamy dip is delightful with fruit, and it can also be used as a fluffy, low-calorie frosting.
—Kim Marie Van Rheenan, Mendota, Illinois

✓ **Uses less fat, sugar or salt. Includes Nutrition Facts and Diabetic Exchanges.**

  1 **cup orange juice**
  1 **package (3.4 ounces) instant vanilla**
    pudding mix
  1 **cup (8 ounces) sour cream**
  1 **carton (8 ounces) frozen whipped topping,**
    thawed
Assorted fresh fruit

In a large bowl, whisk orange juice and pudding mix. Whisk in sour cream. Fold in whipped topping. Transfer to a serving bowl; serve with fruit. Refrigerate leftovers. **Yield:** 4-1/2 cups.

Nutrition Facts: 1/4 cup (prepared with sugar-free pudding, reduced-fat sour cream and reduced-fat whipped topping; calculated without fruit) equals 118 calories, 3 g fat (3 g saturated fat), 5 mg cholesterol,

Sunrise Slushies

(Pictured above)

Prep/Total Time: 10 min.

I came up with this yummy breakfast beverage full of fruity goodness, and my teenage daughters love it.
—Linda Evancoe-Coble, Leola, Pennsylvania

✓ **Uses less fat, sugar or salt. Includes Nutrition Facts and Diabetic Exchanges.**

  2 **cups orange juice**
  1 **cup reduced-calorie cranberry juice**
  1 **medium tart apple, coarsely chopped**
1/2 **cup cubed peeled mango**
  2 **kiwifruit, peeled, sliced and quartered**
  2 **cups halved fresh strawberries**
  8 **to 10 ice cubes**

In a blender, place half of each ingredient; cover and process until smooth. Pour into chilled glasses. Repeat with remaining ingredients. Serve immediately. **Yield:** 8 servings.

Nutrition Facts: 1 cup equals 73 calories, trace fat (trace saturated fat), 0 cholesterol, 2 mg sodium, 18 g carbohydrate, 2 g fiber, 1 g protein. **Diabetic Exchange:** 1 fruit.

Raspberry Fondue Dip

(Pictured on page 4)

Prep/Total Time: 25 min.

It's a breeze to delight my guests with this fun, unusual fondue. —Edna Hoffman, Hebron, Indiana

1 package (10 ounces) frozen sweetened raspberries
1 cup apple butter
1 tablespoon red-hot candies
2 teaspoons cornstarch
Assorted fresh fruit

Place raspberries in a bowl; set aside to thaw. Strain raspberries, reserving 1 tablespoon juice; discard seeds.

In a small saucepan, combine strained berries, apple butter and red-hots; cook over medium heat until candies are dissolved, stirring occasionally. In a small bowl, combine cornstarch and reserved juice until smooth; stir into berry mixture. Bring to a boil; cook and stir over medium heat for 1-2 minutes or until thickened.

Transfer to a serving dish, fondue pot or 1-1/2-qt. slow cooker. Serve warm or cold with fruit. **Yield:** 1 cup.

Bacon-Wrapped Cajun Jalapenos

Prep: 20 min.   **Bake:** 25 min.

These peppers are so addictive that if I want any for myself, I need to either make a double batch or hide some. The jalapenos are not that spicy after they are baked (I take out the seeds and white membrane), but have a wonderful flavor. —Linda Foreman, Locust Grove, Oklahoma

8 large jalapeno peppers
1 package (3 ounces) cream cheese, softened
1/2 cup finely shredded cheddar cheese
1 teaspoon Cajun seasoning
8 thick-sliced peppered bacon strips

Cut jalapenos in half lengthwise; remove seeds and center membrane. In a small mixing bowl, combine the cream cheese, cheddar cheese and Cajun seasoning. Stuff about 1-1/2 teaspoonfuls into each pepper half.

Cut bacon strips in half widthwise. In a large skillet, cook bacon until partially cooked. Wrap a bacon piece around each pepper; secure with a toothpick.

Place on a wire rack in a shallow baking pan. Bake, uncovered, at 350° for 25-30 minutes or until bacon is crisp. Discard toothpicks. Serve immediately. **Yield:** 16 appetizers.

Editor's Note: When cutting or seeding hot peppers, use rubber or plastic gloves to protect your hands. Avoid touching your face.

Garlic Garbanzo Bean Spread

(Pictured at right)

Prep/Total Time: 10 min.

You can't go wrong with this 10-minute dip. Friends and family always ask me for it, and I'm happy to oblige. —Lisa Moore, Clay, New York

✓ **Uses less fat, sugar or salt. Includes Nutrition Facts and Diabetic Exchanges.**

1 can (15 ounces) garbanzo beans *or* chickpeas, rinsed and drained
1/2 cup olive oil
2 tablespoons minced fresh parsley
1 tablespoon lemon juice
1 green onion, cut into three pieces
1 to 2 garlic cloves, peeled
1/4 teaspoon salt
Assorted fresh vegetables and baked pita chips

In a food processor or blender, combine the first seven ingredients; cover and process until blended. Transfer to a bowl. Refrigerate until serving. Serve with vegetables and pita chips. **Yield:** 1-1/2 cups.

Nutrition Facts: 2 tablespoons equals 114 calories, 10 g fat (1 g saturated fat), 0 cholesterol, 96 mg sodium, 6 g carbohydrate, 1 g fiber, 1 g protein. **Diabetic Exchanges:** 1-1/2 fat, 1/2 starch.

Phyllo Crab Cups

(Pictured above right)

Prep: 15 min.   **Bake:** 20 min.

These delicious appetizers taste scrumptious in their phyllo tart shells. Horseradish sauce and paprika add a nice kick. —Cheryl Spiropoulos, Hales Corners, Wisconsin

1 package (8 ounces) cream cheese, softened
2 to 3 tablespoons horseradish sauce
3/4 cup chopped imitation crabmeat
1 tablespoon chopped green onion
2 packages (2.1 ounces *each*) frozen miniature phyllo tart shells
Paprika

In a small mixing bowl, beat the cream cheese and horseradish until smooth. Stir in the crab and onion. Spoon 2-3 teaspoonfuls into each phyllo tart shell; sprinkle with paprika. Place on a baking sheet. Bake at 350° for 16-18 minutes or until the tops begin to brown. **Yield:** 2-1/2 dozen.

GET YOUR PARTY STARTED with an appetizer table featuring irresistible Garlic Garbanzo Bean Spread, Phyllo Crab Cups and Olive Veggie Pizza (shown above).

Olive Veggie Pizza

(Pictured above)

Prep: 15 min. + rising **Bake:** 20 min.

My husband is in the Navy, and I often feed some of his fellow officers. I have to make several of these pizzas to satisfy them! —Becky Fore, El Cajon, California

- 1 loaf (1 pound) frozen bread dough, thawed
- 1 tablespoon olive oil
- 1 teaspoon garlic salt
- 3 tablespoons blue cheese *or* ranch salad dressing
- 2 cups (8 ounces) shredded part-skim mozzarella cheese
- 1 cup (4 ounces) shredded Colby-Monterey Jack cheese
- 4 ounces provolone cheese, shredded
- 3 medium tomatoes, thinly sliced
- 1 medium green pepper, thinly sliced into rings
- 1 small onion, thinly sliced and separated into rings
- 1 can (2-1/4 ounces) sliced ripe olives, drained
- 15 pimiento-stuffed olives, sliced
- 1 can (4 ounces) mushroom stems and pieces, drained
- 1 teaspoon salt
- 1/2 teaspoon dried basil
- 1/2 teaspoon dried oregano
- 1/2 teaspoon pepper
- 1/2 cup grated Parmesan cheese

On a lightly floured surface, roll dough into a 16-in. x 11-in. rectangle. Transfer to a greased 15-in. x 10-in. x 1-in. baking pan. Build up edges slightly. Cover and let rise for 30 minutes.

Brush oil over dough; sprinkle with garlic salt. Spread with a thin layer of salad dressing. Combine the shredded cheeses; sprinkle over dressing. Layer with tomatoes, green pepper, onion, olives and mushrooms. Sprinkle with salt, basil, oregano, pepper and Parmesan cheese.

Bake at 425° for 20-25 minutes or until crust is golden brown and cheese is melted. Cut into squares. **Yield:** 24 slices.

Asparagus Cheese Triangles

(Pictured below)

Prep: 30 min. **Bake:** 40 min.

I came up with this takeoff on Greek spanakopita (spinach pie) when I had an overabundance of asparagus. Sometimes I add leftover chopped chicken and cut larger triangles for meals. —Colette Gerow, Raytown, Missouri

> 8 cups water
> 2 pounds fresh asparagus, trimmed and chopped
> 2 cups (8 ounces) shredded part-skim mozzarella cheese
> 1 cup (8 ounces) ricotta cheese
> 1 small onion, chopped
> 1/2 teaspoon garlic powder
> 1/4 teaspoon salt
> 1/8 teaspoon pepper
> 9 tablespoons butter, melted
> 30 sheets phyllo dough (18 inches x 14 inches)

In a large saucepan, bring water to a boil; add asparagus. Cover and cook for 4-6 minutes or until crisp-tender. Drain and immediately rinse with cold water; drain and pat dry. In a large bowl, combine the asparagus, cheeses, onion, garlic powder, salt and pepper.

Brush a 15-in. x 10-in. x 1-in. baking pan with some of the butter. Unroll phyllo sheets; trim to 15 in. x 10 in. Cover dough with plastic wrap and a damp cloth while assembling. Place two sheets of phyllo in pan; brush with butter. Repeat eight times. Spread with asparagus mixture. Layer with remaining phyllo sheets, brushing each with butter.

Bake at 350° for 40-45 minutes or until golden brown. Cool on a wire rack for 5 minutes. Cut into 2-1/2-in. squares; cut each square in half diagonally. Serve warm. Refrigerate leftovers. **Yield:** 4 dozen.

Honey-Mustard Chicken Wings

Prep: 20 min. **Bake:** 1 hour

Mustard adds excellent flavor to the sticky sauce for these wings. They're a sure hit with company and family alike—great for a gathering to watch a football game or other event on TV. —Susan Seymour, Valatie, New York

> 4 pounds whole chicken wings
> 1/2 cup spicy brown mustard
> 1/2 cup honey
> 1/4 cup butter, cubed
> 2 tablespoons lemon juice
> 1/4 teaspoon ground turmeric

Line two 15-in. x 10-in. x 1-in. baking pans with foil; grease the foil. Cut chicken wings into three sections; discard wing tips. Place wings in prepared pans.

In a small saucepan, combine the mustard, honey, butter, lemon juice and turmeric. Bring to a boil. Pour over chicken wings; turn to coat. Bake at 400° for 1 to 1-1/4 hours or until chicken juices run clear and glaze is set, turning once. **Yield:** about 3 dozen.

Meatballs in Plum Sauce

Prep: 1 hour **Bake:** 30 min.

A tasty sauce made of plum jam and chili sauce coats these moist meatballs beautifully. Make sure these delightful appetizers are on your holiday menus. —Mary Poninski, Whittington, Illinois

> 1/2 cup milk
> 1 cup soft bread crumbs
> 1 egg, lightly beaten
> 1 tablespoon Worcestershire sauce
> 1 medium onion, finely chopped
> 1/4 teaspoon salt
> 1/4 teaspoon pepper
> 1/8 teaspoon ground cloves
> 1/2 pound lean ground beef
> 1/2 pound ground pork
> 1/2 pound ground veal
> 2 tablespoons vegetable oil
> 1/2 teaspoon beef bouillon granules
> 1/2 cup boiling water
> 3 tablespoons all-purpose flour
> 1 cup plum jam
> 1/2 cup chili sauce

In a large bowl, pour milk over bread crumbs; let stand for 10 minutes. Add the egg, Worcestershire sauce, onion, salt, pepper and cloves. Crumble beef, pork and veal over mixture; mix well (mixture will be soft). Shape into 1-in. balls.

In a large skillet, brown meatballs in oil in batches. Drain on paper towels. Place in a greased 13-in. x 9-in. x 2-in. baking dish.

In a small bowl, dissolve bouillon in water. Stir flour into pan drippings until blended; add bouillon mixture, jam and chili sauce. Bring to a boil; cook and stir for 1-2 minutes or until thickened. Pour over meatballs. Cover and bake at 350° for 30-45 minutes or until meat is no longer pink and sauce is bubbly. **Yield:** 10-12 servings.

Mustard Pretzel Dip

Prep: 10 min. + chilling

This flavorful dip is addictive, so be careful! It's also delicious served with pita chips, crackers and fresh veggies.
—*Iola Egle, Bella Vista, Arkansas*

- 1 cup (8 ounces) sour cream
- 1 cup mayonnaise
- 1 cup prepared mustard
- 1/2 cup sugar
- 1/4 cup dried minced onion
- 1 envelope ranch salad dressing mix
- 1 tablespoon prepared horseradish
- Sourdough pretzel nuggets

In a bowl, combine the first seven ingredients. Cover and refrigerate for at least 30 minutes. Serve with pretzels. Refrigerate leftovers. **Yield:** 3-1/2 cups.

Effortless Eggnog

Prep/Total Time: 5 min.

This wonderful holiday beverage brings back memories of the old-fashioned eggnog my mother used to make.
—*Paula Zsiray, Logan, Utah*

- 1/2 gallon cold milk, *divided*
- 1 package (3.4 ounces) instant French vanilla pudding mix
- 1/4 cup sugar
- 2 teaspoons vanilla extract
- 1/2 teaspoon ground cinnamon
- 1/2 teaspoon ground nutmeg

In a large bowl, whisk 3/4 cup milk and pudding mix until smooth. Whisk in the sugar, vanilla, cinnamon and nutmeg. Stir in the remaining milk. Refrigerate until serving. **Yield:** 16 servings (2 quarts).

Imagination Punch

(Pictured above)
Prep: 35 min. + freezing

Floating ice-cube "faces" in this fun punch stimulate the curiosity of folks at our Independence Day gatherings.
—*Kathy Kittell, Lenexa, Kansas*

ICE CUBES:
- 18 disposable plastic cups (3 ounces)
- 18 maraschino cherries
- 36 fresh blueberries
- 1-1/2 cups cold distilled water, *divided*

PUNCH:
- 2 packages (3 ounces *each*) berry blue gelatin
- 2 cups boiling water
- 4 cups cold water
- 2 cups unsweetened pineapple juice
- 1 can (12 ounces) frozen lemonade concentrate, thawed
- 2 liters ginger ale, chilled

Place plastic cups in muffin pans. From each cherry, cut out a mouth shape; pat dry. Place one cherry mouth and two blueberries for eyes in the bottom of each cup. Pour 1 teaspoon distilled water into each cup. Freeze for 30 minutes or until solid.

Pour 1 tablespoon distilled water into each cup. Return to freezer; freeze for 3 hours or until solid.

For punch, in a large bowl, dissolve gelatin in boiling water. Stir in cold water, pineapple juice and lemonade concentrate. Refrigerate for 1-1/2 hours or until chilled.

Just before serving, transfer to a 5-qt. punch bowl. Stir in ginger ale. Remove ice cubes from cups; place face side up in punch bowl. **Yield:** 18 servings (about 1 gallon).

Fresh Peach Mango Salsa

(Pictured above)

Prep/Total Time: 20 min.

This colorful, freshly made salsa tastes wonderful on fish tacos. The garlic and veggies nicely complement the peach and mango flavors. —Marina Castle-Henry
Burbank, California

✓ **Uses less fat, sugar or salt. Includes Nutrition Facts and Diabetic Exchanges.**

1-1/2 cups chopped fresh tomatoes
   3/4 cup chopped peeled fresh peaches
   1/2 cup chopped red onion
   1/2 cup chopped sweet yellow pepper
   1/2 cup chopped peeled mango
     2 tablespoons chopped seeded jalapeno pepper
     3 garlic cloves, minced
1-1/2 teaspoons lime juice
   1/2 teaspoon minced fresh cilantro
Tortilla chips

In a large bowl, combine the first nine ingredients. Cover and refrigerate until serving. Serve with tortilla chips. **Yield:** 4 cups.

Nutrition Facts: 1/4 cup (calculated without chips) equals 14 calories, trace fat (trace saturated fat), 0 cholesterol, 2 mg sodium, 3 g carbohydrate, 1 g fiber, trace protein. **Diabetic Exchange:** Free food.

Editor's Note: When cutting or seeding hot peppers, use rubber or plastic gloves to protect your hands. Avoid touching your face.

Red Pepper Green Bean Roll-Ups

Prep: 45 min. + marinating

Here's a pleasing appetizer that's a yummy way to eat green beans. Plus, the roll-ups can be prepared ahead of time. —Marie Rizzio, Traverse City, Michigan

✓ **Uses less fat, sugar or salt. Includes Nutrition Facts and Diabetic Exchanges.**

   1/2 pound fresh green beans, trimmed
   1/2 cup Italian salad dressing
    15 slices white bread
   1/4 cup mayonnaise
     2 tablespoons spicy brown mustard
     1 jar (7-1/4 ounces) roasted sweet red peppers, well drained
   1/3 cup butter, melted
   1/2 cup packed minced fresh parsley

Place green beans in a large saucepan and cover with water. Bring to a boil; cook, uncovered, for 6-8 minutes or until crisp-tender. Drain and rinse in cold water. Pat dry with paper towels.

Place the beans in a large resealable plastic bag; add the salad dressing. Seal the bag and toss to coat; refrigerate overnight.

Trim crusts from bread. With a rolling pin, flatten each slice slightly. Combine mayonnaise and mustard; spread about 1 teaspoon on each slice of bread.

Cut roasted peppers into 1/2-in. slices. Drain and discard marinade from beans. Place three green beans and two pepper slices on each slice of bread.

Roll up each from a long side and secure with a toothpick. Brush with butter; roll in parsley. Cover and refrigerate until serving. Just before serving, discard the toothpicks and cut each roll into three pieces. **Yield:** 45 appetizers.

Nutrition Facts: 3 appetizers (prepared with fat-free Italian dressing, fat-free mayonnaise and reduced-fat butter) equals 104 calories, 3 g fat (2 g saturated fat), 8 mg cholesterol, 384 mg sodium, 16 g carbohydrate, 1 g fiber, 3 g protein. **Diabetic Exchanges:** 1 starch, 1/2 fat.

Crab 'n' Brie Strudel Slices

Prep: 45 min.   **Bake:** 20 min.

Mouth-watering Brie, succulent crab and a hint of pears make this delicate pastry a favorite. —Jennifer Pfaff
Indianapolis, Indiana

   1/2 pound fresh crabmeat
     6 ounces Brie *or* Camembert cheese, rind removed and cut into 1/4-inch cubes
2-1/2 cups finely chopped peeled ripe pears
   1/2 cup thinly sliced green onions

1/2 cup diced fully cooked ham
2 teaspoons lemon juice
1 garlic clove, minced
Dash pepper
14 sheets phyllo dough (14 inches x 9 inches)
3/4 cup butter, melted

In a large bowl, combine the first eight ingredients; set aside.

Place a piece of plastic wrap larger than a sheet of phyllo on a work surface. Place one phyllo sheet on plastic wrap; brush with butter. (Keep remaining phyllo covered until ready to use.) Repeat six times. Spread half of crab filling to within 1 in. of edges. Fold the two short sides over filling. Using the plastic wrap to lift one long side, roll up jelly-roll style.

Transfer to a greased 15-in. x 10-in. x 1-in. baking pan; discard plastic wrap. Brush top with butter; score top lightly at 1-in. intervals. Repeat with remaining phyllo, butter and filling.

Bake at 375° for 20-25 minutes or until golden brown. Let stand for 5 minutes. Cut into slices along scored lines. **Yield:** 2 dozen.

Prosciutto Chicken Kabobs

Prep: 30 min. + marinating   **Grill:** 10 min.

Everyone will think you spent hours preparing these clever grilled wraps, served with a guacamole-like dip.
—*Elaine Sweet, Dallas, Texas*

3/4 cup five-cheese Italian salad dressing
1/4 cup lime juice
2 teaspoons white Worcestershire sauce for chicken
1/2 pound boneless skinless chicken breasts, cut into 3-inch x 1/2-inch strips
12 thin slices prosciutto
24 fresh basil leaves
AVOCADO DIP:
2 medium ripe avocados, peeled
1/4 cup minced fresh cilantro
2 green onions, chopped
2 tablespoons lime juice
2 tablespoons mayonnaise
1-1/2 teaspoons prepared horseradish
1 garlic clove, minced
1/4 teaspoon salt

In a large resealable plastic bag, combine the salad dressing, lime juice and Worcestershire sauce; add chicken. Seal bag and turn to coat; refrigerate for 1 hour.

Drain and discard marinade. Fold prosciutto slices in half; top each with two basil leaves and a chicken strip. Roll up jelly-roll style, starting with a short side. Thread onto metal or soaked wooden skewers. Grill,

covered, over medium heat for 5 minutes on each side or until chicken juices run clear.

Meanwhile, in a small bowl, mash avocados. Stir in cilantro, onions, lime juice, mayonnaise, horseradish, garlic and salt. Serve with kabobs. **Yield:** 12 appetizers.

Herbed Leek Tart

(Pictured below)

Prep: 25 min. **Bake:** 20 min. + cooling

I love serving this savory, nontraditional tart. It's different yet delicious.   —*Jean Ecos, Hartland, Wisconsin*

3 cups thinly sliced leeks (about 4 medium)
1/2 cup chopped sweet red pepper
4 garlic cloves, minced
2 tablespoons olive oil
1-1/2 cups (6 ounces) shredded Swiss cheese
2 tablespoons Dijon mustard
1 teaspoon herbes de Provence
1 package (15 ounces) refrigerated pie pastry
1 teaspoon milk
2 tablespoons chopped almonds *or* walnuts, optional

In a large skillet, saute the leeks, red pepper and garlic in oil until tender. Remove from the heat; cool for 5 minutes. Stir in cheese, mustard and herbs; set aside.

On a lightly floured surface, roll each sheet of pastry into a 12-in. circle. Transfer to parchment paper-lined baking sheets. Spoon leek mixture over pastry to within 2 in. of edges. Fold edges of pastry over filling, leaving center uncovered. Brush folded pastry with milk; sprinkle with nuts if desired.

Bake at 375° for 20-25 minutes or until crust is golden and filling is bubbly. Using parchment paper, slide tarts onto wire racks. Cool for 10 minutes before cutting. Serve warm. Refrigerate leftovers. **Yield:** 2 tarts (8 servings each).

Salads & Dressings

Just the right mix of ingredients is the secret to sensational side and main-dish salads. These fresh selections are ripe for the picking.

IT'S A TOSS-UP. Clockwise from upper left: Honey-Mustard Potato Salad (p. 26), Strawberry Vinaigrette (p. 30), Garlic Anchovy Salad Dressing (p. 33), Grilled Apple Tossed Salad (p. 29), Chicken Broccoli Toss (p. 24) and Spiral Pasta Salad (p. 24).

Hawaiian Ham Salad

(Pictured above)

Prep: 15 min. + chilling

Sometimes I substitute celery for the water chestnuts in this fruity medley. —*Vickie Lowrey, Fallon, Nevada*

   1 **can (8 ounces) unsweetened pineapple chunks**
   3 **cups cooked brown rice**
   2 **cups cubed fully cooked ham**
   1 **can (8 ounces) sliced water chestnuts, drained and halved**
1/4 **cup finely chopped red onion**
1/2 **cup plain yogurt**
1/2 **teaspoon salt**
   1 **medium apple, chopped**
Lettuce leaves
1/3 **cup chopped macadamia nuts, toasted**
1/4 **cup flaked coconut, toasted**

Drain pineapple, reserving 1 tablespoon of juice. In a large bowl, combine pineapple, rice, ham, water chestnuts and onion. Cover; refrigerate for at least 2 hours.

In a small bowl, combine the yogurt, salt and reserved pineapple juice. Pour over ham mixture and toss to coat. Stir in apple. Serve on lettuce-lined plates; sprinkle with macadamia nuts and coconut. **Yield:** 4 servings.

Spiral Pasta Salad

(Pictured on page 22)

Prep/Total Time: 25 min.

I cook with homegrown herbs, and marjoram is the star here. —*Sue Gronholz, Beaver Dam, Wisconsin*

✓ **Uses less fat, sugar or salt. Includes Nutrition Facts and Diabetic Exchanges.**

   1 **package (12 ounces) spiral pasta**
   3 **plum tomatoes, seeded and chopped**
   1 **medium green pepper, chopped**
   1 **small onion, thinly sliced**
   1 **can (2-1/4 ounces) sliced ripe olives, drained**
MARJORAM VINAIGRETTE:
   3 **tablespoons white wine vinegar**
   2 **tablespoons honey**
   1 **tablespoon minced fresh marjoram *or***
   1 **teaspoon dried marjoram**
1-1/2 **teaspoons minced fresh basil *or***
   1/2 **teaspoon dried basil**
   1 **teaspoon Dijon mustard**
3/4 **teaspoon salt**
1/8 **teaspoon pepper**
1/2 **cup olive oil**

Cook pasta according to package directions; drain and rinse in cold water. In a large bowl, combine the pasta, tomatoes, green pepper, onion and olives.

In a small bowl, combine the vinegar, honey, marjoram, basil, mustard, salt and pepper. Gradually whisk in oil. Pour over pasta mixture and toss to coat. Cover and refrigerate until serving. **Yield:** 12 servings.

Nutrition Facts: 1 cup equals 212 calories, 10 g fat (1 g saturated fat), 0 cholesterol, 208 mg sodium, 27 g carbohydrate, 1 g fiber, 4 g protein. **Diabetic Exchanges:** 2 fat, 1-1/2 starch.

Chicken Broccoli Toss

(Pictured on page 22)

Prep/Total Time: 20 min.

This fruit, veggie and chicken salad is a favorite of my family. The golden raisins make it a little different. —*Marie Hattrup, The Dalles, Oregon*

✓ **Uses less fat, sugar or salt. Includes Nutrition Facts and Diabetic Exchanges.**

   4 **cups fresh broccoli florets**
   3 **cups torn romaine**
   2 **cups sliced cooked chicken breast**
   1 **medium apple, chopped**
1/2 **cup fat-free Italian salad dressing**
1/4 **cup pecan halves, toasted**
   2 **tablespoons golden raisins**

Place broccoli in a steamer basket; place in a large saucepan over 1 in. of water. Bring to a boil; cover and steam for 5-8 minutes or until crisp-tender. Drain and rinse in cold water; pat dry with paper towels.

Divide romaine among four salad plates. In a bowl, combine the chicken, apple and broccoli; drizzle with dressing and toss to coat. Spoon onto romaine. Sprinkle with pecans and raisins. **Yield:** 4 servings.

Nutrition Facts: 1-1/2 cups equals 248 calories, 9 g fat (2 g saturated fat), 60 mg cholesterol, 507 mg sodium, 18 g carbohydrate, 5 g fiber, 26 g protein. **Diabetic Exchanges:** 3 lean meat, 1 vegetable, 1 fruit.

Special Spinach Salad

Prep/Total Time: 15 min.

With dried cranberries and crunchy walnuts, this spinach salad is perfect at Christmastime. The creamy homemade dressing adds just the right finishing touch.
—Laurene Hunsicker, Canton, Pennsylvania

      1/3 **cup olive oil**
        3 **tablespoons sugar**
        2 **tablespoons white wine vinegar**
        2 **tablespoons sour cream**
      1/2 **teaspoon ground mustard**
        1 **package (6 ounces) fresh baby spinach**
      1/2 **cup chopped walnuts, toasted**
      1/2 **cup dried cranberries**

In a jar with a tight-fitting lid, combine the oil, sugar, vinegar, sour cream and mustard; shake well. Divide spinach among four salad plates; drizzle with dressing. Sprinkle with walnuts and cranberries. **Yield:** 4 servings.

Asparagus Tomato Salad

(Pictured below right)
Prep/Total Time: 15 min.

This colorful, light salad was a hit at our church's cooking club. ———*Dorothy Buhr, Ogden, Illinois*

✓ **Uses less fat, sugar or salt. Includes Nutrition Facts and Diabetic Exchanges.**

        1 **pound fresh asparagus, trimmed and cut into 1-inch pieces**
        1 **small zucchini, halved and cut into 1/4-inch slices**
        1 **cup grape *or* cherry tomatoes**
      1/4 **cup sliced green onions**
      1/4 **cup minced fresh parsley**
        3 **tablespoons olive oil**
        2 **tablespoons red wine vinegar**
        1 **garlic clove, minced**
      1/4 **teaspoon seasoned salt**
      1/4 **teaspoon Dijon mustard**
      1/4 **cup shredded Parmesan cheese, optional**
        2 **tablespoons sunflower kernels, toasted, optional**

Place the asparagus and zucchini in a steamer basket; place in a saucepan over 1 in. of water. Bring to a boil; cover and steam for 2 minutes. Rinse in cold water.

In a large bowl, combine the asparagus, zucchini, tomatoes, onions and parsley. In a small bowl, whisk the oil, vinegar, garlic, seasoned salt and mustard. Pour over asparagus mixture and toss to coat. Sprinkle with Parmesan cheese and sunflower kernels if desired. **Yield:** 6 servings.

Nutrition Facts: 3/4 cup (calculated without Parmesan cheese and sunflower kernels) equals 81 calories, 7 g fat (1 g saturated fat), 0 cholesterol, 78 mg sodium, 4 g carbohydrate, 1 g fiber, 2 g protein. **Diabetic Exchanges:** 1 vegetable, 1 fat.

Creamy Grape Salad

Prep/Total Time: 25 min.

I've been bringing this refreshing salad to potlucks recently, and everyone raves about it. A sprinkle of brown sugar and chopped pecans makes a special accent.
—Marge Elling, Jenison, Michigan

        1 **package (8 ounces) cream cheese, softened**
        1 **cup (8 ounces) sour cream**
      1/3 **cup sugar**
        2 **teaspoons vanilla extract**
        2 **pounds seedless green grapes**
        2 **pounds seedless red grapes**
        3 **tablespoons brown sugar**
        3 **tablespoons chopped pecans**

In a large mixing bowl, beat the cream cheese, sour cream, sugar and vanilla until blended. Add grapes and toss to coat. Transfer to a serving bowl. Cover and refrigerate until serving. Sprinkle with brown sugar and pecans just before serving. **Yield:** 21-24 servings.

Shrimp Pasta Salad

(Pictured below)

Prep: 20 min. + chilling

I adore shrimp, so to have it sneak into a pasta salad is a real treat for me. The combination of lemon-dill sauce over chilled pasta is a refreshing taste in the hot summer.
—*Traci Wynne, Bear, Delaware*

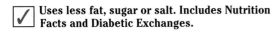 **Uses less fat, sugar or salt. Includes Nutrition Facts and Diabetic Exchanges.**

- 4 cups cooked small pasta shells
- 1 pound cooked large shrimp, peeled, deveined and cut into thirds
- 1 cup frozen peas
- 1/2 cup chopped green onions
- 1/4 cup minced fresh parsley
- 1 cup (8 ounces) plain yogurt
- 1 cup mayonnaise
- 1/4 cup lemon juice
- 2 tablespoons snipped fresh dill
- 1/2 teaspoon salt
- 1/4 teaspoon white pepper

In a large bowl, combine the pasta, shrimp, peas, onions and parsley. In a small bowl, combine the yogurt, mayonnaise, lemon juice, dill, salt and pepper. Pour over pasta mixture and toss gently. Cover and refrigerate for at least 2 hours before serving. **Yield:** 10 servings.

Nutrition Facts: 3/4 cup (prepared with reduced-fat yogurt and fat-free mayonnaise) equals 158 calories, 2 g fat (1 g saturated fat), 92 mg cholesterol, 447 mg sodium, 21 g carbohydrate, 2 g fiber, 14 g protein. **Diabetic Exchanges:** 1-1/2 starch, 1 very lean meat.

Greek Seafood Salad

Prep: 25 min. + chilling

This mix of ingredients never fails to elicit wows. It's great accompanied by a fresh baguette for a picnic.
—*Maryalice Wood, Langley, British Columbia*

- 2 medium cucumbers, peeled, seeded and coarsely chopped
- 1 large tomato, coarsely chopped
- 1 large onion, coarsely chopped
- 1 large green pepper, coarsely chopped
- 1 large sweet yellow pepper, coarsely chopped
- 8 ounces frozen cooked small shrimp, thawed
- 1 can (6 ounces) pitted ripe olives, drained and sliced
- 1/2 cup cubed part-skim mozzarella cheese
- 2 cans (6 ounces *each*) chunk tuna, drained

DRESSING:
- 1/4 cup white vinegar
- 1/4 cup crumbled feta cheese
- 2 tablespoons minced fresh parsley
- 2 tablespoons minced fresh oregano
- 1 garlic clove, minced
- 1/4 teaspoon salt
- 1/4 teaspoon pepper
- 1/2 cup olive oil

In a large bowl, combine the first eight ingredients. Gently stir in the tuna. In a small bowl, combine the vinegar, feta cheese, parsley, oregano, garlic, salt and pepper. Whisk in the oil. Pour over salad; do not toss. Cover and refrigerate for at least 1 hour. Toss just before serving. **Yield:** 10 servings.

Honey-Mustard Potato Salad

(Pictured on page 22)

Prep: 30 min. + chilling

Whenever there is a potluck or cookout, I'm asked to bring this potato salad. It's tangy and a little different.
—*Alicia Quadrozzi, Escondido, California*

- 5 pounds red potatoes
- 2 cups chopped celery
- 1 cup chopped sweet red pepper
- 4 hard-cooked eggs, chopped
- 2 green onions, chopped

1/2 cup mayonnaise
1/2 cup honey mustard
1/2 cup prepared mustard
1/4 cup sour cream
3/4 teaspoon salt
1/4 teaspoon pepper

Place potatoes in a saucepan and cover with water. Bring to a boil. Reduce heat; cover and cook for 15-20 minutes or until tender. Drain and cool.

Cut potatoes into quarters; place in a large bowl. Add the celery, red pepper, hard-cooked eggs and onions. In a small bowl, combine the remaining ingredients. Pour over potato mixture and toss to coat. Cover and refrigerate for at least 1 hour. **Yield:** 16 servings.

Glazed Fruit Medley

Prep: 20 min. + chilling

The orange dressing on this salad complements the fresh fruit flavors beautifully. I like it at a spring or summer brunch. —*Karen Bourne, Magrath, Alberta*

1 cup sugar
2 tablespoons cornstarch
2 cups orange juice
3 cups cubed honeydew
3 medium firm bananas, sliced
2 cups green grapes
2 cups halved fresh strawberries

For glaze, in a small saucepan, combine the sugar, cornstarch and orange juice until smooth. Bring to a boil; cook and stir for 2 minutes or until thickened. Transfer to a bowl. Cover and chill for 2 hours.

In a large serving bowl, combine the honeydew, bananas, grapes and strawberries. Add glaze and gently toss to coat. **Yield:** 10 servings.

Traditional Greek Salad

(Pictured above right)

Prep/Total Time: 20 min.

This tart and crispy salad goes well with a variety of entrees, from casseroles and meats to pasta and pizza. —*Valerie Belley, St. Louis, Missouri*

☑ Uses less fat, sugar or salt. Includes Nutrition Facts and Diabetic Exchanges.

1 medium head iceberg lettuce, torn
2 medium cucumbers, sliced
3 small tomatoes, cut into wedges
2 cans (2-1/4 ounces *each*) sliced ripe olives, drained
2 green onions, chopped
2 packages (4 ounces *each*) crumbled feta cheese
DRESSING:
1/4 cup olive oil
3 tablespoons red wine vinegar
1 teaspoon dried oregano
1/2 teaspoon salt
1/8 teaspoon pepper

In a large salad bowl, combine the lettuce, cucumbers, tomatoes, olives, onions and feta cheese. In a small bowl, whisk the dressing ingredients. Drizzle over salad and toss to coat. **Yield:** 12 servings.

Nutrition Facts: 3/4 cup equals 119 calories, 9 g fat (3 g saturated fat), 10 mg cholesterol, 380 mg sodium, 5 g carbohydrate, 3 g fiber, 5 g protein. **Diabetic Exchanges:** 1-1/2 fat, 1 vegetable.

♪ *Aromatic Oregano*

If you are familiar with the taste and aroma of oregano, you might be surprised to know that this pungent, peppery herb enjoyed in many types of dishes is a member of the mint family. It's also closely related to marjoram, which is milder and sweeter than oregano.

You can purchase oregano fresh in bunches or dried. When shopping for fresh oregano, make sure the leaves are not wilted. To keep them fresh, put the stems in a glass of water, and they should last a week.

As with other herbs, store the dried version of oregano in an airtight container in a cool, dark place away from humidity.

In a small skillet, saute the green pepper, onion, carrot and garlic in oil until crisp-tender. Add to rice. Stir in the corn, beans, tomatoes, peanuts and cilantro.

In a small bowl, combine the oil, lemon juice, cayenne and cumin. Pour over rice mixture and stir to coat. Cover and refrigerate until serving. **Yield:** 12 servings.

Green Goddess Salad Dressing

Prep/Total Time: 10 min.

It's no trick to fix this time-honored dressing at home. Made with fresh ingredients, it's excellent—a real treat compared to store-bought dressing.
—Page Alexander
Baldwin City, Kansas

> 1 **cup mayonnaise**
> 1/2 **cup sour cream**
> 1/4 **cup chopped green pepper**
> 1/4 **cup packed fresh parsley sprigs**
> 3 **anchovy fillets**
> 2 **tablespoons lemon juice**
> 2 **green onion tops, coarsely chopped**
> 1 **garlic clove, peeled**
> 1/4 **teaspoon pepper**
> 1/8 **teaspoon Worcestershire sauce**

Place all ingredients in a blender; cover and process until smooth. Transfer to a bowl or jar; cover and store in the refrigerator. **Yield:** 2 cups.

Southwestern Rice Salad

(Pictured above)
Prep/Total Time: 30 min.

The recipe for this delicious, colorful salad has been in my family for years. My mother used to bring it to many different functions, and I'm carrying on her tradition.
—Ruth Bianchi, Apple Valley, Minnesota

> 1-1/3 **cups water**
> 2/3 **cup uncooked long grain rice**
> 3/4 **cup chopped green pepper**
> 1/2 **cup chopped red onion**
> 1 **medium carrot, chopped**
> 3 **garlic cloves, minced**
> 1 **tablespoon vegetable oil**
> 1 **package (16 ounces) frozen corn, thawed**
> 1 **can (15 ounces) black beans, rinsed and drained**
> 2 **medium plum tomatoes, chopped**
> 1 **cup salted peanuts**
> 1/3 **cup minced fresh cilantro**
> 2/3 **cup olive oil**
> 1/3 **cup lemon juice**
> 1/2 to 1-1/2 **teaspoons cayenne pepper**
> 1/2 **teaspoon ground cumin**

In a large saucepan, bring water and rice to a boil. Reduce heat; cover and simmer for 15 minutes. Remove from the heat. Let stand for 5 minutes or until rice is tender. Rinse rice with cold water and drain. Place in a large bowl.

Salad with Grilled Chicken

Prep: 20 min. + marinating **Grill:** 15 min.

I feel like I am serving fine restaurant-quality food with this dish. Every single guest asked for the recipe when I made it for a get-together.
—Diana Wissinger
Lawrenceburg, Indiana

> 3/4 **cup olive oil**
> 1/4 **cup red wine vinegar**
> 2 **tablespoons minced fresh parsley**
> 4-1/2 **teaspoons Dijon mustard**
> 1 **green onion, chopped**
> 1 **tablespoon minced fresh tarragon *or***
> 1 **teaspoon dried tarragon**
> 1 **garlic clove, minced**
> 1/2 **teaspoon salt**
> 1/4 **teaspoon pepper**
> 4 **boneless skinless chicken breast halves (4 ounces *each*)**
> 4 **cups shredded romaine**

6 **bacon strips, cooked and crumbled**
1 **large tomato, chopped**
1/2 **cup sliced fresh mushrooms**
1/3 **cup chopped walnuts, toasted**

For vinaigrette, in a jar with a tight-fitting lid, combine the first nine ingredients; shake well. Place the chicken in a large resealable plastic bag; add 6 tablespoons vinaigrette. Seal the bag and turn to coat the chicken; refrigerate for 2 hours. Cover and refrigerate the remaining vinaigrette until serving.

Drain and discard marinade. Grill chicken, uncovered, over medium-low heat for 6-8 minutes on each side or until juices run clear. Cut into strips.

In a large bowl, combine the romaine, bacon, tomato, mushrooms, walnuts, chicken and reserved vinaigrette; toss to coat. **Yield:** 4 servings.

Grilled Apple Tossed Salad

(Pictured above right and on page 22)

Prep: 15 min. + marinating   **Grill:** 15 min.

The grilled apples in this salad combine so well with the blue cheese, walnuts and balsamic dressing. I like to serve it on pink Depression glass dessert plates from my great-grandmother. —Paul Soska, Toledo, Ohio

6 **tablespoons olive oil**
1/4 **cup orange juice**
1/4 **cup white balsamic vinegar**
1/4 **cup minced fresh cilantro**
2 **tablespoons honey**
1/2 **teaspoon salt**
1/2 **teaspoon chili sauce**
1 **garlic clove, minced**
2 **large apples, cut into wedges**
1 **package (5 ounces) spring mix salad greens**
1 **cup walnut halves**
1/2 **cup crumbled blue cheese**

For dressing, in a bowl, combine the first eight ingredients. Pour 1/4 cup into a large resealable plastic bag; add apples. Seal bag and turn to coat; refrigerate for at least 10 minutes. Cover and refrigerate remaining dressing until serving.

Drain apples, reserving marinade for basting. Thread onto six metal or soaked wooden skewers. Grill apples, covered, over medium heat for 6-8 minutes or until golden brown, basting frequently. Turn and grill 6-8 minutes longer or until golden and tender.

In a large salad bowl, combine the greens, walnuts and blue cheese. Add apples. Drizzle with reserved dressing and toss to coat. **Yield:** 4 servings.

Choosing the Right Apple

According to the U.S. Apple Association, these are the top 10 varieties of apples produced in the United States:

• **Red Delicious:** Full-flavored, sweet taste and crisp texture. Best for fresh eating and snacks.

• **Golden Delicious:** Smooth, sweet taste and tender. Best for eating raw, cutting up in salads, and making applesauce, cider and desserts.

• **Gala:** Crisp and snappy with mellow sweetness. Best for fresh eating or in salads and sauces.

• **Fuji:** Sweet-tart flavor; stays crisp for weeks. Good all-purpose apple that's best for fresh eating, salads and applesauce.

• **Granny Smith:** Crisp with sour apple flavor. Good all-purpose apple.

• **McIntosh:** Juicy with lightly tart flavor and fresh apple aroma. Excellent in applesauce, cider and salad or for fresh eating. Also used in pies.

• **Rome:** Mild, sweet flavor and firm texture. Most popular for baking.

• **Ida Red:** Tangy-tart flavor. Favored for sauces, pies and desserts.

• **Jonathan:** Juicy flavor with a spicy tang and tender texture. Use for fresh eating and cooking.

• **Empire:** Sweet-tart taste and extra crisp. Use for fresh-cut slices, candy and caramel apples, and baking. Excellent lunch-box snack.

Beef Kabob Spinach Salad

(Pictured below)

Prep: 10 min. + marinating **Grill:** 10 min.

I found this easy recipe many years ago, and we never grow tired of it. I like to serve the zippy main-dish medley with roasted potatoes, rolls and a mandarin orange salad.
—Gail Reinford, Souderton, Pennsylvania

  1/4 **cup packed brown sugar**
    4 **teaspoons white vinegar**
    2 **teaspoons chili powder**
    1 **teaspoon salt**
    1 **teaspoon vegetable oil**
  1/2 **to 1 teaspoon hot pepper sauce**
    2 **pounds boneless beef sirloin steak, cut into 1-inch cubes**
    1 **cup (8 ounces) plain yogurt**
  1/3 **cup chopped green onions**
    1 **garlic clove, minced**
    1 **package (10 ounces) fresh baby spinach**

In a large resealable bag, combine the brown sugar, vinegar, chili powder, salt, oil and hot pepper sauce. Add beef; seal bag and turn to coat. Refrigerate for 30 minutes. Meanwhile, in a small bowl, combine the yogurt, onions and garlic; cover and refrigerate until serving.

Drain and discard marinade. Thread the beef cubes onto eight metal or soaked wooden skewers. Grill, covered, over medium heat for 4-6 minutes on each side or until meat reaches desired doneness. Serve over spinach with yogurt sauce. **Yield:** 8 servings.

Seasoned Croutons

Prep/Total Time: 30 min.

These toppers are easy to make using day-old bread and seasonings. You'll never want store-bought croutons again!
—Shelley McKinney, New Castle, Indiana

    2 **tablespoons butter**
    1 **tablespoon olive oil**
  1/4 **teaspoon garlic powder**
  1/4 **teaspoon onion powder**
  1/4 **teaspoon dried oregano**
  1/4 **teaspoon dried basil**
Pinch salt
    6 **slices day-old bread, cubed**

In an ungreased 13-in. x 9-in. x 2-in. baking pan, combine the first seven ingredients. Place in a 300° oven until butter is melted.

Remove from the oven; stir to combine. Add the bread cubes and toss to coat. Bake for 10-15 minutes or until bread is lightly browned, stirring frequently. Cool. Store croutons in the refrigerator in an airtight container. **Yield:** 3 cups.

Strawberry Vinaigrette

(Pictured on page 22)

Prep/Total Time: 10 min.

I enjoy using strawberries in a variety of ways, including featuring them in this pretty, sweet-tart dressing.
—Carolyn McMunn, Angelo, Texas

☑ **Uses less fat, sugar or salt. Includes Nutrition Facts and Diabetic Exchanges.**

    1 **package (16 ounces) frozen unsweetened strawberries, thawed**
    6 **tablespoons lemon juice**
  1/4 **cup sugar**
    2 **tablespoons cider vinegar**
    2 **tablespoons olive oil**
  1/8 **teaspoon poppy seeds**

Place the strawberries in a blender; cover and process until smooth. Add lemon juice and sugar. While processing, gradually add vinegar and oil in a steady stream; process until thickened. Stir in poppy seeds. Transfer to a bowl or jar; cover and store in the refrigerator. **Yield:** 2-1/2 cups.

Nutrition Facts: 2 tablespoons (prepared with sugar substitute) equals 23 calories, 1 g fat (trace saturated fat), 0 cholesterol, 1 mg sodium, 3 g carbohydrate, trace fiber, trace protein. **Diabetic Exchange:** Free food.

Using a slotted spoon, spoon onto a lettuce-lined serving platter or salad plates. Garnish with tomatoes. **Yield:** 6 servings.

Nutrition Facts: 3/4 cup equals 224 calories, 6 g fat (1 g saturated fat), 115 mg cholesterol, 571 mg sodium, 22 g carbohydrate, 4 g fiber, 19 g protein. **Diabetic Exchanges:** 2 very lean meat, 1 starch, 1 vegetable, 1 fat.

Caesar Salad

(Pictured below)

Prep/Total Time: 20 min.

The light dressing that coats this classic salad has a flavorful balance of garlic, lemon and anchovy.
— *Phyllis Schmalz, Kansas City, Kansas*

  4 **teaspoons lemon juice**
  3 **anchovy fillets**
  1 **garlic clove, peeled**
1/2 **teaspoon Worcestershire sauce**
1/4 **teaspoon pepper**
1/4 **cup olive oil**
  8 **cups torn romaine**
  1 **medium red onion, thinly sliced**
  1 **cup salad croutons**
1/2 **cup shredded Parmesan cheese**

For dressing, place the first five ingredients in a blender; cover and process until blended. While processing, gradually add oil in a steady stream.

In a large salad bowl, combine the romaine, onion, croutons and Parmesan cheese. Drizzle with dressing and toss to coat. **Yield:** 6 servings.

Black Bean Shrimp Salad

(Pictured above)

Prep: 15 min. + chilling

I lived in Venezuela for years and love this Caribbean-style salad. — *Rosemarie Forcum, White Stone, Virginia*

☑ Uses less fat, sugar or salt. Includes Nutrition Facts and Diabetic Exchanges.

  1 **pound cooked medium shrimp, peeled and deveined**
  1 **can (15 ounces) black beans, rinsed and drained**
  1 **small green pepper, julienned**
  1 **small onion, thinly sliced**
1/2 **cup chopped celery**
2/3 **cup picante sauce**
  2 **tablespoons minced fresh cilantro**
  2 **tablespoons lime juice**
  2 **tablespoons olive oil**
  2 **tablespoons honey**
1/2 **teaspoon salt**
1/8 **teaspoon grated lime peel, optional**
  6 **lettuce leaves**
  1 **cup halved cherry tomatoes**

In a large bowl, combine the first five ingredients. In a small bowl, whisk the picante sauce, cilantro, lime juice, oil, honey, salt and lime peel if desired. Pour over shrimp mixture and toss to coat. Cover and refrigerate for at least 2 hours.

Blue Cheese Bacon Dressing

(Pictured below)

Prep/Total Time: 10 min.

This dressing is absolutely fantastic—I've made it again and again. It has just about everything we like in it, from rich sour cream and chives to a pinch of garlic.
—Marion Karlin, Waterloo, Iowa

    1 cup mayonnaise
1/2 cup sour cream
    5 to 6 tablespoons milk
    1 tablespoon white wine vinegar
1/2 teaspoon sugar
1/4 teaspoon salt
1/4 teaspoon garlic powder
1/4 teaspoon white pepper
    1 cup (4 ounces) crumbled blue cheese
1/4 cup crumbled cooked bacon
1/4 cup minced chives

In a small bowl, whisk the mayonnaise, sour cream, milk, vinegar, sugar, salt, garlic powder and pepper until blended. Stir in the blue cheese, bacon and chives. Cover and store in the refrigerator. **Yield:** 2 cups.

Grape Broccoli Salad

(Pictured above and on front cover)

Prep/Total Time: 30 min.

Our nephew recently told me this salad, which has a wide variety of ingredients, is his favorite. But the first time he ate it at my house, he thought I was cleaning out the fridge! —Lavonne Hartel, Williston, North Dakota

    6 cups fresh broccoli florets
    6 green onions, sliced
    1 cup diced celery
    1 cup green grapes
    1 cup seedless red grapes
    1 cup mayonnaise
1/3 cup sugar
    1 tablespoon cider vinegar
1/2 pound sliced bacon, cooked and crumbled
    1 cup slivered almonds, toasted

In a large salad bowl, combine the broccoli, onions, celery and grapes. In another bowl, whisk the mayonnaise, sugar and vinegar; pour over broccoli mixture and toss to coat. Cover and refrigerate until serving. Stir in bacon and almonds just before serving. **Yield:** 15 servings.

Garlic Anchovy Salad Dressing

(Pictured on page 22)

Prep/Total Time: 10 min.

This is one of the best dressings I've ever tasted. It's thick, creamy and terrific with greens and vegetables.
—*Lois Taylor Caron, Bainsville, Ontario*

　2 tablespoons lemon juice
　2 tablespoons sour cream
　2 tablespoons mayonnaise
　2 to 3 anchovy fillets
　1/3 cup grated Parmesan cheese
　2 garlic cloves, peeled
　1/4 teaspoon pepper
　1/8 teaspoon hot pepper sauce
　1/8 teaspoon Worcestershire sauce
　1/3 cup vegetable oil

Place the first nine ingredients in a blender; cover and process until smooth. While processing, gradually add oil in a steady stream. Transfer to a small bowl or jar; cover and store in the refrigerator. **Yield:** 2/3 cup.

Sesame Salad Dressing

(Pictured at left)

Prep/Total Time: 5 min.

To give greens a pleasant, fresh Asian flavor, just try this super-easy mixture.　—*Jean Ecos, Hartland, Wisconsin*

　6 tablespoons sesame oil
　1/4 cup rice wine vinegar
　1/4 cup soy sauce
　3 tablespoons sugar

In a bowl, whisk all of the ingredients. Cover and store in the refrigerator. **Yield:** 1 cup.

ʃ Rice Wine Vinegar

Also known simply as rice vinegar, rice wine vinegar is produced by adding bacteria to rice wine. Compared to white vinegar, rice wine vinegar is mild and slightly sweet. It is best used in salad dressings for delicate greens or to add slight acidity to cooked dishes.

Seasoned rice vinegar, which has been seasoned with sugar and salt, is a different product and should not be substituted when a recipe calls for rice vinegar or rice wine vinegar.

Autumn Tossed Salad

(Pictured above)

Prep: 30 min. + chilling

When you take this wonderful salad to a holiday gathering or serve it at home, you will get rave reviews and many requests for the recipe.　—*Edie DeSpain, Logan, Utah*

　1/2 cup lemon juice
　1/2 cup sugar
　2 teaspoons finely chopped onion
　1 teaspoon Dijon mustard
　1/2 teaspoon salt
　2/3 cup vegetable oil
　1 tablespoon poppy seeds
　1 bunch romaine, torn
　1 cup (4 ounces) shredded Swiss cheese
　1 cup unsalted cashews
　1 medium apple, chopped
　1 medium pear, chopped
　1/4 cup dried cranberries

In a blender, combine the lemon juice, sugar, onion, mustard and salt. While processing, gradually add oil in a steady stream. Stir in poppy seeds. Transfer to a small pitcher or bowl. Cover and refrigerate for 1 hour or until chilled.

In a large salad bowl, combine the romaine, cheese, cashews, apple, pear and cranberries. Drizzle with dressing and toss to coat. **Yield:** 10 servings.

Soups & Sandwiches

What goes together better than a steaming bowl of soup and a stacked-high sandwich? Look right here for tasty twosomes.

CLASSIC COMFORT FOODS. Clockwise from upper left: Salsa Ranch Chicken Wraps (p. 40), Healthy Tomato Soup (p. 39), Firecracker Burgers (p. 38), Pizza Meatball Subs (p. 36) and Broccoli Chowder (p. 38).

1 meaty ham bone *or* **2 smoked ham hocks**
1/4 cup minced fresh parsley

Place beans in a Dutch oven or soup kettle; add water to cover by 2 in. Bring to a boil; boil for 2 minutes. Remove from the heat; cover and let stand for 1 hour.

Drain and rinse beans, discarding liquid. In the same pan, saute onions in oil for 2 minutes. Add celery; cook until tender. Stir in the beans, water, ham, potatoes, carrot, Worcestershire sauce, salt, thyme, pepper and bay leaves. Add ham bone. Bring to a boil. Reduce heat; cover and simmer for 1-1/4 to 1-1/2 hours or until beans are tender.

Remove the ham bone; when cool enough to handle, remove ham from bone and cut into cubes. Return to soup. Discard bone and bay leaves. Garnish soup with parsley. **Yield:** 10 servings.

Pizza Meatball Subs

(Pictured on page 34)

Prep: 30 min. **Bake:** 25 min.

I made these sandwiches one evening for my family, and they were a huge hit with everyone, including the picky eaters. There's plenty of sauce and cheese to complement the baked meatballs. —Heather Begin, Athens, Maine

   1 egg, lightly beaten
1/3 cup steak sauce
   1 cup crushed saltines
   1 teaspoon onion powder
1/4 teaspoon seasoned salt
1/8 teaspoon pepper
1-1/2 pounds ground beef
   6 to 7 tablespoons mayonnaise
   6 to 7 submarine buns, split
   9 to 11 slices process American cheese, cut into strips
   1 jar (14 ounces) pizza sauce
   2 cups (8 ounces) shredded part-skim mozzarella cheese

In a large bowl, combine the egg, steak sauce, saltines, onion powder, salt and pepper. Crumble the beef over the mixture and mix well. Shape into 1-1/2-in. meatballs.

Place the meatballs on a greased rack in a foil-lined 15-in. x 10-in. x 1-in. baking pan. Bake at 375° for 20-25 minutes or until no longer pink. Drain meatballs on paper towels.

Spread the mayonnaise over the bun bottoms; top each with American cheese, 1 tablespoon pizza sauce, meatballs and remaining pizza sauce. Sprinkle with mozzarella cheese. Place on a baking sheet. Bake for 5-10 minutes or until the cheese is melted. **Yield:** 6-7 servings.

Ham and Bean Soup

(Pictured above)

Prep: 30 min. + soaking **Cook:** 1-1/4 hours

I learned to make this soup when we lived in Pennsylvania near several Amish families. It's a great way to use up ham and mashed potatoes, and it freezes well, too. —Amanda Reed, Milford, Delaware

   1 pound dried navy beans
   2 medium onions, chopped
   2 teaspoons vegetable oil
   2 celery ribs, chopped
10 cups water
   4 cups cubed fully cooked ham
   1 cup mashed potatoes (without added milk and butter)
1/2 cup shredded carrot
   2 tablespoons Worcestershire sauce
   1 teaspoon salt
1/2 teaspoon dried thyme
1/2 teaspoon pepper
   2 bay leaves

Chicken Broccoli Calzones

(Pictured below)

Prep: 20 min.   **Bake:** 20 min.

Smoked mozzarella cheese and golden raisins add to the excellent flavor of the broccoli and chicken in these easy-to-fix calzones.   —*Iola Egle, Bella Vista, Arkansas*

- 1 package (10 ounces) frozen chopped broccoli
- 1/2 teaspoon rubbed sage
- 1 small onion, finely chopped
- 3 garlic cloves, minced
- 1 tablespoon olive oil
- 2 cups shredded cooked chicken breast
- 1/2 pound smoked mozzarella cheese, shredded
- 1/3 cup chopped fresh basil
- 1/3 cup golden raisins
- 1 loaf (1 pound) frozen bread dough, thawed
- 1 egg
- 1 tablespoon water

Cook broccoli according to package directions; drain. Sprinkle with sage; set aside. In a large saucepan, saute onion and garlic in oil until tender. Remove from the heat. Stir in the broccoli, chicken, cheese, basil and raisins; set aside.

On a lightly floured surface, divide dough into four pieces. Roll each piece into a 10-in. circle. Carefully place one circle on a lightly greased baking sheet. Spoon a fourth of the chicken mixture onto half of the circle. Brush edges of dough with water; fold dough over filling and pinch edges to seal. Repeat with remaining dough and filling.

With a sharp knife, make two slashes on each cal-

zone. Beat egg and water; brush over calzones. Bake at 400° for 18-22 minutes or until golden brown. **Yield:** 4 calzones.

Apple 'n' Prosciutto Sandwiches

(Pictured above)

Prep/Total Time: 20 min.

Prepared on an indoor grill, these Italian-style sandwiches are spread with homemade rosemary pesto. They're wonderful on a cool day with a bowl of butternut squash soup.   —*Elizabeth Bennett, Mill Creek, Washington*

- 1/4 cup olive oil
- 1/2 cup chopped walnuts
- 2 tablespoons grated Parmesan cheese
- 2 tablespoons minced fresh rosemary
- 1 loaf (12 ounces) focaccia bread
- 8 thin slices prosciutto
- 1 medium apple, sliced
- 6 ounces Brie cheese, rind removed and sliced

In a blender, combine the oil, walnuts, Parmesan cheese and rosemary; cover and process until blended and nuts are finely chopped. With a bread knife, split focaccia into two horizontal layers. Spread rosemary mixture over cut sides of bread.

On bottom of bread, layer prosciutto, apple and Brie; replace bread top. Cut into quarters. Cook on an indoor grill for 2-3 minutes or until bread is browned and cheese is melted. To serve, cut each wedge in half. **Yield:** 8 servings.

Spanish Gazpacho

(Pictured below)
Prep: 30 min. + chilling

There's a bounty of vegetables in this tantalizing chilled soup. Its refreshing flavor makes it an ideal addition to summer meals. —Dave Schmitt, Hartland, Wisconsin

✓ **Uses less fat, sugar or salt. Includes Nutrition Facts and Diabetic Exchanges.**

 5 pounds tomatoes, peeled and quartered
 3 medium carrots, quartered
 1 large cucumber, peeled and quartered
 1 large sweet red pepper, quartered
 1 large green pepper, quartered
 1 sweet onion, quartered
 2 garlic cloves, minced
 1/3 cup olive oil
 3 tablespoons balsamic vinegar
 1-1/2 teaspoons salt
 1/2 teaspoon pepper

In batches, place ingredients in a blender; cover and process until soup reaches desired texture. Pour into a large bowl. Cover and refrigerate for 1-2 hours before serving. **Yield:** 12 servings (3 quarts).
 Nutrition Facts: 1 cup equals 118 calories, 7 g fat (1 g saturated fat), 0 cholesterol, 320 mg sodium, 15 g carbohydrate, 4 g fiber, 2 g protein. **Diabetic Exchanges:** 3 vegetable, 1 fat.

Firecracker Burgers

(Pictured on page 34)
Prep: 20 min. **Grill:** 15 min.

These tasty stuffed burgers are perfect fare for July 4. They're great with a cool, creamy macaroni salad and an icy cold drink! —Kelly Williams, La Porte, Indiana

 1 pound lean ground beef
 1/4 cup chunky salsa
 4 frozen breaded cheddar cheese jalapeno peppers, thawed
 1/4 cup guacamole
 4 hamburger buns, split and toasted
 4 lettuce leaves
 1/4 cup salsa con queso dip
 1/4 cup sliced plum tomatoes
 2 tablespoons sliced ripe olives
 4 thin slices sweet onion

In a bowl, combine beef and salsa. Shape into four patties. Place a jalapeno in center of each; wrap beef around jalapeno, forming a ball. Reshape into patties, about 3-1/2 in. to 4 in. in diameter and 1 in. thick.
 Grill, covered, over medium-hot heat for 7-8 minutes on each side or until meat is no longer pink. Spread guacamole over toasted side of bun tops. On each bun bottom, layer lettuce, a burger, dip, tomatoes, olives and onion; replace tops. **Yield:** 4 servings.

Broccoli Chowder

(Pictured on page 34)
Prep: 20 min. **Cook:** 15 min.

My family loves this tasty, satisfying soup, so I serve it often. —Esther Shank, Harrisonburg, Virginia

✓ **Uses less fat, sugar or salt. Includes Nutrition Facts and Diabetic Exchanges.**

 4 cups fresh small broccoli florets
 2 medium potatoes, diced
 1-1/2 cups water
 2 medium carrots, thinly sliced
 1 large onion, chopped
 1 celery rib, finely chopped
 4 cups milk, *divided*
 2 teaspoons chicken bouillon granules
 1 teaspoon Worcestershire sauce
 3/4 teaspoon salt
 1/2 teaspoon pepper
 1/3 cup all-purpose flour
 1 cup cubed process cheese (Velveeta)

In a large saucepan, combine the first six ingredients. Bring to a boil. Reduce heat; cover and simmer for 8-10 minutes or until vegetables are tender. Add 3 cups milk and bouillon, Worcestershire sauce, salt and pepper.

In a small bowl, combine flour and remaining milk until smooth; gradually stir into soup. Bring to a boil; cook and stir for 2 minutes or until thickened. Remove from the heat; stir in cheese just until melted. **Yield:** 6 servings.

Nutrition Facts: 1-1/3 cups (prepared with fat-free milk, reduced-sodium bouillon and reduced-fat cheese) equals 233 calories, 3 g fat (2 g saturated fat), 11 mg cholesterol, 838 mg sodium, 39 g carbohydrate, 6 g fiber, 15 g protein. **Diabetic Exchanges:** 1 vegetable, 1 starch, 1 fat-free milk.

Open-Faced Meatball Sandwiches

(Pictured at right)

Prep: 30 min.   **Cook:** 10 min.

My husband and I both like meatball subs. I came up with this version that's easy to make after a hard day.
—Karen Barthel, North Canton, Ohio

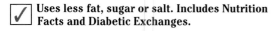 **Uses less fat, sugar or salt. Includes Nutrition Facts and Diabetic Exchanges.**

  1/4 cup egg substitute
  1/2 cup soft bread crumbs
  1/4 cup finely chopped onion
    2 garlic cloves, minced
  1/2 teaspoon onion powder
  1/2 teaspoon dried oregano
  1/2 teaspoon dried basil
  1/4 teaspoon pepper
Dash salt
 1-1/4 pounds lean ground turkey
    2 cups garden-style pasta sauce
    4 submarine buns (6 inches *each*), split
    2 tablespoons shredded part-skim mozzarella cheese
Shredded Parmesan cheese, optional

In a large bowl, combine first nine ingredients. Crumble turkey over mixture; mix well. Shape into 40 meatballs, 1 in. each. In a large skillet coated with nonstick cooking spray, brown meatballs in batches; drain.

Place meatballs in a large saucepan. Add the pasta sauce; bring to a boil. Reduce heat; cover and simmer for 10-15 minutes or until meat is no longer pink. Spoon meatballs and sauce onto bun halves; sprinkle with mozzarella cheese and Parmesan cheese if desired. **Yield:** 8 servings.

Nutrition Facts: 1 sandwich equals 231 calories, 9 g fat (2 g saturated fat), 60 mg cholesterol, 488 mg sodium, 21 g carbohydrate, 2 g fiber, 17 g protein. **Diabetic Exchanges:** 2 lean meat, 1 starch, 1 vegetable.

Healthy Tomato Soup

(Pictured on page 34)

Prep: 5 min.   **Cook:** 5 hours

I season this slow-cooked soup with spices and herbs rather than salt. —Heather Campbell, Lawrence, Kansas

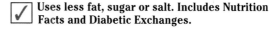 **Uses less fat, sugar or salt. Includes Nutrition Facts and Diabetic Exchanges.**

    1 can (46 ounces) tomato juice
    1 can (8 ounces) tomato sauce
  1/2 cup water
  1/2 cup chopped onion
    1 celery rib with leaves, chopped
    2 tablespoons sugar
  1/2 teaspoon dried basil
    3 to 5 whole cloves
    1 bay leaf

In a 3-qt. slow cooker, combine all of the ingredients. Cover and cook on low for 5-6 hours or until heated through. Discard cloves and bay leaf before serving. **Yield:** 6 servings.

Nutrition Facts: 1-1/4 cups equals 69 calories, trace fat (trace saturated fat), 0 cholesterol, 964 mg sodium, 17 g carbohydrate, 2 g fiber, 2 g protein. **Diabetic Exchange:** 1 starch.

duced-sodium broth) equals 182 calories, 4 g fat (2 g saturated fat), 26 mg cholesterol, 808 mg sodium, 22 g carbohydrate, 3 g fiber, 13 g protein. **Diabetic Exchanges:** 1-1/2 vegetable, 1 starch, 1 lean meat.

Salsa Ranch Chicken Wraps

(Pictured on page 34)

Prep/Total Time: 25 min.

I came up with this easy wrap while working at a deli during college. The combination of salsa and ranch dressing adds a unique twist, and the chicken pieces are nice and tender. —Amanda Rasner, Ellis, Kansas

 4 **tablespoons salsa**
 4 **tablespoons ranch salad dressing**
 4 **tomato basil tortillas (10 inches)**
 2 **boneless skinless chicken breast halves (4 ounces *each*), grilled and cut into strips**
 12 **slices cucumber**
 8 **slices tomato**
 1/2 **cup julienned green pepper**
 6 **slices Swiss cheese**
 2 **tablespoons butter, *divided***

Spread 1 tablespoon of salsa and 1 tablespoon of ranch dressing over each tortilla. Place the chicken, cucumber, tomato and green pepper down each center; top with 1-1/2 slices of cheese. Fold ends of each tortilla over filling.

 In a large skillet, melt 1 tablespoon butter. Place two wraps folded side down in skillet. Cook over medium heat for 3-4 minutes on each side or until lightly browned and cheese is melted. Repeat with remaining wraps and butter. **Yield:** 4 servings.

Vegetarian Chili

Prep: 20 min.   **Cook:** 50 min.

This filling meatless chili is loaded with nutritious beans, veggies and seasonings. You might serve it as a light main course or a zippy, satisfying side with your favorite sandwiches. —Bill Hughes, Raleigh, North Carolina

 Uses less fat, sugar or salt. Includes Nutrition Facts and Diabetic Exchanges.

 1 **large onion, chopped**
 1 **large green pepper, chopped**
 1 **large sweet red pepper, chopped**
 3 **medium carrots, thinly sliced**
 6 **garlic cloves, minced**
 2 **tablespoons olive oil**
 1 **can (28 ounces) crushed tomatoes, undrained**

Hamburger Vegetable Soup

(Pictured above)

Prep: 10 min.   **Cook:** 40 min.

Oregano really shines in this chock-full soup. It smells delicious while it's cooking and makes a great lunch or dinner. —Traci Wynne, Bear, Delaware

 Uses less fat, sugar or salt. Includes Nutrition Facts and Diabetic Exchanges.

 1 **pound ground beef**
 1 **medium onion, chopped**
 1/2 **large green pepper, diced**
 4 **garlic cloves, minced**
 8 **cups beef broth**
 2 **cans (14-1/2 ounces *each*) Italian stewed tomatoes**
 1 **package (9 ounces) frozen cut green beans**
 1 **can (8 ounces) tomato sauce**
 1 **cup ditalini *or* other small pasta**
 1 **tablespoon Worcestershire sauce**
 2 **teaspoons dried oregano**
 1 **teaspoon dried basil**
 1/2 **teaspoon pepper**

In a Dutch oven or soup kettle, cook the beef, onion, green pepper and garlic over medium heat until meat is no longer pink; drain.

 Stir in the remaining ingredients. Bring to a boil. Reduce heat; cover and simmer for 30 minutes or until vegetables and pasta are tender. **Yield:** 10 servings (3-3/4 quarts).

 Nutrition Facts: 1-1/2 cups (prepared with re-

1 can (16 ounces) hominy, rinsed and
  drained
1 can (16 ounces) kidney beans, rinsed and
  drained
1 can (15 ounces) pinto beans, rinsed and
  drained
1 can (15 ounces) garbanzo beans *or*
  chickpeas, rinsed and drained
2 cups water
1 can (8 ounces) tomato paste
3 tablespoons chili powder
2 tablespoons Worcestershire sauce
1 tablespoon ground cumin
2 teaspoons dried thyme
2 teaspoons dried parsley flakes
1/2 teaspoon salt
1/2 teaspoon pepper

In a Dutch oven or soup kettle, saute the onion, peppers, carrots and garlic in oil for 15 minutes or until vegetables are tender.

Stir in the remaining ingredients. Bring to a boil. Reduce heat; cover and simmer for 30 minutes or until heated through. **Yield:** 12 servings (4 quarts).

Nutrition Facts: 1-1/4 cups equals 204 calories, 4 g fat (trace saturated fat), 0 cholesterol, 569 mg sodium, 37 g carbohydrate, 10 g fiber, 8 g protein. **Diabetic Exchanges:** 2 starch, 1 vegetable, 1/2 very lean meat.

Meat Loaf Gyros

(Pictured at right)

Prep: 30 min. **Bake:** 1 hour + chilling

I always wanted to learn to make Greek gyros at home, but I was intimidated. Then I tried this recipe, and they were great. I slice leftover meat in individual portions and freeze them for any time I crave a gyro.
— *Sharon Rawlings, Tampa, Florida*

1 egg, lightly beaten
6 garlic cloves, minced
3 tablespoons dried oregano
1-1/2 teaspoons kosher salt
1 teaspoon pepper
1 pound ground lamb
1 pound ground beef
TZATZIKI SAUCE:
1 cup (8 ounces) plain yogurt
1 medium cucumber, peeled, seeded and
  chopped
2 tablespoons lemon juice
2 garlic cloves, minced
1/2 teaspoon salt
1/4 teaspoon pepper

8 whole gyro-style pitas (6 inches)
3 tablespoons olive oil, *divided*
16 slices tomato
8 slices sweet onion, halved

In a large bowl, combine the egg, garlic, oregano, kosher salt and pepper. Crumble lamb and beef over mixture; mix well.

Pat mixture into an ungreased 9-in. x 5-in. x 3-in. loaf pan. Bake, uncovered, at 350° for 60-70 minutes or until no pink remains and a meat thermometer reads 160°. Cool completely on a wire rack. Refrigerate for 1-2 hours.

For sauce, in a small bowl, combine the yogurt, cucumber, lemon juice, garlic, salt and pepper. Cover and refrigerate until serving.

Brush the pita breads with 1 tablespoon oil; heat on a lightly greased griddle for 1 minute on each side or until warmed. Cut the meat loaf into very thin slices. In a large skillet, fry the meat loaf in the remaining oil in batches until crisp.

On each pita bread, layer tomato, onion and meat loaf slices; top with some tzatziki sauce. Carefully fold the pitas in half. Serve with the remaining sauce. **Yield:** 8 servings.

Red Pepper Carrot Soup

(Pictured below)

Prep: 40 min.   **Cook:** 40 min. + cooling

This colorful soup is a tasty way to have a serving of vegetables without a lot of fat. Even my discerning teenagers lap it up happily. —Anna Hartle, Loveland, Ohio

> 1 medium sweet red pepper
> 1 pound carrots, sliced
> 1 medium onion, chopped
> 2 tablespoons uncooked long grain rice
> 2 tablespoons butter
> 2 cans (14-1/2 ounces *each*) chicken broth
> 2 cups water
> 1/3 cup orange juice
> 4-1/2 teaspoons snipped fresh dill
> 2 teaspoons grated orange peel
> 1/2 teaspoon salt
> 1/2 teaspoon *each* dried marjoram, thyme and rosemary, crushed
> 1/2 teaspoon rubbed sage
> 1/4 teaspoon pepper

Broil red pepper 4 in. from the heat until skin is blistered, about 6 minutes. With tongs, rotate pepper a quarter turn. Broil and rotate until all sides are blistered and blackened. Immediately place pepper in a bowl; cover and let stand for 15-20 minutes. Peel and discard charred skin. Remove stem and seeds; set pepper aside.

Cream of Cauliflower Soup

(Pictured above)

Prep: 30 min.   **Cook:** 3-1/2 hours

When a chill is in the air, I like to make soups for the family. Cheddar cheese adds flavor and heartiness to this one, which is my own recipe. —Ruth Worden Mossena, New York

> 1 large head cauliflower, broken into florets
> 2 cups chicken broth
> 2 tablespoons reduced-sodium chicken bouillon granules
> 2 cups half-and-half cream
> 2 cups milk
> 1 medium carrot, shredded
> 2 bay leaves
> 1/4 teaspoon garlic powder
> 1/2 cup mashed potato flakes
> 2 cups (8 ounces) shredded cheddar cheese

Paprika

In a large saucepan, combine the cauliflower, broth and bouillon. Bring to a boil. Reduce heat; cover and cook for 20 minutes or until tender.

Mash cauliflower. Transfer to a 3-qt. slow cooker. Stir in the cream, milk, carrot, bay leaves and garlic powder. Cover and cook on low for 3 hours. Stir in potatoes; cook 30 minutes longer or until thickened. Discard bay leaves. Cool slightly.

In a blender, process soup in batches until smooth. Return to the slow cooker; stir in cheese. Cook until soup is heated through and cheese is melted. Garnish with paprika. **Yield:** 8 servings (2 quarts).

In a large saucepan, cook the carrots, onion and rice in butter until onion is tender. Stir in the broth, water, orange juice, dill, orange peel, salt, marjoram, thyme, rosemary, sage and pepper. Bring to a boil. Reduce heat; cover and simmer for 20-25 minutes or until carrots and rice are tender. Cool for 10 minutes.

In a blender, puree carrot mixture and roasted pepper in small batches. Return to the pan; heat through. **Yield:** 4 servings.

Italian Wedding Soup

(Pictured at right)

Prep: 30 min. **Cook:** 45 min.

I enjoyed a similar soup for lunch at work one day and decided to re-create it at home. I love the combination of meatballs, vegetables and pasta. —Noelle Myers
Grand Forks, North Dakota

- 2 eggs, lightly beaten
- 1/2 cup seasoned bread crumbs
- 1 pound ground beef
- 1 pound bulk Italian sausage
- 3 medium carrots, sliced
- 3 celery ribs, diced
- 1 large onion, chopped
- 3 garlic cloves, minced
- 4-1/2 teaspoons olive oil
- 4 cans (14-1/2 ounces *each*) reduced-sodium chicken broth
- 2 cans (14-1/2 ounces *each*) beef broth
- 1 package (10 ounces) frozen chopped spinach, thawed and squeezed dry
- 1/4 cup minced fresh basil
- 1 envelope onion soup mix
- 4-1/2 teaspoons ketchup
- 1/2 teaspoon dried thyme
- 3 bay leaves
- 1-1/2 cups uncooked penne *or* medium tube pasta

In a large bowl, combine eggs and bread crumbs. Crumble beef and sausage over mixture; mix well. Shape into 3/4-in. balls.

Place meatballs on a greased rack in a foil-lined 15-in. x 10-in. x 1-in. baking pan. Bake at 350° for 15-18 minutes or until no longer pink. Meanwhile, in a soup kettle or Dutch oven, saute carrots, celery, onion and garlic in oil until tender. Stir in the broth, spinach, basil, soup mix, ketchup, thyme and bay leaves.

Drain meatballs on paper towels. Bring soup to a boil; add meatballs. Reduce heat; simmer, uncovered, for 30 minutes. Add pasta; cook 13-15 minutes longer or until tender, stirring occasionally. Discard bay leaves before serving. **Yield:** 10 servings (2-1/2 quarts).

Beef Gyros

Prep: 15 min. + marinating **Cook:** 5 min.

I found this Greek-style recipe years ago. When I altered a few ingredients, I knew I had a tasty and good-for-you meal. —Didi Trowbridge, Wilkesport, Ontario

✓ **Uses less fat, sugar or salt. Includes Nutrition Facts.**

- 1/2 cup reduced-sodium beef broth
- 2 tablespoons olive oil
- 1 garlic clove, minced
- 1/2 teaspoon salt
- 1/2 teaspoon dried oregano
- Dash pepper
- 1 pound boneless beef sirloin steak, cut into thin strips
- 2/3 cup reduced-fat cucumber ranch salad dressing
- 1 teaspoon sugar
- 5 whole gyro-style pitas (6 inches), warmed
- 2 cups chopped lettuce
- 1 cup chopped tomato
- 1 small cucumber, peeled and sliced
- 1 small red onion, sliced

In a large resealable plastic bag, combine the first six ingredients; add beef. Seal bag and turn to coat; refrigerate for up to 24 hours.

In a small bowl, combine dressing and sugar; refrigerate until serving. Drain and discard marinade. In a large nonstick skillet coated with nonstick cooking spray, saute beef for 3-4 minutes or until no longer pink. Serve on pitas with lettuce, tomato, cucumber and onion; drizzle with dressing. **Yield:** 5 servings.

Nutrition Facts: 1 gyro equals 396 calories, 14 g fat (3 g saturated fat), 51 mg cholesterol, 1,046 mg sodium, 41 g carbohydrate, 3 g fiber, 24 g protein.

Side Dishes & Condiments

Whether it's Thanksgiving dinner or a weekday supper, the can't-miss sides and condiments here will make your meal complete.

PLEASING PLATE-FILLERS. Clockwise from upper left: Sweet 'n' Tangy Carrots (p. 51), Parmesan Potato Wedges (p. 48), Kohlrabi 'n' Carrot Bake (p. 53), Strawberry Freezer Jam (p. 51) and Lemon-Scented Broccoli (p. 46).

White Cheddar Scalloped Potatoes

(Pictured above)

Prep: 40 min.   **Bake:** 70 min.

This recipe has evolved over the past 8 years. After I added the thyme, ham and sour cream, my husband declared, "This is it!"   —Hope Toole, Muscle Shoals, Alabama

- 1 **medium onion, finely chopped**
- 1/4 **cup butter, cubed**
- 1/4 **cup all-purpose flour**
- 1 **teaspoon dried parsley flakes**
- 1 **teaspoon salt**
- 1/2 **teaspoon pepper**
- 1/2 **teaspoon dried thyme**
- 3 **cups milk**
- 1 **can (10-3/4 ounces) condensed cream of mushroom soup, undiluted**
- 1 **cup (8 ounces) sour cream**
- 8 **cups thinly sliced peeled potatoes**
- 3-1/2 **cups cubed fully cooked ham**
- 2 **cups (8 ounces) shredded white cheddar cheese**

In a large saucepan, saute onion in butter until tender. Stir in the flour, parsley, salt, pepper and thyme until blended. Gradually add milk. Bring to a boil; cook and stir for 2 minutes or until thickened. Stir in the soup. Remove from the heat; stir in sour cream until blended.

In a large bowl, combine the potatoes and ham. In a greased 13-in. x 9-in. x 2-in. baking dish, layer half of the potato mixture, cheese and white sauce. Repeat layers. Cover and bake at 375° for 30 minutes. Uncover; bake 40-50 minutes longer or until potatoes are tender. **Yield:** 6-8 servings.

Lemon-Scented Broccoli

(Pictured on page 44)

Prep/Total Time: 25 min.

If you do not like broccoli, you might change your mind after tasting this saucy dish. It is simple yet elegant.
—Dorothy Pritchett, Wills Point, Texas

✓ **Uses less fat, sugar or salt. Includes Nutrition Facts and Diabetic Exchanges.**

- 1/4 **cup coarsely chopped pecans**
- 1-1/2 **teaspoons butter**
- 1 **medium bunch broccoli, trimmed and cut into spears**
- 1 **tablespoon sugar**
- 2 **teaspoons cornstarch**
- 1/2 **cup chicken broth**
- 3 to 4 **tablespoons lemon juice**
- 1 **teaspoon grated lemon peel**
- 1/4 **teaspoon pepper**

In a small skillet, saute pecans in butter until golden brown; set aside. Place broccoli in a large saucepan; add 1 in. of water. Bring to a boil. Reduce heat; cover and cook for 5-8 minutes or until crisp-tender.

Meanwhile, in a small saucepan, combine the sugar, cornstarch, broth and lemon juice until smooth. Cook and stir over medium heat for 1 minute or until thickened. Remove from the heat; stir in the lemon peel and pepper. Drain broccoli and place in a serving bowl; top with lemon sauce and pecans. **Yield:** 6 servings.

Nutrition Facts: 1 cup (prepared with reduced-fat butter and reduced-sodium broth) equals 82 calories, 4 g fat (1 g saturated fat), 2 mg cholesterol, 85 mg sodium, 10 g carbohydrate, 4 g fiber, 4 g protein. **Diabetic Exchanges:** 2 vegetable, 1 fat.

Ribboned Vegetables

Prep/Total Time: 25 min.

This easy medley makes the most of summer produce. The colorful veggie strips, seasoned with lemon and horseradish, will add zip to just about any menu.
—Julie Gwinn, Hershey, Pennsylvania

✓ **Uses less fat, sugar or salt. Includes Nutrition Facts and Diabetic Exchanges.**

- 2 **medium carrots**
- 2 **small zucchini**
- 2 **small yellow summer squash**
- 1 **tablespoon butter**
- 2 **teaspoons lemon juice**
- 1 **teaspoon prepared horseradish**
- 1/2 **teaspoon salt**
- 1/8 **teaspoon pepper**

With a vegetable peeler or metal cheese slicer, cut very thin slices down the length of each carrot, zucchini and yellow squash, making long ribbons.

In a large skillet, saute vegetables in butter for 2 minutes. Stir in the remaining ingredients. Cook 2-4 minutes longer or until vegetables are crisp-tender, stirring occasionally. **Yield:** 4 servings.

Nutrition Facts: 3/4 cup equals 67 calories, 3 g fat (2 g saturated fat), 8 mg cholesterol, 342 mg sodium, 9 g carbohydrate, 4 g fiber, 2 g protein. **Diabetic Exchanges:** 2 vegetable, 1/2 fat.

Mustard-Glazed Carrots

Prep/Total Time: 25 min.

Ever since I served these carrots on Thanksgiving a couple of years ago, this recipe is my most requested side dish at family dinners. —Kelly Kirby, Westville, Nova Scotia

☑ **Uses less fat, sugar or salt. Includes Nutrition Facts and Diabetic Exchanges.**

- 1 package (16 ounces) fresh baby carrots
- 2 tablespoons honey mustard
- 1 tablespoon snipped fresh dill *or*
    1 teaspoon dill weed
- 2 teaspoons butter

Place 1 in. of water in a large saucepan; add carrots. Bring to a boil. Reduce heat; cover and simmer for 15-20 minutes or until crisp-tender. Drain. Add the mustard, dill and butter; stir until butter is melted. **Yield:** 4-6 servings.

Nutrition Facts: 3/4 cup equals 74 calories, 3 g fat (1 g saturated fat), 5 mg cholesterol, 172 mg sodium, 13 g carbohydrate, 2 g fiber, 1 g protein. **Diabetic Exchanges:** 2 vegetable, 1/2 fat.

ʃ More on Mustard

Pepping up a hot dog at a sporting event or adding a distinctive tang to side dishes, mustard is a great flavor booster. Popular prepared mustard styles and flavors include American ballpark, Dijon, honey and spicy brown.

When the jar's empty and you need prepared mustard for a recipe, try this blend: Mix 1 tablespoon ground mustard, 1 teaspoon cider vinegar and up to 1 teaspoon sugar to equal 1 tablespoon of prepared mustard. Let it stand for 15 minutes so the flavors can develop.

If you're adding mustard to a wet or liquid mixture, 1 teaspoon ground mustard is equal to 1 tablespoon prepared mustard.

Pecan Sweet Potato Bake

(Pictured below)

Prep: 20 min.   **Bake:** 30 min.

The recipe for this luscious side dish was handed down through my husband's family, and it's become a tradition for me to serve it during the holidays. Everyone loves it!
—Nanci Keatley, Salem, Oregon

- 3 cups mashed sweet potatoes
- 2 eggs
- 1/2 cup sugar
- 1/4 cup half-and-half cream
- 1/4 cup butter, softened
- 2 teaspoons vanilla extract
- 1/8 teaspoon salt

TOPPING:
- 1/2 cup packed brown sugar
- 2 tablespoons all-purpose flour
- 1/4 cup cold butter
- 1/2 cup chopped pecans

In a large mixing bowl, combine the first seven ingredients; beat until light and fluffy. Transfer to a greased 11-in. x 7-in. x 2-in. baking dish.

For topping, combine the brown sugar and flour in a bowl; cut in butter until crumbly. Fold in pecans. Sprinkle over sweet potato mixture. Bake, uncovered, at 350° for 30-35 minutes or until a knife inserted near the center comes out clean. **Yield:** 6-8 servings.

Candied Fruit Cranberry Chutney

(Pictured below)

Prep: 10 min.   **Cook:** 20 min. + cooling

I serve this sweet-tart condiment with turkey, chicken and pork, and find it a nice little gift to share with family and friends at holiday time. —Heather Hewgill, Elora, Ontario

> **4 cups fresh *or* frozen cranberries**
> **2 cups packed brown sugar**
> **1 medium apple, peeled and diced**
> **3/4 cup white vinegar**
> **3/4 cup chopped mixed candied fruit**
> **1/2 teaspoon ground ginger**
> **1/4 teaspoon ground allspice**
> **1/4 teaspoon ground mustard**
> **1/8 to 1/4 teaspoon ground cloves**

In a large saucepan, combine all ingredients. Bring to a boil. Reduce heat; simmer, uncovered, for 20-25 minutes or until slightly thickened, stirring occasionally. Cool. Transfer to a bowl; cover and refrigerate until serving. **Yield:** 5 cups.

Parmesan Potato Wedges

(Pictured on page 44)

Prep: 10 min.   **Bake:** 30 min.

These simple-to-fix potato wedges are great with burgers, chicken sandwiches, fish and other entrees.
—Barbara Trautmann, Ham Lake, Minnesota

✓ Uses less fat, sugar or salt. Includes Nutrition Facts and Diabetic Exchanges.

> **4 medium baking potatoes (1 pound)**
> **1 tablespoon olive oil**
> **1/3 cup grated Parmesan cheese**

> **1/2 teaspoon Cajun seasoning**
> **1/2 teaspoon dried parsley flakes**
> **1/4 teaspoon onion powder**
> **1/4 teaspoon garlic powder**
> **1/8 teaspoon pepper**

Cut each potato into eight wedges; place in a large resealable plastic bag. Add oil; seal bag and shake to coat. In another resealable bag, combine the Parmesan cheese and seasonings; add potatoes, a few at a time, and shake to coat.

Place in a single layer in a 15-in. x 10-in. x 1-in. baking pan coated with nonstick cooking spray. Bake, uncovered, at 375° for 30-35 minutes or until golden brown, turning once. **Yield:** 4 servings.

Nutrition Facts: 8 wedges equals 151 calories, 5 g fat (2 g saturated fat), 5 mg cholesterol, 214 mg sodium, 21 g carbohydrate, 2 g fiber, 5 g protein. **Diabetic Exchanges:** 1-1/2 starch, 1/2 fat.

Honey Almond Butter

(Pictured above)

Prep: 10 min. + chilling

To me, nothing tastes better than a warm homemade muffin right from the oven and topped with this yummy flavored butter. It's also wonderful on toast, English muffins, scones, quick breads, biscuits...you name it!
—Pat Hockett, Wrangell, Alaska

> **1 cup butter, softened**
> **1/4 cup honey**
> **1 tablespoon brown sugar**
> **1/2 teaspoon almond extract**

In a small mixing bowl, beat butter, honey, brown sugar and extract until light and fluffy. Transfer to a sheet of plastic wrap; roll into a log. Refrigerate until chilled. Unwrap and slice or place on a butter dish. **Yield:** 1-1/2 cups.

Corn Bread Pudding

Prep: 5 min.   **Bake:** 40 min.

I adapted this from my mother's recipe and don't need much convincing to whip up a big dishful.
—Bob Gebhardt, Wausau, Wisconsin

  2 eggs
  1 cup (8 ounces) sour cream
  1 can (15-1/4 ounces) whole kernel corn, drained
  1 can (14-3/4 ounces) cream-style corn
1/2 cup butter, melted
  1 package (8-1/2 ounces) corn bread/muffin mix
1/4 teaspoon paprika

In a large bowl, combine the first five ingredients. Stir in corn bread mix just until blended. Pour into a greased 3-qt. baking dish. Sprinkle with paprika.

Bake, uncovered, at 350° for 40-45 minutes or until a toothpick inserted near the center comes out clean. Serve warm. **Yield:** 12 servings.

Broccoli Scalloped Potatoes

(Pictured above right)

Prep: 20 min.   **Bake:** 1 hour

I love it that I can cook the entire meal—vegetables and all—in one dish. Created in my kitchen, this is a twist on traditional scalloped potatoes and ham.
—Denell Syslo, Fullerton, Nebraska

  2 tablespoons chopped onion
  4 garlic cloves, minced
1/4 cup butter, cubed
  5 tablespoons all-purpose flour
1/4 teaspoon white pepper
1/8 teaspoon salt
2-1/2 cups milk
  2 cups (8 ounces) shredded Swiss cheese, *divided*
  2 pounds medium potatoes, peeled and thinly sliced
  2 cups julienned fully cooked ham
  2 cups frozen broccoli florets, thawed and patted dry

In a large skillet, saute onion and garlic in butter for 3-4 minutes or until crisp-tender. Stir in the flour, pepper and salt until blended. Gradually stir in milk. Bring to a boil; cook and stir for 2 minutes or until thickened. Stir in 1 cup of cheese. Reduce heat; cook for 1-2 minutes or until cheese is melted (sauce will be thick).

Remove from the heat; gently stir in the potatoes, ham and broccoli. Transfer to a greased 13-in. x 9-in.

x 2-in. baking dish. Cover and bake at 350° for 40 minutes. Sprinkle with remaining cheese. Bake, uncovered, 20-25 minutes longer or until potatoes are tender and cheese is melted. **Yield:** 8 servings.

Shredded Potato Casserole

Prep: 10 min.   **Bake:** 45 min.

This potato dish is perfect with prime rib and many other entrees. Make it ahead and have it ready to pop into the oven for a party. The topping of cornflake crumbs and Parmesan adds crunch. *—Paula Zsiray, Logan, Utah*

  1 can (10-3/4 ounces) condensed cream of mushroom soup, undiluted
  1 cup (8 ounces) sour cream
1/2 cup milk
  1 cup (4 ounces) shredded cheddar cheese
1/2 cup butter, melted, *divided*
  1 package (30 ounces) frozen shredded hash brown potatoes, thawed
  1 cup cornflake crumbs
1/4 cup grated Parmesan cheese

In a large bowl, combine the soup, sour cream, milk, cheddar cheese and 1/4 cup butter. Stir in the hash browns. Transfer to a greased 13-in. x 9-in. x 2-in. baking dish. Combine the cornflake crumbs, Parmesan cheese and remaining butter; sprinkle over top. Bake, uncovered, at 325° for 45-50 minutes or until heated through. **Yield:** 6-8 servings.

(2 g saturated fat), 9 mg cholesterol, 396 mg sodium, 39 g carbohydrate, 9 g fiber, 9 g protein. **Diabetic Exchanges:** 2 starch, 2 vegetable, 1/2 fat.

Turkey Sausage Patties

(Pictured below)

Prep: 10 min. + chilling   **Cook:** 15 min.

I always try to eat smart—relying on delicious but light recipes like this homemade turkey sausage. It's great not only for breakfast but also for lunch or dinner. If you're a fan of garlic, try substituting it for the sage.
— *Janice Wuertzer, Dubuque, Iowa*

☑ **Uses less fat, sugar or salt. Includes Nutrition Facts and Diabetic Exchanges.**

   1 small onion, finely chopped
1/4 cup dry bread crumbs
   1 teaspoon rubbed sage
1/2 teaspoon salt
1/2 teaspoon paprika
1/4 teaspoon pepper
   1 pound lean ground turkey
   2 teaspoons canola oil

In a large bowl, combine the onion, bread crumbs, sage, salt, paprika and pepper. Crumble turkey over mixture and mix well. Shape into six patties. Cover and refrigerate for 2 hours.

In a large nonstick skillet over medium heat, cook patties in oil for 7 minutes on each side or until meat is no longer pink. **Yield:** 6 patties.

Nutrition Facts: 1 patty equals 150 calories, 8 g fat (2 g saturated fat), 60 mg cholesterol, 307 mg sodium, 4 g carbohydrate, trace fiber, 14 g protein. **Diabetic Exchanges:** 1-1/2 lean meat, 1 vegetable, 1 fat.

Springtime Barley

(Pictured above)

Prep/Total Time: 30 min.

While working as a sorority housemother, I occasionally filled in for the cook. The girls really appreciated this low-fat medley.   — *Sharon Helmick, Colfax, Washington*

☑ **Uses less fat, sugar or salt. Includes Nutrition Facts and Diabetic Exchanges.**

   1 small onion, chopped
   1 medium carrot, chopped
   1 tablespoon butter
   1 cup quick-cooking barley
   2 cups reduced-sodium chicken broth, *divided*
1/2 pound fresh asparagus, trimmed and cut into 1-inch pieces
1/4 teaspoon dried marjoram
1/8 teaspoon pepper
   2 tablespoons shredded Parmesan cheese

In a large skillet, saute onion and carrot in butter until crisp-tender. Stir in the barley; cook and stir for 1 minute. Stir in 1 cup broth. Bring to a boil. Reduce heat; cook and stir until liquid is absorbed.

Add asparagus. Cook for 15-20 minutes or until barley is tender and liquid is absorbed, stirring occasionally and adding more broth as needed. Stir in marjoram and pepper; sprinkle with Parmesan cheese. **Yield:** 4 servings.

Nutrition Facts: 3/4 cup equals 226 calories, 5 g fat

Sweet 'n' Tangy Carrots

(Pictured on page 44)

Prep/Total Time: 20 min.

I dress up carrots with a brown sugar and mustard sauce as a side dish for my New Year's holiday meal. Garnished with a little bright green parsley, the carrots add color to the dinner plate. —*Paula Zsiray, Logan, Utah*

  2 **pounds carrots, sliced**
1/4 **teaspoon salt**
1/2 **cup packed brown sugar**
  3 **tablespoons butter**
  2 **tablespoons Dijon mustard**
1/4 **teaspoon white pepper**
  2 **tablespoons minced fresh parsley**

Place the carrots in a large saucepan; sprinkle with salt and cover with water. Bring to a boil. Reduce heat; cover and simmer until tender, about 8 minutes. Drain well.

Return carrots to the pan; add brown sugar, butter, mustard and pepper. Cook and stir over low heat until well coated. Sprinkle with parsley. Serve with a slotted spoon. **Yield:** 6-8 servings.

Strawberry Freezer Jam

(Pictured on page 44)

Prep: 40 min. + freezing

Strawberry season is in early June here in Indiana. A dear friend of mine gave me this recipe when we were living in Germany. It is good on ice cream, too! —*Mary Jean Ellis, Indianapolis, Indiana*

    2 **quarts fresh strawberries**
5-1/2 **cups sugar**
    1 **cup light corn syrup**
  1/4 **cup lemon juice**
  3/4 **cup water**
    1 **package (1-3/4 ounces) powdered fruit pectin**

Wash and mash the berries, measuring out enough mashed berries to make 4 cups; place in a large bowl. Stir in the sugar, corn syrup and lemon juice. Let stand for 10 minutes.

In a small saucepan, bring water and pectin to a boil, stirring constantly. Cook and stir for 1 minute. Add to fruit mixture; stir for 3 minutes.

Pour into jars or freezer containers, leaving 1/2-in. headspace. Cover and let stand overnight or until set, but not longer than 24 hours. Refrigerate for up to 3 weeks or freeze for up to 1 year. **Yield:** 4-1/2 pints.

Tangy Rhubarb Chutney

(Pictured above)

Prep: 25 min.   **Cook:** 40 min. + chilling

My mother-in-law shared with me a great chutney recipe that I experiment with by changing ingredients. This version is a bit different, but I love the pear, onion and rhubarb combination. The longer it sets, the better it tastes! —*Barbara Estabrook, Rhinelander, Wisconsin*

  3 **cups chopped fresh *or* frozen rhubarb**
  1 **cup packed brown sugar**
  1 **cup white balsamic vinegar**
  1 **cup finely chopped onion**
3/4 **cup golden raisins**
  1 **tablespoon Worcestershire sauce**
  2 **teaspoons minced fresh gingerroot**
  1 **teaspoon salt**
3/4 **teaspoon curry powder**
1/4 **teaspoon ground nutmeg**
  2 **medium pears, peeled and diced**
  2 **tablespoons minced fresh mint**

In a large saucepan, combine the rhubarb, brown sugar, vinegar, onion, raisins, Worcestershire sauce, ginger, salt, curry and nutmeg. Cook and stir until mixture comes to a boil. Reduce heat; simmer, uncovered, for 25-30 minutes or until rhubarb is tender, stirring occasionally.

Add pears. Simmer, uncovered, 10-15 minutes longer or until pears are tender. Cool to room temperature. Stir in mint. Transfer to a bowl. Cover and refrigerate for at least 6 hours before serving. May be stored in the refrigerator up to 1 week. **Yield:** 4 cups.

Maple Vegetable Medley

(Pictured below)

Prep: 20 min. **Grill:** 25 min.

Terrific for summer, this recipe calls for fresh vegetables brushed with a maple glaze and grilled to perfection.
—*Lorraine Caland, Thunder Bay, Ontario*

✓ **Uses less fat, sugar or salt. Includes Nutrition Facts and Diabetic Exchanges.**

- 1/3 **cup balsamic vinegar**
- 1/3 **cup maple syrup**
- 1 **large red onion**
- 1 **pound fresh asparagus, trimmed**
- 1 **pound baby carrots**
- 2 **medium zucchini, cut lengthwise into thirds and seeded**
- 1 **medium sweet red pepper, cut into eight pieces**
- 1 **medium sweet yellow pepper, cut into eight pieces**
- 2 **tablespoons olive oil**
- 1 **tablespoon minced fresh thyme** *or* 1 **teaspoon dried thyme**
- 1/2 **teaspoon salt**
- 1/2 **teaspoon pepper**

For glaze, in a saucepan, bring vinegar and syrup to a boil. Reduce heat; cook and stir over medium heat for 6-8 minutes or until thickened. Remove from the heat; set aside.

Cut onion into eight wedges to 1/2 in. of the bottom. Place the onion, asparagus, carrots, zucchini and peppers in a large bowl. Drizzle with oil and sprinkle with seasonings; toss to coat.

Coat grill rack with nonstick cooking spray before starting the grill. Arrange vegetables on rack. Grill, covered, over medium heat for 10 minutes on each side. Brush with half of the glaze; grill 5-8 minutes longer or until crisp-tender. Before serving, brush with remaining glaze. **Yield:** 8 servings.

Nutrition Facts: 1 cup equals 120 calories, 4 g fat (1 g saturated fat), 0 cholesterol, 201 mg sodium, 21 g carbohydrate, 3 g fiber, 2 g protein. **Diabetic Exchanges:** 2 vegetable, 1/2 starch, 1/2 fat.

Lemon Green Beans

Prep/Total Time: 15 min.

Delicately seasoned with lemon and dill, these tender green beans taste fresh and inviting. They're a great accompaniment to almost any dinner entree.
—*Karalee Helminak, South Milwaukee, Wisconsin*

✓ **Uses less fat, sugar or salt. Includes Nutrition Facts and Diabetic Exchanges.**

- 1 **pound fresh green beans, trimmed**
- 2 **tablespoons lemon juice**
- 2 **tablespoons olive oil**
- 2 **tablespoons snipped fresh dill**
- 1/4 **teaspoon salt**

Place beans in a steamer basket; place in a large saucepan over 1 in. of water. Bring to a boil; cover and steam for 8-10 minutes or until crisp-tender.

In a jar with a tight-fitting lid, combine the lemon juice, oil, dill and salt; shake well. Transfer beans to a serving dish; add dressing and toss to coat. **Yield:** 6 servings.

Nutrition Facts: 2/3 cup equals 62 calories, 5 g fat (1 g saturated fat), 0 cholesterol, 103 mg sodium, 5 g carbohydrate, 2 g fiber, 1 g protein. **Diabetic Exchanges:** 1 vegetable, 1 fat.

Creamy Turkey Gravy

Prep/Total Time: 20 min.

With my easy recipe, even someone who has never made homemade gravy before can be assured of success.
—*Phyllis Schmalz, Kansas City, Kansas*

- 2 **tablespoons cornstarch**
- 2 **tablespoons turkey** *or* **chicken drippings**
- 2 **cups chicken broth**
- 1/4 **cup milk**

1/8 teaspoon salt
1/8 teaspoon pepper

In a small saucepan, whisk cornstarch and drippings until smooth. Gradually stir in the broth, milk, salt and pepper. Bring to a boil; cook and stir for 2 minutes or until thickened. Serve with turkey or chicken. **Yield:** 2-1/3 cups.

Curried Butternut Squash Kabobs

(Pictured at right)

Prep: 30 min. + cooling   **Grill:** 10 min.

These baked squash cubes pick up a mouth-watering grilled taste along with a mild curry butter flavor.
—*Mary Relyea, Canastota, New York*

1 butternut squash (2 pounds), peeled, seeded and cut into 1-inch cubes
3 tablespoons butter, melted
1 teaspoon curry powder
1/4 teaspoon salt

Place squash in a greased 13-in. x 9-in. x 2-in. baking dish. Combine the butter, curry powder and salt; drizzle over squash and toss to coat. Bake, uncovered, at 450° for 20-25 minutes or until tender and lightly browned, stirring twice. Cool on a wire rack.

Thread squash cubes onto 12 metal or soaked wooden skewers. Grill, covered, over medium heat for 3-5 minutes on each side or until heated through. **Yield:** 12 servings.

Kohlrabi 'n' Carrot Bake

(Pictured on page 44)

Prep: 35 min.   **Bake:** 20 min.

We love kohlrabies, but there don't seem to be many recipes that use them. This oven-baked one is wonderful!
—*Dianne Bettin, Truman, Minnesota*

3 medium kohlrabies, peeled and sliced
4 medium carrots, sliced
1/4 cup chopped onion
3 tablespoons butter, *divided*
2 tablespoons all-purpose flour
1/2 teaspoon salt
Dash pepper
1-1/2 cups milk
1/4 cup minced fresh parsley
1 tablespoon lemon juice
3/4 cup soft bread crumbs

Place kohlrabies and carrots in a large saucepan and cover with water. Bring to a boil. Reduce heat; cover and cook for 15-20 minutes or until tender. Drain well; set aside. In a large skillet, saute onion in 2 tablespoons butter until tender. Stir in flour, salt and pepper until blended. Gradually whisk in milk. Bring to a boil; cook and stir for 2 minutes or until thickened.

Remove from the heat. Stir in the vegetable mixture, parsley and lemon juice. Transfer to a shallow 2-qt. baking dish coated with nonstick cooking spray.

In a small skillet, melt remaining butter over medium heat. Add bread crumbs; cook and stir for 2-3 minutes or until lightly browned. Sprinkle over vegetable mixture. Bake, uncovered, at 350° for 20-25 minutes or until heated through. **Yield:** 6 servings.

Kabob Cues

Keep these tips in mind when preparing kabobs on the grill:
• Cut foods in uniform-size pieces.
• Don't bunch up the ingredients on the skewer. Leave a small space in between (1/4 inch) so each piece cooks thoroughly.
• Choose foods with similar cooking times, or add ingredients such as cherry tomatoes near the end of the cooking time.
• Remove food from skewers before serving. Use a fork to gently slide off the pieces.

cinnamon; set aside.

Unfold pastry sheets on a lightly floured surface. Roll each pastry to 1/8-in. thickness; transfer each to an ungreased baking sheet. Sprinkle with pecan mixture. Arrange squash slices to within 1-1/2 in. of edges, alternating slices of butternut and acorn squash.

Fold up edges of pastry over filling, leaving center uncovered. Brush pastry with egg. Dot squash with butter. Bake at 375° for 35-40 minutes or until golden brown. **Yield:** 2 tarts (8 servings each).

Editor's Note: This recipe was tested in a 1,100-watt microwave.

Rustic Squash Tarts

(Pictured above)

Prep: 30 min. **Bake:** 35 min.

Of all the delicious Thanksgiving side dishes we've tested, this recipe has been the biggest surprise. These rustic-looking and flaky pastry shells hold a sweet and spicy pecan layer under the squash slices. —Ann Marie Moch Kintyre, North Dakota

> 1 **medium butternut squash, peeled, seeded and cut into 1/8-inch slices**
> 1 **medium acorn squash, peeled, seeded and cut into 1/8-inch slices**
> 2 **tablespoons water**
> 1/4 **cup olive oil**
> 1 **tablespoon minced fresh thyme**
> 1 **tablespoon minced fresh parsley**
> 1/2 **teaspoon salt**
> 1/4 **teaspoon pepper**
> 1/2 **cup all-purpose flour**
> 1/2 **cup ground pecans**
> 6 **tablespoons sugar**
> 1/2 **teaspoon ground nutmeg**
> 1/2 **teaspoon ground cinnamon**
> 1 **package (17.3 ounces) frozen puff pastry, thawed**
> 1 **egg, beaten**
> 2 **tablespoons butter**

In a large microwave-safe bowl, combine squash and water. Cover and cook on high for 5 minutes or until crisp-tender. Drain; transfer to a large resealable plastic bag. Add the oil, thyme, parsley, salt and pepper; seal bag and shake to coat. Set aside. In a small bowl, combine the flour, pecans, sugar, nutmeg and

Potato Gnocchi

(Pictured below)

Prep: 30 min. **Cook:** 10 min. per batch

My Italian mother remembers how her mother made these dumplings for special occasions. She still has the bowl Grandma mixed the dough in, which will be passed down to me someday. —Tina Repak, Johnstown, Pennsylvania

> 4 **medium potatoes, peeled and quartered**
> 1 **egg, lightly beaten**
> 1-1/2 **teaspoons salt,** *divided*
> 1-3/4 **to 2 cups all-purpose flour**
> 3 **quarts water**
> **Spaghetti sauce, warmed**

Place potatoes in a saucepan and cover with water. Bring to a boil. Reduce heat; cover and cook for 15-20 minutes or until tender. Drain and mash.

Place 2 cups mashed potatoes in a large mixing bowl (save any remaining mashed potatoes for an-

other use). Stir in the egg and 1 teaspoon salt. Gradually beat in the flour until blended (the dough will be firm and elastic).

Turn onto a lightly floured surface; knead 15 times. Roll into 1/2-in.-wide ropes. Cut ropes into 1-in. pieces. Press down with a lightly floured fork.

In a Dutch oven, bring water and remaining salt to a boil. Add gnocchi in small batches; cook for 8-10 minutes or until gnocchi float to the top and are cooked through. Remove with a slotted spoon. Serve immediately with spaghetti sauce. **Yield:** 6-8 servings.

Italian-Style Broccoli

(Pictured below right)

Prep/Total Time: 30 min.

It's not a lot of fuss to dress up broccoli for Thanksgiving dinner with this tasty recipe. The bright broccoli adds lovely color to the table, too. —*Phyllis Schmalz South Milwaukee, Wisconsin*

    1/3 **cup finely chopped onion**
      1 **garlic clove, minced**
      2 **tablespoons olive oil**
  1-1/2 **pounds fresh broccoli, cut into 2-inch
          spears**
    1/4 **cup water**
    1/2 **teaspoon salt**
    1/4 **teaspoon chili powder**

In a large skillet, saute onion and garlic in oil for 2-3 minutes or until onion is tender. Stir in the broccoli, water, salt and chili powder. Bring to a boil. Reduce heat; cover and cook for 10-15 minutes or until broccoli is crisp-tender. **Yield:** 4 servings.

Gnocchi Notes

Gnocchi (pronounced NYOH-kee) are classic Italian dumplings often served with a tomato sauce. Many creative cooks like to put their own spin on this old-world recipe.

Traditionally, gnocchi are made with potatoes and flour or farina. Eggs and seasonings are added before the dough is shaped into long ropes and cut into small pieces. A fork, cheese grater or special gnocchi board is used to make small ridges in the pieces of dough. The indentations hold the sauce on the gnocchi and help them cook faster.

It's not difficult to make these favorite Italian dumplings for your own family. Just try Potato Gnocchi (recipe above left) and see!

Peppery Parsnip Fries

Prep: 15 min.   **Bake:** 20 min.

Looking for creative ways to use parsnips? These crispy bites are a healthier take on popular french fries. —*Sandy Abrams, Greenville, New York*

✓ **Uses less fat, sugar or salt. Includes Nutrition Facts and Diabetic Exchanges.**

      8 **medium parsnips, peeled**
      1 **tablespoon olive oil**
    1/4 **cup grated Parmesan cheese**
    1/2 **teaspoon salt**
    1/4 **teaspoon pepper**
    1/8 **teaspoon ground nutmeg**

Cut parsnips lengthwise into 2-1/2-in. x 1/2-in. sticks. In a large resealable plastic bag, combine the oil, Parmesan cheese, salt, pepper and nutmeg. Add parsnips, a few sticks at a time, and shake to coat.

Line two 15-in. x 10-in. x 1-in. baking pans with foil; coat the foil with nonstick cooking spray. Place the parsnips in a single layer in the pans. Bake at 425° for 20-25 minutes or until tender, turning several times. **Yield:** 8 servings.

Nutrition Facts: 1/2 cup equals 156 calories, 3 g fat (1 g saturated fat), 2 mg cholesterol, 210 mg sodium, 31 g carbohydrate, 6 g fiber, 3 g protein. **Diabetic Exchange:** 2 starch.

Parsnip Sweet Potato Pancakes

(Pictured below)

Prep: 20 min.   **Cook:** 30 min.

Golden brown sweet potatoes make these cakes pretty to look at and even better to eat. The green onions and thyme add an extra boost. —Amy Short
Lesage, West Virginia

- 1 cup all-purpose flour
- 3 tablespoons minced fresh thyme
- 2 teaspoons salt
- 1/4 teaspoon pepper
- 4 eggs, beaten
- 2 pounds sweet potatoes, peeled and grated
- 1 pound parsnips, peeled and grated
- 12 green onions, sliced diagonally
- 1/2 cup vegetable oil

In a large bowl, combine the flour, thyme, salt and pepper. Stir in eggs until blended. Add the sweet potatoes, parsnips and onions; toss to coat.

In an electric skillet or deep-fat fryer, heat oil to 375°. Drop batter by 1/4 cupfuls, a few at a time, into hot oil; press lightly to flatten. Fry for 3-4 minutes on each side or until golden brown. Drain on paper towels. Serve warm. **Yield:** 2 dozen.

German-Style Mashed Potatoes

(Pictured above)

Prep: 20 min.   **Cook:** 20 min.

Comforting and filling, these tangy potatoes will warm up any meal, especially one with a German flair. They're a fitting accompaniment to sausages like bratwurst. —Alena Horn, Austin, Texas

- 3 pounds red potatoes, peeled and cubed
- 2 large tart apples, peeled and chopped
- 4 bacon strips, diced
- 2 medium onions, sliced
- 1 tablespoon sugar
- 1 tablespoon cider vinegar
- 3/4 teaspoon salt

Place potatoes in a large saucepan and cover with water. Bring to a boil. Reduce heat; cover and cook for 10 minutes. Add apples; cook 10 minutes longer or until potatoes and apples are tender.

Meanwhile, in a large skillet, cook bacon over medium heat until crisp. Using a slotted spoon, remove to paper towels; drain, reserving 1 tablespoon drippings. In the drippings, saute onions until lightly browned.

Drain potatoes and apples. Add sugar, vinegar and salt; mash slightly. Transfer to a serving bowl. Top with onions and bacon. **Yield:** 7 servings.

Orange Rhubarb Spread

(Pictured below)

Prep: 5 min.   **Cook:** 20 min. + standing

This tangy spread is easy to make and tastes especially good on hot, buttered cinnamon toast. The recipe makes enough to have on hand well beyond the growing season.
—*Betty Nyenhuis, Oostburg, Wisconsin*

- **4 cups diced fresh *or* frozen rhubarb**
- **2 cups water**
- **1 can (6 ounces) frozen orange juice concentrate, thawed**
- **1 package (1-3/4 ounces) powdered fruit pectin**
- **4 cups sugar**

In a large saucepan, bring the rhubarb and water to a boil. Reduce heat; simmer, uncovered, for 7-8 minutes or until the rhubarb is tender. Drain and reserve cooking liquid. Cool rhubarb and liquid to room temperature.

Place the rhubarb in a blender; cover and process until pureed. Transfer to a 4-cup measuring cup; add enough reserved cooking liquid to measure 2-1/3 cups. Return to the saucepan.

Add orange juice concentrate and pectin; bring to a full rolling boil, stirring constantly. Stir in sugar. Return to a full rolling boil; boil and stir for 1 minute. Remove from the heat; skim off foam.

Pour into jars or freezer containers; cool to room temperature, about 1 hour. Cover and let stand overnight or until set, but not longer than 24 hours. Refrigerate or freeze. **Yield:** 5 half-pints.

Sprouts with Water Chestnuts

(Pictured above)

Prep/Total Time: 30 min.

This tasty side dish has become a family favorite at Thanksgiving, as well as throughout the year. A creamy sauce and water chestnuts give the sprouts a nice lift.
—*Genelle Smith, Hanover, Pennsylvania*

- **2 pounds fresh brussels sprouts, trimmed and halved**
- **2 tablespoons butter**
- **2 tablespoons all-purpose flour**
- **1/4 teaspoon salt**
- **1/4 teaspoon pepper**
- **1 cup chicken broth**
- **1 can (8 ounces) sliced water chestnuts, drained**

Place sprouts in a steamer basket; place in a large saucepan over 1 in. of water. Bring to a boil; cover and steam for 9-11 minutes or until crisp-tender.

Meanwhile, in a small saucepan, melt butter; stir in flour, salt and pepper until smooth. Gradually stir in broth. Bring to a boil; cook and stir for 2 minutes or until thickened. Stir in water chestnuts. Transfer brussels sprouts to a serving dish; top with water chestnut mixture. **Yield:** 9 servings.

Main Dishes

On every mealtime menu, the star attraction is the main course. When you need an outstanding entree to take center stage on the table, look no further than this chock-full chapter!

STANDOUT SELECTIONS. Clockwise from upper left: Spinach Venison Quiche (p. 81), Pecan Apple Pancakes (p. 87), Meat Loaf Wellington (p. 86), Dad's Swedish Meatballs (p. 82) and Veggie Turkey Pizza (p. 89).

Stuffed Ham with Raisin Sauce

(Pictured above)

Prep: 30 min.   **Bake:** 1-3/4 hours

I've served this impressive ham most often for brunch, but it also makes a great centerpiece for a holiday dinner.
—Jeanne Miller, Big Sky, Montana

  1 **boneless fully cooked ham (6 to 7 pounds)**
  1 **large onion, chopped**
1/4 **cup butter, cubed**
  2 **cups corn bread stuffing mix**
1-1/2 **cups chopped pecans, toasted**
1/2 **cup minced fresh parsley**
1/4 **cup egg substitute**
  2 **tablespoons prepared mustard**
1/2 **cup honey**
  2 **tablespoons orange juice concentrate**
RAISIN SAUCE:
1/2 **cup packed brown sugar**
  2 **tablespoons all-purpose flour**
1/2 **teaspoon ground mustard**
1/2 **cup raisins**

1-1/2 **cups water**
1/4 **cup cider vinegar**

Using a sharp knife and beginning at one end of ham, carefully cut a 2-1/2-in. circle about 6 in. deep; remove cutout. Cut a 1-1/2-in. slice from end of removed piece; set aside. Continue cutting a 2-1/2-in. tunnel halfway through ham, using a spoon to remove ham pieces (save for another use). Repeat from opposite end, until a tunnel has been cut through ham.

In a skillet, saute onion in butter until tender. In a large bowl, combine the next five ingredients. Stir in onion. Stuff ham; cover end openings with reserved ham slices. Place in a shallow roasting pan.

Bake, uncovered, at 325° for 1-1/4 hours. In a small saucepan, combine honey and orange juice concentrate; cook and stir for 1-2 minutes or until blended. Brush over ham. Bake 30 minutes longer or until a meat thermometer reads 140°.

For sauce, combine the brown sugar, flour, mustard and raisins in a saucepan. Gradually add water and vinegar. Bring to a boil; cook and stir for 1-2 minutes or until thickened. Serve with ham. **Yield:** 12-14 servings.

Oven Beef Stew

Prep: 20 min.   **Cook:** 2-1/4 hours

This is a great cold-weather meal—simply add a green salad. —Bettina Turner, Kernersville, North Carolina

✓ **Uses less fat, sugar or salt. Includes Nutrition Facts.**

1/4 **cup all-purpose flour**
1/4 **teaspoon salt, optional**
1/4 **teaspoon pepper**
1-1/2 **pounds boneless beef chuck roast, cut into 1-inch cubes**
  1 **medium onion, chopped**
  3 **garlic cloves, minced**
  1 **tablespoon canola oil**
  3 **cups beef broth**
  1 **can (14-1/2 ounces) stewed tomatoes, cut up**
3/4 **teaspoon dried thyme**
  3 **large potatoes, peeled and cut into 1-inch cubes**
  3 **medium carrots, cut into 1/4-inch slices**
1/2 **cup frozen peas, thawed**

In a large resealable plastic bag, combine the flour, salt if desired and pepper. Add beef, a few pieces at a time, and shake to coat. Save any remaining flour mixture.

In a Dutch oven, cook the beef, onion and garlic in oil over medium-high heat until meat is browned.

Stir in the reserved flour mixture until blended. Gradually stir in the broth, tomatoes and thyme. Cover and bake at 350° for 1-1/4 hours.

Add the potatoes and carrots. Cover and bake 1 hour longer or until meat and vegetables are tender. Stir in peas; cover and let stand for 5 minutes before serving. **Yield:** 6 servings.

Nutrition Facts: 1-1/2 cups (prepared with reduced-sodium broth; calculated without salt) equals 439 calories, 13 g fat (5 g saturated fat), 76 mg cholesterol, 426 mg sodium, 50 g carbohydrate, 6 g fiber, 30 g protein.

Chicken and Asparagus Kabobs

Prep: 25 min. + marinating   **Grill:** 10 min.

These Oriental-flavored kabobs, served with a delicious dipping sauce, are special enough to serve guests at your next backyard get-together. Sometimes I substitute chunks of salmon for the chicken. —Kelly Townsend
Syracuse, Nebraska

DIPPING SAUCE:
  2 cups mayonnaise
  1/4 cup sugar
  1/4 cup soy sauce
  2 tablespoons sesame seeds, toasted
  1 tablespoon sesame oil
  1/2 teaspoon white pepper
KABOBS:
  1/4 cup soy sauce
  2 tablespoons brown sugar
  2 tablespoons water
  1 tablespoon sesame oil
  1 teaspoon crushed red pepper flakes
  1 teaspoon minced fresh gingerroot
  1-1/2 pounds boneless skinless chicken
    breasts, cut into 1-1/2-inch pieces
  1 pound fresh asparagus, trimmed and cut
    into 2-inch pieces
  2 tablespoons olive oil
  1/2 teaspoon salt

In a bowl, combine the sauce ingredients. Cover and refrigerate for 2-4 hours.

In a large resealable plastic bag, combine the soy sauce, brown sugar, water, sesame oil, pepper flakes and ginger. Add the chicken; seal bag and turn to coat. Refrigerate for 2 hours, turning occasionally.

Drain and discard marinade. In a bowl, toss the asparagus with olive oil and salt. On six metal or soaked wooden skewers, alternately thread one chicken piece and two asparagus pieces. Grill, covered, over medium heat for 4-5 minutes on each side or until chicken juices run clear and asparagus is crisp-tender. Serve with dipping sauce. **Yield:** 6 servings.

Pretty Penne Ham Skillet

(Pictured below)
Prep/Total Time: 30 min.

I enjoy experimenting with herbs and spices to cut down on salt and sugar. Parsley, basil and oregano season this tasty main dish. —Kathy Stephan, West Seneca, New York

  1 pound uncooked penne *or* medium tube
    pasta
  3 cups cubed fully cooked ham
  1 large sweet red pepper, diced
  1 medium onion, chopped
  1/4 cup minced fresh parsley
  2 garlic cloves, minced
  1-1/2 teaspoons minced fresh basil *or* 1/2
    teaspoon dried basil
  1-1/2 teaspoons minced fresh oregano *or* 1/2
    teaspoon dried oregano
  1/4 cup olive oil
  3 tablespoons butter
  1 can (14-1/2 ounces) chicken broth
  1 tablespoon lemon juice
  1/2 cup shredded Parmesan cheese

Cook pasta according to package directions. Meanwhile, in a large skillet, saute the ham, red pepper, onion, parsley, garlic, basil and oregano in oil and butter for 4-6 minutes or until ham is browned and vegetables are tender.

Stir in broth and lemon juice. Bring to a boil. Reduce heat; simmer, uncovered, for 10-15 minutes or until liquid is reduced by half. Drain pasta; stir into ham mixture. Sprinkle with Parmesan cheese. **Yield:** 6 servings.

Red Snapper with Orange Sauce

(Pictured below)
Prep/Total Time: 30 min.

The tangy sauce really brings out the best in these red snapper fillets. —Barbara Nowakowski, Mesa, Arizona

✓ **Uses less fat, sugar or salt. Includes Nutrition Facts and Diabetic Exchanges.**

    2 pounds red snapper fillets
1/4 teaspoon salt
1/8 teaspoon pepper
    2 garlic cloves, minced
    1 tablespoon butter
    3 tablespoons orange juice
    1 teaspoon grated orange peel
ORANGE SAUCE:
    1 garlic clove, peeled
    2 tablespoons butter
    3 tablespoons orange juice
1/8 teaspoon ground ginger
    2 tablespoons minced fresh parsley

Place the fish in a single layer in a 13-in. x 9-in. x 2-in. baking dish coated with nonstick cooking spray; sprinkle with salt and pepper. In a small saucepan over medium heat, cook the garlic in butter for 1 minute; pour over fish. Drizzle with orange juice; sprinkle with orange peel. Bake, uncovered, at 400° for 10-15 minutes or until fish flakes easily with a fork.

In a small saucepan over medium heat, cook garlic in butter for 2-3 minutes or until golden brown; discard garlic. Stir orange juice and ginger into butter; heat through. Cut fish into serving-size pieces; drizzle with orange sauce. Sprinkle with parsley. **Yield:** 6 servings.

Nutrition Facts: About 5 ounces cooked fish equals 206 calories, 8 g fat (4 g saturated fat), 69 mg cholesterol, 222 mg sodium, 2 g carbohydrate, trace fiber, 30 g protein. **Diabetic Exchanges:** 4-1/2 very lean meat, 1 fat.

Waldorf Stuffed Ham

Prep: 35 min. **Bake:** 1-1/4 hours + standing

I couldn't resist trying something new for Taste of Home's "Ham It Up" contest, and this recipe came into my head. When I served it to my husband, he said it's a keeper. —Colleen Vrooman, Waukesha, Wisconsin

1-1/2 cups unsweetened apple juice
1/4 cup butter, cubed
    1 package (6 ounces) pork stuffing mix
    1 medium tart apple, finely chopped
1/4 cup chopped sweet onion
1/4 cup chopped celery
1/4 cup chopped walnuts
    1 fully cooked spiral-sliced ham (8 pounds)
    1 can (21 ounces) apple pie filling
1/4 teaspoon ground cinnamon

In a large saucepan, bring apple juice and butter to a boil. Remove from the heat; stir in the stuffing mix, apple, onion, celery and walnuts.

Place ham on a rack in a shallow roasting pan. Spoon stuffing by tablespoonfuls between ham slices. Spoon pie filling over the ham; sprinkle with cinnamon.

Bake, uncovered, at 325° for 1-1/4 to 1-3/4 hours or until a meat thermometer reads 140°. Let stand for 10 minutes before serving. **Yield:** 14-16 servings.

Prime Rib with Horseradish Sauce

Prep: 5 min. **Bake:** 3 hours

To ring in the New Year, we invite friends for dinner. This tender prime rib is festive yet simple to prepare. A pepper rub and mild horseradish sauce complement the beef's great flavor. —Paula Zsiray, Logan, Utah

    1 semi-boneless beef rib roast (4 to 6 pounds)
    1 tablespoon olive oil
    1 to 2 teaspoons coarsely ground pepper
HORSERADISH SAUCE:
    1 cup (8 ounces) sour cream
    3 to 4 tablespoons prepared horseradish
    1 teaspoon coarsely ground pepper
1/8 teaspoon Worcestershire sauce

Brush roast with oil; rub with pepper. Place roast, fat side up, in a shallow roasting pan. Bake, uncovered, at 450° for 15 minutes.

Reduce heat to 325°. Bake for 2-3/4 hours or until meat reaches desired doneness (for medium-rare, a meat thermometer should read 145°; medium, 160°; well-done, 170°), basting with pan drippings every 30 minutes.

Let stand for 10-15 minutes before slicing. Meanwhile, in a small bowl, combine the sauce ingredients. Serve with beef. **Yield:** 6-8 servings.

Mock Manicotti

(Pictured below)

Prep: 25 min. **Bake:** 45 min.

When my son tried manicotti at a restaurant and liked it, I created this version. It was a hit. —Deanne Schwarting
North English, Iowa

✓ **Uses less fat, sugar or salt. Includes Nutrition Facts and Diabetic Exchanges.**

- 3 cups (24 ounces) fat-free cottage cheese, drained
- 1 package (10 ounces) frozen chopped spinach, thawed and squeezed dry
- 1 package (8 ounces) reduced-fat cream cheese
- 1/2 cup reduced-fat sour cream
- 1 teaspoon garlic powder
- 1/8 teaspoon salt
- 1/8 teaspoon pepper
- 8 lasagna noodles, cooked, rinsed and drained
- 1 cup (4 ounces) shredded part-skim mozzarella cheese
- 1 cup meatless spaghetti sauce, optional

In a bowl, combine the cottage cheese, spinach, cream cheese, sour cream, garlic powder, salt and pepper. Spread 1/2 cup over each noodle; roll up jelly-roll style. Place seam side down in an 11-in. x 7-in. x 2-in. baking dish coated with nonstick cooking spray. Sprinkle with mozzarella cheese.

Cover and bake at 350° for 35 minutes. Uncover; drizzle with spaghetti sauce if desired. Bake 10 minutes longer or until heated through. **Yield:** 8 servings.

Nutrition Facts: 1 serving (calculated without spaghetti sauce) equals 287 calories, 10 g fat (7 g saturated fat), 37 mg cholesterol, 545 mg sodium, 26 g carbohydrate, 2 g fiber, 22 g protein. **Diabetic Exchanges:** 3 lean meat, 2 vegetable, 1 starch.

Roasted Chicken with Veggies

(Pictured above)

Prep: 20 min. **Bake:** 1-1/2 hours

Thyme accents this moist, golden brown chicken surrounded by bright, tender vegetables. It's an appealing meal-in-one. —Mary Beth Hansen, Columbia, Tennessee

✓ **Uses less fat, sugar or salt. Includes Nutrition Facts and Diabetic Exchanges.**

- 1 broiler/fryer chicken (3 to 3-1/2 pounds)
- 1 tablespoon canola oil
- 1/8 teaspoon salt
- 1/8 teaspoon pepper
- 6 medium carrots, cut into 1-inch pieces
- 4 celery ribs, cut into 1-inch pieces
- 3 medium baking potatoes, cut into 1-1/2-inch pieces
- 2 medium onions, cut into wedges
- 2 tablespoons butter, melted
- 4 teaspoons minced fresh thyme *or* 1 teaspoon dried thyme

Place chicken, breast side up, in a shallow roasting pan. Rub with oil; sprinkle with salt and pepper. Bake, uncovered, at 375° for 45 minutes.

Arrange the carrots, celery, potatoes and onions around chicken. Combine butter and thyme; drizzle over chicken and vegetables. Cover and bake 45-60 minutes longer or until a meat thermometer reads 180° and vegetables are tender. **Yield:** 6 servings.

Nutrition Facts: About 4 ounces cooked chicken (skin removed) with 1/2 cup vegetables (prepared with reduced-fat butter) equals 329 calories, 10 g fat (3 g saturated fat), 80 mg cholesterol, 187 mg sodium, 31 g carbohydrate, 5 g fiber, 28 g protein. **Diabetic Exchanges:** 3 lean meat, 2 vegetable, 1-1/2 starch.

(1 g saturated fat), 36 mg cholesterol, 785 mg sodium, 27 g carbohydrate, 8 g fiber, 23 g protein. **Diabetic Exchanges:** 2 lean meat, 1-1/2 starch, 1 vegetable.

Editor's Note: When cutting or seeding hot peppers, use rubber or plastic gloves to protect your hands. Avoid touching your face.

Beef Fajitas with Cilantro Sauce

(Pictured at left)

Prep: 15 min. + marinating   **Grill:** 25 min.

I found this recipe in the newspaper and made some variations. The jalapeno gives a bit of zing to the sauce.
—Rebecca Sodergren, Wichita Falls, Texas

✓ Uses less fat, sugar or salt. Includes Nutrition Facts and Diabetic Exchanges.

- 4 tablespoons lime juice, *divided*
- 3 tablespoons olive oil, *divided*
- 2 tablespoons minced fresh thyme
- 1 tablespoon hot pepper sauce
- 1 boneless beef sirloin steak (1-1/2 pounds)
- 1-1/2 cups fat-free plain yogurt
- 1/2 cup fresh cilantro leaves
- 1 jalapeno pepper, seeded
- 2 large green peppers, halved
- 2 large onions, thickly sliced
- 8 flour tortillas (6 inches), warmed

Shredded lettuce, tomato wedges and sliced ripe olives, optional

In a large resealable plastic bag, combine 3 tablespoons lime juice, 2 tablespoons oil, thyme and hot pepper sauce. Add the beef; seal bag and turn to coat. Refrigerate for at least 2 hours.

For sauce, place the yogurt, cilantro, jalapeno and remaining lime juice in a blender; cover and process until smooth. Transfer to a bowl; refrigerate until serving. Brush the green peppers and onions with the remaining oil; set aside.

Drain and discard the marinade. Grill the beef, uncovered, over medium-hot heat for 6-7 minutes on each side or until meat reaches desired doneness (for medium-rare, a meat thermometer should read 145°; medium, 160°; well-done, 170°). Let stand for 10 minutes before slicing.

Meanwhile, grill the green peppers and onions, uncovered, over medium-hot heat for 5 minutes on each side or until crisp-tender. Cut into strips; spoon onto tortillas. Top with the beef. Serve with the cilantro sauce. Garnish with lettuce, tomato and olives if desired. **Yield:** 8 servings.

Nutrition Facts: 1 beef fajita with 1/4 cup sauce (calculated without the optional ingredients) equals

White Bean Chicken Stew

(Pictured above)

Prep: 15 min.   **Cook:** 20 min.

I dreamed up this hearty stew chock-full of white beans and chicken chunks. For a spicier version, simply add more peppers. —LaDonna Reed, Ponca City, Oklahoma

✓ Uses less fat, sugar or salt. Includes Nutrition Facts and Diabetic Exchanges.

- 1 medium onion, chopped
- 1 jalapeno pepper, seeded and chopped
- 4 garlic cloves, minced
- 1 tablespoon canola oil
- 4 cups reduced-sodium chicken broth
- 2 cans (15-1/2 ounces *each*) great northern beans, rinsed and drained
- 1-1/4 teaspoons ground cumin
- 2 tablespoons cornstarch
- 1/4 cup cold water
- 2 cups cubed cooked chicken breast
- 2 tablespoons minced fresh parsley

In a large saucepan, saute the onion, jalapeno and garlic in oil until tender. Add the broth, beans and cumin. Bring to a boil. Reduce heat; cover and simmer for 10-15 minutes or until heated through.

Combine cornstarch and water until smooth; stir into stew. Bring to a boil; cook and stir for 2 minutes or until thickened. Add chicken and parsley; heat through. **Yield:** 6 servings.

Nutrition Facts: 1 cup equals 243 calories, 4 g fat

265 calories, 10 g fat (2 g saturated fat), 49 mg cholesterol, 291 mg sodium, 23 g carbohydrate, 2 g fiber, 22 g protein. **Diabetic Exchanges:** 2-1/2 lean meat, 1 starch, 1 vegetable.

Editor's Note: When cutting or seeding hot peppers, use rubber or plastic gloves to protect your hands. Avoid touching your face.

Bacon Honey Walleye

Prep: 20 min.   **Grill:** 15 min.

The texture and flavor of these fillets are enhanced by the savory-sweet topping.   —*Linda Neumann*
Algonac, Michigan

   16 bacon strips, partially cooked
    4 walleye fillets (2-1/2 pounds)
    1 cup thinly sliced onion
  1/4 cup butter, melted
    2 tablespoons honey
  1/2 teaspoon salt
  1/4 teaspoon pepper

Fold four 18-in. x 15-in. pieces of heavy-duty aluminum foil in half; fold up edges to make pans about 12 in. x 7 in. Place four strips of bacon in each foil pan; top each with a fillet and 1/4 cup onion. Drizzle with butter and honey. Sprinkle with salt and pepper.

Grill the fillets, covered, over medium heat for 12-15 minutes or until the fish flakes easily with a fork. Cut the fillets in half; serve each with two bacon strips. **Yield:** 8 servings.

Smoked Salmon Pizza

Prep/Total Time: 25 min.

This is great for a light supper. It's easy, too, so put away that frozen pizza!   —*Kathy Petty, Portland, Oregon*

    1 prebaked thin Italian bread shell crust
       (10 ounces)
  1/2 cup ranch salad dressing
    6 slices tomato
  1/2 cup crumbled feta cheese
    1 package (3 ounces) smoked cooked
       salmon
    4 slices provolone cheese, cut in half

Place crust on an ungreased 14-in. pizza pan. Spread with ranch dressing; top with tomato, feta cheese and salmon. Arrange provolone cheese over top. Bake at 425° for 15-20 minutes or until cheese is melted. **Yield:** 6-8 slices.

Beef Stir-Fry on a Stick

(Pictured below)

Prep: 20 min.   **Grill:** 15 min.

A thick Oriental sauce coats these tender beef and vegetable kabobs that are served over rice. They're fun to eat and always a big hit.   —*Gwendolyn Lambert*
Frisco City, Alabama

  1/2 cup hoisin sauce
    3 tablespoons water
    2 tablespoons vegetable oil
    1 tablespoon soy sauce
    1 garlic clove, minced
  1/4 to 1/2 teaspoon crushed red pepper flakes
    3 cups large fresh broccoli florets
    2 medium yellow summer squash, cut into
       3/4-inch slices
    1 large sweet red pepper, cut into 1-inch
       pieces
    1 pound beef tenderloin, cut into 1-inch
       cubes
Hot cooked rice

For glaze, in a small bowl, combine the hoisin sauce, water, oil, soy sauce, garlic and pepper flakes.

On four metal or soaked wooden skewers, alternately thread the broccoli, squash, red pepper and beef. Brush with 1/3 cup of glaze. Grill, covered, over medium heat for 6-7 minutes on each side or until meat reaches desired doneness and vegetables are tender, basting once with remaining glaze. Serve with rice. **Yield:** 4 servings.

Spiral Ham with Cranberry Glaze

(Pictured above and on front cover)

Prep: 15 min.   **Bake:** 3 hours

The sweet tangy glaze that complements this ham looks so pretty, and the cranberry flavor pairs well with the meat. It's been a tradition in my home for as long as I can remember.   —Pattie Prescott, Manchester, New Hampshire

  1 **fully cooked spiral-sliced ham (8 pounds)**
  1 **can (16 ounces) whole-berry cranberry sauce**
  1 **package (12 ounces) fresh *or* frozen cranberries**
  1 **jar (12 ounces) red currant jelly**
  1 **cup light corn syrup**
1/2 **teaspoon ground ginger**

Place ham on a rack in a shallow roasting pan. Cover and bake at 325° for 2-1/2 hours. Meanwhile, for glaze, combine the remaining ingredients in a saucepan. Bring to a boil. Reduce heat; simmer, uncovered, until cranberries pop, stirring occasionally. Remove from the heat; set aside.

Uncover ham; bake 30 minutes longer or until a meat thermometer reads 140°, basting twice with 1-1/2 cups glaze. Serve remaining glaze with ham. **Yield:** 12-16 servings.

Sausage-Stuffed Pork Roast

Prep: 30 min.   **Bake:** 1-3/4 hours + standing

I'm a truck driver who likes to cook, much to my wife's delight! This savory roast is unique with its sausage and carrot filling, and it cuts nicely, too.   —William Boothe, Hillsboro, Oregon

1-1/2 **pounds bulk pork sausage**
  1/2 **cup dry bread crumbs**
  1/2 **cup ricotta cheese**
  1/2 **cup shredded carrot**
    6 **garlic cloves, minced**
    1 **tablespoon dried parsley flakes**
    1 **boneless whole pork loin roast (3 to 4 pounds)**
  1/2 **teaspoon salt**
  1/8 **teaspoon pepper**
    2 **tablespoons vegetable oil**

In a large skillet, cook sausage over medium heat until no longer pink; drain. Transfer to a large bowl. Add the bread crumbs, ricotta cheese, carrot, garlic and parsley; set aside.

Starting about a third in from one side, make a lengthwise slit in the roast to within 1/2 in. of bottom. Turn roast over and make another lengthwise slit, starting from about a third in from the opposite side. Open roast so it lies flat; cover with plastic wrap. Flatten to 3/4-in. thickness. Remove plastic wrap.

Spread sausage mixture over meat to within 1 in. of edges. Sprinkle with salt and pepper. Roll up jelly-roll style, starting with a long side. Tie several times with kitchen string and secure ends with toothpicks. Place seam side down on a rack in a shallow roasting pan. Rub oil over roast.

Cover and bake at 350° for 45 minutes. Uncover; bake 60-70 minutes longer or until a meat thermometer reads 160°. Discard toothpicks. Let stand for 10-15 minutes before slicing. **Yield:** 12-14 servings.

Creamy Ham 'n' Macaroni

Prep: 20 min.   **Bake:** 20 min.

The original comfort food, macaroni and cheese gets a mouth-watering makeover with the addition of cubed ham and grated Parmesan in this recipe. Kids will love it!   —Christy Looper, Colorado Springs, Colorado

  2 **cups uncooked elbow macaroni**
1/4 **cup butter, cubed**
1/4 **cup all-purpose flour**
  2 **cups milk**
  4 **teaspoons chicken bouillon granules**
1/4 **teaspoon pepper**

2 cups (8 ounces) shredded cheddar
   cheese, *divided*
1-1/2 cups cubed fully cooked ham
1/4 cup grated Parmesan cheese

Cook macaroni according to package directions; drain and set aside. In a large saucepan, melt butter over low heat; whisk in flour until smooth. Whisk in the milk, bouillon and pepper. Bring to a boil; cook and stir for 2 minutes or until thickened. Remove from the heat. Stir in 1 cup cheddar cheese, ham, Parmesan cheese and macaroni.

Transfer to a greased 2-qt. baking dish. Sprinkle with remaining cheddar cheese. Bake, uncovered, at 350° for 20-25 minutes or until bubbly. Let stand for 5 minutes before serving. **Yield:** 6 servings.

Chicken in Mushroom Sauce

Prep/Total Time: 30 min.

You won't need to heat the oven for this tasty microwave entree. —Betty Claycomb, Alverton, Pennsylvania

✓ **Uses less fat, sugar or salt. Includes Nutrition Facts and Diabetic Exchanges.**

1/2 pound sliced fresh mushrooms
1/2 cup chopped green onions
  1 tablespoon butter
  2 tablespoons all-purpose flour
1/2 cup reduced-fat plain yogurt
1/4 cup water
  2 tablespoons reduced-sodium chicken broth
  1 teaspoon reduced-sodium chicken
     bouillon granules
1/8 teaspoon pepper
  4 boneless skinless chicken breast halves
     (5 ounces *each*)

In a 2-qt. microwave-safe dish, combine mushrooms and onions. Cover and microwave on high for 2-4 minutes or until mushrooms are tender; drain. Set aside.

In the same dish, melt the butter. Stir in flour until smooth; add the yogurt, water, broth, bouillon and pepper. Stir in the mushroom mixture.

Arrange chicken in another 2-qt. microwave-safe dish; top with mushroom sauce. Cover and microwave at 50% power for 15-20 minutes or until juices run clear, stirring sauce twice. **Yield:** 4 servings.

Nutrition Facts: 1 chicken breast half with about 1/2 cup sauce equals 232 calories, 7 g fat (3 g saturated fat), 88 mg cholesterol, 220 mg sodium, 9 g carbohydrate, 1 g fiber, 33 g protein. **Diabetic Exchanges:** 4 lean meat, 1/2 starch.

Editor's Note: This recipe was tested in a 1,100-watt microwave.

Cranberry Ham Loaf

(Pictured below)

Prep: 20 min.   **Bake:** 70 min.

A cranberry sauce topping makes this easy-to-prepare loaf festive enough for a holiday dinner. I find it's a great way to use up leftover ham. —Ronald Heffner
Pawleys Island, South Carolina

  1 egg, lightly beaten
  1 cup milk
  2 medium onions, chopped
  1 medium green pepper, chopped
  1 cup soft bread crumbs
1-1/2 pounds ground fully cooked ham
  1 pound bulk pork sausage
  1 can (16 ounces) whole-berry cranberry
     sauce
1/4 cup water
  1 tablespoon light corn syrup

In a large bowl, combine the egg, milk, onions, green pepper and bread crumbs. Crumble ham and sausage over mixture; mix well.

Pat into an ungreased 9-in. x 5-in. x 3-in. loaf pan (pan will be full). Place on a baking sheet. Bake, uncovered, at 350° for 70-80 minutes or until a meat thermometer reads 160°.

In a small saucepan, combine the cranberry sauce, water and corn syrup. Bring to a boil. Reduce heat; simmer, uncovered, for 5 minutes or until thickened. Remove ham loaf to a serving platter; top with cranberry sauce. **Yield:** 8 servings.

Warm Up with Savory Stews

WANT TO KNOW how to chase away winter's chill? Try hot helpings of these hearty stews chock-full of meat, veggies and more. With each satisfying spoonful, you'll feel cozy and content no matter how cold it may be outside.

Choose a down-home stew brimming with chunks of chicken, pork or beef. No matter which recipe you select, you'll soon have a meal-in-one fresh from the stove, slow cooker or oven...and guaranteed to please even the hungriest among your bunch.

Chicken Stew

(Pictured at far right)

Prep: 10 min.   **Cook:** 35 min.

Farm-fresh cream gave old-fashioned chicken stews a wonderful richness. This version uses half-and-half cream to cut the fat while keeping the home-style taste.
—*Ruby Williams, Bogalusa, Louisiana*

✓ **Uses less fat, sugar or salt. Includes Nutrition Facts.**

   1 broiler/fryer chicken (3 pounds), cut up
   4 cups water, *divided*
   2 teaspoons dill weed
 1/2 teaspoon salt
 1/4 teaspoon pepper
   4 medium carrots, cut into 1/2-inch slices
   2 medium potatoes, peeled and cut into 1-inch cubes
   2 medium parsnips, peeled and cut into 1/2-inch slices
   5 tablespoons all-purpose flour
 1/3 cup half-and-half cream

Remove and discard skin from chicken; rinse and pat dry. Place chicken pieces in a Dutch oven; add 3-1/2 cups water, dill, salt and pepper. Bring to a boil. Reduce heat; cover and simmer for 5 minutes. Add the carrots, potatoes and parsnips. Cover; simmer for 20 minutes or until the chicken juices run clear.

Using a slotted spoon, remove chicken and vegetables to a large bowl; keep warm. Bring cooking juices to a boil. In a small bowl, combine flour, half-and-half cream and remaining water until smooth; gradually stir into juices. Cook and stir for 2 minutes or until thickened. Pour over chicken and vegetables. **Yield:** 4 servings.

Nutrition Facts: 1-1/4 cups (prepared with fat-free half-and-half) equals 460 calories, 9 g fat (3 g saturated fat), 110 mg cholesterol, 442 mg sodium, 51 g carbohydrate, 7 g fiber, 42 g protein.

Creamy Cabbage-Pork Stew

(Pictured at right)

Prep: 20 min.   **Cook:** 6 hours

Savory flavors blend beautifully in this hearty stew that cooks in a slow cooker. In a pinch, I use chunks of garlic bologna in place of the cubed pork shoulder.
—*Ruth Ann Stelfox, Raymond, Alberta*

   1 pound boneless pork shoulder, cut into 3/4-inch cubes
   1 tablespoon vegetable oil
   2 cans (10-3/4 ounces *each*) condensed cream of celery soup, undiluted
1-1/2 cups apple juice
   2 medium red potatoes, cut into 1-inch chunks
   3 medium carrots, sliced
 1/4 teaspoon caraway seeds
 1/4 teaspoon pepper
   3 cups coarsely chopped cabbage
 1/2 cup milk

In a large skillet over medium-high heat, brown pork in oil; drain. Place in a 3-qt. slow cooker; stir in the soup, apple juice, potatoes, carrots, caraway and pepper. Cover and cook on high for 3-1/2 hours.

Add the cabbage and milk. Cover and cook 2-1/2 hours longer or until meat and vegetables are tender. **Yield:** 6 servings.

Ground Beef Biscuit Stew

(Pictured above right)

Prep: 10 min.   **Bake:** 30 min.

For a change of pace, I sometimes add a little chili powder to the meat mixture and top this meal-in-one with a prepared corn bread mix. I've been making this for over 25 years. —*Darlene Brenden, Salem, Oregon*

   1 pound ground beef
   1 medium onion, chopped
   1 can (14-1/2 ounces) stewed tomatoes, cut up

SURE TO SATISFY. Chicken Stew, Creamy Cabbage-Pork Stew and Ground Beef Biscuit Stew (shown above) are *Taste of Home* readers' hearty favorites.

    1 package (10 ounces) frozen mixed
      vegetables
    1 can (8 ounces) tomato sauce
BISCUITS:
    1 cup all-purpose flour
1-1/2 teaspoons baking powder
    2 tablespoons shortening
  2/3 cup milk
    1 teaspoon prepared mustard
  1/2 cup shredded cheddar cheese, *divided*

In a large skillet, cook beef and onion over medium heat until meat is no longer pink; drain. Stir in the tomatoes, mixed vegetables and tomato sauce. Transfer to a greased 11-in. x 7-in. x 2-in. baking dish. Cover and bake at 400° for 15 minutes.

For biscuits, in a bowl, combine flour and baking powder. Cut in shortening until mixture resembles coarse crumbs. With a fork, stir in milk and mustard until mixture forms a soft dough. Add 6 tablespoons cheese. Drop by tablespoonfuls onto stew. Bake for 15-20 minutes or until golden brown; sprinkle with remaining cheese. **Yield:** 6 servings.

Stew Savvy

Speaking of stews, here are a few hints you may find helpful:

- If your stew needs just a little extra thickening, stir in a few tablespoons of fresh white, whole wheat or rye bread crumbs.
- Great garnishes for stew include shredded cheese, sour cream, minced chives, bacon bits and chopped celery.
- Use leftover stew to fill a meat pie. Line a 9-inch deep-dish pie plate with pastry; fill it with about 5 cups of stew and top it with pastry. Cut a vent for steam and bake at 375° until golden brown, for 30-45 minutes.
- Wondering what to serve with stew? No matter how you slice it, bread is a perfect complement. Pick up a loaf of your favorite kind from your grocer's bakery. Corn bread or corn muffins are another tasty option.
- You could also pair stew with a green salad. Just toss one together and enjoy a full meal.

Crispy Fried Chicken

(Pictured below)

Prep: 10 min.   **Cook:** 10 min. per batch

Always a picnic favorite, this chicken is delicious hot or cold. It's such a mouth-watering classic, no one can resist a piece...and most folks come back for seconds!
—Jeanne Schnitzler, Lima, Montana

> 4 **cups all-purpose flour,** *divided*
> 2 **tablespoons garlic salt**
> 1 **tablespoon paprika**
> 3 **teaspoons pepper,** *divided*
> 2-1/2 **teaspoons poultry seasoning**
> 2 **eggs**
> 1-1/2 **cups water**
> 1 **teaspoon salt**
> 2 **broiler/fryer chickens (3-1/2 to 4 pounds** *each***), cut up**
> **Oil for deep-fat frying**

In a large resealable plastic bag, combine 2-2/3 cups flour, garlic salt, paprika, 2-1/2 teaspoons pepper and poultry seasoning. In a shallow bowl, beat eggs and water; add salt and remaining flour and pepper. Dip chicken in egg mixture, then place in the bag, a few pieces at a time, and shake until coated.

In a deep-fat fryer, heat oil to 375°. Fry chicken, several pieces at a time, for 5-6 minutes on each side or until golden brown and crispy and juices run clear. Drain on paper towels. **Yield:** 8 servings.

Cauliflower Ham Casserole

Prep: 20 min.   **Bake:** 40 min.

Cauliflower replaces the potatoes in this comforting casserole, which I've been making for 30 years. Whenever we have leftover ham, my husband asks me to make this dish.
—Sue Herlund, White Bear Lake, Minnesota

> 4 **cups chopped fresh cauliflower**
> 1/4 **cup butter, cubed**
> 1/3 **cup all-purpose flour**
> 2 **cups milk**
> 1 **cup (4 ounces) shredded cheddar cheese**
> 1/2 **cup sour cream**
> 2 **cups cubed fully cooked ham**
> 1 **jar (4-1/2 ounces) sliced mushrooms, drained**

TOPPING:
> 1 **cup soft bread crumbs**
> 1 **tablespoon butter, melted**

Place cauliflower in a large saucepan; cover with water. Bring to a boil. Reduce heat; cover and simmer for 5-10 minutes or until tender.

Meanwhile, in another large saucepan, melt butter. Stir in flour until smooth; gradually add milk. Bring to a boil; cook and stir for 2 minutes or until thickened. Remove from the heat. Stir in the cheese and sour cream until melted.

Drain cauliflower. In a large bowl, combine the cauliflower, ham and mushrooms. Add cheese sauce and toss to coat.

Transfer to a greased 2-qt. baking dish. Combine topping ingredients; sprinkle over casserole. Bake, uncovered, at 350° for 40-45 minutes or until heated through. **Yield:** 6 servings.

Spicy Salmon Kabobs

Prep: 15 min. + marinating   **Grill:** 10 min.

I first prepared these kabobs for a team of archaeologists excavating a site in the Aleutian Islands. We used fresh sockeye salmon, but other varieties of salmon work well, too.
—Terri Mach, Homer, Alaska

> 1-1/2 **pounds salmon fillets, cut into 1-1/2-inch cubes**
> 1 **tablespoon brown sugar**
> 1 **teaspoon salt**
> 1 **teaspoon garlic powder**
> 1 **teaspoon celery seed**
> 1 **teaspoon pepper**
> 1 **teaspoon paprika**
> 1/2 **teaspoon onion powder**

1/2 teaspoon cayenne pepper
1/4 teaspoon chili powder
1/8 teaspoon fennel seed, crushed
1/8 teaspoon ground cumin

Place the salmon in a large resealable plastic bag. Combine the remaining ingredients; sprinkle over salmon. Seal bag and toss to coat; refrigerate for 30 minutes.

Thread the salmon onto six metal or soaked wooden skewers. Grill, covered, over medium heat for 4-6 minutes on each side or until fish flakes easily with a fork. **Yield:** 6 servings.

Chicken Fajita Pizza

Prep: 20 min.   **Bake:** 20 min.

Pizza takes a southwest turn in this version. I made this recipe on the first date—an evening of cooking at my apartment—with my husband, Gary.   *—Tricia Longo*
Spencer, Massachusetts

✓ **Uses less fat, sugar or salt. Includes Nutrition Facts and Diabetic Exchanges.**

  1 tube (13.8 ounces) refrigerated pizza crust
1/2 pound boneless skinless chicken breasts, cut into strips
  2 tablespoons olive oil
1/2 cup sliced onion
1/2 cup julienned green pepper
  3 garlic cloves, minced
  1 teaspoon chili powder
1/4 teaspoon salt
1/8 teaspoon pepper
  1 cup salsa
  2 cups (8 ounces) shredded Mexican cheese blend

Unroll crust into a greased 15-in. x 10-in. x 1-in. baking pan; flatten dough and build up edges slightly. Bake at 400° for 8-10 minutes or until lightly browned.

Meanwhile, in a large skillet, saute chicken in oil until lightly browned. Add onion, green pepper, garlic, chili powder, salt and pepper. Cook and stir until the vegetables are tender and chicken is no longer pink.

Spread salsa over crust. Top with 1 cup cheese, chicken mixture and remaining cheese. Bake at 400° for 10-15 minutes or until cheese is bubbly and golden brown. **Yield:** 12 slices.

Nutrition Facts: 1 slice (prepared with reduced-fat cheese) equals 191 calories, 8 g fat (2 g saturated fat), 24 mg cholesterol, 505 mg sodium, 19 g carbohydrate, 2 g fiber, 14 g protein. **Diabetic Exchanges:** 1-1/2 lean meat, 1 starch, 1 vegetable.

Vegetarian Penne

(Pictured above)
Prep/Total Time: 20 min.

I've served this satisfying, quick meal for both friends and relatives who are vegetarians. They love it!
—Shirley Brazel, Rocklin, California

✓ **Uses less fat, sugar or salt. Includes Nutrition Facts and Diabetic Exchanges.**

  2 cups uncooked penne *or* medium tube pasta
  1 cup baby carrots, halved lengthwise
  1 garlic clove, minced
  1 tablespoon canola oil
  2 cans (14-1/2 ounces *each*) stewed tomatoes
  2 cups frozen cut green beans
  2 teaspoons dried basil
1/2 teaspoon dried oregano
  3 tablespoons cornstarch
1/4 cup water
  1 tablespoon minced fresh parsley

Cook pasta according to package directions. Meanwhile, in a large nonstick skillet, saute carrots and garlic in oil until tender. Add tomatoes, beans, basil and oregano; bring to a boil. Reduce the heat; simmer, uncovered, until vegetables are tender.

Combine cornstarch and water until smooth; stir into vegetables. Bring to a boil; cook and stir for 2 minutes or until thickened. Drain pasta; stir into the vegetables. Sprinkle with parsley. **Yield:** 8 servings.

Nutrition Facts: 1 cup equals 125 calories, 2 g fat (trace saturated fat), 0 cholesterol, 237 mg sodium, 24 g carbohydrate, 3 g fiber, 3 g protein. **Diabetic Exchanges:** 2 vegetable, 1 starch.

Sweet Cherry French Toast

Prep: 15 min. + chilling   **Bake:** 15 min.

You'll be proud to serve this tasty brunch bake. The cherry topping and dollop of yogurt make each bite a yummy treat.   —*Elisa Lochridge, Aloha, Oregon*

>   8 slices French bread (1 inch thick)
>   6 eggs
> 1-1/2 cups milk
>   1/3 cup maple syrup
>   2 tablespoons sugar
>   1 tablespoon grated orange peel
>   1/8 teaspoon salt
> **CHERRY TOPPING:**
>   4 cups fresh *or* frozen pitted sweet cherries
>   1/2 cup orange juice
>   1 tablespoon sugar
>   4 teaspoons cornstarch
>   4 teaspoons cold water
> **Vanilla yogurt**

Place the bread in a greased 15-in. x 10-in. x 1-in. baking pan. In a bowl, whisk the eggs, milk, syrup, sugar, orange peel and salt. Pour over bread; turn to coat. Cover and refrigerate overnight. In a bowl, combine the cherries, orange juice and sugar. Cover and refrigerate overnight.

Transfer bread slices to another greased 15-in. x 10-in. x 1-in. baking pan. Discard any remaining egg mixture. Bake at 400° for 15-18 minutes or until golden brown, turning once.

Meanwhile, in a small saucepan, combine cornstarch and water until smooth. Stir in the reserved cherry mixture. Bring to a boil; cook and stir for 2 minutes or until thickened. Serve over French toast; drizzle with yogurt. **Yield:** 4 servings.

Cornmeal Ham Cakes

(Pictured above)

Prep/Total Time: 30 min.

These cakes are terrific for breakfast, but my husband and I also enjoy them in the evening. It's a fantastic way to use up extra ham from yesterday's dinner.
—*Priscilla Gilbert, Indian Harbour Beach, Florida*

>   1/2 cup all-purpose flour
>   1/2 cup cornmeal
>   2 tablespoons sugar
>   1/2 teaspoon baking powder
>   1/4 teaspoon baking soda
>   1/8 teaspoon salt
>   2 eggs
>   1 cup buttermilk
>   3 tablespoons butter, melted
>   1 teaspoon vanilla extract
> 1-1/2 cups diced fully cooked ham
> **PINEAPPLE MAPLE SYRUP:**
>   1 cup diced fresh pineapple
>   1/4 teaspoon ground cinnamon
>   1 tablespoon butter
>   1 cup maple syrup

In a large bowl, combine the first six ingredients. Combine the eggs, buttermilk, butter and vanilla; stir into dry ingredients until well blended. Fold in ham. Pour batter by 1/4 cupfuls onto a greased hot griddle. Turn when bubbles form on top; cook until second side is golden brown.

For syrup, in a small saucepan, saute pineapple and cinnamon in butter for 4-6 minutes or until pineapple is browned. Stir in maple syrup. Serve with pancakes. **Yield:** 4 servings.

Avocado Eggs Benedict

Prep/Total Time: 20 min.

Fresh avocado slices and a special creamy sauce really dress up this classic egg dish. It's great any time of day and never fails to impress guests.   —*Deborah Hilpipre
Eden Prairie, Minnesota*

>   1/2 cup butter
>   1/4 cup all-purpose flour
>   2 cups milk
>   2 cups (8 ounces) shredded cheddar cheese
>   1 tablespoon grated Romano cheese
>   1/2 teaspoon salt
>   1/8 teaspoon garlic powder
>   1/8 teaspoon dried thyme
>   1/8 teaspoon *each* ground mustard, coriander
>   and pepper

1 tablespoon white vinegar
6 eggs
6 slices Canadian bacon, warmed
1 large ripe avocado, peeled and sliced
3 English muffins, split and toasted

In a large saucepan, melt butter. Stir in flour until smooth; gradually add milk. Bring to a boil; cook and stir for 2 minutes or until thickened. Reduce heat; stir in the cheeses and seasonings. Cook and stir until cheese is melted; keep warm.

Place 2-3 in. of water in a large skillet with high sides; add vinegar. Bring to a boil; reduce heat and simmer gently.

Break cold eggs, one at a time, into a custard cup or saucer; holding the cup close to the surface of the water, slip each egg into water. Cook, uncovered, until whites are completely set and yolks begin to thicken (but are not hard), about 4 minutes.

Place Canadian bacon and avocado on each muffin half. With a slotted spoon, lift each egg out of the water and place over avocado. Top with cheese sauce. **Yield:** 6 servings.

Tropical Mahi Mahi

Prep: 15 min.   **Cook:** 30 min.

I enjoy cooking so much, I own over 400 cookbooks! The tropical fruit and cilantro make this a wonderful, aromatic dish.   —Bob Gebhardt, Wausau, Wisconsin

2 cups all-purpose flour
1 teaspoon seasoned salt, *divided*
1/2 teaspoon pepper, *divided*
6 mahi mahi fillets (4 ounces *each*)
2 tablespoons butter
2 tablespoons olive oil
1 cup fresh cilantro leaves, chopped
1 cup white grape juice
1-1/2 cups heavy whipping cream
1 can (15-1/4 ounces) mixed tropical fruit, drained
1/2 cup chopped macadamia nuts

In a large resealable plastic bag, combine the flour, 1/2 teaspoon seasoned salt and 1/4 teaspoon pepper; add fillets. Seal bag and turn to coat.

In a large skillet, heat butter and oil. Cook mahi mahi over medium-high heat for 2-3 minutes on each side. Remove and keep warm.

Saute cilantro in pan drippings for 1 minute. Add grape juice; cook until reduced by half. Add cream; cook until reduced by half. Stir in the fruit, and remaining seasoned salt and pepper; heat through. Serve over mahi mahi; sprinkle with macadamia nuts. **Yield:** 6 servings.

Cheddar Ham Strata

(Pictured below)

Prep: 20 min. + chilling   **Bake:** 1 hour + standing

I put together this ham and egg dish on Christmas Eve and refrigerate it. Then, while we open presents on Christmas morning, I pop it in the oven for breakfast. It's a family tradition.   —Ann Pool, Jerome, Idaho

10 slices day-old bread, crusts removed and cubed
1 medium onion, finely chopped
4 medium fresh mushrooms, finely chopped
1/4 cup butter, cubed
4 cups (16 ounces) shredded cheddar cheese
2 cups cubed fully cooked ham
2 tablespoons all-purpose flour
8 eggs
3 cups milk
2 tablespoons prepared mustard
1 teaspoon garlic powder
1/2 teaspoon salt

Place the bread cubes in a greased 13-in. x 9-in. x 2-in. baking dish. In a small skillet, saute onion and mushrooms in butter; spoon over bread. Sprinkle with cheese, ham and flour. In a large bowl, whisk the eggs, milk, mustard, garlic powder and salt. Pour over ham and cheese. Cover and refrigerate overnight.

Remove from the refrigerator 30 minutes before baking. Bake, uncovered, at 350° for 60-70 minutes or until a knife inserted near the center comes out clean. Let stand for 10 minutes before serving. **Yield:** 12 servings.

Hearty Bean Stew

(Pictured below)
Prep: 10 min. **Cook:** 50 min.

A Canadian prairie winter can be bone-chilling. A bowl of this meatless stew over couscous or rice or with corn bread is all it takes to warm us up. It's hearty, tasty and—unbeknownst to your family—healthy, too!
—*Penny Giles, Regina, Saskatchewan*

☑ **Uses less fat, sugar or salt. Includes Nutrition Facts.**

1-1/2 **cups chopped onions**
    4 **garlic cloves, minced**
    1 **tablespoon canola oil**
    1 **can (28 ounces) diced tomatoes, drained**
    3 **large carrots, chopped**
    3 **celery ribs, chopped**
1-1/4 **cups beef broth**
    1 **tablespoon Worcestershire sauce**
    1 **can (16 ounces) kidney beans, rinsed and drained**
    1 **can (15 ounces) garbanzo beans *or* chickpeas, rinsed and drained**
    1 **can (15 ounces) black beans, rinsed and drained**
    1 **can (6 ounces) tomato paste**
    1 **tablespoon chili powder**
  1/4 **teaspoon pepper**

In a large saucepan, saute onions and garlic in oil until tender. Add the tomatoes, carrots, celery, broth and Worcestershire sauce. Bring to a boil. Reduce heat; cover and simmer for 15 minutes. Stir in the beans, tomato paste, chili powder and pepper. Cover and simmer for 30 minutes, stirring occasionally. **Yield:** 6 servings.

Nutrition Facts: 1-1/3 cups (calculated with reduced-sodium broth) equals 314 calories, 4 g fat (trace saturated fat), 1 mg cholesterol, 708 mg sodium, 57 g carbohydrate, 16 g fiber, 15 g protein.

Southwestern Fried Perch

Prep/Total Time: 30 min.

This is my favorite way to fix the sweet, tender perch I land. Taco seasoning and cornmeal make the coating zesty and unique. —*Jim Lord, Manchester, New Hampshire*

    1 **envelope taco seasoning**
    1 **pound lake perch fillets**
    1 **egg**
  1/2 **cup yellow cornmeal**
  1/4 **cup all-purpose flour**
    3 **tablespoons vegetable oil**

Place taco seasoning in a large resealable bag; add perch fillets, one at a time, and shake to coat. In a shallow bowl, lightly beat the egg. Combine cornmeal and flour in another shallow bowl. Dip fillets in egg, then coat with cornmeal mixture. Place in a single layer on a plate; refrigerate for 15 minutes.

In a large skillet, heat oil over medium-high heat. Fry fillets for 2-3 minutes on each side or until fish flakes easily with a fork. **Yield:** 4 servings.

Turkey Chop Suey

Prep/Total Time: 20 min.

I make good use of leftover turkey with this fast-to-fix chop suey. Sliced celery, canned bean sprouts and water chestnuts add a nice crunch to the savory mix.
—*Ruth Peterson, Jenison, Michigan*

☑ **Uses less fat, sugar or salt. Includes Nutrition Facts and Diabetic Exchanges.**

    1 **small onion, sliced**
    2 **celery ribs, sliced**
    1 **tablespoon butter**
    2 **cups cubed cooked turkey breast**
    1 **can (8 ounces) sliced water chestnuts, drained**
1-1/4 **cups reduced-sodium chicken broth**
    2 **tablespoons cornstarch**
  1/4 **cup cold water**
    3 **tablespoons reduced-sodium soy sauce**
    1 **can (14 ounces) canned bean sprouts, drained**
Hot cooked rice

In a large skillet, saute onion and celery in butter until tender. Add turkey, water chestnuts and broth; bring to a boil. Reduce heat.

In a small bowl, combine cornstarch, water and soy sauce until smooth; add to turkey mixture. Bring to a boil; cook and stir for 2 minutes or until thickened.

Add bean sprouts. Serve over rice. **Yield:** 4 servings.

Nutrition Facts: 1-1/4 cups (calculated without rice) equals 204 calories, 4 g fat (2 g saturated fat), 68 mg cholesterol, 762 mg sodium, 17 g carbohydrate, 3 g fiber, 25 g protein. **Diabetic Exchanges:** 3 very lean meat, 2 vegetable, 1/2 starch.

Honey-Ginger Turkey Kabobs

Prep: 30 min. + marinating **Grill:** 10 min.

Lime juice and pineapple lend an island flair to these fun kabobs, served with seasoned rice. I got the recipe from a friend and make it often. —Pam Thomas, Marion, Iowa

 2 tablespoons chopped green onion
 2 tablespoons soy sauce
 1 tablespoon honey
 1 tablespoon minced fresh gingerroot
 1 teaspoon lime juice
 2 garlic cloves, minced
 1 pound turkey breast tenderloins, cut into 1-inch cubes
 2 cups cubed fresh pineapple
 1 medium sweet red pepper, cut into 1-inch pieces
 1 medium red onion, cut into chunks
 1 medium lime, cut into wedges
PINEAPPLE RICE:
 2-1/2 cups water
 1 cup uncooked long grain rice
 1/2 cup chopped dried pineapple
 2 teaspoons butter
 1/2 teaspoon grated lime peel
 1/4 teaspoon salt
 1/4 cup minced fresh cilantro
 1/4 cup chopped green onions
 2 tablespoons lime juice

In a large resealable plastic bag, combine the first six ingredients; add turkey. Seal bag and turn to coat; refrigerate for at least 2 hours.

Drain and discard marinade. On eight metal or soaked wooden skewers, alternately thread the turkey, pineapple, red pepper, red onion and lime wedges; set aside.

In a large saucepan, bring water to a boil. Stir in the rice, dried pineapple, butter, lime peel and salt. Reduce heat; cover and simmer for 15-20 minutes or until tender.

Meanwhile, grill kabobs, covered, over medium heat for 5-6 minutes on each side or until turkey juices run clear and vegetables are tender. Stir the cilantro, onions and lime juice into the rice. Serve with kabobs. **Yield:** 4 servings.

Spicy Barbecued Chicken

(Pictured above)
Prep/Total Time: 30 min.

This zesty chicken is fantastic served with basil-buttered, grilled corn on the cob and fresh coleslaw.
—Rita Wintrode, Corryton, Tennessee

✓ Uses less fat, sugar or salt. Includes Nutrition Facts and Diabetic Exchanges.

 2 garlic cloves, minced
 1 tablespoon canola oil
 1/2 cup chili sauce
 3 tablespoons brown sugar
 2 teaspoons salt-free seasoning blend, *divided*
 3/4 teaspoon cayenne pepper, *divided*
 2 teaspoons ground mustard
 2 teaspoons chili powder
 8 boneless skinless chicken breast halves (4 ounces *each*)

In a small saucepan, saute garlic in oil for 1 minute. Add the chili sauce, brown sugar, 1 teaspoon seasoning blend and 1/4 teaspoon cayenne. Bring to a boil; cook and stir for 1 minute. Remove from the heat; set aside.

Prepare grill for indirect heat. Coat grill rack with nonstick cooking spray before starting the grill. Combine the mustard, chili powder, and remaining seasoning blend and cayenne; rub over chicken. Grill, covered, over indirect medium-hot heat for 3 minutes. Turn and baste with chili sauce mixture. Grill 6-8 minutes longer or until juices run clear, basting occasionally. **Yield:** 8 servings.

Nutrition Facts: 1 chicken breast half equals 179 calories, 5 g fat (1 g saturated fat), 63 mg cholesterol, 293 mg sodium, 10 g carbohydrate, trace fiber, 23 g protein. **Diabetic Exchanges:** 3 very lean meat, 1/2 starch, 1/2 fat.

Positively Pasta!

PUT SOME WATER on the boil and try these delicious possibilities for fettuccine, manicotti and angel hair pasta. You and your family will be glad you did!

Indonesian Pasta

(Pictured at far right)

Prep/Total Time: 20 min.

My family truly enjoys this delectable asparagus dish. The flavors blend to create an interesting taste.
—*Jolene Caldwell, Council Bluffs, Iowa*

- 1/2 **cup chicken broth**
- 2 **jalapeno peppers, seeded and chopped**
- 2 **tablespoons soy sauce**
- 2 **tablespoons peanut butter**
- 1 **tablespoon dried minced onion**
- 1 **tablespoon lemon juice**
- 1/4 **teaspoon brown sugar**
- 18 **fresh asparagus spears, trimmed and cut into 1-inch pieces**
- 1/2 **medium sweet red pepper, julienned**
- 2 **teaspoons olive oil**
- 6 **ounces uncooked angel hair pasta**
- 1/2 **cup sliced green onions**

In a small saucepan, combine the first seven ingredients. Bring to a boil, stirring constantly. Remove from the heat; keep warm.

In a large skillet, saute asparagus and red pepper in oil for 6-8 minutes. Meanwhile, cook pasta according to package directions. Add green onions to the asparagus mixture; saute for 2-3 minutes or until vegetables are crisp-tender. Drain pasta; toss with vegetable mixture and reserved sauce. **Yield:** 4 servings.

Editor's Note: When cutting or seeding hot peppers, use rubber or plastic gloves to protect your hands. Avoid touching your face.

Meaty Manicotti

(Pictured above far right)

Prep: 20 min.   **Bake:** 45 min.

This simple meal-in-one has been popular at family gatherings and potlucks. You can assemble it ahead of time.
—*Lori Thompson, New London, Texas*

- 14 **uncooked manicotti shells**
- 1 **pound bulk Italian sausage**
- 3/4 **pound ground beef**
- 2 **garlic cloves, minced**
- 2 **cups (8 ounces) shredded part-skim mozzarella cheese**
- 1 **package (3 ounces) cream cheese, cubed**
- 1/4 **teaspoon salt**
- 4 **cups meatless spaghetti sauce, *divided***
- 1/4 **cup grated Parmesan cheese**

Cook manicotti shells according to package directions. Meanwhile, in a large skillet, cook the sausage, beef and garlic over medium heat until meat is no longer pink; drain. Remove from the heat. Cool for 10 minutes.

Drain shells and rinse in cold water. Stir the mozzarella, cream cheese and salt into meat mixture. Spread 2 cups spaghetti sauce into a greased 13-in. x 9-in. x 2-in. baking dish.

Stuff each shell with about 1/4 cup meat mixture; arrange over sauce. Pour the remaining sauce over top. Sprinkle with the Parmesan cheese.

Cover; bake at 350° for 40 minutes. Uncover; bake 5-10 minutes longer or until bubbly and heated through. **Yield:** 7 servings.

Fettuccine Primavera

(Pictured at right)

Prep/Total Time: 30 min.

Colorful, crisp-tender vegetables give plenty of eye appeal to this pasta dish. Low-fat ingredients complement the rich taste of the sauce. —*Mel Miller, Perkins, Oklahoma*

☑ **Uses less fat, sugar or salt. Includes Nutrition Facts and Diabetic Exchanges.**

- 8 **ounces uncooked fettuccine**
- 1-1/4 **cups chicken broth, *divided***
- 1 **small zucchini, coarsely chopped**
- 1 **small yellow summer squash, coarsely chopped**
- 1 **cup fresh broccoli florets**
- 1 **small sweet red pepper, coarsely chopped**
- 1 **medium carrot, coarsely chopped**
- 1 **small onion, chopped**
- 3 **teaspoons dried basil**
- 1/2 **teaspoon salt**
- 4 **teaspoons cornstarch**
- 2 **plum tomatoes, cut into wedges**
- 1/2 **cup sour cream**
- 1/2 **cup grated Parmesan cheese**
- 1/4 **cup minced fresh parsley**

Cook fettuccine according to package directions. Meanwhile, in a large saucepan, bring 3/4 cup broth to

PICK YOUR PASTA. Indonesian Pasta, Meaty Manicotti and Fettuccine Primavera (shown above) are three delicious choices your family is sure to request time and again.

a boil. Add the zucchini, yellow squash, broccoli, red pepper, carrot, onion, basil and salt. Return to a boil. Reduce heat; cover and simmer for 6-8 minutes or until vegetables are crisp-tender.

In a small bowl, combine the cornstarch and remaining broth until smooth; stir into the vegetable mixture. Bring to a boil; cook and stir for 2 minutes or until slightly thickened. Remove from the heat; stir in the tomatoes and sour cream.

Drain fettuccine; place in a large bowl. Add the vegetable mixture, Parmesan cheese and parsley; toss to coat. **Yield:** 6 servings.

Nutrition Facts: 1 cup (prepared with reduced-sodium chicken broth and reduced-fat sour cream) equals 229 calories, 5 g fat (3 g saturated fat), 12 mg cholesterol, 488 mg sodium, 37 g carbohydrate, 4 g fiber, 12 g protein. **Diabetic Exchanges:** 2 starch, 1 vegetable, 1 fat.

tershire sauce, garlic, pepper and salt. Place chicken in a large resealable plastic bag; add half of the marinade. Place onions and sweet potatoes in another large resealable plastic bag; add remaining marinade. Seal bags and turn to coat; refrigerate for 30 minutes.

In a small bowl, combine the butter, molasses, chipotle peppers and lemon peel. Cover and refrigerate until serving.

Drain and discard marinade. On 12 metal or soaked wooden skewers, alternately thread the chicken, sweet potatoes and onions. Grill, covered, over medium-hot heat for 6-8 minutes on each side or until chicken juices run clear. Serve with chipotle molasses butter. **Yield:** 6 servings.

Editor's Note: This recipe was tested in a 1,100-watt microwave.

Skewered Chicken 'n' Sweet Potatoes

(Pictured above)

Prep: 20 min. + marinating   **Grill:** 15 min.

For a deliciously different main dish, try this quick and simple recipe. The chipotle molasses butter adds an appealing accent to the chicken, sweet potatoes and sweet onions.
—Janice Elder, Charlotte, North Carolina

  4 **medium sweet potatoes, peeled and cut into 1-inch cubes**
  2 **tablespoons water**
1/4 **cup olive oil**
  2 **tablespoons lemon juice**
  2 **tablespoons Worcestershire sauce**
  2 **garlic cloves, minced**
1/2 **teaspoon pepper**
1/4 **teaspoon salt**
1-1/2 **pounds boneless skinless chicken breasts, cut into 1-inch cubes**
  2 **large sweet onions, cut into chunks**
CHIPOTLE MOLASSES BUTTER:
1/2 **cup butter, softened**
  2 **tablespoons molasses**
  2 **teaspoons chipotle peppers in adobo sauce**
  1 **teaspoon grated lemon peel**

Place sweet potatoes and water in a large microwave-safe dish. Cover and microwave on high for 8 minutes or until tender; drain and set aside.

In a small bowl, combine the oil, lemon juice, Worces-

Zippy Peanut Steak Kabobs

Prep: 40 min. + marinating   **Grill:** 10 min.

If you like kabobs with a kick, you're sure to savor these meaty versions seasoned with habanero pepper sauce. The zippy steak is balanced with refreshing pineapple and red peppers. Sometimes, I substitute chicken for the beef.
—Sheri Nutter, Oneida, Kentucky

3/4 **cup packed brown sugar**
3/4 **cup water**
  1 **cup chunky peanut butter**
  1 **cup reduced-sodium soy sauce**
3/4 **cup honey barbecue sauce**
1/3 **cup vegetable oil**
  1 **to 2 tablespoons habanero pepper sauce**
  3 **garlic cloves, minced**
  2 **pounds boneless beef sirloin steak, cut into thin strips**
  2 **teaspoons ground ginger**
  1 **fresh pineapple, cut into 1-inch cubes**
  2 **large sweet red peppers, cut into 1-inch pieces**
Hot cooked jasmine rice

In a small saucepan, combine brown sugar and water. Cook and stir over low heat until sugar is completely dissolved. Remove from the heat. Whisk in peanut butter until blended. Stir in the soy sauce, barbecue sauce, oil, pepper sauce and garlic.

Pour 3 cups of the marinade into a large resealable plastic bag; add beef. Seal bag and turn to coat; refrigerate for 4 hours. Cover and refrigerate remaining marinade until serving.

Drain and discard marinade. Sprinkle ginger over pineapple. On 16 metal or soaked wooden skewers, alternately thread the beef, pineapple and red peppers. Grill, covered, over medium heat for 5-7 minutes on each side or until meat reaches desired doneness. Serve with rice and reserved marinade for dipping. **Yield:** 8 servings.

Asparagus Ham Crepes

Prep: 25 min. + chilling   **Bake:** 20 min.

I recommend these rich and tender crepes stuffed with a cheesy filling for a Sunday brunch. They're so pretty, too!
—Sue Erickson, Loveland, Colorado

  1/2 cup milk
    1 egg
    1 tablespoon vegetable oil
  1/4 cup all-purpose flour
  1/2 teaspoon baking powder
  1/4 teaspoon salt
   24 fresh asparagus spears, trimmed
    8 thin slices deli ham
    8 slices Swiss cheese
MUSHROOM CHEESE SAUCE:
    3 tablespoons butter
    3 tablespoons all-purpose flour
    1 teaspoon chicken bouillon granules
    1 cup water
  1/4 cup shredded cheddar cheese
  1/3 cup half-and-half cream
    1 can (4 ounces) mushroom stems and
      pieces, drained
    1 tablespoon minced chives

In a blender, combine the first six ingredients; cover and process mixture until smooth. Refrigerate mixture for 1 hour.

Heat a lightly greased 8-in. nonstick skillet; pour 2 tablespoons batter into center of skillet. Lift and tilt pan to evenly coat bottom. Cook until top appears dry; turn and cook 15-20 seconds longer. Remove to a wire rack. Repeat with remaining batter, greasing skillet as needed. When cool, stack crepes with waxed paper or paper towels in between.

In a large skillet, bring 1/2 in. of water to a boil. Add the asparagus spears; cover and cook for 3 minutes. Drain and immediately place the asparagus in ice water; drain and pat dry.

On each crepe, layer a ham slice, Swiss cheese slice and three asparagus spears. Roll up and place in a greased 11-in. x 7-in. x 2-in. baking dish.

In a saucepan, melt butter. Stir in flour and bouillon. Gradually stir in water. Bring to a boil over medium heat; cook and stir for 2 minutes or until thickened. Reduce heat; stir in cheddar cheese until melted. Stir in the cream, mushrooms and chives. Pour over crepes. Bake, uncovered, at 350° for 20-25 minutes or until heated through. **Yield:** 8 crepes.

Pork Fajita Kabobs

(Pictured below)

Prep/Total Time: 30 min.

This has become my favorite way to cook pork loin. The grilled vegetable and meat chunks, seasoned with a home-made, Southwestern-style spice blend, are appropriately served in a flour tortilla. Just top with salsa and enjoy!
—Bea Westphal, Slidell, Louisiana

    2 teaspoons paprika
1-1/2 teaspoons ground cumin
1-1/2 teaspoons dried oregano
    1 teaspoon garlic powder
  1/8 to 1/4 teaspoon crushed red pepper flakes
1-1/2 pounds boneless pork loin chops, cut into
      1-inch cubes
    1 small green pepper, cut into 1-inch pieces
    1 small onion, cut into eight wedges
    8 large fresh mushrooms
   16 grape tomatoes
    8 flour tortillas (8 inches), warmed
  3/4 cup chunky salsa

In a large resealable plastic bag, combine the paprika, cumin, oregano, garlic powder and pepper flakes; add pork. Seal bag and toss to coat. On eight metal or soaked wooden skewers, alternately thread the pork, green pepper, onion, mushrooms and tomatoes.

Grill kabobs, covered, over medium heat for 5-8 minutes on each side or until meat is no longer pink and vegetables are tender. Place each kabob in a tortilla; remove skewers and fold tortillas in half. Serve with salsa. **Yield:** 4 servings.

Pizza Bianco

(Pictured below)

Prep: 20 min. + standing **Bake:** 35 min.

Here's the perfect pizza for cheese lovers. Served with a green salad, it makes a satisfying meal. You can use store-bought dough if you don't have a bread machine.
—*Christine Omar, Harwich Port, Massachusetts*

✓ **Uses less fat, sugar or salt. Includes Nutrition Facts and Diabetic Exchanges.**

DOUGH:
- 1 cup water (70° to 80°)
- 1 tablespoon olive oil
- 1 teaspoon sugar
- 1 teaspoon salt
- 3 cups all-purpose flour
- 1 package (1/4 ounce) active dry yeast

TOPPING:
- 2 cups sliced fresh mushrooms
- 1/2 cup chopped onion
- 3 garlic cloves, minced
- 3 tablespoons olive oil
- 2 tablespoons minced fresh basil

FILLING:
- 2 cups (8 ounces) shredded part-skim mozzarella cheese
- 1 cup (8 ounces) ricotta cheese
- 1/4 cup grated Romano cheese
- 1 tablespoon minced fresh parsley

In bread machine pan, place dough ingredients in order suggested by manufacturer. Select dough setting (check dough after 5 minutes of mixing; add 1 to 2 tablespoons of water or flour if needed).

When cycle is completed, turn dough onto a lightly floured surface. Punch down; cover and let stand for 10 minutes. Press dough into a 13-in. x 9-in. x 2-in. baking dish coated with nonstick cooking spray; build up edges slightly.

In a large skillet, saute the mushrooms, onion and garlic in oil for 3-5 minutes or until onion is crisp-tender. Stir in basil. Combine the filling ingredients; spread over crust. Sprinkle with vegetable topping. Bake at 400° for 35-45 minutes or until crust is golden brown. **Yield:** 12-16 slices.

Nutrition Facts: 1 piece (prepared with fat-free ricotta) equals 385 calories, 16 g fat (5 g saturated fat), 25 mg cholesterol, 512 mg sodium, 42 g carbohydrate, 2 g fiber, 17 g protein. **Diabetic Exchanges:** 2 starch, 1 lean meat, 1 reduced-fat milk, 1 fat.

Minted Lamb 'n' Veggie Kabobs

Prep: 30 min. + marinating **Grill:** 10 min.

Mint leaves give these lamb kabobs an enticing flavor and aroma. The eye-catching meat and vegetable chunks look and taste special enough to dish up for company.
—*Michael Rose, Grand Prairie, Texas*

- 3 tablespoons olive oil
- 2 tablespoons lemon juice
- 4 garlic cloves, minced
- 2 teaspoons dried basil
- 1 teaspoon dried oregano
- 1 teaspoon pepper
- 1/2 teaspoon salt
- 1/2 teaspoon dried thyme
- 1 pound boneless leg of lamb, cut into 1-inch cubes
- 1 medium sweet red pepper, cut into 1-inch pieces
- 1 medium sweet yellow pepper, cut into 1-inch pieces
- 1 medium zucchini, cut into 1/4-inch slices

1 small red onion, cut into chunks
16 medium fresh mushrooms
1 cup fresh mint leaves
Hot cooked brown rice

In a large resealable plastic bag, combine the oil, lemon juice, garlic, basil, oregano, pepper, salt and thyme; add lamb. Seal bag and turn to coat; refrigerate for 30 minutes.

On eight metal or soaked wooden skewers, alternately thread the lamb and vegetables with mint leaves. Grill, covered, over medium heat for 4-5 minutes on each side or until meat reaches desired doneness and vegetables are tender. Serve with rice. **Yield:** 4 servings.

Cajun Shrimp Skewers

(Pictured at right)

Prep: 20 min. + marinating   **Grill:** 5 min.

Fresh herbs and Cajun seasoning enhance these delicious shrimp, accompanied by spicy butter. Serve them as an entree or as appetizers—you'll love them either way!
—*Dwayne Veretto, Roswell, New Mexico*

3/4 cup vegetable oil
1 medium onion, finely chopped
2 tablespoons Cajun seasoning
6 garlic cloves, minced
2 teaspoons ground cumin
1 teaspoon minced fresh rosemary
1 teaspoon minced fresh thyme
2 pounds uncooked large shrimp, peeled and deveined
CAJUN BUTTER:
1 cup butter, cubed
1 teaspoon minced fresh basil
1 teaspoon minced fresh tarragon
1 teaspoon Cajun seasoning
1/2 teaspoon garlic powder
3 drops hot pepper sauce

In a small bowl, combine the first seven ingredients. Place the shrimp in a large resealable plastic bag; add half of the marinade. Seal bag and turn to coat; refrigerate for 1-2 hours. Cover and refrigerate remaining marinade for basting.

In a small saucepan, combine the Cajun butter ingredients; heat until butter is melted. Keep warm. Drain and discard marinade. Thread shrimp onto eight metal or soaked wooden skewers. Grill, uncovered, over medium heat for 2-4 minutes on each side or until shrimp turn pink, basting once with reserved marinade. Serve with Cajun butter. **Yield:** 8 servings.

Spinach Venison Quiche

(Pictured on page 58)

Prep: 20 min.   **Bake:** 45 min.

This exceptional quiche is a favorite of ours. The spinach and venison are an unbeatable match, and the feta adds savory goodness.
—*Gloria Long*
Morehead City, North Carolina

1 unbaked pastry shell (9 inches)
1/2 pound ground venison
1/2 pound sliced fresh mushrooms
1/2 cup chopped onion
1/2 cup chopped green pepper
1 package (10 ounces) frozen chopped spinach, thawed and squeezed dry
1 package (4 ounces) crumbled feta cheese
6 eggs
3/4 cup half-and-half cream
1 teaspoon pepper
1/2 teaspoon salt

Line unpricked pastry shell with a double thickness of heavy-duty foil. Bake at 450° for 8 minutes. Remove foil; bake 5 minutes longer.

Meanwhile, in a large skillet, cook the venison, mushrooms, onion and green pepper for 5-6 minutes or until meat is no longer pink; drain. Spoon into crust; top with spinach and feta cheese. In a bowl, whisk the eggs, cream, pepper and salt; pour over cheese.

Cover edges loosely with foil. Bake at 350° for 45-50 minutes or until a knife inserted near the center comes out clean. Let stand for 5 minutes before cutting. **Yield:** 8 servings.

Taco Meat Loaves

(Pictured below)

Prep: 25 min.   **Bake:** 1 hour + standing

We live in Texas and love the Southwest style of cooking. This recipe spices up plain ol' meat loaf so it tastes like a filling for tacos.   —Susan Garoutte, Georgetown, Texas

      3 eggs, lightly beaten
      2 cups picante sauce, *divided*
      1 can (16 ounces) kidney beans, rinsed and
         drained
      1 can (11 ounces) Mexicorn, drained
      1 medium onion, chopped
      2 cans (2-1/4 ounces *each*) sliced ripe
         olives, drained
   3/4 cup dry bread crumbs
      1 envelope taco seasoning
      1 teaspoon ground cumin
      1 teaspoon chili powder
      2 pounds ground beef
      2 cups (8 ounces) shredded cheddar cheese
Additional picante sauce, optional

In a large bowl, combine the eggs, 1/2 cup picante sauce, beans, corn, onion, olives, bread crumbs, taco seasoning, cumin and chili powder. Crumble beef over mixture and mix well.

Pat into two ungreased 9-in. x 5-in. x 3-in. loaf pans. Bake, uncovered, at 350° for 50-55 minutes or until no pink remains and a meat thermometer reads 160°.

Spoon remaining picante sauce over each meat loaf; sprinkle with cheese. Bake 10-15 minutes longer or until cheese is melted. Let stand for 10 minutes before slicing. Serve with additional picante sauce if desired. **Yield:** 2 meat loaves (6 servings each).

Dad's Swedish Meatballs

(Pictured on page 58)

Prep: 30 min.   **Cook:** 35 min.

My father used to make these tender meatballs every year for Christmas when I was a kid. Now I carry on the tradition.   —Michelle Lizotte, Cumberland, Rhode Island

      1 egg, lightly beaten
   1/2 cup milk
      1 cup soft bread crumbs
   1/2 cup finely chopped onion
      1 teaspoon salt
   1/4 teaspoon ground nutmeg
   1/4 teaspoon pepper
      1 pound ground beef
   1/2 pound ground pork
   1/4 cup butter, cubed
DILL CREAM SAUCE:
      2 tablespoons all-purpose flour
      1 cup heavy whipping cream
      1 cup beef broth
      1 teaspoon salt
   1/2 teaspoon dill seed

In a large bowl, combine the first seven ingredients. Crumble beef and pork over mixture; mix well. Shape into 1-1/2-in. balls. In a large skillet, cook meatballs in butter in batches until no longer pink. Remove and keep warm.

In a bowl, combine the sauce ingredients until blended. Stir into skillet. Bring to a boil; cook and stir for 2 minutes or until thickened. Serve over meatballs. **Yield:** 6 servings.

Colorful Chicken Fettuccine

(Pictured at right)

Prep/Total Time: 30 min.

This surefire entree is a delicious option if you ever find yourself in a time crunch. I like to prepare and freeze fresh veggies ahead of time for use in recipes like this one. Then, the rest is as easy as 1-2-3! —Ginger Kelly
Cranberry Township, Pennsylvania

- **10 ounces uncooked fettuccine**
- **1 pound boneless skinless chicken breasts, cut into strips**
- **1 tablespoon vegetable oil**
- **1 cup julienned carrots**
- **1 medium sweet red pepper, julienned**
- **1 medium green pepper, julienned**
- **2 cups fresh broccoli florets**
- **4 teaspoons cornstarch**
- **1 can (14-1/2 ounces) chicken broth**
- **1 tablespoon lemon juice**
- **1/2 teaspoon salt**
- **1/2 teaspoon dried thyme**
- **2 tablespoons sour cream**
- **1/2 cup shredded Parmesan cheese**

Cook fettuccine according to package directions. Meanwhile, in a large skillet, saute chicken in oil until no longer pink. Remove and keep warm. In the same pan, saute carrots for 1 minute. Add peppers and broccoli; saute 3-4 minutes longer or until vegetables are crisp-tender.

In a small bowl, combine the cornstarch, broth, lemon juice, salt and thyme until blended; stir into vegetables. Bring to a boil; cook and stir for 2 minutes. Remove from heat. Stir in sour cream.

Drain fettuccine; place in a large bowl. Add the chicken, vegetable mixture and Parmesan cheese; toss to coat. **Yield:** 4-6 servings.

Chicago-Style Stuffed Pizza

Prep: 30 min. + rising   **Bake:** 30 min.

"Excellent" is the rating I give this hearty double-crust pizza. Favorite fillings are tucked inside, and tasty tomato sauce tops the pie. —Edie DeSpain, Logan, Utah

- **1 teaspoon active dry yeast**
- **1 cup warm water (110° to 115°)**
- **2 teaspoons sugar**
- **2 tablespoons vegetable oil**
- **1-1/2 teaspoons salt**
- **2-1/2 to 3 cups all-purpose flour**
- **1/2 cup yellow cornmeal**
- **1/2 pound bulk Italian sausage**
- **1 small green pepper, diced**
- **1 small onion, diced**
- **3 garlic cloves, peeled and sliced**
- **2 cups (8 ounces) shredded part-skim mozzarella cheese**
- **1/3 cup chopped pepperoni**
- **1/4 cup grated Parmesan cheese**
- **1 teaspoon dried oregano**
- **1/4 cup tomato sauce**

In a large mixing bowl, dissolve yeast in warm water. Add sugar; let stand for 5 minutes. Add oil and salt. Add 1-1/2 cups flour and cornmeal; beat until smooth. Stir in enough remaining flour to form a soft dough.

Turn onto a floured surface; knead until smooth and elastic, about 4-5 minutes. Place in a greased bowl; turn once to grease top. Cover and let rise in a warm place until doubled, about 1 hour.

Punch dough down; let rest for 5 minutes. Divide into two portions, one slightly larger than the other. On a lightly floured surface, roll out larger portion to a 12-in. circle. Press onto the bottom and up the sides of a greased 10-in. ovenproof skillet.

In a large skillet, cook sausage, green pepper, onion and garlic over medium heat until meat is no longer pink; drain. Stir in the mozzarella, pepperoni, Parmesan and oregano. Spread over crust.

On a lightly floured surface, roll remaining dough into an 11-in. circle. Place over pizza; seal edges. Cut four slits in top. Bake at 375° for 30-35 minutes or until crust is golden brown. Spread with tomato sauce. **Yield:** 8 slices.

Prosciutto-Stuffed Meat Loaf

(Pictured below)

Prep: 45 min.   **Bake:** 1-1/4 hours

A mouth-watering blend of flavors—including prosciutto, sun-dried tomatoes, fresh herbs and cheese—makes this rolled loaf something special. —Carole Hermenau
Oviedo, Florida

- 1 **cup finely chopped red onion**
- 1 **tablespoon olive oil**
- 1 **tablespoon butter**
- 2 **garlic cloves, minced**
- 1/2 **pound whole fresh mushrooms, coarsely chopped**
- 3/4 **teaspoon salt**
- 1/2 **teaspoon pepper**
- 2 **eggs, lightly beaten**
- 1-3/4 **cups soft sourdough bread crumbs**
- 3/4 **cup grated Parmesan cheese**
- 1/3 **cup minced fresh parsley**
- 1 **teaspoon minced fresh thyme**
- 1-1/2 **pounds lean ground beef**
- 3/4 **pound bulk Italian sausage**

FILLING:
- 3 **ounces thinly sliced prosciutto**
- 5 **ounces thinly sliced Havarti cheese**
- 1-1/4 **cups loosely packed basil leaves, cut into thin strips**
- 1/3 **cup oil-packed sun-dried tomatoes, drained and cut into strips**

In a large skillet, saute onion in oil and butter for 2 minutes. Add garlic; cook 1 minute longer. Add mushrooms; cook 6-8 minutes longer or until mushrooms are tender and no liquid remains. Stir in salt and pepper.

In a large bowl, combine the eggs, bread crumbs, Parmesan cheese, parsley, thyme and mushroom mixture. Crumble beef and sausage over mixture; mix well.

On a large piece of heavy-duty foil, pat beef mixture into a 15-in. x 10-in. rectangle. Layer the prosciutto, Havarti, basil and tomatoes to within 1 in. of edges. Roll up jelly-roll style, starting with a short side and peeling foil away while rolling. Seal seams and ends.

Place seam side down in a greased 13-in. x 9-in. x 2-in. baking dish. Bake, uncovered, at 350° for 75-85 minutes or until no pink remains and a meat thermometer reads 160°. Let stand for 5 minutes. Using two large spatulas, carefully transfer meat loaf to a serving platter. **Yield:** 6-8 servings.

Apple-Stuffed French Toast

(Pictured above)

Prep: 20 min. + chilling   **Bake:** 35 min.

This is a great dish to assemble ahead of time for holidays or Sunday brunch. I run a bed-and-breakfast and tearoom cafe, and this is often requested by customers.
—Kay Clark, Lawrenceburg, Kentucky

- 1 **cup packed brown sugar**
- 1/2 **cup butter, cubed**
- 2 **tablespoons light corn syrup**
- 1 **cup chopped pecans**
- 12 **slices Italian bread (1/2 inch thick)**
- 2 **large tart apples, peeled and thinly sliced**
- 6 **eggs**
- 1-1/2 **cups milk**
- 1-1/2 **teaspoons ground cinnamon**
- 1 **teaspoon vanilla extract**
- 1/4 **teaspoon salt**
- 1/4 **teaspoon ground nutmeg**

CARAMEL SAUCE:
- 1/2 **cup packed brown sugar**
- 1/4 **cup butter, cubed**
- 1 **tablespoon light corn syrup**

In a small saucepan, combine the brown sugar, butter and corn syrup; cook and stir over medium heat until thickened. Pour into a greased 13-in. x 9-in. x 2-in. baking dish; top with half of the pecans, a single layer of bread and remaining pecans. Arrange apples and remaining bread over the top.

In a large bowl, whisk the eggs, milk, cinnamon, vanilla, salt and nutmeg. Pour over bread. Cover and refrigerate overnight.

Remove from the refrigerator 30 minutes before baking. Bake, uncovered, at 350° for 35-40 minutes or until lightly browned.

In a small saucepan, combine the sauce ingredients. Cook and stir over medium heat until thickened. Serve with French toast. **Yield:** 6 servings.

Dad's Favorite Pizza

Prep: 30 min. + rising   **Bake:** 30 min.

Our daughter, Stephanie, makes this pizza for her dad whenever he has a craving for it. Meat eaters will definitely get their fill with a slice of this deep-dish delight.
—Nancy Jo Leffler, Depauw, Indiana

- 1 package (1/4 ounce) active dry yeast
- 1/2 cup warm water (110° to 115°)
- 1/2 cup butter, melted and cooled
- 3 eggs
- 1/4 cup grated Parmesan cheese
- 1 teaspoon salt
- 3 to 3-1/2 cups bread flour
- 2 tablespoons yellow cornmeal
- 1/2 pound ground beef
- 1/2 pound bulk Italian sausage
- 1 small onion, chopped
- 2 cans (8 ounces *each*) pizza sauce
- 1 can (4-1/2 ounces) sliced mushrooms, drained
- 1 package (3 ounces) sliced pepperoni
- 1/2 pound deli ham, cubed
- 1/2 cup chopped pitted green olives
- 1 can (2-1/4 ounces) chopped ripe olives, drained
- 1-1/2 cups (6 ounces) shredded part-skim mozzarella cheese
- 1/2 cup shredded Parmesan cheese

In a large mixing bowl, dissolve yeast in warm water. Add butter, eggs, grated Parmesan and salt. Add 2 cups flour; beat until smooth. Stir in enough remaining flour to form a soft dough.

Turn onto a floured surface; knead until smooth and elastic, about 5 minutes. Place in a greased bowl; turn once to grease top. Cover and let rise in a warm place until doubled, about 1 hour.

Punch dough down; let rest for 5 minutes. Grease a 14-in. deep-dish pizza pan; sprinkle bottom with cornmeal. Press dough into pan; build up edges slightly.

In a skillet, cook beef, sausage and onion over medium heat until meat is no longer pink; drain. Spread pizza sauce over dough; sprinkle with meat mixture. Top with mushrooms, pepperoni, ham, olives, mozzarella and shredded Parmesan. Bake at 400° for 30-35 minutes or until crust is golden brown. **Yield:** 8 slices.

Mozzarella-Stuffed Meatballs

(Pictured below)

Prep: 20 min.   **Cook:** 15 min.

It's fun to watch my friends eat these for the first time. They're pleasantly surprised to find melted cheese in the middle. The meatballs are also good in a hot sub sandwich.   *—Michaela Rosenthal, Woodland Hills, California*

- 1 egg, lightly beaten
- 1/4 cup prepared Italian salad dressing
- 1-1/2 cups cubed bread
- 2 tablespoons minced fresh parsley
- 2 garlic cloves, minced
- 1/2 teaspoon dried oregano
- 1/2 teaspoon pepper
- 1/4 teaspoon salt
- 1/2 pound ground pork
- 1/2 pound ground sirloin
- 3 ounces fresh mozzarella cheese
- 2 tablespoons vegetable oil
- 1 jar (26 ounces) marinara sauce

Hot cooked pasta

In a large bowl, combine the first eight ingredients. Crumble pork and beef over mixture; mix well. Cut mozzarella into eighteen 1/2-in. cubes. Divide meat mixture into 18 portions; shape each around a cheese cube.

In a large skillet, cook meatballs in oil in batches until no pink remains; drain. In a large saucepan, heat marinara sauce; add meatballs and heat through. Serve over pasta. **Yield:** 6 servings.

On a lightly floured surface, roll dough into a 14-in. circle. Transfer to a greased 12-in. pizza pan, letting dough drape 2 in. over the edge. Place string cheese around edge of pan; fold dough over cheese and pinch to seal. Prick dough thoroughly with a fork. Bake at 425° for 10 minutes.

Meanwhile, in a large skillet, cook sausage and green pepper over medium heat until meat is no longer pink; drain.

In a small bowl, combine the tomato sauce, oregano, pepper and garlic powder; spread over crust. Sprinkle with meat mixture, mushrooms and mozzarella. Bake for 15-20 minutes or until cheese is melted and crust is golden brown. **Yield:** 6-8 slices.

Stuffed-Crust Pizza

(Pictured above)

Prep: 25 min.   **Bake:** 25 min.

String cheese is the secret to success for this popular stuffed-crust pizza. Prebaking the crust before you add the toppings assures that the cheese inside will melt completely.   —Terri Kearns, Oklahoma City, Oklahoma

- 2 to 2-1/2 cups all-purpose flour
- 1 package (1/4 ounce) quick-rise yeast
- 1 teaspoon salt
- 1 cup water
- 2 tablespoons vegetable oil
- 8 pieces string cheese
- 1/2 pound bulk Italian sausage
- 1 medium green pepper, diced
- 1 cup tomato sauce
- 1 teaspoon dried oregano
- 1/4 teaspoon pepper
- 1/8 teaspoon garlic powder
- 1 jar (4-1/2 ounces) sliced mushrooms, drained
- 1-1/2 cups (6 ounces) shredded part-skim mozzarella cheese

In a large mixing bowl, combine 2 cups flour, yeast and salt. In a saucepan, heat water and oil to 120°-130°. Add to dry ingredients; beat just until moistened. Stir in enough remaining flour to form a soft dough. Let rest for 5 minutes.

Meat Loaf Wellington

(Pictured on page 58)

Prep: 20 min.   **Bake:** 1-1/4 hours

I took what I liked from a few different recipes and came up with this cheese-filled loaf. I make it for neighbors or friends who are sick or need a hand. It's a pleaser!
—Janine Talbot, Santaquin, Utah

- 1 egg, lightly beaten
- 1 cup meatless spaghetti sauce, *divided*
- 1/4 cup dry bread crumbs
- 1/2 teaspoon salt
- 1/4 teaspoon pepper
- 1-1/2 pounds ground beef
- 2 cups (8 ounces) shredded part-skim mozzarella cheese, *divided*
- 1 tablespoon minced fresh parsley
- 1 tube (8 ounces) refrigerated crescent rolls

In a large bowl, combine the egg, 1/3 cup spaghetti sauce, bread crumbs, salt and pepper. Crumble beef over mixture and mix well.

On a piece of heavy-duty foil, pat beef mixture into a 12-in. x 8-in. rectangle. Sprinkle 1 cup cheese and parsley to within 1 in. of edges. Roll up jelly-roll style, starting with a long side and peeling foil away while rolling. Seal seam and ends. Place seam side down in a greased 13-in. x 9-in. x 2-in. baking dish.

Bake, uncovered, at 350° for 1 hour; drain. Unroll crescent dough; seal seams and perforations. Drape dough over meat loaf to cover the top, sides and ends; seal ends. Bake 15-20 minutes longer or until a meat thermometer reads 160° and crust is golden brown. Let stand for 5 minutes.

Using two large spatulas, carefully transfer the meat loaf to a serving platter. Sprinkle with the remaining cheese and serve with the remaining spaghetti sauce. **Yield:** 8 servings.

Pecan Apple Pancakes

(Pictured on page 58)

Prep: 15 min.   **Cook:** 10 min. per batch

Leisurely weekend breakfasts are a big deal here in my part of Texas, and these sweet, nicely spiced pancakes make any breakfast seem extra-special.
—*Sharon Richardson, Dallas, Texas*

       2 cups all-purpose flour
       1 cup sugar
       2 teaspoons baking powder
       1 teaspoon baking soda
       1 teaspoon ground cinnamon
     1/2 teaspoon salt
     1/2 teaspoon ground ginger
     1/2 teaspoon ground mace
     1/2 teaspoon ground cloves
       2 eggs
 1-3/4 cups buttermilk
       3 tablespoons vegetable oil
 1-3/4 cups shredded peeled apples
     1/2 cup chopped pecans

In a large bowl, combine the first nine ingredients. In another bowl, combine the eggs, buttermilk and oil; stir into dry ingredients just until blended. Stir in apples and pecans.

Pour the batter by 1/4 cupfuls onto a greased griddle over medium-low heat. Turn when bubbles form on top; cook until second side is golden brown. **Yield:** 1-1/2 dozen.

Turkey with Apple Stuffing

(Pictured at right)

Prep: 20 min.   **Bake:** 3-3/4 hours + standing

Complementing a golden-brown bird, my well-seasoned bread stuffing is sparked by a festive sweetness from apples and raisins. This beautiful and impressive entree is a staple on my Thanksgiving menu.
—*Nancy Zimmerman, Cape May Court House, New Jersey*

 1-1/2 cups chopped celery
     3/4 cup chopped onion
     3/4 cup butter, cubed
       9 cups day-old cubed whole wheat bread
       3 cups finely chopped apples
     3/4 cup raisins
 1-1/2 teaspoons salt
 1-1/2 teaspoons dried thyme
     1/2 teaspoon rubbed sage
     1/4 teaspoon pepper
       1 turkey (14 to 16 pounds)
Additional butter, melted

In a Dutch oven, saute celery and onion in butter until tender. Remove from the heat; stir in the bread cubes, apples, raisins, salt, thyme, sage and pepper.

Just before baking, loosely stuff turkey with 4 cups of stuffing. Place remaining stuffing in a greased 2-qt. baking dish; refrigerate until ready to bake. Skewer the turkey openings; tie the drumsticks together. Place breast side up on a rack in a roasting pan. Brush with melted butter.

Bake, uncovered, at 325° for 3-3/4 to 4 hours or until a meat thermometer reads 180° for the turkey and 165° for the stuffing, basting occasionally with the pan drippings. (Cover loosely with foil if the turkey browns too quickly.)

Bake additional stuffing, covered, for 20-30 minutes. Uncover; bake 10 minutes longer or until lightly browned. Cover turkey and let stand for 20 minutes before removing stuffing and carving. If desired, thicken pan drippings for gravy. **Yield:** 10-12 servings.

Editor's Note: Stuffing may be prepared as directed and baked separately in a greased 3-qt. baking dish. Cover and bake at 325° for 30 minutes. Uncover and bake 10 minutes longer or until lightly browned.

Pork Chops with Onions

(Pictured below)

Prep: 20 min.   **Bake:** 40 min.

My mother-in-law shared this simple main dish recipe with me, and it's always well-received. —*Jill Van Nuis Marietta, Georgia*

✓ **Uses less fat, sugar or salt. Includes Nutrition Facts and Diabetic Exchanges.**

   6 bone-in pork loin chops (7 ounces *each*)
   1 tablespoon canola oil
 3/4 teaspoon salt
 1/2 teaspoon pepper
   2 medium sweet onions, sliced and
     separated into rings
   1 cup reduced-sodium beef broth
   1 tablespoon cornstarch
   2 tablespoons cold water

In a large nonstick skillet, brown pork chops in oil over medium-high heat. Sprinkle with salt and pepper. Transfer to an ungreased 13-in. x 9-in. x 2-in. baking dish.

   In the drippings, saute onions until tender. Spoon over chops; add broth. Cover and bake at 325° for 40-45 minutes or until juices run clear. Remove pork chops and onions; keep warm.

   In a small saucepan, combine cornstarch and water until smooth; stir in pan juices. Bring to a boil; cook and stir for 1-2 minutes or until thickened. Serve with pork and onions. **Yield:** 6 servings.

   Nutrition Facts: 1 serving equals 252 calories, 11 g fat (3 g saturated fat), 87 mg cholesterol, 433 mg

sodium, 6 g carbohydrate, 1 g fiber, 31 g protein. **Diabetic Exchanges:** 5 very lean meat, 1 vegetable, 1 fat.

Beef Stew with Dilly Dumplings

Prep: 40 min.   **Cook:** 2 hours

For a comforting meal, try this savory stew. The combination of well-seasoned dumplings, tender meat and vegetables is so good, you'll want to serve it to guests. —*Bernadine Dirmeyer, McComb, Ohio*

✓ **Uses less fat, sugar or salt. Includes Nutrition Facts.**

 1/3 cup all-purpose flour
1-1/8 teaspoons salt, *divided*
 1/4 teaspoon pepper
   2 pounds lean beef stew meat, cut into
     1-inch cubes
   2 tablespoons canola oil
   4 cups water
   2 cups sliced fresh carrots
   2 cups cubed peeled potatoes
   2 medium onions, chopped
1-1/2 cups sliced celery
   2 tablespoons minced fresh parsley
 1/2 teaspoon dried thyme
   1 bay leaf
DUMPLINGS:
1-1/2 cups all-purpose flour
   1 tablespoon minced fresh parsley
   3 teaspoons baking powder
 1/2 teaspoon salt
 1/4 teaspoon dried thyme
 1/4 teaspoon dill weed
   1 egg, lightly beaten
 2/3 cup fat-free milk
   1 tablespoon canola oil

In a large resealable plastic bag, combine the flour, 1/8 teaspoon salt and pepper. Add meat; seal bag and shake to coat. In a Dutch oven, brown beef in oil in batches. Add water, stirring to loosen browned bits from pan. Return meat to the pan. Bring to a boil. Reduce heat; cover and simmer for 1 hour.

   Add the carrots, potatoes, onions, celery, parsley, thyme, bay leaf and remaining salt. Bring to a boil. Reduce the heat; cover and simmer for 45 minutes or until the meat and vegetables are tender. Discard the bay leaf.

   For dumplings, in a bowl, combine the flour, parsley, baking powder, salt, thyme and dill. Combine egg, milk and oil; stir into dry ingredients just until moistened. Drop by tablespoonfuls onto simmering stew. Cover and simmer for 15-20 minutes or until a toothpick inserted in a dumpling comes out clean (do not lift the

cover while simmering). **Yield:** 8 servings.

Nutrition Facts: 1-1/4 cups stew with 2 dumplings equals 407 calories, 14 g fat (4 g saturated fat), 97 mg cholesterol, 699 mg sodium, 41 g carbohydrate, 4 g fiber, 28 g protein.

Veggie Turkey Pizza

(Pictured on page 58)

Prep: 40 min. + rising   **Bake:** 15 min.

This is the best pizza I've ever eaten! I sometimes mix walnuts with the pine nuts, but you can use your favorites.
—Marina Castle-Henry, Burbank, California

   1 **package (1/4 ounce) active dry yeast**
1-1/2 **cups warm water (110° to 115°)**
   1 **teaspoon sugar**
   5 **tablespoons olive oil,** *divided*
1/3 **cup pine nuts, chopped**
   3 **tablespoons minced fresh basil**
1-1/2 **teaspoons salt,** *divided*
   4 **cups bread flour**
   1 **package (20 ounces) ground turkey**
   1 **medium onion, chopped**
   1 **medium green pepper, diced**
   1 **medium sweet red pepper, diced**
   1 **cup sliced fresh mushrooms**
   2 **garlic cloves, minced**
   1 **envelope ranch salad dressing mix**
1/2 **teaspoon pepper**
   1 **can (3.8 ounces) sliced ripe olives, drained**
1/2 **cup shredded Parmesan cheese**
   3 **cups (12 ounces) shredded part-skim mozzarella cheese**

In a large mixing bowl, dissolve yeast in warm water. Add sugar; let stand for 5 minutes. Stir in 1 tablespoon oil, pine nuts, basil and 1/2 teaspoon salt. Add 2 cups flour; beat until smooth. Stir in enough remaining flour to form a soft dough.

Turn onto a floured surface; knead until smooth and elastic, about 5-6 minutes. Place in a greased bowl; turn once to grease top. Cover and let rise in a warm place until doubled, about 1 hour.

Punch dough down; let rest for 5 minutes. Divide dough in half; press each portion into a greased 12-in. pizza pan.

In a large skillet, cook the turkey, onion, peppers, mushrooms and garlic in 2 tablespoons oil over medium heat until meat is no longer pink; drain. Sprinkle with salad dressing mix, pepper and remaining salt.

Brush remaining oil over dough. Top with turkey mixture, olives and cheeses. Bake at 425° for 15-20 minutes or until cheese is melted and crust is golden brown. **Yield:** 2 pizzas (8 slices each).

Curried Shrimp and Apples

(Pictured above)

Prep/Total Time: 30 min.

Apples and shrimp, seasoned with curry powder, combine beautifully in this appealing main dish. If you like, try making it with chicken instead of the shrimp.
—Lynda Mack, Neptune Beach, Florida

✓ Uses less fat, sugar or salt. Includes Nutrition Facts and Diabetic Exchanges.

   1 **medium onion, chopped**
   2 **celery ribs, chopped**
1/4 **cup butter, cubed**
   2 **medium apples, sliced**
   2 **teaspoons all-purpose flour**
3/4 **teaspoon curry powder**
3/4 **cup water**
   1 **teaspoon chicken bouillon granules**
3/4 **pound uncooked medium shrimp, peeled and deveined**
Hot cooked rice

In a large skillet, saute the onion and celery in butter for 2 minutes. Stir in apples; saute 1-2 minutes longer or until crisp-tender.

Sprinkle with the flour and curry powder. Gradually whisk in the water and bouillon until smooth. Add shrimp; bring to a boil. Reduce heat; simmer for 2-3 minutes or until shrimp turn pink and sauce is thickened. Serve over the rice. **Yield:** 4 servings.

Nutrition Facts: 1 cup (prepared with reduced-fat butter; calculated without rice) equals 181 calories, 7 g fat (4 g saturated fat), 146 mg cholesterol, 311 mg sodium, 16 g carbohydrate, 3 g fiber, 16 g protein. **Diabetic Exchanges:** 2 lean meat, 1 vegetable, 1 fruit.

Curried Honey Chicken

(Pictured above)

Prep: 15 min. **Bake:** 1 hour

A friend gave me this recipe, and it always receives lots of compliments. The curry-citrus sauce is the perfect accent for the golden-baked chicken. —Joanna Burks
Marshfield, Missouri

    1/4 cup butter, melted
    1/4 cup orange juice
    1/4 cup honey
      2 tablespoons lemon juice
      1 tablespoon prepared mustard
      1 to 2 teaspoons curry powder
      1 teaspoon salt
      6 bone-in chicken breast halves (8 ounces
        each)
      1 teaspoon cornstarch
    1/3 cup cold water

In a large bowl, combine the first seven ingredients; set aside 1/3 cup for basting. Dip chicken in remaining butter mixture; place in a well-greased 13-in. x 9-in. x 2-in. baking dish. Bake, uncovered, at 350° for 1 hour, basting occasionally with reserved butter mixture.

Remove the chicken and keep warm. In a small saucepan, combine cornstarch and water until smooth. Stir in the pan drippings. Bring to a boil; cook and stir for 2 minutes or until thickened. Drizzle over chicken. **Yield:** 6 servings.

Cinnamon Raisin Strata

Prep: 20 min. + chilling **Bake:** 40 min.

This delightful dish, made with day-old raisin bread, is full of cinnamon flavor. —Barbara Tritch, Hope, Idaho

    1/4 cup butter, softened
      3 tablespoons ground cinnamon
      8 slices day-old raisin bread
      4 tablespoons brown sugar, *divided*
      6 eggs
  1-1/2 cups milk
      3 tablespoons maple syrup
      1 teaspoon vanilla extract
Additional maple syrup

In a small bowl, combine butter and cinnamon; spread over one side of each slice of bread. Place four slices, buttered side up, in a greased 8-in. square baking dish (trim to fit if necessary). Sprinkle with 2 tablespoons brown sugar. Repeat with remaining bread and brown sugar. In a large bowl, whisk eggs, milk, syrup and vanilla; pour over bread. Cover and refrigerate overnight.

Remove from refrigerator 30 minutes before baking. Bake, uncovered, at 350° for 40-50 minutes or until golden and puffed. Serve with syrup. **Yield:** 4 servings.

Tortilla-Salsa Meat Loaf

Prep: 15 min. **Bake:** 1-1/4 hours

I'm asked to make this recipe at least once a month during winter, especially for birthday dinners. My guests like it with asparagus and garlic mashed potatoes.
—Steven Espinosa, Salt Lake City, Utah

      2 slices day-old white bread
      2 eggs, lightly beaten
      1 cup salsa
    1/2 cup crushed tortilla chips
    1/2 cup *each* chopped green pepper, onion
        and celery
      1 jalapeno pepper, seeded and chopped
      6 garlic cloves, minced
      1 teaspoon pepper
    1/2 teaspoon Italian seasoning
    1/4 teaspoon seasoned salt
      1 pound ground beef
      1 pound ground pork

Place bread in an ungreased 9-in. x 5-in. x 3-in. loaf pan; set aside. In a bowl, combine the eggs, salsa, tortilla chips, green pepper, onion, celery, jalapeno, garlic, pepper, Italian seasoning and seasoned salt. Crumble beef and pork over mixture; mix well. Pat into prepared pan.

Bake, uncovered, at 375° for 1-1/4 to 1-1/2 hours

or until no pink remains and a meat thermometer reads 160°. Invert meat loaf onto a serving platter; discard bread. Let stand for 5 minutes before slicing. **Yield:** 8 servings.

Editor's Note: When cutting or seeding hot peppers, use rubber or plastic gloves to protect your hands. Avoid touching your face.

Venison Parmigiana

Prep: 25 min.   **Bake:** 1 hour

While looking for an alternative to pan-frying our venison steak, we decided to give it a little Italian flair. Our idea turned out to be a big hit with our family and friends.
—*Phil Zipp, Tomahawk, Wisconsin*

    2 **pounds boneless venison steaks**
    1 **egg**
    1 **tablespoon milk**
  2/3 **cup seasoned bread crumbs**
  1/3 **cup grated Parmesan cheese**
    5 **tablespoons olive oil**
    1 **small onion, finely chopped**
    2 **cups hot water**
    1 **can (6 ounces) tomato paste**
    1 **teaspoon pepper**
  1/2 **teaspoon salt**
  1/2 **teaspoon sugar**
  1/2 **teaspoon dried marjoram**
    2 **cups (8 ounces) shredded part-skim mozzarella cheese**

Pound steaks to 1/4-in. thickness; cut into serving-size pieces. In a shallow bowl, beat egg and milk. In another bowl, combine bread crumbs and Parmesan cheese. Dip venison in egg mixture, then coat with crumb mixture.

In a large skillet, brown meat in oil on both sides. Place in a greased 13-in. x 9-in. x 2-in. baking dish. In the drippings, saute onion for 2-3 minutes or until tender. Stir in the water, tomato paste, pepper, salt, sugar and marjoram. Bring to a boil. Reduce heat; simmer, uncovered, for 5 minutes. Pour over venison.

Cover and bake at 350° for 50 minutes or until meat is tender. Uncover; sprinkle with cheese. Bake 10-15 minutes longer or until cheese is melted. **Yield:** 6 servings.

Meatball Stew

(Pictured at right)

Prep: 1 hour   **Cook:** 30 min.

Hearty and homey, this saucy stew is chock-full of tender meatballs and vegetables that are sure to warm you and your family up when there's an autumn chill in the air.
—*Joan Chasse, Berlin, Connecticut*

    3 **eggs, lightly beaten**
  2/3 **cup seasoned bread crumbs**
  1/3 **cup grated Parmesan cheese**
Dash pepper
  1/2 **pound *each* ground beef, pork and veal**
    4 **medium potatoes, peeled and cut into small chunks**
    3 **medium carrots, sliced**
1-1/2 **cups chopped celery**
    1 **medium onion, cut into wedges**
    1 **garlic clove, minced**
    1 **envelope onion soup mix**
2-1/4 **cups water**
    1 **cup frozen peas, thawed**
4-1/2 **teaspoons minced fresh parsley**

In a large bowl, combine the eggs, bread crumbs, Parmesan cheese and pepper. Crumble beef, pork and veal over mixture; mix well. Shape into 1-1/2-in. balls.

Place meatballs on a greased rack in a foil-lined 15-in. x 10-in. x 1-in. baking pan. Bake at 350° for 20-25 minutes or until no longer pink. Drain on paper towels.

Place the meatballs, potatoes, carrots, celery, onion and garlic in a soup kettle or Dutch oven. In a small bowl, combine soup mix and water; pour over meatball mixture. Bring to a boil. Reduce heat; cover and simmer for 25-30 minutes or until vegetables are tender. Stir in peas and parsley; heat through. **Yield:** 10 servings (2-1/2 quarts).

Breads, Rolls & Muffins

The tempting aroma of these golden brown braids, pastries and other goodies will draw everyone to the oven, so be sure to bake plenty!

FRESH-BAKED FAVORITES. Clockwise from upper left: Spiced Cake Doughnuts (p. 100), Basil-Cheese Bread Strips (p. 94), Almond Pastry Puffs (p. 101), Grilled Vegetable Cheese Bread (p. 98) and Lemon Pound Cake Muffins (p. 99).

Cranberry Almond Muffins

(Pictured above)

Prep: 20 min.   **Bake:** 20 min.

My youngest daughter, Elaine, served these delightful muffins for breakfast when my husband and I were visiting her in Virginia. We just loved them, so I got the recipe and now make them often at our home.
— *Janice Pletscher, Basking Ridge, New Jersey*

- 1-1/2 **cups all-purpose flour**
- 1/2 **cup sugar**
- 1 **teaspoon baking powder**
- 1/4 **teaspoon baking soda**
- 1/4 **teaspoon salt**
- 2 **eggs**
- 1/2 **cup sour cream**
- 1/4 **cup butter, melted**
- 1/4 **teaspoon almond extract**
- 3/4 **cup sliced almonds, *divided***
- 1/2 **cup whole-berry cranberry sauce**

In a bowl, combine the flour, sugar, baking powder, baking soda and salt. In another bowl, whisk the eggs, sour cream, butter and extract; stir into dry ingredients just until moistened. Fold in 1/2 cup almonds.

Fill greased or paper-lined muffin cups half full; drop 1 tablespoon cranberry sauce into the center of each muffin. Cover with enough batter to fill cups three-fourths full; sprinkle with remaining almonds.

Bake at 375° for 20-25 minutes or until a toothpick inserted 1 in. from the edge comes out clean. Cool for 5 minutes before removing from pan to a wire rack. Serve warm. **Yield:** 8 muffins.

Basil-Cheese Bread Strips

(Pictured on page 92)

Prep: 15 min. + standing   **Bake:** 15 min.

Tender and chewy, these breadsticks always go fast. My three daughters could eat every last one.
— *Melinda Rhoads, Slippery Rock, Pennsylvania*

✓ **Uses less fat, sugar or salt. Includes Nutrition Facts and Diabetic Exchanges.**

- 2-1/2 **cups all-purpose flour**
- 1/4 **cup toasted wheat germ**
- 1 **package (1/4 ounce) active dry yeast**
- 1 **cup warm water (120° to 130°)**
- 2 **tablespoons olive oil, *divided***
- 1 **tablespoon honey**
- 1/2 **teaspoon salt**
- 2 **garlic cloves, minced**
- 1/4 **cup shredded part-skim mozzarella cheese**
- 2 **tablespoons grated Parmesan cheese**
- 2 **tablespoons minced fresh parsley**
- 10 **fresh basil leaves**

In a large mixing bowl, combine 1-1/2 cups flour, wheat germ, yeast, warm water, 1 tablespoon oil, honey and salt; beat for 2 minutes. Stir in enough remaining flour to make a soft dough. Turn onto a floured surface; knead for 5-6 minutes. Cover and let rest for 10 minutes.

Coat a 15-in. x 10-in. x 1-in. baking pan with nonstick cooking spray. Pat dough into pan. Bake at 425° for 10 minutes or until golden brown. In a small bowl, combine garlic and remaining oil; brush over bread. Sprinkle with cheeses, parsley and basil. Bake 5 minutes longer or until cheese is melted. Cut into strips. Refrigerate leftovers. **Yield:** 2 dozen.

Nutrition Facts: 2 bread strips equals 141 calories, 3 g fat (1 g saturated fat), 2 mg cholesterol, 126 mg sodium, 23 g carbohydrate, 1 g fiber, 5 g protein. **Diabetic Exchanges:** 1-1/2 starch, 1/2 fat.

Feta 'n' Chive Muffins

Prep: 15 min.   **Bake:** 20 min.

This is a "spring" variation on a savory muffin recipe that my husband has made for years. It has a light texture and tastes best eaten warm right from the oven.
— *Angela Buchanan, Boulder, Colorado*

✓ **Uses less fat, sugar or salt. Includes Nutrition Facts and Diabetic Exchanges.**

- 1-1/2 **cups all-purpose flour**
- 3 **teaspoons baking powder**
- 1/4 **teaspoon salt**

2 eggs
1 cup milk
2 tablespoons butter, melted
1/2 cup crumbled feta cheese
3 tablespoons minced chives

In a bowl, combine the flour, baking powder and salt. In another bowl, whisk the eggs, milk and butter; stir into dry ingredients just until moistened. Fold in the feta cheese and chives.

Fill greased or paper-lined muffin cups two-thirds full. Bake at 400° for 18-22 minutes or until a toothpick comes out clean. Cool for 5 minutes before removing from pan to a wire rack. Serve warm. Refrigerate leftovers. **Yield:** 1 dozen.

Nutrition Facts: 1 muffin equals 105 calories, 4 g fat (2 g saturated fat), 43 mg cholesterol, 235 mg sodium, 13 g carbohydrate, 1 g fiber, 4 g protein. **Diabetic Exchanges:** 1 starch, 1/2 fat.

Miniature Orange Muffins

Prep: 30 min.   **Bake:** 10 min. per batch

Orange peel and orange juice flavor these fun streusel-topped muffins that are perfect for a buffet table. The accompanying orange marmalade butter really makes them special. —Bonita Kinney, Firth, Nebraska

1-1/2 cups plus 2 tablespoons all-purpose flour, *divided*
1/2 cup sugar
2 teaspoons baking powder
1/2 teaspoon salt
1 egg
1 cup milk
9 tablespoons butter, melted, *divided*
3 tablespoons orange juice concentrate
2-1/2 teaspoons grated orange peel, *divided*
1/4 cup packed brown sugar
1/4 cup chopped pecans
ORANGE BUTTER:
1/2 cup butter, softened
1/4 cup sweet orange marmalade
1 teaspoon honey

In a large bowl, combine 1-1/2 cups flour, sugar, baking powder and salt. In another bowl, whisk the egg, milk, 8 tablespoons butter, orange juice concentrate and 2 teaspoons orange peel; stir into dry ingredients just until moistened.

Fill greased miniature muffin cups half full. Combine the brown sugar, pecans and remaining flour, butter and orange peel; sprinkle over batter. Bake at 400° for 10-12 minutes or until a toothpick comes out clean. Cool for 5 minutes before removing from pans

to wire racks.

In a small mixing bowl, beat the orange butter ingredients until blended. Serve with muffins. **Yield:** 4-1/2 dozen.

Sunday Morning Coffee Cake

(Pictured below)

Prep: 20 min.   **Bake:** 25 min. + cooling

This easy, old-fashioned coffee cake boasts a cinnamon-sugar streusel topping and cuts nicely for company. Your family is sure to love it, too. Serve slices for a weekend brunch or as a midafternoon dessert with a cup of coffee or tea. —Lavonn Bormuth, Westerville, Ohio

2 tablespoons butter, softened
1/2 cup sugar
1/2 teaspoon salt
1 egg
2/3 cup milk
1 teaspoon vanilla extract
1-1/2 cups all-purpose flour
3 teaspoons baking powder
TOPPING:
1/4 cup sugar
2 tablespoons all-purpose flour
1 tablespoon ground cinnamon
1/4 cup cold butter

In a small mixing bowl, beat butter, sugar and salt until crumbly. Add the egg, milk and vanilla; mix well. Combine flour and baking powder; add to butter mixture. Transfer to a greased 8-in. square baking dish.

For topping, in a small bowl, combine the sugar, flour and cinnamon; cut in butter until mixture is crumbly. Sprinkle over batter. Bake at 350° for 25-30 minutes or until a toothpick inserted near the center comes out clean. Cool on a wire rack for 10 minutes. Serve warm if desired. **Yield:** 9 servings.

White Chocolate Macadamia Muffins

(Pictured below)

Prep: 20 min.   **Bake:** 15 min.

I love making muffins because they are so versatile and everyone loves them. These nutty treats remind me of one of my favorite cookies. They're real kid-pleasers.
—*Lorie Roach, Buckatunna, Mississippi*

 1-3/4 cups all-purpose flour
  3/4 cup sugar
 2-1/2 teaspoons baking powder
  1/2 teaspoon salt
    1 egg
  1/2 cup milk
  1/4 cup butter, melted
  3/4 cup vanilla *or* white chips
  3/4 cup chopped macadamia nuts
GLAZE:
  1/2 cup vanilla *or* white chips
    2 tablespoons heavy whipping cream

In a bowl, combine the flour, sugar, baking powder and salt. In another bowl, whisk the egg, milk and butter; stir into dry ingredients just until moistened. Fold in the chips and nuts.

Fill paper-lined muffin cups two-thirds full. Bake at 400° for 15-18 minutes or until a toothpick comes out clean. Cool for 5 minutes before removing from pan to a wire rack.

For glaze, in a small microwave-safe bowl, melt chips with cream; stir until smooth. Drizzle over warm muffins. **Yield:** 1 dozen.

Cloverleaf Bran Rolls

(Pictured above)

Prep: 40 min. + rising   **Bake:** 15 min.

These tender, delicious rolls are great for a gathering. They're especially good served warm!
—*Marvel Herriman, Hayesville, North Carolina*

    1 cup All-Bran
    1 cup boiling water
    2 packages (1/4 ounce *each*) active dry yeast
    1 cup warm water (110° to 115°)
    1 cup shortening
  3/4 cup sugar
    1 teaspoon salt
    2 eggs, beaten
    6 cups all-purpose flour

In a small bowl, combine bran and boiling water; set aside. In another bowl, dissolve yeast in warm water. In a large mixing bowl, cream shortening, sugar and salt. Add eggs and yeast mixture; mix well. Add bran mixture and 2 cups flour; beat well. Gradually add enough remaining flour to form a soft dough.

Turn onto a lightly floured surface; knead until smooth and elastic, about 6-8 minutes. Place in a greased bowl, turning once to grease top. Cover and let rise until doubled, about 1 hour.

Punch dough down. Turn onto a lightly floured surface. Divide into six portions; divide each into 12 pieces. Shape each into a ball; place three balls in each greased muffin cup. Cover and let rise until doubled, about 1 hour.

Bake at 350° for 15-18 minutes or until lightly browned. Remove from pans to wire racks. **Yield:** 2 dozen.

Lemon-Thyme Tea Bread

(Pictured below right)

Prep: 20 min. **Bake:** 40 min. + cooling

I received this recipe as part of a gift, along with a lemon thyme plant and a loaf of this pound cake-like bread. Everyone who tries it asks for the recipe.
—*Jeannette Mango, Parkesburg, Pennsylvania*

     3/4 **cup milk**
        1 **tablespoon minced fresh thyme** *or*
        1 **teaspoon dried thyme**
     1/2 **cup butter, softened**
        1 **cup sugar**
        2 **eggs**
        2 **cups all-purpose flour**
    1-1/2 **teaspoons baking powder**
     1/4 **teaspoon salt**
        1 **tablespoon lemon juice**
        1 **tablespoon grated lemon peel**
GLAZE:
     1/2 **cup confectioners' sugar**
        1 **tablespoon lemon juice**

In a microwave-safe bowl, combine milk and thyme. Microwave, uncovered, on high for 1-2 minutes or until bubbly; cover and let stand for 5 minutes. Cool to room temperature.

In a large mixing bowl, cream butter and sugar. Add eggs, one at a time, beating well after each addition. Combine the flour, baking powder and salt; add to creamed mixture alternately with reserved milk mixture. Stir in lemon juice and lemon peel.

Pour into a greased 9-in. x 5-in. x 3-in. loaf pan. Bake at 350° for 40-45 minutes or until a toothpick inserted near the center comes out clean. Cool for 10 minutes before removing from pan to a wire rack.

In a small bowl, combine glaze ingredients until smooth; drizzle over bread. **Yield:** 1 loaf.

Gingerbread Muffins

Prep: 45 min. **Bake:** 15 min.

Growing up, I adored my mom's gingerbread cake with lemon sauce, so I re-created the combination for my family. These spice- and molasses-flavored muffins spread with homemade lemon curd have become a favorite.
—*Kelly Trupkiewicz, Fort Collins, Colorado*

LEMON CURD:
     2/3 **cup sugar**
     3/4 **teaspoon cornstarch**
     1/3 **cup lemon juice**
        5 **egg yolks, lightly beaten**
     1/4 **cup butter, cubed**
        2 **teaspoons grated lemon peel**

MUFFINS:
        2 **cups all-purpose flour**
     1/4 **cup sugar**
    2-1/2 **teaspoons baking powder**
        2 **teaspoons ground ginger**
        1 **teaspoon ground cinnamon**
     1/4 **teaspoon salt**
     1/4 **teaspoon ground cloves**
        1 **egg**
     3/4 **cup milk**
     1/4 **cup vegetable oil**
     1/4 **cup molasses**

In a heavy saucepan, combine the sugar, cornstarch and lemon juice until smooth. Bring to a boil; cook and stir for 2 minutes or until slightly thickened. Stir a small amount into egg yolks. Return all to the pan; bring to a gentle boil, stirring constantly. Cook and stir 1-2 minutes longer or until mixture reaches 160° and coats the back of a metal spoon.

Remove from heat; gently stir in butter and lemon peel until blended. Pour into a bowl; cover surface with plastic wrap. Cover and refrigerate until serving.

In a bowl, combine the flour, sugar, baking powder, ginger, cinnamon, salt and cloves. In another bowl, whisk the egg, milk, oil and molasses until smooth; stir into dry ingredients just until moistened.

Fill paper-lined muffin cups half full. Bake at 375° for 15-20 minutes or until a toothpick comes out clean. Cool for 5 minutes before removing from pan to a wire rack. Serve warm with lemon curd. **Yield:** 1 dozen (1 cup lemon curd).

Tricolor Braid

(Pictured below)

Prep: 1 hour + rising   **Bake:** 25 min. + cooling

These exquisite and eye-catching loaves are wonderfully dense and chewy. They take some time to prepare, but the results are always well worth the extra effort.
—*Cindi Paulson, Anchorage, Alaska*

✓ **Uses less fat, sugar or salt. Includes Nutrition Facts and Diabetic Exchanges.**

    2 packages (1/4 ounce *each*) active dry yeast
2-1/3 cups warm water (110° to 115°)
  1/4 cup butter, softened
    2 tablespoons honey
    3 teaspoons salt
3-1/3 to 3-2/3 cups all-purpose flour
WHEAT DOUGH:
    2 tablespoons toasted wheat germ
    2 tablespoons molasses
    1 cup plus 2 to 5 tablespoons whole wheat
      flour
PUMPERNICKEL DOUGH:
    2 tablespoons baking cocoa
    2 tablespoons molasses
    1 cup plus 2 to 5 tablespoons rye flour
    1 egg white
    1 tablespoon water

In a large mixing bowl, dissolve yeast in warm water. Add the butter, honey, salt and 2-1/3 cups flour; beat for 2 minutes. Divide evenly among three mixing bowls.

To the first bowl, add enough remaining all-purpose flour to make a stiff dough; mix well. Turn onto a floured surface; knead until smooth and elastic, about 6-8 minutes. Place in a greased bowl, turning once to grease top. Cover and set aside.

Add wheat germ and molasses to the second bowl; mix well. Gradually add enough whole wheat flour to make a stiff dough. Turn onto a floured surface; knead until smooth and elastic, about 6-8 minutes. Place in a greased bowl, turning once to grease top. Cover and set aside.

Add cocoa and molasses to the third bowl; mix well. Gradually add enough rye flour to make a stiff dough. Turn onto a floured surface; knead until smooth and elastic, about 6-8 minutes. Place in a greased bowl, turning once to grease top. Cover. Let all three bowls rise in a warm place until doubled, about 1 hour.

Punch doughs down; divide each in half. Shape each portion into a 15-in. rope. Place a rope of each dough on a greased baking sheet and braid; seal ends. Repeat with remaining ropes. Cover and let rise until doubled, about 45 minutes.

Beat the egg white and water; brush over the braided dough. Bake at 350° for 25-30 minutes or until golden brown. Remove to wire racks to cool. **Yield:** 2 loaves (12 slices each).

Nutrition Facts: 1 slice equals 146 calories, 2 g fat (1 g saturated fat), 5 mg cholesterol, 319 mg sodium, 28 g carbohydrate, 2 g fiber, 4 g protein. **Diabetic Exchanges:** 2 starch, 1/2 fat.

Editor's Note: Use all-purpose flour on kneading surfaces for all three doughs.

Grilled Vegetable Cheese Bread

(Pictured on page 92)

Prep: 20 min.   **Grill:** 15 min.

Here in the Deep South, tomatoes are ripe and delicious on the Fourth of July. They're especially good on this loaf, which tastes great any time you fire up the grill.
—*Sundra Hauck, Bogalusa, Louisiana*

    1 loaf (1 pound) French bread, sliced
      lengthwise
  1/4 cup olive oil
    3 large tomatoes, thinly sliced
    2 cups thinly sliced zucchini
    1 cup (4 ounces) shredded cheddar cheese
    1 jar (4 ounces) sliced pimientos, drained
    1 can (2-1/4 ounces) chopped ripe olives,
      drained

2 teaspoons Creole seasoning
1/4 cup grated Parmesan cheese

Brush cut sides of bread with oil. Layer with tomatoes and zucchini; sprinkle with cheddar cheese, pimientos, olives and Creole seasoning.

Prepare grill for indirect heat. Place bread on grill rack. Grill, covered, over indirect medium heat for 10-12 minutes or until zucchini is crisp-tender. Sprinkle with Parmesan cheese; grill 2-4 minutes longer or until melted. **Yield:** 8 servings.

Berry Cheesecake Muffins

(Pictured at right)

Prep: 30 min.   **Bake:** 25 min. per batch

I adapted this recipe over the years. Not only are these muffins delicious, but they're bursting with color, too.
—*Jeanne Bilhimer, Midland, Michigan*

1/3 cup butter, softened
3/4 cup sugar
2 eggs
1-1/2 cups all-purpose flour
1-1/2 teaspoons baking powder
1 teaspoon ground cinnamon
1/3 cup milk
CREAM CHEESE FILLING:
2 packages (3 ounces *each*) cream cheese, softened
1/3 cup sugar
1 egg
3/4 cup fresh raspberries
3/4 cup fresh blueberries
STREUSEL TOPPING:
1/4 cup all-purpose flour
2 tablespoons brown sugar
1/2 teaspoon ground cinnamon
1 tablespoon cold butter

In a large mixing bowl, cream butter and sugar. Add eggs; beat well. Combine flour, baking powder and cinnamon; add to creamed mixture alternately with milk. Fill greased or paper-lined muffin cups one-third full.

For filling, in a small mixing bowl, beat cream cheese, sugar and egg until smooth. Fold in berries. Drop a rounded tablespoonful into center of each muffin. For topping, combine flour, brown sugar and cinnamon in a small bowl; cut in butter until crumbly. Sprinkle over batter. (Muffin cups will be full.)

Bake at 375° for 25-30 minutes or until a toothpick comes out clean. Cool for 5 minutes before removing from pans to wire racks. Serve warm. Refrigerate leftovers. **Yield:** 21 muffins.

Lemon Pound Cake Muffins

(Pictured on page 92)

Prep: 15 min.   **Bake:** 20 min.

I make these lemony muffins for all kinds of occasions. My family always requests them when we have a brunch. They're so good!   —*Lola Baxter, Winnebago, Minnesota*

1/2 cup butter, softened
1 cup sugar
2 eggs
1 teaspoon vanilla extract
1/2 teaspoon lemon extract
1-3/4 cups all-purpose flour
1/2 teaspoon salt
1/4 teaspoon baking soda
1/2 cup sour cream
GLAZE:
2 cups confectioners' sugar
3 tablespoons lemon juice

In a large mixing bowl, cream the butter and sugar. Add the eggs and extracts; beat well. Combine the flour, salt and baking soda; add to creamed mixture alternately with sour cream.

Fill greased or paper-lined muffin cups three-fourths full. Bake at 400° for 18-20 minutes or until a toothpick comes out clean. Cool for 5 minutes before removing from pan to a wire rack. Combine the glaze ingredients; drizzle over muffins. Serve warm. **Yield:** 1 dozen.

Nut Roll Coffee Cakes

(Pictured above)

Prep: 45 min. + rising   **Bake:** 20 min. + cooling

My parents moved to America from Slovenia in the early 1900s. With them came this special recipe that has been cherished and enjoyed by more than four generations.
—*Louise Gasper, Northville, Michigan*

  1 package (1/4 ounce) active dry yeast
1/4 cup warm water (110° to 115°)
  1 cup butter, melted and cooled
1/2 cup warm milk (110° to 115°)
  3 egg yolks
  2 tablespoons sugar
1/2 teaspoon salt
  3 cups all-purpose flour
FILLING:
  3 egg whites
  1 teaspoon vanilla extract
3/4 cup sugar
 2-1/4 cups ground walnuts
ICING:
3/4 cup confectioners' sugar
  1 teaspoon butter, softened
  1 teaspoon vanilla extract
  3 to 4 teaspoons milk

In a large mixing bowl, dissolve yeast in warm water. Add the butter, milk, egg yolks, sugar, salt and flour;

beat until smooth. Do not knead. Cover and refrigerate overnight.

For filling, in a small mixing bowl, beat egg whites and vanilla on medium speed until soft peaks form. Gradually beat in sugar, 1 tablespoon at a time, on high until stiff glossy peaks form and sugar is dissolved. Fold in walnuts; set aside.

Turn dough onto a lightly floured surface. Let stand for 10 minutes or until easy to handle. Divide into thirds. Roll each portion into a 15-in. x 13-in. rectangle. Spread filling over rectangles to within 1/2 in. of edges. Roll up jelly-roll style, starting with a long side; pinch seams to seal.

Place seam side down on greased baking sheets. Cover and let rise until doubled, about 45 minutes. Bake at 350° for 20-25 minutes or until golden brown. Remove from pans to wire racks to cool. Combine glaze ingredients; drizzle over coffee cakes. **Yield:** 3 loaves.

Spiced Cake Doughnuts

(Pictured on page 92)

Prep: 30 min. + chilling
Cook: 5 min. per batch + cooling

As part of our family's Halloween tradition, I make these delicious frosted doughnuts to serve with warm, spiced cider. Grated apples give them a scrumptious flavor and texture.   —*Katherine Nelson, Centerville, Utah*

1/4 cup shortening
  1 cup sugar
  3 eggs
  1 teaspoon vanilla extract
  5 cups all-purpose flour
  3 teaspoons baking powder
  2 teaspoons salt
  1 teaspoon baking soda
  1 teaspoon ground cinnamon
  1 teaspoon ground nutmeg
1/4 teaspoon ground mace
1/2 cup buttermilk
  1 cup grated peeled apples
Oil for deep-fat frying
BROWNED BUTTER FROSTING:
1/2 cup packed brown sugar
  3 tablespoons butter
1/4 cup heavy whipping cream
 1-3/4 cups confectioners' sugar
Colored sprinkles

In a large mixing bowl, cream the shortening and sugar. Beat in the eggs and vanilla. Combine the flour, baking powder, salt, baking soda, cinnamon, nutmeg and mace; add to the creamed mixture alternately with the buttermilk. Fold in the apples. Cover and refrigerate for at least 2 hours.

On a lightly floured surface, roll dough to 1/2-in. thickness. Cut with a floured 2-1/2-in. doughnut cutter. In an electric skillet or deep-fat fryer, heat oil to 375°. Fry doughnuts, a few at a time, until golden brown on both sides. Drain on paper towels.

In a small saucepan, bring brown sugar and butter to a boil. Cook and stir for 1 minute or until slightly thickened. Pour into a small mixing bowl; let stand for 10 minutes. Add cream; beat until smooth. Gradually add confectioners' sugar, 1/4 cup at a time, beating well after each addition until frosting achieves desired consistency. Frost doughnuts; top with sprinkles. **Yield:** 22 doughnuts.

Almond Pastry Puffs

(Pictured on page 92)

Prep: 40 min.   **Bake:** 20 min. + cooling

This tender, nutty coffee cake is one of my favorite brunch treats. It's good that the recipe makes two!
—Betty Claycomb, Alverton, Pennsylvania

  2 **cups all-purpose flour,** *divided*
1/4 **teaspoon salt**
  1 **cup cold butter,** *divided*
  2 **tablespoons plus 1 cup cold water,** *divided*
1/4 **teaspoon almond extract**
  3 **eggs**
FROSTING:
1-1/2 **cups confectioners' sugar**
  2 **tablespoons butter, softened**
  4 **teaspoons water**
1/4 **teaspoon almond extract**
2/3 **cup chopped almonds, toasted**

In a large bowl, combine 1 cup flour and salt; cut in 1/2 cup butter until mixture resembles coarse crumbs. Add 2 tablespoons cold water; stir with a fork until blended. Shape dough into a ball; divide in half. Place dough 3 in. apart on an ungreased baking sheet; pat each into a 12-in. x 3-in. rectangle.

In a large saucepan, bring remaining butter and water to a boil. Remove from the heat; stir in extract and remaining flour until a smooth ball forms. Remove from the heat; let stand for 5 minutes. Add eggs, one at a time, beating well after each addition. Continue beating until mixture is smooth and shiny.

Spread over rectangles. Bake at 400° for 18-20 minutes or until topping is lightly browned. Cool for 5 minutes before removing from pan to wire racks.

For frosting, in a small mixing bowl, combine the confectioners' sugar, butter, water and extract; beat until smooth. Spread over pastries; sprinkle with almonds. **Yield:** 2 pastries (11 servings each).

Italian Herb Muffins

(Pictured below)

Prep: 20 min.   **Bake:** 15 min.

My husband enjoys garlic bread with pasta dishes. While preparing spaghetti for dinner one day, I realized I was out of bread and thought, Why not make an herb muffin instead? I created this cheesy recipe, and it was a hit.
—Cyndee Page, Reno, Nevada

  2 **cups all-purpose flour**
  2 **tablespoons grated Parmesan cheese**
  1 **tablespoon sugar**
  1 **tablespoon Italian seasoning**
  3 **teaspoons baking powder**
  1 **teaspoon salt**
  1 **egg**
3/4 **cup milk**
1/2 **cup vegetable oil**
1/4 **cup butter, softened**
1/2 **teaspoon garlic powder**

In a bowl, combine the flour, Parmesan cheese, sugar, Italian seasoning, baking powder and salt. In another bowl, whisk the egg, milk and oil; stir into dry ingredients just until moistened.

Fill greased or paper-lined muffin cups three-fourths full. Bake at 400° for 15-20 minutes or until a toothpick comes out clean. Cool for 5 minutes before removing from pan to a wire rack. In a small bowl, combine the butter and garlic powder. Serve with the warm muffins. **Yield:** 10 muffins.

Blueberry Sour Cream Coffee Cake

(Pictured below)

Prep: 25 min. **Bake:** 55 min. + cooling

Holidays would not be the same at our house without this treat. —Susan Walschlager, Anderson, Indiana

        3/4 cup butter, softened
    1-1/2 cups sugar
        4 eggs
        1 teaspoon vanilla extract
        3 cups all-purpose flour
    1-1/2 teaspoons baking powder
        3/4 teaspoon baking soda
        1/4 teaspoon salt
        1 cup (8 ounces) sour cream
FILLING:
        1/4 cup packed brown sugar
        1 tablespoon all-purpose flour
        1/2 teaspoon ground cinnamon
        2 cups fresh *or* frozen blueberries
GLAZE:
        1 cup confectioners' sugar
        2 to 3 tablespoons milk

In a large mixing bowl, cream butter and sugar. Add eggs, one at a time, beating well after each addition. Beat in vanilla. Combine the flour, baking powder, baking soda and salt; add to creamed mixture alternately with sour cream.

Spoon a third of the batter into a greased and floured 10-in. tube pan. Combine brown sugar, flour and cinnamon; sprinkle half over batter. Top with half of the berries. Repeat layers. Top with remaining batter.

Bake at 350° for 55-65 minutes or until a toothpick inserted near the center comes out clean. Cool for 10 minutes before removing from pan to a wire rack to cool completely. Combine glaze ingredients; drizzle over cake. **Yield:** 10-12 servings.

Editor's Note: If you are using frozen blueberries, do not thaw.

Garden Biscuits

(Pictured above)

Prep/Total Time: 30 min.

These flaky yeast biscuits—speckled with carrot, parsley and green onion—smell wonderful while baking.
        —Kerry Dority, Camdenton, Missouri

☑ **Uses less fat, sugar or salt. Includes Nutrition Facts and Diabetic Exchanges.**

    2-1/2 cups all-purpose flour
        1 tablespoon sugar
        1 package (1/4 ounce) active dry yeast
    1-1/2 teaspoons baking powder
        1/2 teaspoon baking soda
        1/4 teaspoon salt
        1/2 cup shortening
        1 cup buttermilk
        2 tablespoons water
        1/4 cup finely shredded carrot
        2 tablespoons minced fresh parsley
        2 tablespoons finely chopped green onion

In a large mixing bowl, combine the flour, sugar, yeast, baking powder, baking soda and salt. Cut in shortening until mixture resembles coarse crumbs. In a small saucepan, heat buttermilk and water to 120°-130°. Add buttermilk mixture, carrot, parsley and onion to yeast mixture; stir just until moistened.

Turn onto a lightly floured surface; knead until a soft dough forms, about 6-8 minutes. Pat or roll out to 1/2-in. thickness; cut with a floured 2-1/2-in. biscuit cutter. Place 1 in. apart on ungreased baking sheets. Bake at 450° for 8-10 minutes or until golden brown. Serve warm. **Yield:** 15 biscuits.

Nutrition Facts: 1 biscuit equals 147 calories, 7 g fat (2 g saturated fat), 1 mg cholesterol, 140 mg sodium, 18 g carbohydrate, 1 g fiber, 3 g protein. **Diabetic Exchanges:** 1-1/2 fat, 1 starch.

Editor's Note: Warmed buttermilk will appear curdled.

Apple Streusel Muffins

Prep: 20 min.   **Bake:** 15 min. + cooling

My husband and children just love these coffee cake-like muffins.   *—Dulcy Grace, Roaring Spring, Pennsylvania*

- 2 cups all-purpose flour
- 1 cup sugar
- 1 teaspoon baking powder
- 1/2 teaspoon baking soda
- 1/2 teaspoon salt
- 2 eggs
- 1/2 cup butter, melted
- 1-1/4 teaspoons vanilla extract
- 1-1/2 cups chopped peeled tart apples

STREUSEL TOPPING:
- 1/3 cup packed brown sugar
- 1 tablespoon all-purpose flour
- 1/8 teaspoon ground cinnamon
- 1 tablespoon cold butter

GLAZE:
- 1-1/2 cups confectioners' sugar
- 1 to 2 tablespoons milk
- 1 teaspoon butter, melted
- 1/4 teaspoon vanilla extract
- 1/8 teaspoon salt

In a bowl, combine the flour, sugar, baking powder, baking soda and salt. In another bowl, whisk the eggs, butter and vanilla; stir into dry ingredients just until moistened (batter will be stiff). Fold in apples.

Fill greased or paper-lined muffin cups three-fourths full. In a small bowl, combine the brown sugar, flour and cinnamon; cut in the butter until crumbly. Sprinkle over the batter.

Bake at 375° for 15-20 minutes or until a toothpick comes out clean. Cool for 5 minutes before removing from pan to a wire rack to cool completely. Combine glaze ingredients; drizzle over muffins. **Yield:** 1 dozen.

Walnut Raspberry Muffins

(Pictured below)

Prep: 25 min.   **Bake:** 20 min. per batch

Raspberries are my favorite berry, so this recipe is tops with me. The walnuts give the muffins a nice crunch. You can dress them up by using foil liners instead of paper.
—Elisa Lochridge, Tigard, Oregon

- 2/3 cup cream cheese, softened
- 1/3 cup butter, softened
- 1-1/2 cups sugar
- 2 egg whites
- 1 egg
- 1-1/2 teaspoons vanilla extract
- 2 cups all-purpose flour
- 1 teaspoon baking powder
- 1/4 teaspoon baking soda
- 1/2 cup buttermilk
- 2 cups fresh *or* frozen raspberries
- 1/4 cup chopped walnuts

In a large mixing bowl, beat the cream cheese, butter and sugar until light and fluffy. Add the egg whites, egg and vanilla; beat well. Combine the flour, baking powder and baking soda; add to creamed mixture alternately with buttermilk. Fold in the raspberries and walnuts.

Fill paper-lined muffin cups three-fourths full. Bake at 350° for 20-24 minutes or until a toothpick comes out clean. Cool for 5 minutes before removing from pans to wire racks. Serve warm. **Yield:** 1-1/2 dozen.

Editor's Note: If you are using frozen raspberries, do not thaw before adding to batter.

Beat in vanilla. Combine the flour, baking powder, baking soda, salt, ginger and nutmeg; add to creamed mixture alternately with orange juice. Fold in the rhubarb, almonds and orange peel.

Transfer to a greased 9-in. x 5-in. x 3-in. loaf pan. Bake at 350° for 55-65 minutes or until a toothpick inserted near the center comes out clean. Cool for 10 minutes before removing from pan to a wire rack. **Yield:** 1 loaf.

Editor's Note: If using frozen rhubarb, measure rhubarb while still frozen, then thaw completely. Drain in a colander, but do not press liquid out.

Golden Raisin Bran Muffins

Prep/Total Time: 30 min.

I tried many bran muffin recipes before coming up with this one. My family and friends say these moist goodies, featuring applesauce, golden raisins and cinnamon, are the best they have ever tasted. —Joanne Foote
Harbour Breton, Newfoundland

> 1 cup unsweetened applesauce
> 1/3 cup vegetable oil
> 1/4 cup milk
> 1 egg, lightly beaten
> 1 cup All-Bran
> 3/4 cup all-purpose flour
> 3/4 cup whole wheat flour
> 1/3 cup packed brown sugar
> 3 teaspoons baking powder
> 1 teaspoon ground cinnamon
> 1/2 teaspoon baking soda
> 1/4 teaspoon salt
> 1/2 cup golden raisins

In a bowl, combine the applesauce, oil, milk and egg. Stir in bran; let stand for 5 minutes. In another bowl, combine the flours, brown sugar, baking powder, cinnamon, baking soda and salt; stir in the bran mixture just until blended. Fold in the raisins (the batter will be thick).

Fill greased or paper-lined muffin cups two-thirds full. Bake at 375° for 15-20 minutes or until a toothpick comes out clean. Cool for 5 minutes before removing from pan to a wire rack. Serve the muffins warm. **Yield:** 1 dozen.

Orange-Rhubarb Breakfast Bread

(Pictured above)

Prep: 20 min. **Bake:** 55 min. + cooling

I love starting my day with a slice of this fabulous sweet bread alongside eggs, sausage and orange juice. It's full of tangy flavor and crunchy slivered almonds.
—Sonya Goergen, Moorhead, Minnesota

> 1/3 cup butter, softened
> 1 cup sugar
> 2 eggs
> 1 teaspoon vanilla extract
> 2 cups all-purpose flour
> 1-1/2 teaspoons baking powder
> 1/2 teaspoon baking soda
> 1/2 teaspoon salt
> 1/4 teaspoon ground ginger
> 1/4 teaspoon ground nutmeg
> 1/2 cup orange juice
> 1 cup chopped fresh *or* frozen rhubarb
> 1/2 cup slivered almonds
> 2 teaspoons grated orange peel

In a large mixing bowl, cream butter and sugar. Add eggs, one at a time, beating well after each addition.

Jumbo Caramel Banana Muffins

Prep: 20 min. **Bake:** 25 min. + cooling

Like banana bread? These flavorful muffins, drizzled with sweet caramel icing, will fill the bill in a big way.
—Katherine McClelland, Deep Brook, Nova Scotia

1/4 cup shortening
1 cup sugar
1 egg
1-1/2 cups mashed ripe bananas (about 3 large)
1 teaspoon vanilla extract
1-1/2 cups all-purpose flour
1 teaspoon baking soda
1/4 teaspoon salt

CARAMEL ICING:
2 tablespoons butter
1/4 cup packed brown sugar
1 tablespoon milk
1/2 cup confectioners' sugar

In a small mixing bowl, cream shortening and sugar. Add egg; beat well. Add bananas and vanilla; mix well. Combine the flour, baking soda and salt; add to creamed mixture.

Fill paper-lined jumbo muffin cups three-fourths full. Bake at 350° for 23-28 minutes or until a toothpick comes out clean. Cool for 5 minutes before removing from pan to a wire rack to cool completely.

For icing, in a small saucepan, melt butter over medium heat. Stir in brown sugar and milk; bring to a boil. Cool slightly. Whisk in confectioners' sugar. Transfer to a small resealable plastic bag; cut a small hole in a corner of bag and drizzle over muffins. **Yield:** 6 muffins.

Mini Maple Cinnamon Rolls

(Pictured at right)

Prep: 20 min. + rising   **Bake:** 20 min.

Maple syrup sweetens these lovely cinnamon buns. I make the dough in my bread machine before popping the rolls in the oven. My husband prefers them warm.
—Juanita Carlsen, North Bend, Oregon

2/3 cup milk
1/3 cup maple syrup
1/3 cup butter, softened
1 egg
3/4 teaspoon salt
3 cups bread flour
1 package (1/4 ounce) active dry yeast

FILLING:
1/2 cup packed brown sugar
2 tablespoons bread flour
4 teaspoons ground cinnamon
6 tablespoons cold butter

MAPLE ICING:
1 cup confectioners' sugar
3 tablespoons butter, melted
3 tablespoons maple syrup
1 to 2 teaspoons milk

In bread machine pan, place the first seven ingredients in order suggested by the manufacturer. Select dough setting (check dough after 5 minutes of mixing; add 1 to 2 tablespoons of water or bread flour if needed).

When the cycle is completed, turn dough onto a lightly floured surface. Roll into two 12-in. x 7-in. rectangles. In a small bowl, combine the brown sugar, flour and cinnamon; cut in butter until mixture resembles coarse crumbs. Sprinkle half over each rectangle. Roll up jelly-roll style, starting from a long side; pinch seam to seal.

Cut each roll into 12 slices. Place cut side down in one greased 13-in. x 9-in. x 2-in. baking pan. Cover and let rise in a warm place until doubled, about 20 minutes.

Bake at 375° for 20-25 minutes or until golden brown. Cool on a wire rack for 5 minutes. In a small mixing bowl, combine the confectioners' sugar, butter, syrup and enough milk to achieve desired consistency. Spread over warm rolls. **Yield:** 2 dozen.

Editor's Note: If your bread machine has a time-delay feature, we recommend you do not use it for this recipe.

Cookies, Bars & Candies

Prepare plenty of the buttery cutouts, rich brownies and other decadent delights here. They're certain to disappear fast!

GRAB SOME GOODIES. Clockwise from upper left: Almond-Butter Cookie Bouquet (p. 111), Chippy Peanut Butter Cookies (p. 113), Shamrock Toffee Fudge (p. 112), Chunky Drop Cookies (p. 115) and Rhubarb Oat Bars (p. 114).

maining dough. Bake at 350° for 7-9 minutes or until edges begin to brown. Remove to wire racks to cool.

In a microwave-safe bowl, melt white chocolate; stir until smooth. Tint with food coloring. Transfer to a heavy-duty resealable plastic bag; cut a small hole in a corner of bag. Pipe designs on cookies. **Yield:** 6 dozen.

Berry-Almond Sandwich Cookies

(Pictured at left)

Prep: 30 min. **Bake:** 10 min. per batch + cooling

These almond shortbread cookies have a delightful berry filling and are irresistible on a Christmas cookie tray.
—Helga Schlape, Florham Park, New Jersey

        1-1/2 **cups butter, softened**
            1 **cup sugar**
            1 **teaspoon vanilla extract**
        2-3/4 **cups all-purpose flour**
          1/2 **teaspoon salt**
            2 **cups ground almonds**
          3/4 **cup raspberry filling**
Edible glitter *or* confectioners' sugar

In a large mixing bowl, cream the butter and sugar. Beat in vanilla. Combine the flour and salt; gradually add to creamed mixture. Stir in almonds.

On a heavily floured surface, roll out dough to 1/8-in. thickness. Cut into desired shapes with floured 2-1/2-in. cookie cutters. Place 1 in. apart on ungreased baking sheets. Bake at 325° for 10-12 minutes or until edges begin to brown. Remove to wire racks to cool.

Spread 1 teaspoon raspberry filling over the bottom of half of the cookies; top with the remaining cookies. Sprinkle with edible glitter or confectioners' sugar. Store in an airtight container. **Yield:** 3 dozen.

Christmas Cutouts

(Pictured above)

Prep: 1-1/4 hours
Bake: 10 min. per batch + cooling

I made these cookies for my daughter's Winter Gala sorority event. They look exquisite with their smooth glaze of tinted white chocolate...and they taste great, too!
—Kathy Witherup, Villa Hills, Kentucky

          1/3 **cup butter, softened**
          1/3 **cup butter-flavored shortening**
          3/4 **cup sugar**
            1 **egg**
            4 **teaspoons milk**
            1 **teaspoon vanilla extract**
            2 **cups all-purpose flour**
        1-1/2 **teaspoons baking powder**
          1/4 **teaspoon salt**
            8 **squares (1 ounce *each*) white baking**
              chocolate
Food coloring

In a large mixing bowl, cream the butter, shortening and sugar until light and fluffy. Beat in egg, milk and vanilla. Combine the flour, baking powder and salt; gradually add to creamed mixture.

Divide the dough in half. On a lightly floured surface, roll out one portion to 1/8-in. thickness. Cut into desired shapes with floured 2-in. cookie cutters. Place 1 in. apart on ungreased baking sheets. Repeat with re-

Peanut Crescents

(Pictured above left)

Prep: 25 min. + chilling
Bake: 15 min. per batch + cooling

I've been making these festive crescents for 30 years. They freeze well and are especially nice for the holidays.
—Kay Brantley, Shaver Lake, California

            1 **cup butter, softened**
          1/3 **cup sugar**
            1 **tablespoon water**
            1 **teaspoon vanilla extract**
            2 **cups all-purpose flour**
          1/2 **cup finely chopped salted peanuts**
Confectioners' sugar

In a small mixing bowl, cream the butter and sugar. Beat in water and vanilla. Gradually add flour. Stir in the peanuts. Cover and refrigerate for 1 hour or until easy to handle.

Shape rounded tablespoonfuls of dough into 2-1/2-in. crescents. Place 2 in. apart on ungreased baking sheets. Bake at 350° for 15-18 minutes or until set (do not brown). Roll warm cookies in confectioners' sugar; cool completely on wire racks. Roll cooled cookies again in the sugar. **Yield:** about 3 dozen.

Gingerbread Teddy Bears

(Pictured below right)

Prep: 40 min. + chilling
Bake: 10 min. per batch + cooling

These cookies have been a Christmas tradition in my family since I was a little girl. The big bears are so soft and chewy that we can hardly wait until they come out of the oven!   —Elizabeth Manzanares, Gloucester, Virginia

      1 cup butter, cubed
   2/3 cup packed brown sugar
   2/3 cup molasses
      1 egg, beaten
 1-1/2 teaspoons vanilla extract
      4 cups all-purpose flour
 1-1/2 teaspoons ground cinnamon
      1 teaspoon ground ginger
   3/4 teaspoon baking soda
   1/2 teaspoon ground cloves
Miniature chocolate chips
Red decorating frosting

In a small saucepan, combine the butter, brown sugar and molasses. Cook over medium heat until sugar is dissolved. Pour into a large mixing bowl; let stand for 10 minutes. Stir in egg and vanilla.

Combine the flour, cinnamon, ginger, baking soda and cloves; gradually add to butter mixture and mix well. Cover and refrigerate for 2 hours or overnight.

Shape dough into eight balls, 2 in. each; eight balls, 1 in. each; 32 balls, 1/2 in. each; and 16 balls, 3/8 in. each. Place the 2-in. balls on three foil-lined baking sheets for bodies of eight bears; flatten to 1/2-in. thickness. Position the 1-in. balls for heads; flatten to 1/2-in. thickness.

Attach four 1/2-in. balls to each bear for arms and legs. Attach two 3/8-in. balls for ears. Add chocolate chips for eyes, noses and buttons.

Bake at 350° for 10-12 minutes or until set. Cool for 10 minutes before carefully removing to wire racks to cool completely. With frosting, pipe bows on bears. **Yield:** 8 cookies.

Dark Chocolate Butterscotch Brownies

Prep: 25 min.   **Bake:** 25 min. + cooling

My daughters and I experimented with many brownie recipes and came up with this family favorite.
      —Kit Concilus, Meadville, Pennsylvania

      4 squares (1 ounce *each*) unsweetened chocolate
   3/4 cup butter, cubed
      2 cups sugar
      3 egg whites
 1-1/2 teaspoons vanilla extract
      1 cup all-purpose flour
      1 cup 60% cocoa bittersweet chocolate baking chips
      1 cup butterscotch chips
GLAZE:
      1 cup 60% cocoa bittersweet chocolate baking chips
   1/4 cup butter, cubed

In a microwave-safe bowl, melt unsweetened chocolate and the butter; stir until smooth. Cool slightly. In a large bowl, combine sugar and chocolate mixture. Stir in egg whites and vanilla. Stir in flour. Stir in the chips.

Spread into a greased 13-in. x 9-in. x 2-in. baking pan. Bake at 350° for 25-30 minutes or until a toothpick inserted near the center comes out clean. Cool on a wire rack.

For glaze, melt chips and butter; stir until smooth. Immediately spread over brownies. Cool before cutting. **Yield:** about 5 dozen.

Editor's Note: This recipe was tested using Ghirardelli 60% cocoa bittersweet chocolate baking chips. Semisweet chocolate chips may be substituted.

Peanut Butter Spritz Fingers

(Pictured below)

Prep: 25 min. + chilling
Bake: 10 min. per batch + cooling

Everyone in my family craves these fancy-looking, dipped cookies because they satisfy the need for something chocolaty, crunchy, sweet and nutty, all in just one bite!
—Irma Lowery, Reedsburg, Wisconsin

- 1/2 **cup butter, softened**
- 1/2 **cup creamy peanut butter**
- 1/2 **cup sugar**
- 1/2 **cup packed brown sugar**
- 1 **egg**
- 1 **teaspoon vanilla extract**
- 1-1/2 **cups all-purpose flour**
- 3/4 **teaspoon baking soda**
- 1/2 **teaspoon baking powder**
- 1/4 **teaspoon salt**
- 3 **milk chocolate candy bars (4 ounces *each*), chopped**
- 1 **cup finely chopped unsalted peanuts**

In a large mixing bowl, cream the butter, peanut butter and sugars until light and fluffy. Beat in egg and vanilla. Combine the flour, baking soda, baking powder and salt; gradually add to creamed mixture. Cover and refrigerate for 30 minutes or until easy to handle.

Using a cookie press fitted with a star disk, press dough 2 in. apart into long strips on ungreased baking sheets. Cut each strip into 2-in. pieces (do not separate pieces). Bake at 350° for 7-9 minutes or until golden brown. Remove to wire racks to cool.

In a microwave-safe bowl, melt candy bars; stir until smooth. Dip one end of each cookie into chocolate, then into peanuts. Place on waxed paper; let stand until set. **Yield:** about 4 dozen.

Fudgy Mint Cookies

(Pictured below left)

Prep: 10 min.   **Bake:** 10 min. per batch + cooling

Chocolate lovers will get a double dose of their favorite flavor when they taste this cake-like cookie and its chocolate mint middle. These treats are especially popular served with a big scoop of mint chocolate chip ice cream.
—Renee Schwebach, Dumont, Minnesota

- 1 **package (18-1/4 ounces) devil's food cake mix**
- 1/2 **cup butter, softened**
- 1 **tablespoon water**
- 2 **eggs**
- 2 **tablespoons confectioners' sugar**
- 2 **packages (5 ounces *each*) chocolate-covered thin mints**

In a large mixing bowl, combine the cake mix, butter and water. Add eggs; mix well. Shape into 1-in. balls; roll in confectioners' sugar. Place 2 in. apart on ungreased baking sheets.

Bake at 375° for 8-10 minutes or until set. Immediately press a mint into the center of each cookie. Cool for 2 minutes before removing to wire racks to cool completely. **Yield:** about 3 dozen.

Chocolate Pretzels

Prep: 30 min.   **Bake:** 10 min. per batch + cooling

A rich chocolate coating accented with a pretty vanilla drizzle makes these homemade, cocoa-flavored pretzels hard to resist. My grandchildren and I love making them together...and we love eating them just as much!
—Karen Nemeth, Calgary, Alberta

- 1/2 **cup butter, softened**
- 1/2 **cup shortening**
- 1 **cup confectioners' sugar**
- 1 **egg**
- 1-1/2 **teaspoons vanilla extract**
- 2-1/4 **cups all-purpose flour**
- 1/2 **cup baking cocoa**
- 1 **teaspoon salt**
- **GLAZE:**
- 3 **squares (1 ounce *each*) semisweet chocolate**
- 3 **tablespoons butter**
- 3 **cups confectioners' sugar**
- 5 **tablespoons water**
- 1/2 **cup vanilla *or* white chips**

In a large mixing bowl, cream the butter, shortening and confectioners' sugar until light and fluffy. Beat in egg and vanilla. Combine the flour, cocoa and salt; gradually add to creamed mixture.

Shape into 1-in. balls. Roll each into a 7-in. rope. On greased baking sheets, form each rope into a pretzel shape, placing 2 in. apart. Bake at 375° for 8-9 minutes or until firm. Cool for 1 minute before removing to wire racks to cool completely.

For glaze, in a microwave-safe bowl, melt the chocolate and butter; stir until smooth. Stir in confectioners' sugar and water until smooth. Dip pretzels in glaze; place on waxed paper. Melt vanilla chips; drizzle over half of the pretzels. Let stand until completely set. Store in an airtight container. **Yield:** 4 dozen.

Almond-Butter Cookie Bouquet

(Pictured on page 106)

Prep: 2 hours + chilling
Bake: 10 min. per batch + cooling

I like to bake these fun cookie pops often during the year. In the spring, I cut them into flower shapes and insert the pops into a block of foam fitted into a basket. They make a great gift for friends and neighbors.
—*Krissy Fossmeyer, Huntley, Illinois*

  1-1/4 **cups butter, softened**
  1-3/4 **cups confectioners' sugar**
      2 **ounces almond paste**
      1 **egg**
    1/4 **cup milk**
      1 **teaspoon vanilla extract**
      4 **cups all-purpose flour**
    1/2 **teaspoon salt**
Wooden skewers *or* lollipop sticks
ICING:
      1 **cup confectioners' sugar**
      4 **teaspoons evaporated milk**
Food coloring of your choice

In a large mixing bowl, cream butter and confectioners' sugar until light and fluffy; add almond paste. Beat in the egg, milk and vanilla. Combine flour and salt; gradually add to creamed mixture. Cover and refrigerate for 1 hour.

On a lightly floured surface, roll out dough to 1/4-in. thickness. Cut out with floured 3-in. cookie cutters. Place 1 in. apart on ungreased baking sheets. Insert skewers or sticks. Bake at 375° for 7-8 minutes or until firm. Let stand for 2 minutes before removing to wire racks to cool.

In a bowl, whisk the confectioners' sugar and milk. Divide the icing into small bowls; tint with the food coloring. Gently spread the icing over the cookies. Decorate the cookies with other colors of icing if desired. **Yield:** about 2-1/2 dozen.

Frosted Molasses Cookies

(Pictured above)

Prep: 30 min. **Bake:** 10 min. per batch + cooling

These frosted spice cookies are always snatched up at holiday bake sales. —*Muriel Lerdal, Humboldt, Iowa*

      1 **cup butter, softened**
      1 **cup packed brown sugar**
      2 **eggs**
      1 **cup dark molasses**
      1 **teaspoon vanilla extract**
  4-1/2 **cups all-purpose flour**
      1 **tablespoon ground ginger**
      1 **tablespoon ground cinnamon**
      2 **teaspoons baking soda**
      1 **teaspoon salt**
    1/4 **teaspoon ground allspice**
      1 **cup buttermilk**
FROSTING:
    1/4 **cup shortening**
    1/4 **cup butter, softened**
    1/2 **teaspoon vanilla extract**
      2 **cups confectioners' sugar**
    1/4 **teaspoon ground ginger**
      4 **teaspoons milk**
Colored sprinkles, optional

In a large mixing bowl, cream butter and brown sugar. Beat in eggs, molasses and vanilla. Combine flour, ginger, cinnamon, baking soda, salt and allspice; add to creamed mixture alternately with buttermilk.

Drop by tablespoonfuls 2 in. apart onto greased baking sheets. Bake at 375° for 7-9 minutes or until set. Remove to wire racks to cool.

For frosting, in a small mixing bowl, cream shortening and butter. Beat in vanilla. Gradually beat in confectioners' sugar and ginger. Add milk; beat until light and fluffy. Spread over cookies. Decorate with sprinkles if desired. Store in an airtight container. **Yield:** 7-1/2 dozen.

Heart's Delight Cookies

(Pictured above)

Prep: 45 min. + chilling
Bake: 10 min. per batch + cooling

We serve these tender, pretty cookies for afternoon tea at the bed-and-breakfast my husband and I operate with my parents. —Angela Everett, Port Arthur, Texas

- 1 cup butter, softened
- 3 cups sugar
- 3 eggs
- 3 teaspoons vanilla extract
- 7-1/2 cups all-purpose flour
- 2 teaspoons baking powder
- 1 teaspoon baking soda
- 1 cup buttermilk
- Coarse sugar, optional
- 54 ribbons (16 inches x 1/8 inch)

In a large mixing bowl, cream butter and sugar. Add eggs, one at a time, beating well after each addition. Beat in vanilla. Combine the flour, baking powder and baking soda; gradually add to creamed mixture alternately with buttermilk. Cover and refrigerate for 1 hour or until easy to handle.

On a heavily floured surface, roll out dough to 1/4-in. thickness. Cut with a floured 4-in. heart-shaped cookie cutter. Place 1 in. apart on ungreased baking sheets. Sprinkle with coarse sugar if desired.

Bake at 350° for 8-10 minutes or until edges are lightly browned. Cool 2 minutes before removing to wire racks. While still warm, poke two holes into each cookie with a straw. When completely cooled, thread ribbons through holes and tie into bows; trim if necessary. **Yield:** 4-1/2 dozen.

Frosted Rhubarb Cookies

Prep: 30 min. **Bake:** 10 min. per batch + cooling

We have two prolific rhubarb plants, so I'm always looking for new ways to use the harvest. These treats are soft and yummy. —Shauna Schneyder, Idaho Falls, Idaho

- 1 cup shortening
- 1-1/2 cups packed brown sugar
- 2 eggs
- 3 cups all-purpose flour
- 1 teaspoon baking soda
- 1/2 teaspoon salt
- 1-1/2 cups diced fresh *or* frozen rhubarb
- 3/4 cup flaked coconut
- FROSTING:
- 1 package (3 ounces) cream cheese, softened
- 1 tablespoon butter, softened
- 1-1/2 cups confectioners' sugar
- 3 teaspoons vanilla extract

In a large mixing bowl, cream shortening and brown sugar. Beat in eggs. Combine the flour, baking soda and salt; gradually add to creamed mixture and mix well. Fold in the rhubarb and coconut.

Drop by rounded tablespoonfuls 2 in. apart onto greased baking sheets. Bake at 350° for 10-14 minutes or until golden brown. Cool for 1 minute before removing to wire racks to cool completely.

For frosting, in a small mixing bowl, beat cream cheese and butter until fluffy. Beat in confectioners' sugar and vanilla. Spread over cookies. **Yield:** 4 dozen.

Editor's Note: If using frozen rhubarb, measure rhubarb while still frozen, then thaw completely. Drain in a colander, but do not press liquid out.

Shamrock Toffee Fudge

(Pictured on page 106)

Prep: 30 min. + chilling

Tiny toffee bits add a delightful crunch to this creamy fudge. I decorated each piece with a green frosting shamrock for our church's St. Patrick's Day fund-raiser dinner. —Kristine Chayes, Smithtown, New York

- 1 can (14 ounces) sweetened condensed milk
- 2 cups vanilla *or* white chips
- 1 cup milk chocolate chips
- 1 tablespoon butter
- Dash salt
- 3/4 cup chocolate-covered English toffee bits
- 1/8 teaspoon rum extract

1 cup vanilla frosting
Green food coloring

Line a 9-in. square pan with foil and grease the foil; set aside. In a large saucepan, combine the milk and chips. Cook and stir over low heat until chips are melted. Add the butter and salt; stir until smooth. Remove from the heat; stir in toffee bits and extract. Pour into prepared pan. Cover and refrigerate for 2 hours or until firm.

Using foil, remove fudge from pan; carefully remove foil. Cut fudge into 1-in. squares. Place the frosting in a small resealable plastic bag; tint with food coloring. Cut a small hole in a corner of bag; pipe a shamrock onto each square. **Yield:** about 2-1/4 pounds.

Door County Cherry Biscotti

(Pictured below right)

Prep: 40 min.   **Bake:** 50 min. + cooling

Drizzled with chocolate and dotted with dried cherries, this biscotti won a blue ribbon at the county fair.
—*Joanne Surfus, Sturgeon Bay, Wisconsin*

> 3 **eggs**
> 1/2 **cup butter, softened**
> 1 **cup plus 3 tablespoons sugar,** *divided*
> 1 **teaspoon almond extract**
> 3-2/3 **cups all-purpose flour**
> 1/2 **teaspoon baking powder**
> 1/4 **teaspoon baking soda**
> 1 **cup dried cherries**
> 1 **cup slivered almonds, toasted**
> 1 **cup (6 ounces) semisweet chocolate chips**
> 1 **tablespoon plus 2 teaspoons shortening,** *divided*
> 4 **squares (1 ounce** *each*) **white baking chocolate**

Separate one egg; set aside. In a large mixing bowl, cream butter and 1 cup plus 2 tablespoons sugar until light and fluffy. Beat in 2 eggs and reserved egg yolk. Beat in extract. Combine the flour, baking powder and baking soda; gradually add to creamed mixture.

Turn onto a floured surface. Knead in cherries and almonds. Divide dough in half; shape each portion into a 12-in. x 3-in. rectangle. Transfer to a greased baking sheet. Beat reserved egg white; brush over dough. Sprinkle with remaining sugar. Bake at 350° for 28-30 minutes. Cool 10 minutes.

Transfer to a cutting board; with a serrated knife, cut each rectangle diagonally into 18 slices. Place cut side down on greased baking sheets. Bake for 20-25 minutes, turning once. Remove to wire racks to cool.

In a microwave-safe bowl, melt chocolate chips and 1 tablespoon shortening; stir until smooth. Drizzle over both sides of cookies. Place on waxed paper; let stand until set.

Melt white chocolate and remaining shortening; stir until smooth. Drizzle over both sides of cookies. Place on waxed paper; let stand until set. Store in an airtight container. **Yield:** 3 dozen.

Chippy Peanut Butter Cookies

(Pictured on page 106)

Prep: 25 min.   **Bake:** 15 min. per batch

I modified a recipe to create these chewy peanut butter cookies. A fresh-baked batch never lasts very long.
—*Ian Badeer, Hickman, Nebraska*

> 1 **cup butter, softened**
> 1 **cup creamy peanut butter**
> 1 **cup sugar**
> 1 **cup packed brown sugar**
> 2 **eggs**
> 1 **teaspoon vanilla extract**
> 2-1/4 **cups all-purpose flour**
> 2 **teaspoons baking soda**
> 1/4 **teaspoon salt**
> 1 **package (10 ounces) swirled milk chocolate and peanut butter chips**

In a large bowl, cream butter, peanut butter and sugars. Add eggs, one at a time, beating well after each addition. Beat in vanilla. Combine the flour, baking soda and salt; gradually add to creamed mixture. Stir in chips.

Drop by rounded tablespoonfuls onto ungreased baking sheets. Bake at 350° for 12-15 minutes or until golden brown. Cool for 2 minutes before removing to wire racks. **Yield:** about 4 dozen.

Editor's Note: This recipe was tested with Nestlé swirled milk chocolate and peanut butter chips.

Caramel Pecan Candy

(Pictured below)

Prep: 35 min. + cooling

These rich, layered squares are chewy and packed with plenty of crunchy pecans. If you don't have a 9-inch square baking dish handy, make this recipe in a 9-inch pie pan.
—Dick Deacon, Lawrenceville, Georgia

- 1/3 cup plus 1/2 cup butter, *divided*
- 20 cream-filled chocolate sandwich cookies, crushed
- 1 package (14 ounces) caramels
- 3 cups chopped pecans, toasted

TOPPING:

- 3/4 cup semisweet chocolate chips
- 3 tablespoons butter
- 3 tablespoons heavy whipping cream
- 3 tablespoons light corn syrup
- 3/4 teaspoon vanilla extract

Melt 1/3 cup butter; stir in cookie crumbs. Press into an ungreased 9-in. square baking dish. Bake at 325° for 10-12 minutes or until set. Cool on a wire rack. In a saucepan over low heat, melt caramels and remaining butter. Stir in pecans. Pour over crust. Cool.

For the topping, in a saucepan, combine the chocolate chips, butter, cream and corn syrup. Cook and stir over low heat until smooth. Remove from the heat; stir in the vanilla. Pour over the caramel layer. Cool on a wire rack. Refrigerate until chocolate hardens. Let candy stand at room temperature for 5-10 min. before cutting into 1-in. squares. Store in the refrigerator. **Yield:** about 6-1/2 dozen.

Maine Mud Cookies

Prep: 15 min.   **Bake:** 10 min. per batch

Every year, as spring approaches, we here in Maine have what we call "mud season." These cookies make everyone smile.   *—Kathleen Winslow, Naples, Maine*

✓ **Uses less fat, sugar or salt. Includes Nutrition Facts and Diabetic Exchanges.**

- 2-1/3 cups all-purpose flour
- 2/3 cup baking cocoa
- 2/3 cup sugar
- 1/3 cup packed brown sugar
- 3/4 teaspoon baking soda
- 1/4 teaspoon salt
- 1 cup 1% buttermilk
- 1/3 cup unsweetened applesauce

In a bowl, combine the flour, cocoa, sugars, baking soda and salt. Stir in buttermilk and applesauce (dough will be thick and moist).

Drop by tablespoonfuls 2 in. apart on baking sheets coated with nonstick cooking spray. Spread with a fork to make irregular shapes. Bake at 350° for 8-10 minutes or until firm. Remove to wire racks. **Yield:** 4 dozen.

Nutrition Facts: 1 cookie equals 56 calories, 1 g fat (trace saturated fat), trace cholesterol, 44 mg sodium, 12 g carbohydrate, trace fiber, 1 g protein. **Diabetic Exchange:** 1 starch.

Rhubarb Oat Bars

(Pictured on page 106)

Prep: 20 min.   **Bake:** 25 min. + cooling

These treats have just the right amount of tartness and sweetness.   *—Renette Cressey, Fort Mill, South Carolina*

- 1-1/2 cups chopped fresh *or* frozen rhubarb
- 1 cup packed brown sugar, *divided*
- 4 tablespoons water, *divided*
- 1 teaspoon lemon juice
- 4 teaspoons cornstarch
- 1 cup old-fashioned oats
- 3/4 cup all-purpose flour
- 1/2 cup flaked coconut
- 1/2 teaspoon salt
- 1/3 cup butter, melted

In a large saucepan, combine rhubarb, 1/2 cup brown sugar, 3 tablespoons water and lemon juice. Bring to a boil. Reduce heat to medium; cook and stir for 4-5 minutes or until rhubarb is tender.

Combine the cornstarch and remaining water until smooth; gradually stir into rhubarb mixture. Bring to a boil; cook and stir for 2 minutes or until thickened. Remove from the heat; set aside.

In a large bowl, combine oats, flour, coconut, salt and remaining brown sugar. Stir in butter until mixture is crumbly. Press half of mixture into a greased 8-in. square baking dish. Spread with rhubarb mixture. Sprinkle with remaining oat mixture and press down lightly.

Bake at 350° for 25-30 minutes or until golden brown. Cool on a wire rack. Cut into squares. **Yield:** 16 bars.

Editor's Note: If using frozen rhubarb, measure rhubarb while still frozen, then thaw completely. Drain in a colander, but do not press liquid out.

Chunky Drop Cookies

(Pictured on page 106)

Prep: 15 min. **Bake:** 10 min. per batch

Both sweet and salty, these gems are a nice change of pace from the usual chocolate chip cookies.
—*Kelly Ward Hartman, Cape Coral, Florida*

- 1 **cup butter, softened**
- 1 **cup packed brown sugar**
- 1/2 **cup sugar**
- 2 **eggs**
- 3 **teaspoons vanilla extract**
- 2-1/2 **cups all-purpose flour**
- 3/4 **teaspoon baking powder**
- 2 **cups halved pretzel sticks**
- 1 **cup coarsely chopped dry roasted peanuts**
- 1 **cup semisweet chocolate chunks**
- 1 **cup raisins**

In a large mixing bowl, cream butter and sugars. Add eggs, one at a time, beating well after each addition. Beat in vanilla. Combine the flour and baking powder; gradually add to creamed mixture. Stir in the pretzels, peanuts, chocolate chunks and raisins.

Drop by heaping tablespoonfuls 2 in. apart onto ungreased baking sheets. Bake at 350° for 10-14 minutes or until edges are golden brown. Cool for 2 minutes before removing to wire racks. **Yield:** about 6-1/2 dozen.

No-Cook Divinity

Prep: 30 min. + standing

This is the only divinity recipe I've used that will turn out every time.   —*Linda Huffman, Charleston, Arkansas*

- 1 **package (7-1/2 ounces) white frosting mix**
- 1/3 **cup light corn syrup**
- 2 **tablespoons boiling water**
- 1 **teaspoon vanilla extract**
- 3-3/4 **cups confectioners' sugar**

- 6 **tablespoons hot water**
- 1 **cup chopped nuts**

In a large mixing bowl, combine the frosting mix, corn syrup, boiling water and vanilla. Beat on high speed for 5 minutes. Gradually add confectioners' sugar, hot water and nuts; mix well.

Drop by teaspoonfuls onto waxed paper. Let stand at room temperature overnight or until dry to the touch. Store in an airtight container. **Yield:** about 2 pounds.

Pistachio Cranberry Bark

(Pictured above)

Prep: 20 min. + chilling

I was quick to ask for this festive recipe after sampling it at a Christmastime cookie/candy exchange.
—*Susan Wacek, Pleasanton, California*

- 2 **cups (12 ounces) semisweet chocolate chips**
- 5 **ounces white candy coating, chopped**
- 1 **cup chopped pistachios, toasted, *divided***
- 3/4 **cup dried cranberries, *divided***

In a microwave-safe bowl, melt chocolate chips; stir until smooth. Repeat with candy coating. Stir 3/4 cup pistachios and half of the cranberries into semisweet chocolate. Thinly spread onto a waxed paper-lined baking sheet.

Drizzle with candy coating. Cut through with a knife to swirl. Sprinkle with remaining pistachios and cranberries. Chill until firm. Break into pieces. Store in an airtight container in the refrigerator. **Yield:** about 1 pound.

Cakes & Pies

A just-baked pie cooling on the sill...a freshly frosted cake...enjoy these delights any time you like with the winning recipes here.

DOWN-HOME DESSERTS. Clockwise from upper left: Meringue Torte (p. 120), Crumbleberry Pie (p. 132), Chocolate Zucchini Cake (p. 131), Straw-berry Shortbread Pie (p. 128) and Mocha Layer Cake (p. 121).

Cake Blooms with Festive Flavor

THIS CHRISTMAS, serve a real showstopper—this cream-filled cake (shown above) coated with a rich ganache and adorned with edible poinsettias.

Margie Haen from Menomonee Falls, Wisconsin shared the recipe. She suggests making the cake roll the day before and decorating it just prior to serving. (Our home economists added the poinsettias, providing a festive touch for the holidays.)

The flowers are easy to form using the patterns on page 119 and can be made up to 2 weeks in advance.

Poinsettia Cake Roll

Prep: 2 hours + standing   **Bake:** 15 min. + chilling

EDIBLE POINSETTIAS:
- 2 **tablespoons plus 2 teaspoons light corn syrup**
- 1 **cup (5 ounces) red candy coating disks, melted**
- 1 **cup (5 ounces) dark green candy coating disks, melted**
- 2 **tablespoons vanilla *or* white chips**

Yellow paste food coloring
CAKE:
- 4 **eggs, *separated***
- 3/4 **cup cake flour**
- 3/4 **teaspoon baking powder**
- 1/2 **teaspoon salt**
- 3/4 **cup sugar, *divided***
- 1 **teaspoon vanilla extract**

FILLING:
- 1/2 **cup butter, softened**
- 4 **cups confectioners' sugar, *divided***
- 1/2 **cup baking cocoa**
- 7 to 8 **tablespoons milk, *divided***
- 1-1/2 **teaspoons vanilla extract**

GANACHE:
- 1-1/4 **cups semisweet chocolate chips**
- 1 **cup heavy whipping cream**

For poinsettia dough, divide corn syrup between two bowls. Stir red candy coating into one bowl and green into the other just until blended. Spread each mixture onto a sheet of waxed paper to 1/2-in. thickness (about 4 in. square).

Let stand, uncovered, at room temperature for 2-3 hours or until dry to the touch. Remove each mixture from waxed paper and gather into a ball. Wrap tightly in plastic wrap; let stand overnight.

To make leaf and petal patterns, trace patterns at right onto waxed paper and cut out, or use leaf-shaped cookie cutters instead. Knead a portion of green dough until pliable but not soft. Roll between waxed paper to 1/8-in. thickness. Cut out four large and four small leaves; with a toothpick, score veins. Arrange in two circles on waxed paper with center points touching.

Knead and roll out a portion of red dough as above. For each poinsettia, cut out five to seven large flower petals. Shape petals as shown in photos; place in between green leaves. Cut out 10 to 14 smaller flower petals from red dough (use additional dough if needed). Shape as shown; arrange between large red petals.

For flower stamens, form tiny balls of green dough. Place several in center of each flower, covering all petal centers. Melt white chips; stir in yellow food coloring. Transfer to a resealable heavy-duty plastic bag; cut a small hole in corner of bag. Pipe onto green centers. Store the poinsettias in an airtight container at room temperature.

For cake, let egg whites stand at room temperature for 30 minutes. Meanwhile, sift flour, baking powder and salt; set aside. In a large mixing bowl, beat egg yolks until slightly thickened. Gradually add 1/4 cup sugar, beating until thick and lemon-colored. Beat in vanilla. Add sifted ingredients; mix well.

In another mixing bowl, beat the egg whites on medium speed until soft peaks form. Gradually add the remaining sugar, beating until stiff peaks form. Fold a fourth of the egg whites into batter; fold in the remaining whites.

Line a greased 15-in. x 10-in. x 1-in. baking pan with waxed paper and grease the paper. Spread batter evenly into pan.

Bake at 375° for 12-15 minutes or until cake springs back when lightly touched. Cool for 5 minutes. Turn the cake onto a kitchen towel dusted with confectioners' sugar. Gently peel off waxed paper. Roll up cake in the towel jelly-roll style, starting with a short side. Cool completely on a wire rack.

For filling, in a large mixing bowl, cream butter until fluffy. Beat in 2 cups confectioners' sugar, cocoa, 3 tablespoons milk and vanilla. Add the remaining confectioners' sugar and enough milk to achieve desired consistency. Unroll cake; spread filling evenly to within 1/2 in. of edges. Roll up again. Place on a wire rack over a baking sheet; cover and set aside.

Place chocolate chips in a small bowl. In a heavy saucepan, bring cream to a boil over low heat. Pour over chips; whisk gently until smooth. Chill for 35-45 minutes or until ganache begins to thicken, stirring occasionally.

Pour half of the ganache over cake, allowing excess to drip off. Chill cake and remaining ganache, uncovered, for 30 minutes or until remaining ganache has cooled and a thermometer reads about 62°. Pour ganache slowly in a thin stream over cake; chill until set.

If piping is desired, transfer ganache that dripped from cake into a bowl; chill for 45 minutes. Whisk until thickened, about 1 minute. Place cake on a serving platter. Place thickened ganache in a pastry bag with a #21 star tip; pipe around bottom of cake. Position poinsettias on top of cake; gently press into ganache. Store in the refrigerator. **Yield:** 10 servings.

Poinsettia Patterns

To use the patterns below to shape the edible-clay leaves and petals for the Poinsettia Cake Roll (recipe on page 118), trace each pattern onto waxed paper and cut out each with a scissors.

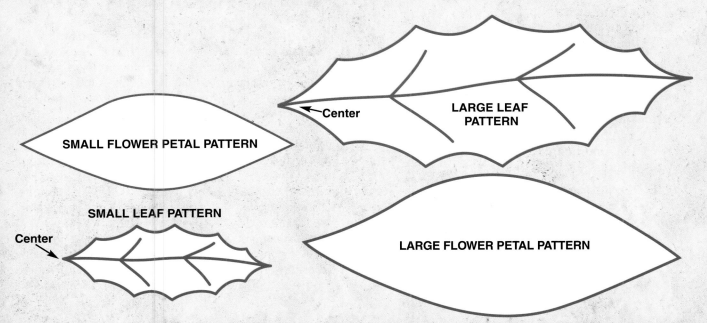

Gingerbread with Chantilly Cream

(Pictured above)

Prep: 15 min.   **Bake:** 35 min.

A blend of ginger, cinnamon and nutmeg makes this old-fashioned dessert extra flavorful...and my guests always comment on the "cute" dollop of whipped cream on top!
—Pam Holloway, Marion, Louisiana

      1/2 **cup shortening**
        2 **tablespoons sugar**
        1 **tablespoon brown sugar**
        1 **egg**
        1 **cup hot water**
        1 **cup molasses**
    2-1/4 **cups all-purpose flour**
        1 **teaspoon baking soda**
        1 **teaspoon ground ginger**
        1 **teaspoon ground cinnamon**
      3/4 **teaspoon salt**
      1/8 **teaspoon ground nutmeg**
CHANTILLY CREAM:
        1 **cup heavy whipping cream**
        1 **teaspoon confectioners' sugar**
      1/4 **teaspoon vanilla extract**

In a large mixing bowl, cream the shortening and sugars. Add egg; mix well. Beat in water and molasses. Combine the flour, baking soda, ginger, cinnamon, salt and nutmeg; gradually add to creamed mixture.

Pour into a greased 9-in. square baking pan. Bake at 350° for 33-37 minutes or until a toothpick inserted near the center comes out clean.

In a small mixing bowl, beat cream until it begins to thicken. Add confectioners' sugar and vanilla; beat until stiff peaks form. Serve with warm gingerbread. **Yield:** 9 servings.

Meringue Torte

(Pictured on page 116)

Prep: 40 min.   **Bake:** 30 min. + cooling

My grandmother, who came here from Sweden when she was 21, used to make this cake for birthdays. It is still a family favorite.   —Ruth Grover, Portland, Connecticut

      3/4 **cup butter, softened**
      3/4 **cup sugar**
        6 **egg yolks**
        1 **teaspoon vanilla extract**
    1-1/2 **cups all-purpose flour**
    1-1/2 **teaspoons baking powder**
        6 **tablespoons milk**
MERINGUE:
        6 **egg whites**
    1-1/2 **cups sugar**
      1/2 **teaspoon vanilla extract**
      1/2 **cup plus 3 tablespoons finely chopped**
           walnuts, *divided*
FILLING:
        2 **cups heavy whipping cream**
      1/4 **cup confectioners' sugar**
        2 **cups fresh raspberries**

In a large mixing bowl, cream butter and sugar until light and fluffy. In a small mixing bowl, beat egg yolks for 3-5 minutes or until light-lemon-colored; beat in vanilla. Add to creamed mixture. Combine flour and baking powder; add to creamed mixture alternately with milk. Pour into three parchment paper-lined 9-in. round baking pans; set aside.

In a mixing bowl, beat egg whites on medium speed until foamy. Gradually beat in sugar, a tablespoon at a time, on high until stiff glossy peaks form and sugar is dissolved. Add vanilla. Fold in 1/2 cup walnuts. Spread meringue evenly over cake batter; sprinkle with remaining walnuts.

Bake at 325° for 30-35 minutes or until meringue is lightly browned. Cool on wire racks for 10 minutes (meringue will crack). Loosen edges of cakes from pans with a knife. Using two large spatulas, carefully remove one cake to a serving plate, meringue side up. Carefully remove remaining cakes, meringue side up, to wire racks.

In a mixing bowl, beat cream until it begins to thicken. Add confectioners' sugar; beat until stiff peaks form. Carefully spread half of the filling over cake on serving plate; top with half of the raspberries. Repeat layers. Top with remaining cake. Store in the refrigerator. **Yield:** 16-18 servings.

Crumb-Topped Cherry Pie

(Pictured below right)

Prep: 25 min. **Bake:** 35 min. + cooling

My mom baked this wonderfully sweet-tart pie frequently for Sunday dinner, and we never tired of it. We had a farm, so Mom made her own butter and ice cream, and she used our fresh dairy products for this pie's great topping.
—Sandy Jenkins, Elkhorn, Wisconsin

1-1/4 **cups all-purpose flour**
  1/2 **teaspoon salt**
  1/2 **cup vegetable oil**
    2 **tablespoons milk**
FILLING:
1-1/3 **cups sugar**
  1/3 **cup all-purpose flour**
    2 **cans (14-1/2 ounces *each*) pitted tart cherries, drained**
  1/4 **teaspoon almond extract**
TOPPING:
  1/2 **cup all-purpose flour**
  1/2 **cup sugar**
  1/4 **cup cold butter**
    1 **cup heavy whipping cream**
    1 **tablespoon confectioners' sugar**
  1/8 **teaspoon vanilla extract**

In a bowl, combine flour and salt. Combine oil and milk; stir into flour mixture with a fork just until blended. Pat evenly onto the bottom and up the sides of a 9-in. pie plate; set aside.

In a bowl, combine filling ingredients; pour into crust. For topping, combine flour and sugar in a small bowl; cut in butter until crumbly. Sprinkle over filling.

Bake at 425° for 35-45 minutes or until crust is golden brown and filling is bubbly. Cool on a wire rack.

Just before serving, in a small mixing bowl, beat cream until it begins to thicken. Add confectioners' sugar and vanilla; beat until soft peaks form. Serve with pie. **Yield:** 6-8 servings.

Mocha Layer Cake

(Pictured on page 116)

Prep: 40 min. **Bake:** 30 min. + cooling

Without a doubt, this is the best chocolate cake I've ever made. I share this decadent dessert with everyone I can!
—Katherine DeLoach, Visalia, California

    1 **cup butter, softened**
    3 **cups packed brown sugar**
    4 **eggs**
    3 **teaspoons vanilla extract**
    3 **cups all-purpose flour**
  3/4 **cup baking cocoa**
    3 **teaspoons baking soda**
  1/2 **teaspoon salt**
1-1/2 **cups brewed coffee, cooled**
1-1/3 **cups sour cream**
FROSTING:
    2 **packages (8 ounces *each*) cream cheese, softened**
  1/2 **cup butter, softened**
    8 **squares (1 ounce *each*) unsweetened chocolate, melted**
  1/2 **cup brewed coffee, cooled**
    3 **teaspoons vanilla extract**
    6 **cups confectioners' sugar**

In a large mixing bowl, cream butter and brown sugar. Add eggs, one at a time, beating well after each addition. Stir in vanilla. Combine the flour, cocoa, baking soda and salt; add to creamed mixture alternately with coffee and sour cream. Pour into three greased and floured 9-in. round baking pans. Bake at 350° for 30-35 minutes or until a toothpick inserted near the center comes out clean. Cool for 10 minutes before removing from pans to wire racks to cool.

In a large mixing bowl, beat cream cheese and butter until fluffy. Beat in chocolate, coffee and vanilla until blended. Gradually beat in confectioners' sugar. Spread between layers and over top and sides of cake. Cover and refrigerate until serving. **Yield:** 14-16 servings.

Rhubarb Upside-Down Cake

(Pictured below)

Prep: 30 min. **Bake:** 50 min. + cooling

This light, airy yellow cake is moist but not too sweet, and the caramelized rhubarb topping adds tangy flavor.
—*Joyce Rowe, Stratham, New Hampshire*

- 2/3 **cup packed brown sugar**
- 3 **tablespoons butter, melted**
- 2-1/4 **cups diced fresh *or* frozen rhubarb**
- 4-1/2 **teaspoons sugar**

BATTER:
- 6 **tablespoons butter, softened**
- 3/4 **cup sugar**
- 2 **eggs, *separated***
- 1 **teaspoon vanilla extract**
- 1 **cup plus 2 tablespoons all-purpose flour**
- 1-1/2 **teaspoons baking powder**
- 1/2 **teaspoon salt**
- 1/4 **cup milk**
- 1/4 **teaspoon cream of tartar**

Whipped cream, optional

In a small bowl, combine brown sugar and butter. Spread into a greased 9-in. round baking pan. Layer with rhubarb; sprinkle with sugar. Set aside.

In a large mixing bowl, cream the butter and sugar. Beat in egg yolks and vanilla. Combine the flour, baking powder and salt; add to creamed mixture alternately with milk. In a small mixing bowl, beat egg whites and cream of tartar on medium speed until stiff peaks form. Gradually fold into creamed mixture, about 1/2 cup at a time. Gently spoon over rhubarb (pan will be full, about 1/4 in. from top of pan).

Bake at 325° for 50-60 minutes or until cake springs back when lightly touched. Cool for 10 minutes before inverting onto a serving plate. Serve warm with whipped cream if desired. **Yield:** 10-12 servings.

Editor's Note: If using frozen rhubarb, measure rhubarb while still frozen, then thaw completely. Drain in a colander, but do not press liquid out.

Lemon Ice Cream Pie

Prep: 25 min. + freezing

Whenever I see the word "lemon" in a recipe, it jumps out at me because lemon is my favorite flavor. It's rightfully up front in this refreshing pie.   —*Barbara Blickensderfer Edgewater, Florida*

- 6 **tablespoons butter**
- 1 **cup sugar**
- 1/2 **cup lemon juice**
- 2 **tablespoons grated lemon peel**

Dash salt
- 2 **eggs**
- 2 **egg yolks**
- 1 **quart vanilla ice cream, softened**
- 1 **pastry shell (9 inches), baked**
- 1 **cup heavy whipping cream**

In a heavy saucepan, melt butter over medium heat. Add the sugar, lemon juice, lemon peel and salt. In a bowl, beat eggs and yolks; add to butter mixture. Cook and stir until filling reaches at least 160° and coats the back of a metal spoon.

Remove from the heat. Cool quickly by placing pan in a bowl of ice water; stir for 2 minutes. Press plastic wrap onto surface of filling. Refrigerate for several hours or overnight.

Spoon half of the ice cream into pastry shell; freeze. Spread with half of the lemon filling; freeze. Repeat layers. In a small mixing bowl, beat cream on high until stiff peaks form. Pipe or spread over pie. Cover and freeze for several hours or overnight. **Yield:** 6-8 servings.

Peaches 'n' Cream Pie

Prep: 20 min. **Bake:** 1 hour + cooling

With a lovely lattice crust, this pie is eye-catching and packed with fruit.   —*Emma Rea, Hermann, Missouri*

- 3 **cups all-purpose flour**
- 1 **teaspoon salt**
- 1 **cup plus 2 tablespoons cold butter**
- 1 **egg**
- 1 **teaspoon cider vinegar**
- 2 to 3 **tablespoons ice water**

FILLING:
- 5 cups sliced peeled peaches
- 1 teaspoon lemon juice
- 3/4 cup plus 1 tablespoon sugar, *divided*
- 3 tablespoons all-purpose flour
- 3/4 teaspoon ground cinnamon
- 1/4 teaspoon salt
- 1/2 cup heavy whipping cream
- 1 tablespoon butter

In a bowl, combine flour and salt; cut in butter until mixture resembles coarse crumbs. Combine egg and vinegar; add to flour mixture. Add water, 1 tablespoon at a time, until dough forms a ball.

Divide dough in half. Roll out one portion to fit a 9-in. pie plate; transfer to pie plate. Trim pastry even with edge; set aside.

In a large bowl, combine peaches and lemon juice. In another bowl, combine 3/4 cup sugar, flour, cinnamon and salt; stir in cream. Pour over peaches; gently toss to coat. Spoon into crust. Dot with butter.

Roll out remaining pastry; make a lattice crust. Seal and flute edges. Sprinkle with remaining sugar. Cover edges loosely with foil.

Bake at 425° for 15 minutes. Reduce heat to 350°; bake for 45-50 minutes or until peaches are tender and crust is golden brown. Cool on a wire rack. **Yield:** 6-8 servings.

Fudge Layer Cake

(Pictured above right)

Prep: 45 min. + chilling   **Bake:** 30 min. + cooling

My mother first made this 40 years ago, and it's still a winner.   —Cheryl Feller, Fort Atkinson, Wisconsin

- 3/4 cup butter, softened
- 2-1/4 cups sugar
- 3 eggs
- 1-1/2 teaspoons vanilla extract
- 3 squares (1 ounce *each*) unsweetened chocolate, melted and cooled
- 3 cups cake flour
- 1-1/2 teaspoons baking soda
- 3/4 teaspoon salt
- 1-1/2 cups water

DATE CREAM FILLING:
- 1/4 cup sugar
- 1 tablespoon all-purpose flour
- 1 cup milk
- 1 egg, beaten
- 1/2 cup chopped dates
- 1/2 cup chopped walnuts
- 1 teaspoon vanilla extract

FUDGE FROSTING:
- 1 cup heavy whipping cream
- 2 tablespoons sugar
- 2 tablespoons light corn syrup
- 16 squares (1 ounce *each*) semisweet chocolate
- 1/4 cup butter, cubed

Line three greased 9-in. round baking pans with waxed paper and grease the paper; set aside. In a mixing bowl, cream butter and sugar until light and fluffy. Beat in eggs and vanilla. Stir in chocolate. Combine the cake flour, baking soda and salt; add to creamed mixture alternately with water.

Pour into prepared pans. Bake at 350° for 30-35 minutes or until a toothpick inserted near the center comes out clean. Cool for 10 minutes before removing from pans to wire racks to cool completely.

In a small saucepan, combine the sugar, all-purpose flour, milk and egg until smooth. Add the dates. Bring to a gentle boil; cook and stir for 2 minutes or until thickened. Remove from the heat. Stir in walnuts and vanilla. Cover and refrigerate.

For frosting, combine cream, sugar and corn syrup in a saucepan. Bring to a full boil over medium heat, stirring constantly. Remove from heat; stir in chocolate and butter until melted. Transfer to a bowl. Refrigerate until spreadable, stirring occasionally.

Place one cake layer on a serving plate; spread with half of the filling. Repeat. Top with remaining cake layer. Spread frosting over top and sides of cake. Store in the refrigerator. **Yield:** 12-14 servings.

FOR THANKSGIVING DINNER or any time you crave a down-home dessert, try Maple-Cream Apple Pie, Caramel Pecan Pie, Eggnog Pumpkin Pie or Pear-Cranberry Lattice Pie (shown above).

Maple-Cream Apple Pie

(Pictured above)

Prep: 25 min. + chilling **Bake:** 20 min. + cooling

A rich maple cream filling topped with cinnamony apples and a crunchy streusel topping make this a heavenly holiday pie. I've also layered the maple cream and streusel from this recipe in parfait glasses for a quick, elegant dessert. —Sue Smith, Norwalk, Connecticut

>   **4 cups thinly sliced peeled tart apples**
> **1/4 cup sugar**
>   **1 teaspoon ground cinnamon**
> **1/4 cup butter, cubed**
>   **1 pastry shell (9 inches), baked**

FILLING:
>   **1 package (8 ounces) cream cheese, softened**
> **1-1/2 cups cold milk**
>   **1 package (3.4 ounces) instant vanilla pudding mix**
>   **1 teaspoon maple extract**

TOPPING:
> **1/4 cup sugar**
>   **3 tablespoons quick-cooking oats**
>   **3 tablespoons all-purpose flour**
> **1/2 teaspoon ground cinnamon**
>   **2 tablespoons butter, melted**

In a large bowl, toss apples, sugar and cinnamon. In a large skillet, cook apple mixture in butter for 10-12 minutes or until tender; cool. Spoon into pastry shell; set aside.

In a small mixing bowl, beat cream cheese until fluffy. In another bowl, whisk milk and pudding mix for 2 minutes. Let stand for 2 minutes or until soft-set. Gradually beat into cream cheese. Stir in extract. Spoon over apple layer. Cover and refrigerate for 2 hours or until set.

Meanwhile, in a small bowl, combine topping ingredients. Spread onto an ungreased baking sheet. Bake at 350° for 20-25 minutes or until crisp and golden brown, stirring three to four times. Cool. Just before serving, sprinkle topping over pie. **Yield:** 6-8 servings.

Eggnog Pumpkin Pie

(Pictured at left)

Prep: 10 min.   **Bake:** 1 hour + cooling

Eggnog gets extra credit for the creamy custard filling in this treasured recipe from my mom. It's the absolute best pumpkin pie I have ever tasted. —Terri Kearns
Oklahoma City, Oklahoma

         1 can (15 ounces) solid-pack pumpkin
    1-1/4 cups eggnog
      2/3 cup sugar
         3 eggs
    1-1/2 teaspoons pumpkin pie spice
      1/4 teaspoon salt
         1 unbaked pastry shell (9 inches)

In a large bowl, combine the pumpkin, eggnog, sugar, eggs, pumpkin pie spice and salt. Pour into pastry shell.

Bake at 375° for 60-65 minutes or until a knife inserted near the center comes out clean. Cool on a wire rack. Refrigerate until serving. **Yield:** 6-8 servings.

Editor's Note: This recipe was tested with commercially prepared eggnog.

Caramel Pecan Pie

(Pictured above left)

Prep: 25 min.   **Bake:** 35 min. + cooling

This is hands down my favorite pecan pie—it's so good, it's scary! I like to share it with everyone on Thanksgiving. Here's a time-saving trick: Toss the bag of caramels to your children or spouse and promise they can eat whatever is left after they unwrap your 36 caramels.
—Dorothy Reinhold, Malibu, California

       36 caramels
      1/4 cup water
      1/4 cup butter, cubed
         3 eggs
      3/4 cup sugar
         1 teaspoon vanilla extract
      1/8 teaspoon salt
    1-1/3 cups chopped pecans, toasted
         1 unbaked deep-dish pastry shell (9 inches)
Pecan halves, optional

In a small heavy saucepan, combine the caramels, water and butter. Cook and stir over low heat until caramels are melted. Remove from the heat and set aside.

In a small mixing bowl, beat the eggs, sugar, vanilla and salt until smooth. Gradually add caramel mixture. Stir in chopped pecans. Pour into pastry shell. If desired, arrange pecan halves over filling.

Bake at 350° for 35-40 minutes or until set. Cool on a wire rack. Refrigerate leftovers. **Yield:** 6-8 servings.

Pear-Cranberry Lattice Pie

(Pictured at far left)

Prep: 25 min.   **Bake:** 55 min. + cooling

This fruit-filled treat is a delightful choice for Thanksgiving, Christmas or any special occasion during fall and winter.
—Marian Platt, Sequim, Washington

Pastry for double-crust pie (9 inches)
      3/4 cup sugar
         3 tablespoons cornstarch
         1 teaspoon ground cinnamon
      1/4 teaspoon ground allspice
         5 cups sliced peeled fresh pears
         2 cups fresh *or* frozen cranberries, thawed
         2 tablespoons butter
         1 egg
         1 tablespoon milk
Additional sugar

Line a 9-in. pie plate with bottom pastry; set aside. In a large bowl, combine the sugar, cornstarch, cinnamon and allspice. Add pears and cranberries; toss to coat. Spoon into crust; dot with butter.

With a fluted pastry wheel, pizza cutter or sharp knife, cut remaining pastry into eight 1-in. strips. Twist strips; position parallel to each other and about 1/2 in. to 3/4 in. apart over filling. Trim strips evenly with pastry edge. Seal and flute edges.

In a small bowl, whisk egg and milk; brush over pastry. Sprinkle with additional sugar. Cover pie loosely with foil to prevent overbrowning.

Bake at 450° for 15 minutes. Reduce heat to 350° and remove foil; bake for 40-45 minutes or until crust is golden brown and filling is bubbly. Cool on a wire rack. **Yield:** 6-8 servings.

Chocolate-Covered Strawberries Cake

(Pictured below)

Prep: 50 min.   **Bake:** 20 min. + cooling

I made this for our Cub Scout cake auction, and I almost didn't take it because it looked so good. It was one of our highest sellers!   —*Carol McCartney, Danville, Ohio*

      2/3 **cup butter, softened**
   1-1/2 **cups sugar,** *divided*
        1 **teaspoon vanilla extract**
   2-1/2 **cups all-purpose flour**
   2-1/2 **teaspoons baking powder**
      1/2 **teaspoon salt**
      3/4 **cup milk**
        4 **egg whites**
        1 **cup sliced fresh strawberries**
FROSTING:
   7-1/2 **cups confectioners' sugar**
   1-1/2 **cups baking cocoa**
      3/4 **cup butter, softened**
        1 **cup milk**
        2 **teaspoons vanilla extract**
      1/2 **cup sliced fresh strawberries**
        8 **whole fresh strawberries**

In a large mixing bowl, cream butter and 1-1/4 cups sugar. Beat in vanilla. Combine flour, baking powder and salt; add to creamed mixture alternately with milk.

In a small mixing bowl, beat egg whites on medium

speed until soft peaks form. Gradually beat in remaining sugar, 1 tablespoon at a time, on high until stiff peaks form and sugar is dissolved. Fold into batter. Fold in strawberries.

Pour into two greased and floured 9-in. round baking pans. Bake at 350° for 20-25 minutes or until a toothpick inserted near the center comes out clean. Cool for 10 minutes before removing from pans to wire racks to cool completely.

For frosting, in a large mixing bowl, combine confectioners' sugar and cocoa. Beat in butter and milk until smooth. Beat in vanilla.

Spread frosting over bottom cake layer; top with sliced strawberries. Top with remaining cake layer; frost top and sides of cake. Dip whole strawberries into frosting; arrange around and on top of cake. Refrigerate leftovers. **Yield:** 16 servings.

Rhubarb-Ribbon Brunch Cake

(Pictured above)

Prep: 30 min.   **Bake:** 60 min. + cooling

My dad has always had a flourishing rhubarb patch, and this recipe is a great way to use his seemingly endless supply. The crumb-topped treat can be served as a coffee cake at breakfast or as an elegant finish to a special meal.
                        —*Mary Blenk, Cumberland, Maine*

      3/4 **cup sugar**
        3 **tablespoons cornstarch**
      1/4 **teaspoon ground cinnamon**
      1/8 **teaspoon ground nutmeg**
      1/3 **cup cold water**

2-1/2 cups sliced fresh *or* frozen rhubarb
3 to 4 drops food coloring
BATTER:
2-1/4 cups all-purpose flour
3/4 cup sugar
3/4 cup cold butter
1/2 teaspoon baking powder
1/2 teaspoon baking soda
1/2 teaspoon salt
1 egg, beaten
1 carton (6 ounces) vanilla yogurt
1 teaspoon vanilla extract
TOPPING:
1 egg, beaten
8 ounces Mascarpone cheese
1/4 cup sugar
1/2 cup chopped pecans
1/4 cup flaked coconut

In a large saucepan, combine the first five ingredients until smooth. Add rhubarb. Bring to a boil; cook and stir for 2 minutes or until thickened. Add food coloring. Set aside.

In a bowl, combine flour and sugar; cut in butter until mixture resembles coarse crumbs. Set aside 1 cup for topping. Add baking powder, baking soda and salt to remaining crumb mixture. Combine egg, yogurt and vanilla; stir into batter until smooth. Spread into a greased 9-in. springform pan.

Combine the egg, Mascarpone cheese and sugar; spoon over batter. Top with rhubarb mixture. Add pecans and coconut to reserved crumb mixture; sprinkle over top. Bake at 350° for 60-65 minutes or until a toothpick comes out clean. Cool on a wire rack for 20 minutes; remove sides of pan. Cool completely. **Yield:** 12 servings.

All About Rhubarb

- Rhubarb is technically a vegetable, but it's mostly used like a fruit in pies and sauces.

- Rhubarb comes in two main varieties: field-grown and hothouse-grown. You'll find field-grown for sale from April through June or July. The hothouse variety is available January through June.

- If you buy rhubarb stalks with the leaves attached, cut off the leaves as soon as you get them home. Never eat the leaves raw or cooked, as they can be poisonous.

- Store stalks in plastic bags in the refrigerator crisper. They'll keep for about a week.

Raspberry Custard Pie

(Pictured below)

Prep: 20 min. **Bake:** 55 min. + cooling

You can substitute other kinds of berries or rhubarb in this pie filling. But I think the raspberries are hard to beat!
—Dorothy Regnier, Kamloops, British Columbia

Pastry for single-crust pie (9 inches)
3 eggs
2 cups sugar
1/2 cup all-purpose flour
1/3 cup evaporated milk
2 teaspoons vanilla extract
Dash salt
5-1/2 cups fresh *or* frozen raspberries
TOPPING:
1/2 cup all-purpose flour
1/4 cup packed brown sugar
1/4 cup cold butter

Line a 9-in. pie plate with pastry; trim to 1/2 in. beyond edge of plate. Flute edges; set aside. In a large mixing bowl, beat eggs. Add the sugar, flour, milk, vanilla and salt; mix well. Gently fold in raspberries. Pour into crust.

For topping, combine flour and brown sugar in a small bowl; cut in butter until crumbly. Sprinkle over filling. Bake at 400° for 10 minutes. Reduce heat to 350°; bake 45-50 minutes longer or until a knife inserted near the center comes out clean. Cool on a wire rack. Refrigerate leftovers. **Yield:** 8 servings.

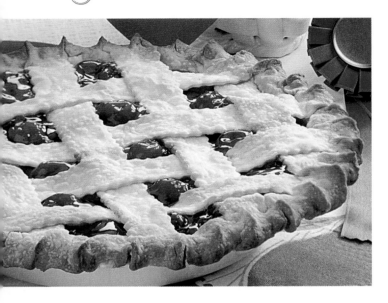

Fresh Cherry Pie

(Pictured above)

Prep: 25 min. **Bake:** 55 min. + cooling

This ruby-red treat is just sweet enough, with a hint of almond flavor and a good level of cinnamon.
—*Josie Bochek, Sturgeon Bay, Wisconsin*

  1-1/4 **cups sugar**
    1/3 **cup cornstarch**
     1 **cup cherry juice**
     4 **cups fresh tart cherries, pitted *or* frozen pitted tart cherries, thawed**
    1/2 **teaspoon ground cinnamon**
    1/4 **teaspoon ground nutmeg**
    1/4 **teaspoon almond extract**
PASTRY:
     2 **cups all-purpose flour**
    1/2 **teaspoon salt**
    2/3 **cup shortening**
     3 **to 4 tablespoons cold water**

In a large saucepan, combine sugar and cornstarch; gradually stir in cherry juice until smooth. Bring to a boil; cook and stir for 2 minutes or until thickened. Remove from the heat. Add the cherries, cinnamon, nutmeg and extract; set aside.

In a bowl, combine flour and salt; cut in shortening until crumbly. Gradually add cold water, tossing with a fork until a ball forms. Divide pastry in half so that one ball is slightly larger than the other.

On a lightly floured surface, roll out larger ball to fit a 9-in. pie plate. Transfer pastry to pie plate; trim even with edge of plate. Add filling. Roll out remaining pastry; make a lattice crust. Trim, seal and flute edges.

Bake at 425° for 10 minutes. Reduce heat to 375°; bake 45-50 minutes longer or until crust is golden brown. Cool on a wire rack. **Yield:** 8 servings.

Pineapple Orange Cake

Prep: 15 min. **Bake:** 25 min. + chilling

I altered the recipe for this moist cake, and now it's nearly guilt-free. —*Pam Sjolund, Columbia, South Carolina*

☑ **Uses less fat, sugar or salt. Includes Nutrition Facts.**

     1 **package (18-1/4 ounces) yellow cake mix**
     1 **can (11 ounces) mandarin oranges, undrained**
     4 **egg whites**
    1/2 **cup unsweetened applesauce**
TOPPING:
     1 **can (20 ounces) crushed pineapple, undrained**
     1 **package (1 ounce) sugar-free instant vanilla pudding mix**
     1 **carton (8 ounces) reduced-fat whipped topping**

In a large bowl, beat cake mix, oranges, egg whites and applesauce on low speed for 2 minutes. Pour into a 13-in. x 9-in. x 2-in. baking dish coated with nonstick cooking spray.

Bake at 350° for 25-30 minutes or until a toothpick inserted near the center comes out clean. Cool on a wire rack. In a bowl, combine pineapple and pudding mix. Fold in whipped topping just until blended. Spread over cake. Refrigerate for at least 1 hour before serving. **Yield:** 15 servings.

Nutrition Facts: 1 piece equals 231 calories, 5 g fat (3 g saturated fat), 0 cholesterol, 310 mg sodium, 43 g carbohydrate, 1 g fiber, 3 g protein.

Strawberry Shortbread Pie

(Pictured on page 116)

Prep: 15 min. + chilling

My husband enjoys this pie so much that I always make one extra! —*Sherry Maurer, Manheim, Pennsylvania*

    3/4 **cup sugar**
     3 **tablespoons cornstarch**
  1-1/2 **cups water**
     1 **package (3 ounces) strawberry gelatin**
     4 **cups sliced fresh strawberries**
     1 **shortbread crust (9 inches)**

In a saucepan, combine sugar, cornstarch and water until smooth. Bring to a boil; cook and stir for 2 minutes or until thickened. Remove from heat; stir in gelatin until dissolved. Transfer to a bowl. Chill until partially set.

Place berries in crust; pour gelatin mixture over berries. Cover; refrigerate until set. **Yield:** 6-8 servings.

Rhubarb Meringue Pie

Prep: 50 min. + chilling **Bake:** 65 min. + cooling

My husband's grandmother was a great cook and didn't always share her secrets, so we are fortunate to have her recipe for rhubarb cream pie. I added one of my favorite crusts and a never-fail meringue. —Elaine Sampson
Colesburg, Iowa

    3/4 cup all-purpose flour
    1/4 teaspoon salt
    1/4 teaspoon sugar
    1/4 cup shortening
      1 tablespoon beaten egg
    1/4 teaspoon white vinegar
      3 to 4-1/2 teaspoons cold water
FILLING:
      3 cups chopped fresh *or* frozen rhubarb
      1 cup sugar
      2 tablespoons all-purpose flour
Dash salt
      3 egg yolks
      1 cup heavy whipping cream
MERINGUE:
      4 teaspoons plus 1/3 cup sugar, *divided*
      2 teaspoons cornstarch
    1/3 cup water
      3 egg whites
    1/8 teaspoon cream of tartar

In a bowl, combine flour, salt and sugar; cut in shortening until crumbly. Combine egg and vinegar; sprinkle over crumb mixture. Gradually add water, tossing with a fork until a ball forms. Cover and chill for 1 hour or until easy to handle.

On a lightly floured surface, roll out the pastry to fit a 9-in. pie plate. Trim to 1/2 in. beyond the edge of plate; flute the edges. Place rhubarb in crust. Whisk the sugar, flour, salt, egg yolks and cream; pour over the rhubarb. Bake at 350° for 50-60 minutes or until a knife comes out clean.

In a small saucepan, combine 4 teaspoons sugar and cornstarch. Gradually stir in water. Bring to a boil, stirring constantly; cook for 1-2 minutes or until thickened. Cool to room temperature. In a small mixing bowl, beat egg whites and cream of tartar until frothy. Add cornstarch mixture; beat on high until soft peaks form. Gradually beat in remaining sugar, 1 tablespoon at a time, on high until stiff glossy peaks form.

Spread evenly over hot filling, sealing edges to crust. Bake for 15 minutes or until meringue is golden brown. Cool on a wire rack for 1 hour. Store in the refrigerator. **Yield:** 6-8 servings.

Editor's Note: If using frozen rhubarb, measure rhubarb while still frozen, then thaw completely. Drain in a colander, but do not press liquid out.

Spring Breeze Cheesecake Pie

(Pictured below)

Prep: 30 min. + chilling **Cook:** 15 min. + cooling

I combined two of my favorites (cheesecake and rhubarb) to come up with this mouth-watering dessert. It's so colorful and creamy that everyone likes it. —Deanna Taylor
Ainsworth, Nebraska

      1 package (8 ounces) cream cheese,
         softened
    1/3 cup sugar
      1 cup (8 ounces) sour cream
      2 teaspoons vanilla extract
      1 carton (8 ounces) frozen whipped
         topping, thawed
      1 graham cracker crust (9 inches)
TOPPING:
      3 cups chopped fresh *or* frozen rhubarb
    1/3 cup sugar
    1/8 teaspoon ground cinnamon
      1 tablespoon cornstarch
      2 tablespoons cold water

In a small mixing bowl, beat cream cheese until smooth. Gradually beat in sugar. Add the sour cream and vanilla; mix well. Set aside 1/2 cup whipped topping for garnish; cover and refrigerate. Beat 1/2 cup whipped topping into cream cheese mixture; fold in remaining whipped topping. Spoon into the crust. Cover and refrigerate for at least 2 hours.

For topping, in a large saucepan, bring the rhubarb, sugar and cinnamon to a boil. Reduce heat; simmer, uncovered, for 5-8 minutes or until rhubarb is tender. In a small bowl, combine cornstarch and cold water until smooth. Gradually stir into rhubarb mixture. Return to a boil; cook and stir for 1-2 minutes or until thickened. Cool to room temperature.

Cut pie into slices; top with the rhubarb sauce and reserved whipped topping. **Yield:** 6-8 servings.

Spread with 1 qt. ice cream; freeze for 30 minutes. Top with remaining sherbet balls. Combine remaining ice cream, pecans and chips; spread over sherbet balls. Cover and freeze overnight.

Run a knife around edge of pan; dip pan in lukewarm water until loosened. Invert cake onto a serving plate. Frost with whipped cream. Return to freezer. Remove from the freezer 10 minutes before serving. Garnish with raspberries and orange and lime slices if desired. **Yield:** 14-16 servings.

Sherbet Cream Cake

(Pictured above and on back cover)

Prep: 30 min. + freezing

For a showstopping summer dessert, serve this colorful, refreshing cake. Family members often request it for their birthdays. —Paula Wipf, Arlington, Virginia

- 3 cups *each* raspberry, orange and lime sherbet
- 3 quarts vanilla ice cream, softened, *divided*
- 2 cups chopped pecans, *divided*
- 2 cups miniature semisweet chocolate chips, *divided*
- 3 cups heavy whipping cream, whipped
- 1 pint fresh raspberries
Orange and lime slices, optional

Using a 1/4-cup ice cream scoop, shape sherbet into balls. Place on a waxed paper-lined baking sheet. Freeze for 1 hour or until firm.

In a large bowl, combine 1 qt. vanilla ice cream, 1 cup pecans and 1 cup chocolate chips. Spread into a 10-in. tube pan. Alternately arrange 12 sherbet balls, four of each color, against the center tube and outer edge of pan. Freeze for 30 minutes.

Lemon Coconut Cake

Prep: 1 hour + cooling   **Bake:** 20 min. + cooling

When I'm pressed for time, I substitute a white cake mix and use the filling and frosting from this recipe.
—LaDonna Reed, Ponca City, Oklahoma

- 5 egg whites
- 3/4 cup shortening
- 1-1/2 cups sugar
- 1-1/2 teaspoons vanilla extract
- 2 cups all-purpose flour
- 2 teaspoons baking powder
- 1 teaspoon salt
- 1 cup milk

FILLING:
- 3/4 cup sugar
- 2 tablespoons cornstarch

Dash salt
- 3/4 cup cold water
- 2 egg yolks
- 3 tablespoons lemon juice
- 1 tablespoon butter

FROSTING:
- 3/4 cup shortening
- 3-3/4 cups confectioners' sugar
- 1 teaspoon vanilla extract
- 1/3 cup water
- 1-1/4 cups flaked coconut

Place egg whites in a small mixing bowl; let stand at room temperature for 30 minutes. In a large mixing bowl, cream shortening and sugar until light and fluffy. Beat in vanilla. Combine flour, baking powder and salt; add to creamed mixture alternately with milk. Beat egg whites until stiff peaks form; fold into creamed mixture.

Pour into three greased and floured 9-in. round baking pans. Bake at 350° for 18-20 minutes or until a toothpick comes out clean. Cool for 10 minutes; remove from pans to wire racks to cool completely.

In a heavy saucepan, combine sugar, cornstarch and salt. Stir in the water until smooth. Cook and stir over medium-high heat until thickened. Reduce heat;

cook and stir 2 minutes longer. Remove from the heat. Stir a small amount of filling into egg yolks; return all to the pan, stirring constantly.

Bring to a boil; cook and stir 2 minutes longer. Remove from the heat. Stir in lemon juice and butter. Cool, without stirring, to room temperature.

In a large mixing bowl, cream shortening and confectioners' sugar until light and fluffy; beat in vanilla. Gradually add water, beating until smooth. Spread filling between cake layers. Frost top and sides of cake; sprinkle with coconut. **Yield:** 12-14 servings.

Chocolate Zucchini Cake

(Pictured on page 116)

Prep: 20 min. **Bake:** 50 min. + cooling

Shredded zucchini makes this cake really moist, and the topping adds a nice crunch. Whenever zucchini is in season, I shred, measure and freeze it in 2-cup amounts for this yummy recipe. —*Lois Holben, Creal Springs, Illinois*

1/2 cup butter, softened
1/2 cup vegetable oil
1-3/4 cups sugar
2 eggs
1 teaspoon vanilla extract
2-1/2 cups all-purpose flour
1/4 cup baking cocoa
1 teaspoon baking soda
1/2 teaspoon baking powder
1/2 teaspoon ground cinnamon
1/2 teaspoon ground cloves
1/2 cup buttermilk
2 cups shredded zucchini
FROSTING:
1 cup flaked coconut
6 tablespoons butter, softened
2/3 cup packed brown sugar
1/2 cup chopped walnuts
1/4 cup milk

In a large mixing bowl, beat the butter, oil and sugar until smooth. Add eggs, one at a time, beating well after each addition. Beat in vanilla. Combine the flour, cocoa, baking soda, baking powder, cinnamon and cloves; add to batter alternately with buttermilk. Fold in zucchini.

Pour into a greased 13-in. x 9-in. x 2-in. baking pan. Bake at 325° for 45-50 minutes or until a toothpick inserted near the center comes out clean. Cool on a wire rack for 10 minutes.

Meanwhile, in a bowl, combine the frosting ingredients. Spread over warm cake. Broil 4-6 in. from the heat for 2-3 minutes or until golden brown. Cool completely. **Yield:** 12-15 servings.

Cinnamon-Sugar Rhubarb Cake

(Pictured below)

Prep: 30 min. **Bake:** 40 min.

A real crowd-pleaser, this tender snack-like cake is chock-full of rhubarb and sprinkled with a sweet cinnamon-sugar topping. Everyone will be asking for the recipe...or seconds! —*Maryls Haber, White, South Dakota*

1/2 cup shortening
1 cup packed brown sugar
1 cup sugar, *divided*
1 egg
1 teaspoon vanilla extract
2 cups all-purpose flour
1 teaspoon baking soda
1/2 teaspoon salt
1 cup buttermilk
2 cups diced fresh *or* frozen rhubarb
1 teaspoon ground cinnamon

In a large mixing bowl, cream the shortening, brown sugar and 1/2 cup sugar until light and fluffy. Add egg and vanilla; beat for 2 minutes. Combine the flour, baking soda and salt; add to creamed mixture alternately with buttermilk, beating well after each addition. Stir in the rhubarb.

Pour into a greased 13-in. x 9-in. x 2-in. baking dish. Combine cinnamon and remaining sugar; sprinkle over batter. Bake at 350° for 40-45 minutes or until a toothpick inserted near the center comes out clean. Serve warm. **Yield:** 12-16 servings.

Editor's Note: If using frozen rhubarb, measure rhubarb while still frozen, then thaw completely. Drain in a colander, but do not press liquid out.

Butternut Squash Cake Roll

(Pictured above)

Prep: 10 min.   **Bake:** 15 min. + chilling

I'm a big fan of squash! This pretty dessert is perfect for a special autumn occasion. —Elizabeth Nelson
Manning, North Dakota

        3 **eggs**
        1 **cup sugar**
    2/3 **cup mashed cooked butternut squash**
    3/4 **cup all-purpose flour**
        1 **teaspoon baking soda**
    1/2 **teaspoon ground cinnamon**
        1 **cup finely chopped walnuts, optional**
Confectioners' sugar
FILLING:
        1 **package (8 ounces) cream cheese,
            softened**
        2 **tablespoons butter, softened**
        1 **cup confectioners' sugar**
    3/4 **teaspoon vanilla extract**
Additional confectioners' sugar

In a large mixing bowl, beat eggs; gradually beat in sugar. Add squash and mix well. Combine the flour, baking soda and cinnamon; add to squash mixture and mix well.

Line a 15-in. x 10-in. x 1-in. baking pan with waxed paper; grease and flour the paper. Spread batter even-ly into pan. Sprinkle with walnuts if desired. Bake at 375° for 13-15 minutes or until a toothpick inserted near the center comes out clean. Cool on a wire rack for 10 minutes.

Turn cake onto a kitchen towel dusted with confec-tioners' sugar. Gently peel off waxed paper. Roll up cake in the towel, jelly-roll style, starting with a short side. Cool completely on a wire rack.

In a small mixing bowl, beat the cream cheese, butter, confectioners' sugar and vanilla until smooth. Unroll cake; spread filling evenly over cake to within 1 in. of edges. Roll up again. Cover and refrigerate for 1 hour. Just before serving, dust with confectioners' sug-ar. **Yield:** 10 servings.

Coconut Chocolate Pie

Prep: 20 min. + chilling

Everyone loves this fudgy pie, made with Almond Joy candy bars. It's attractive, cuts easily and is absolutely delicious. —Cheryl Maczko, Reedville, West Virginia

    1/2 **cup sugar**
    1/3 **cup cornstarch**
    1/4 **cup baking cocoa**
    1/4 **teaspoon salt**
  1-1/2 **cups milk**
      16 **miniature Almond Joy candy bars,
            chopped**
        1 **teaspoon vanilla extract**
        1 **pastry shell (9 inches), baked**
Whipped cream

In a large saucepan, combine the sugar, cornstarch, cocoa and salt. Stir in milk until smooth. Bring to a boil over medium heat; cook and stir for 2 minutes or until thickened (mixture will thicken quickly). Remove from the heat.

Add chopped candy bars and vanilla; stir until chocolate is melted. Pour into pastry shell. Press plastic wrap onto filling. Refrigerate until set, about 4 hours. Remove plastic wrap. Slice and serve with whipped cream. **Yield:** 6-8 servings.

Crumbleberry Pie

(Pictured on page 116)

Prep: 15 min.   **Bake:** 50 min.

Blueberries peek through the golden crumb topping of this tantalizing pear-and-berry pie. It's best served warm.
—Maria Regakis, Somerville, Massachusetts

Pastry for single-crust pie (9 inches)
    6 tablespoons butter, softened
  1/2 cup sugar
    2 eggs
    1 cup finely ground almonds
  1/4 cup all-purpose flour
    1 large pear, peeled and thinly sliced
TOPPING:
  3/4 cup all-purpose flour
  1/3 cup packed brown sugar
  1/4 teaspoon almond extract
  1/3 cup cold butter
    1 cup fresh *or* frozen blueberries

Line a 9-in. pie plate with pastry; set aside. In a small mixing bowl, cream butter and sugar until light and fluffy. Add eggs, one at a time, beating well after each addition. Stir in almonds and flour.

Spread into pastry shell. Arrange pear slices over filling. Bake at 350° for 25-30 minutes or until light golden brown.

For topping, in a bowl, combine the flour, brown sugar and extract; cut in butter until crumbly. Sprinkle blueberries over pears; sprinkle with crumb topping. Bake 25-30 minutes longer or until golden brown. Serve warm. Refrigerate leftovers. **Yield:** 6-8 servings.

Editor's Note: If using frozen blueberries, do not thaw before adding to filling.

Pastry for Extra-Large Double-Crust Pie

Prep/Total Time: 15 min.

Our Test Kitchen home economists adapted one of their 9-inch, double-crust recipes for an 11-1/2- to 12-inch pie plate. Bake an extra-big pie and watch eyes light up!

  2-3/4 cups all-purpose flour
    1 teaspoon salt
    1 cup shortening
    8 to 9 tablespoons water

In a bowl, combine flour and salt; cut in shortening until crumbly. Gradually add water, tossing with a fork until the dough forms a ball. Divide the dough in half so that one ball is slightly larger than the other. Roll out the larger ball to fit an 11-1/2-in. to 12-in. pie plate. Transfer the pastry to the pie plate; trim the pastry even with the edge of the plate.

Pour desired filling into crust. Roll out second ball; cut slits in pastry. Position over filling. Trim pastry to 1 in. beyond edge of pie plate. Fold top crust over bottom crust. Flute edges. Bake according to recipe directions. **Yield:** 8-10 servings.

Chunky Apple Cake

(Pictured below)

Prep: 20 min. **Bake:** 40 min. + cooling

This tender, moist cake is full of old-fashioned comfort, and the yummy brown sugar sauce makes it special. For a festive occasion, add a dollop of whipped cream.
        —Debi Benson, Bakersfield, California

  1/2 cup butter, softened
    2 cups sugar
  1/2 teaspoon vanilla extract
    2 eggs
    2 cups all-purpose flour
 1-1/2 teaspoons ground cinnamon
    1 teaspoon ground nutmeg
  1/2 teaspoon salt
  1/2 teaspoon baking soda
    6 cups chopped peeled tart apples
BUTTERSCOTCH SAUCE:
  1/2 cup packed brown sugar
  1/4 cup butter, cubed
  1/2 cup heavy whipping cream

In a large mixing bowl, cream the butter, sugar and vanilla. Add eggs, one at a time, beating well after each addition. Combine the flour, cinnamon, nutmeg, salt and baking soda; gradually add to creamed mixture and mix well (batter will be stiff). Stir in apples until well combined.

Spread into a greased 13-in. x 9-in. x 2-in. baking dish. Bake at 350° for 40-45 minutes or until top is lightly browned and springs back when lightly touched. Cool for 30 minutes before serving.

Meanwhile, in a small saucepan, combine brown sugar and butter. Cook over medium heat until butter is melted. Gradually add cream. Bring to a slow boil over medium heat, stirring constantly. Remove from the heat. Serve with cake. **Yield:** 12-14 servings.

Just Desserts

Eyes will light up when you surprise everyone at
the dinner table with a creamy cheesecake, fresh fruit crisp or
other decadent delight from this chapter.

HAPPY ENDINGS. Clockwise from upper left: Ultimate Caramel Apples (p. 145), Apple Pizza (p. 144), Hot Fudge Sauce (p. 142), Plum Streusel Kuchen (p. 142) and Berry Cheesecake Dessert (p. 146).

ping on high for 30 seconds or until thin; fold into reserved cream cheese mixture. Carefully spoon over filling; cut through filling with a knife to swirl.

Place pan on a baking sheet. Bake at 350° for 55-65 minutes or until center is almost set. Cool on a wire rack for 10 minutes. Carefully run a knife around edge of pan to loosen; cool 1 hour longer.

Microwave remaining fudge topping for 30 seconds or until warmed; spread over cheesecake. Garnish with peanut butter cups. Refrigerate overnight. Remove sides of pan. **Yield:** 12-14 servings.

Editor's Note: Reduced-fat or generic brands of peanut butter are not recommended for this recipe.

Peanut Butter Cup Cheesecake

(Pictured above)

Prep: 20 min.   **Bake:** 55 min. + chilling

I tried this recipe after saying I'd bring dessert to a holiday party. It tastes and looks lovely!
—Dawn Lowenstein, Hatboro, Pennsylvania

- 1-1/4 cups graham cracker crumbs
- 1/4 cup crushed cream-filled chocolate sandwich cookies
- 1/4 cup sugar
- 6 tablespoons butter, melted
- 3/4 cup creamy peanut butter

FILLING:
- 3 packages (8 ounces *each*) cream cheese, softened
- 1 cup sugar
- 1 cup (8 ounces) sour cream
- 3 eggs, lightly beaten
- 1-1/2 teaspoons vanilla extract
- 1 cup hot fudge ice cream topping, *divided*
- 6 peanut butter cups, cut into small wedges

In a bowl, combine cracker crumbs, cookie crumbs, sugar and butter. Press onto the bottom and 1 in. up the sides of a greased 9-in. springform pan. Place on a baking sheet. Bake at 350° for 7-9 minutes or until set. Cool on a wire rack. In a microwave-safe bowl, heat peanut butter on high for 30 seconds or until softened. Spread over crust to within 1 in. of edges.

In a large mixing bowl, beat cream cheese, sugar and sour cream until smooth. Add eggs; beat on low speed just until combined. Stir in vanilla. Pour 1 cup into a bowl; set aside. Pour remaining filling over peanut butter layer.

In a microwave-safe bowl, heat 1/4 cup fudge top-

Poached Pears with Almond Cream

Prep: 55 min.   **Bake:** 10 min. + cooling

Crisp pastry forms the base for a nicely spiced pear half in this elegant dessert.   —Judy Losecco, Buffalo, New York

- 1-1/3 cups all-purpose flour
- 1/2 teaspoon salt
- 1/2 cup shortening
- 3 to 4 tablespoons cold water

POACHED PEARS:
- 3 large pears
- 2 cups white grape juice
- 1 cinnamon stick (3 inches), halved
- 2 teaspoons thinly sliced candied ginger
- 1/8 teaspoon ground allspice
- 2 tablespoons cornstarch
- 3 tablespoons water

ALMOND CREAM:
- 1 package (8 ounces) cream cheese, softened
- 3 tablespoons sour cream
- 1 tablespoon sugar
- 1 teaspoon almond extract

In a large bowl, combine flour and salt; cut in shortening until mixture is crumbly. Gradually add water, tossing with a fork until mixture forms a ball.

On a lightly floured surface, roll dough to 1/8-in. thickness. Cut into six circles with a 4-in. cookie cutter. Place 1 in. apart on an ungreased baking sheet. Bake at 425° for 7-8 minutes or until edges begin to brown. Remove to a wire rack to cool.

Peel pears and cut in half lengthwise; remove cores. In a large skillet, combine grape juice, cinnamon, ginger and allspice; add pears. Bring to a boil. Reduce heat; cover and simmer for 8-10 minutes or until pears are tender, turning once. Remove pears and set aside.

Combine cornstarch and water; stir into poaching liquid. Bring to a boil; cook and stir for 2 minutes or until thickened. Remove from the heat; discard cinnamon stick.

In a small mixing bowl, combine the almond cream ingredients; beat until smooth. On each dessert plate, place a pear half on a pastry circle; drizzle with poaching liquid. Pipe almond cream over pears. Serve immediately. **Yield:** 6 servings.

Cherry Cheesecake Mousse

(Pictured below)

Prep: 20 min. + chilling

This dessert is perfect for Christmastime, but it's also nice year-round. I freeze fresh cherries in season to have on hand. —*Christine Schmidt, Saskatoon, Saskatchewan*

> 1 **pound fresh *or* frozen pitted sweet cherries**
> 1-1/2 **teaspoons unflavored gelatin**
> 1 **package (8 ounces) cream cheese, softened**
> 1/2 **cup confectioners' sugar**
> 4 **squares (1 ounce *each*) white baking chocolate, melted**
> 2 **teaspoons vanilla extract**
> 1 **cup heavy whipping cream**

Place the cherries in a food processor or blender; cover and process until chopped. Transfer to a saucepan; stir in the gelatin. Let stand for 1 minute.

Bring to a boil; reduce heat. Cook and stir for 1 minute or until the gelatin is dissolved. Transfer to a bowl. Refrigerate for 45 minutes or until the mixture begins to thicken.

In a small mixing bowl, beat cream cheese until smooth. Beat in the confectioners' sugar, chocolate and vanilla until combined. Fold in cherry mixture. In another mixing bowl, beat whipping cream until soft peaks form. Fold into the cherry cream mixture. Pour into dessert dishes. Cover and refrigerate for 3 hours or until set. **Yield:** 10 servings.

Layered Cranberry Dessert

(Pictured above)

Prep: 25 min. + chilling

I like to "fancy up" one of my favorite gelatin desserts with a buttery graham cracker crust and a layer of cream cheese filling. Mandarin oranges add color and pair well with the cranberry gelatin. —*Margery Bryan*
Moses Lake, Washington

> 2 **packages (3 ounces *each*) cranberry gelatin**
> 1-1/2 **cups boiling water**
> 1 **can (16 ounces) whole-berry cranberry sauce**
> 1-1/2 **cups cold water**
> 1-1/2 **cups graham cracker crumbs**
> 1/2 **cup sugar, *divided***
> 1/2 **cup butter, melted**
> 1 **package (8 ounces) cream cheese, softened**
> 1 **carton (16 ounces) frozen whipped topping, thawed, *divided***
> 1 **can (15 ounces) mandarin oranges, drained**

In a large bowl, dissolve gelatin in boiling water. Stir in cranberry sauce and cold water until blended. Refrigerate for 45 minutes or until partially set.

Meanwhile, in a bowl, combine the cracker crumbs, 1/4 cup sugar and butter. Press into an ungreased 13-in. x 9-in. x 2-in. dish. Refrigerate until set.

In a small mixing bowl, beat cream cheese and the remaining sugar until smooth. Fold in half of the whipped topping. Spread over the crust. Fold the oranges into the gelatin mixture; spoon over the cream cheese layer. Refrigerate for 4 hours or until firm. Cut into squares; dollop with remaining whipped topping. **Yield:** 12 servings.

Frozen Raspberry Delight

(Pictured below)

Prep: 30 min. + freezing

This pretty, make-ahead dessert is a light, refreshing ending to a summer meal. I first made it for my aunt's 85th-birthday dinner, and everyone loved it! —Nancy Whitford Edwards, New York

- 2 cups crushed chocolate wafers
- 1/4 cup sugar
- 1/3 cup butter, melted

FILLING:
- 1 cup hot fudge ice cream topping
- 1 quart vanilla ice cream, softened
- 1 pint raspberry sherbet, softened
- 1 package (10 ounces) frozen sweetened raspberries, thawed and drained
- 1 carton (8 ounces) frozen whipped topping, thawed

In a bowl, combine the wafer crumbs, sugar and butter; set aside 1/4 cup. Press the remaining crumb mixture into a 13-in. x 9-in. x 2-in. dish. Cover and refrigerate for 15 minutes.

Place hot fudge topping in a microwave-safe bowl; cover and microwave on high for 15-20 seconds. Spread over crust. Spoon ice cream over fudge layer. Place spoonfuls of sherbet over ice cream; cut through sherbet with a knife to swirl. Top with raspberries. Spread with whipped topping; sprinkle with reserved crumb mixture.

Cover; freeze for 2-3 hours or overnight. Remove from freezer 15 minutes before serving. **Yield:** 12-15 servings.

Peach Rhubarb Crisp

Prep: 20 min.   **Bake:** 30 min.

When a visit to the local farmers market left me with an abundance of quickly ripening peaches and a few stalks of rhubarb, I created this sweet-tart recipe.
—Sandy Kimble, Salinas, California

- 3/4 cup sugar
- 3 tablespoons all-purpose flour
- 1/2 teaspoon ground nutmeg
- 1/2 teaspoon grated lemon peel
- 1/8 teaspoon salt
- 3 cups sliced fresh *or* frozen rhubarb
- 2-1/2 cups chopped peeled fresh peaches *or* frozen unsweetened peach slices, chopped

TOPPING:
- 1/2 cup all-purpose flour
- 1/2 cup old-fashioned oats
- 1/2 cup packed brown sugar
- 3/4 teaspoon ground cinnamon
- 1/8 teaspoon salt
- 5 tablespoons cold butter

In a large bowl, combine the sugar, flour, nutmeg, lemon peel, salt, rhubarb and peaches. Transfer to a greased 11-in. x 7-in. x 2-in. baking dish.

In a bowl, combine the flour, oats, brown sugar, cinnamon and salt. Cut in butter until mixture resembles coarse crumbs; sprinkle over the rhubarb mixture. Bake at 375° for 30-35 minutes or until bubbly and fruit is tender. Serve warm or cold. **Yield:** 6-8 servings.

Editor's Note: If using frozen rhubarb, measure rhubarb while still frozen, then thaw completely. Drain in a colander, but do not press liquid out.

Lemon Cake Custard

Prep: 20 min. + standing   **Bake:** 25 min.

This old-fashioned dessert still makes a wonderful finale for a meal. Folks of all ages really enjoy it.
—Brenda Sanders, Hampstead, North Carolina

- 3 eggs
- 1 cup sugar, *divided*
- 1/4 cup all-purpose flour
- 1/4 teaspoon salt
- 1-1/4 cups milk
- 1/3 cup lemon juice
- 2 tablespoons butter, melted
- 1 tablespoon grated lemon peel

Separate eggs and let stand at room temperature for 30 minutes. In a large bowl, combine 1/2 cup sugar, flour and salt. Stir in the milk, lemon juice, butter and lemon peel. Beat egg yolks; add to lemon mixture.

In a small mixing bowl, beat egg whites on medium speed until soft peaks form. Gradually add remaining sugar, 2 tablespoons at a time, beating on high until stiff peaks form and sugar is dissolved. Fold into lemon mixture.

Spoon into six greased 8-oz. ramekins. Place in a 13-in. x 9-in. x 2-in. baking pan. Add 1 in. of hot water

to pan. Bake, uncovered, at 350° for 25-30 minutes or until a toothpick inserted near the center comes out clean. Serve immediately or chill. **Yield:** 6 servings.

Fruit 'n' Pudding Dessert

Prep: 30 min. + chilling

My family is mixed in their taste for holiday desserts. Some look forward to pumpkin flavors and others prefer layered pudding desserts like this deliciously creamy treat.
—*Shirley Glaab, Hattiesburg, Mississippi*

  1 cup graham cracker crumbs
1/2 cup ground pecans
1/3 cup butter, melted
1/4 cup sugar
  1 can (8 ounces) crushed pineapple
  3 medium firm bananas, peeled and cut into 1/4-inch slices
  1 package (8 ounces) cream cheese, softened
3-1/2 cups cold milk
  2 packages (3.4 ounces *each*) instant lemon pudding mix
TOPPING:
  1 carton (8 ounces) frozen whipped topping, thawed
1/2 cup finely chopped pecans

In a bowl, combine the graham cracker crumbs, pecans, butter and sugar. Press into an ungreased 13-in. x 9-in. x 2-in. dish.

Drain pineapple, reserving juice; set pineapple aside. Place bananas in a small bowl; add reserved juice. Let stand for 5-10 minutes; drain. Arrange bananas in a single layer over crust.

In a large mixing bowl, beat cream cheese until smooth. Gradually beat in milk. Add pudding mixes; beat on low speed just until combined. Spread over bananas; top with pineapple. Spread with whipped topping; sprinkle with pecans. Cover and refrigerate for at least 2 hours before serving. **Yield:** 15 servings.

Cranberry Cheesecake Tart

(Pictured above right)

Prep: 35 min. + chilling

I created this recipe to reduce the sugar and fat in the original high-calorie version. Although it uses sugar substitute and reduced-fat ingredients, you can't tell the difference between this dessert and the original.
—*Diane Halferty, Corpus Christi, Texas*

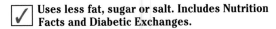 **Uses less fat, sugar or salt. Includes Nutrition Facts and Diabetic Exchanges.**

Pastry for single-crust pie (9 inches)
1/3 cup sugar
  2 tablespoons cornstarch
2/3 cup water
  3 cups fresh *or* frozen cranberries
Sugar substitute equivalent to 1 tablespoon sugar
  1 package (8 ounces) reduced-fat cream cheese
1-1/2 cups reduced-fat whipped topping, *divided*
  1 teaspoon grated lemon peel

Press the pie pastry onto the bottom and up the sides of a 10-in. tart pan with a removable bottom. Bake at 400° for 9-11 minutes or until lightly browned. Cool on a wire rack.

In a large saucepan, combine the sugar, cornstarch and water until smooth. Add cranberries. Bring mixture to a boil over medium heat.

Reduce heat to low; cook and stir for 3-5 minutes or until thickened and the berries have popped. Remove from the heat; cool to room temperature. Stir in the sugar substitute.

In a small mixing bowl, beat cream cheese and 1 cup whipped topping until smooth; add lemon peel. Spread over the pastry; top with the cranberry mixture. Refrigerate for 2-4 hours or until set. Garnish with remaining whipped topping. **Yield:** 10 servings.

Nutrition Facts: 1 slice equals 223 calories, 12 g fat (7 g saturated fat), 20 mg cholesterol, 177 mg sodium, 26 g carbohydrate, 1 g fiber, 3 g protein. **Diabetic Exchanges:** 2 fat, 1 starch, 1 fruit.

Editor's Note: This recipe was tested with Splenda No Calorie Sweetener.

Grandmother's Bread Pudding

(Pictured above)

Prep: 10 min.   **Bake:** 45 min.

Comforting is the best way to describe this homey, flavorful bread pudding. —Edna Butler, Los Fresnos, Texas

    5 eggs
    3 cups milk
1-1/4 cups sugar
    1 cup half-and-half cream
  1/4 cup butter, melted and cooled
    2 teaspoons vanilla extract
    1 teaspoon almond extract
  1/2 teaspoon ground nutmeg
    4 cups cubed day-old white bread
    4 cups cubed day-old wheat bread
  1/3 cup raisins
LEMON SAUCE:
1-1/2 cups sugar
  1/3 cup cornstarch
  1/4 teaspoon salt
2-1/4 cups cold water
    3 egg yolks, beaten
  1/3 cup lemon juice
    2 tablespoons butter

In a large mixing bowl, combine the first eight ingredients. Stir in bread cubes and raisins. Transfer to a greased 13-in. x 9-in. x 2-in. baking dish. Bake, uncovered, at 350° for 45-55 minutes or until a knife inserted near the center comes out clean.

For sauce, combine the sugar, cornstarch, salt and water in a large saucepan until smooth. Bring to a boil over medium heat, stirring constantly.

Remove from heat. Stir a small amount of hot filling into egg yolks; return all to pan, stirring constantly. Bring to a gentle boil; cook and stir for 2 minutes. Remove from the heat; gently stir in lemon juice and butter. Serve with bread pudding. Refrigerate leftovers. **Yield:** 12-15 servings.

Strawberry Ice Cream Dessert

(Pictured below)

Prep: 30 min. + freezing

This pretty, refreshing treat has been served many times at our church showers. We just love it. —Teresa Ryherd
Fairbank, Iowa

    2 cups graham cracker crumbs
    6 tablespoons butter, melted
    1 quart strawberry ice cream, softened
1-1/2 cups milk
    2 packages (3.3 ounces *each*) instant white chocolate pudding mix
    1 teaspoon vanilla extract
    1 carton (16 ounces) frozen whipped topping, thawed, *divided*

In a bowl, combine cracker crumbs and butter; set aside 2 tablespoons for garnish. Press remaining crumb mixture onto the bottom of an ungreased 10-in. springform pan. Place on a baking sheet. Bake at 375° for 8 minutes or until edges begin to brown. Cool on a wire rack.

In a large mixing bowl, combine the ice cream, milk, pudding mixes and vanilla; beat until smooth. Fold in half of the whipped topping. Pour over crust. Cover and freeze for 1 hour or until firm.

Spread with remaining whipped topping and sprinkle with reserved crumb mixture. Freeze for at least 3 hours or until firm. Remove from the freezer 15 minutes before serving. **Yield:** 12 servings.

Puff Pastry Hearts

(Pictured at right)

Prep: 1 hour + chilling
Bake: 10 min. per batch + cooling

Try these adorable cream-filled hearts for Valentine's Day or any time you want to serve a special treat.
— *Sarah Vasques, Milford, New Hampshire*

    3/4 cup sugar, *divided*
    3   tablespoons cornstarch
    1/4 teaspoon salt
    6   egg yolks, beaten
    1-1/2 cups milk
    1/2 to 1 teaspoon rum extract
    1/2 teaspoon vanilla extract
    1-1/2 cups heavy whipping cream
    2   packages (17.3 ounces *each*) frozen puff
         pastry, thawed
    1   jar (12 ounces) seedless raspberry
         preserves
    2   cups fresh raspberries
  Confectioners' sugar

In a bowl, whisk 1/2 cup sugar, cornstarch, salt and egg yolks. In a large saucepan, bring the milk and remaining sugar to a boil; remove from the heat. Stir a small amount into egg yolk mixture; return all to the pan, stirring constantly. Bring to a gentle boil; cook and stir for 2 minutes. Remove from the heat; stir in extracts. Cover and refrigerate for 2-3 hours or until chilled.

In a large mixing bowl, beat the cream until soft peaks form. Fold into custard. Cover and refrigerate until serving.

Roll out pastry on a lightly floured surface. Cut with a 3-1/2-in. heart-shaped cookie cutter. Place 1 in. apart on parchment paper-lined baking sheets. Bake at 400° for 8-10 minutes or until golden brown. Remove to wire racks to cool.

Just before serving, warm preserves in a small saucepan; drizzle some onto dessert plates. Split puff pastry hearts in half. Place bottom halves on plates; spread each with 2 tablespoons of filling. Replace tops; drizzle with remaining preserves. Garnish with raspberries and confectioners' sugar. **Yield:** 3 dozen.

Chocolate-Filled Meringue Shells

Prep: 25 min. + standing   **Bake:** 30 min. + cooling

This has been a favorite Easter dessert of ours for years. It looks special and tastes that way, too!
— *Janis Plourde, Smooth Rock Falls, Ontario*

    2   egg whites
    1/2 cup sugar

    1/4 teaspoon ground cinnamon
    1/2 teaspoon cider vinegar
    1/4 teaspoon salt
  FILLING:
    1   cup (6 ounces) semisweet chocolate chips
    1-1/2 cups heavy whipping cream, *divided*
    1/4 cup sugar
    1/4 teaspoon ground cinnamon
  Toasted chopped pecans

Place egg whites in a small mixing bowl; let stand at room temperature for 30 minutes. In a small bowl, combine sugar and cinnamon. Add vinegar and salt to egg whites; beat on medium speed until soft peaks form. Gradually beat in cinnamon-sugar, 1 tablespoon at a time, on high until glossy peaks form and sugar is dissolved.

Line two baking sheets with parchment paper. Spoon meringue into eight mounds on paper. Using the back of a spoon, shape into 3-in. cups. Bake at 250° for 30 minutes. Turn the oven off and do not open door; let meringues dry in oven for 1 hour. Cool on baking sheets on wire racks.

In a microwave-safe bowl, melt chocolate chips; stir until smooth. Spread 2 teaspoonfuls over bottom of each meringue shell. Whisk 1/2 cup cream into remaining melted chocolate. Cover; chill about 20 minutes.

In a small mixing bowl, beat remaining cream until soft peaks form. Gradually add sugar and cinnamon, beating until stiff peaks form; set aside half of cream mixture. Fold remaining cream mixture into chilled chocolate mixture; pipe into meringue shells. Dollop with reserved cream mixture; sprinkle with pecans. **Yield:** 8 servings.

Rhubarb Swirl Cheesecake

(Pictured above)

Prep: 40 min.   **Bake:** 1 hour + chilling

I love cheesecake and my husband loves chocolate, so this is a favorite of ours. The tart rhubarb complements the sweet flavors. —Carol Witczak, Tinley Park, Illinois

- 2-1/2 **cups thinly sliced fresh** *or* **frozen rhubarb**
- 1/3 **cup plus 1/2 cup sugar,** *divided*
- 2 **tablespoons orange juice**
- 1-1/4 **cups graham cracker crumbs**
- 1/4 **cup butter, melted**
- 3 **packages (8 ounces** *each***) cream cheese, softened**
- 2 **cups (16 ounces) sour cream**
- 1 **tablespoon cornstarch**
- 2 **teaspoons vanilla extract**
- 1/2 **teaspoon salt**
- 3 **eggs, lightly beaten**
- 8 **squares (1 ounce** *each***) white baking chocolate, melted**

In a large saucepan, bring rhubarb, 1/3 cup sugar and orange juice to a boil. Reduce heat; cook and stir until thickened and rhubarb is tender. Set aside.

In a bowl, combine cracker crumbs and butter. Press onto the bottom of a greased 9-in. springform pan. Place on a baking sheet. Bake at 350° for 7-9 minutes or until lightly browned. Cool on a wire rack.

In a large mixing bowl, beat cream cheese, sour cream, cornstarch, vanilla, salt and remaining sugar until smooth. Add eggs; beat just until combined. Fold in white chocolate. Pour half of the filling into crust. Top with half of the rhubarb sauce; cut through batter with

a knife to gently swirl rhubarb. Layer with remaining filling and rhubarb sauce; cut through top layers with a knife to gently swirl rhubarb.

Place pan on a double thickness of heavy-duty foil (about 16 in. square). Securely wrap foil around pan. Place in a large baking pan; add 1 in. of hot water to larger pan. Bake at 350° for 60-70 minutes or until center is almost set. Cool on a wire rack for 10 minutes. Carefully run a knife around edge of pan to loosen; cool 1 hour longer. Cover and chill overnight. Remove sides of pan. Refrigerate leftovers. **Yield:** 12-14 servings.

Editor's Note: If using frozen rhubarb, measure rhubarb while still frozen, then thaw completely. Drain in a colander, but do not press liquid out.

Hot Fudge Sauce

(Pictured on page 134)

Prep/Total Time: 20 min.

Rich and dark, this topping is heavenly on peppermint ice cream, coffee ice cream and lots of other flavors! —Paula Zsiray, Logan, Utah

- 2 **cups sugar**
- 1/4 **cup baking cocoa**
- 1 **can (5 ounces) evaporated milk**
- 1/2 **cup butter, cubed**
- 1 **teaspoon vanilla extract**

In a small saucepan, combine sugar and cocoa. Stir in the milk; add butter. Bring to a boil over medium heat, stirring constantly. Reduce heat; cook and stir for 1 minute or until slightly thickened. Remove from the heat; stir in vanilla. Serve warm. Refrigerate leftovers.

To reheat: Place the sauce in a small saucepan; bring to a boil, stirring until smooth. **Yield:** 2 cups.

Plum Streusel Kuchen

(Pictured on page 134)

Prep: 25 min.   **Bake:** 35 min.

This recipe is actually called platz in German, meaning "flat," and has been in my family since before I was born. —Lisa Warkentin, Winnipeg, Manitoba

- 2 **cups all-purpose flour**
- 1/4 **cup sugar**
- 2 **teaspoons baking powder**
- 2 **tablespoons shortening**
- 1 **egg**
- 1 **cup heavy whipping cream**
- 6 **fresh plums, halved and sliced**

TOPPING:
- 2/3 cup all-purpose flour
- 2/3 cup sugar
- 2 tablespoons cold butter
- 2 tablespoons heavy whipping cream

In a large bowl, combine the flour, sugar and baking powder; cut in shortening until mixture resembles fine crumbs. In another bowl, beat the egg and cream; add to crumb mixture, tossing gently with a fork until mixture forms a ball.

Press dough into a greased 13-in. x 9-in. x 2-in. baking dish. Arrange plums over crust.

For topping, in a bowl, combine the flour and sugar; cut in the butter until the mixture resembles fine crumbs. Add the whipping cream, mixing gently with a fork until moist crumbs form. Sprinkle over plums. Bake at 350° for 35-40 minutes or until lightly browned. **Yield:** 12-15 servings.

Pizza for Dessert

Prep: 30 min.   **Bake:** 10 min. + cooling

At first glance, people might think this colorful "pizza" is a savory snack. But truth comes in the tasting! Kids get a kick out of the fun candy toppings.   —Sandy Gibbons
Ocean Park, Washington

- 1 tube (18 ounces) refrigerated chocolate chip cookie dough, softened
- 1-1/2 cups flaked coconut
- 1-1/2 teaspoons water
- 8 drops yellow food coloring
- 1 drop red food coloring
- 3 to 5 *each* large green, red and white gumdrops
- 1 cup (6 ounces) semisweet chocolate chips
- 1 cup peanut butter
- 10 to 15 small black jelly beans

Press cookie dough onto a greased 12-in. pizza pan. Bake at 350° for 10-15 minutes or until golden brown. Cool on a wire rack.

Place coconut in a resealable plastic bag; add water, and yellow and red food coloring. Seal bag and shake well to tint; set aside. Cut green gumdrops in half. Flatten red and white gumdrops. Using a 1/2-in. round cookie cutter, cut out the center of each white gumdrop.

In a microwave-safe bowl, melt chocolate chips; stir until smooth. Place peanut butter in another microwave-safe bowl; microwave, uncovered, on high for 1 minute or until slightly softened. Spread chocolate over cookie crust; spread with peanut butter.

Sprinkle with "cheese" (tinted coconut). Top with "green peppers," "tomatoes" and "onions" (green, red

and white gumdrops), and "olives" (black jelly beans); press down gently. **Yield:** 8-10 slices.

Berry-Patch Brownie Pizza

(Pictured below)

Prep: 20 min.   **Bake:** 15 min. + chilling

I just love the combination of fruit, almonds and chocolate that makes this brownie so unique. The fruit lightens the chocolate a bit and adds some wholesome goodness.
—Sue Kauffman, Columbia City, Indiana

- 1 package fudge brownie mix (13-inch x 9-inch pan size)
- 1/3 cup chopped unblanched almonds
- 1 teaspoon almond extract
- 1 package (8 ounces) cream cheese, softened
- 1 tablespoon sugar
- 1 teaspoon vanilla extract
- 1/2 teaspoon grated lemon peel
- 2 cups whipped topping

Mixed fresh berries

Prepare brownie batter according to package directions for fudge-like brownies, adding almonds and extract. Spread into a greased 14-in. pizza pan. Bake at 375° for 15-18 minutes or until a toothpick inserted near the center comes out clean. Cool on a wire rack.

In a large mixing bowl, beat the cream cheese, sugar, vanilla and lemon peel until smooth. Fold in whipped topping. Spread over crust to within 1/2 in. of edges. Top with berries. Refrigerate for 2-3 hours before serving. **Yield:** 12-14 servings.

Absolutely Apples!

APPLE PIE may be the all-American dessert, but apples can be used to make an endless variety of tempting treats. Just try these recipes and see!

Cinnamon Apple Cheesecake

(Pictured below and on front cover)

Prep: 40 min.   **Bake:** 40 min. + chilling

An attractive topping of cinnamon-spiced apple slices and a homemade oat-and-walnut crust make this creamy dessert a definite showstopper. —*Emily Ann Young*
Kenai, Alaska

    1/2 cup butter, softened
    1/4 cup packed brown sugar
      1 cup all-purpose flour
    1/4 cup quick-cooking oats
    1/4 cup finely chopped walnuts
    1/2 teaspoon ground cinnamon
FILLING:
      2 packages (8 ounces *each*) cream cheese,
         softened
      1 can (14 ounces) sweetened condensed
         milk
    1/2 cup apple juice concentrate
      3 eggs, lightly beaten
TOPPING:
      2 medium apples, peeled and sliced
      1 tablespoon butter
      1 teaspoon cornstarch
    1/4 teaspoon ground cinnamon
    1/4 cup apple juice concentrate

In a small mixing bowl, cream butter and brown sugar. Gradually add flour, oats, walnuts and cinnamon; mix well. Press onto bottom and 1-1/2 in. up the sides of a greased 9-in. springform pan. Place on a baking sheet. Bake at 325° for 10 minutes or until set. Cool on a wire rack.

In a large mixing bowl, beat cream cheese until fluffy. Beat in milk and apple juice concentrate until smooth. Add eggs; beat on low speed just until combined (batter will be thin). Pour into crust. Return pan to baking sheet. Bake at 325° for 40-45 minutes or until center is almost set. Cool on a wire rack for 10 minutes. Carefully run a knife around edge of pan to loosen; cool 1 hour longer. Refrigerate overnight.

In a large skillet, cook and stir apples in butter over medium heat until crisp-tender, about 5 minutes. Cool to room temperature. Arrange over cheesecake. In a small saucepan, combine cornstarch, cinnamon and apple juice concentrate until smooth. Bring to a boil, stirring constantly. Boil for 1 minute or until thickened. Immediately brush over apples. Refrigerate for 1 hour or until chilled. Remove sides of pan. Refrigerate leftovers. **Yield:** 12 servings.

Apple Pizza

(Pictured on page 134)

Prep: 40 min.   **Bake:** 20 min.

I tailored an apple pizza recipe I found to fit my family's tastes. —*Brenda Mowrey, Taylors, South Carolina*

2-1/3 to 3 cups all-purpose flour
      3 tablespoons sugar
      1 package (1/4 ounce) active dry yeast
    1/2 teaspoon salt
    1/2 cup water
    1/4 cup milk
    1/4 cup butter, cubed
TOPPINGS:
      4 cups sliced peeled tart apples
      2 tablespoons butter
    1/2 cup sugar
      2 tablespoons all-purpose flour
      1 teaspoon ground cinnamon
      4 ounces cream cheese, softened
    1/4 cup packed brown sugar
      2 tablespoons caramel ice cream topping
    2/3 cup all-purpose flour
    1/3 cup sugar
    1/4 cup cold butter

In a large mixing bowl, combine 1-1/2 cups flour, sugar, yeast and salt. In a saucepan, heat water, milk and butter to 120°-130°. Add to dry ingredients; beat for 2 minutes. Stir in enough remaining flour to form a firm dough. Turn onto a floured surface; cover and let rest for 15 minutes.

In a large skillet, cook and stir apples in butter over medium heat for 2 minutes. Combine sugar, flour and cinnamon; stir into skillet. Cook 3 minutes more. Reduce heat to low; cook, uncovered, for 4-6 minutes or until apples are tender, stirring frequently.

In a small mixing bowl, combine the cream cheese, brown sugar and topping. In another small bowl, combine flour and sugar; cut in butter until crumbly.

Pat dough onto a greased 14-in. pizza pan, building up edges slightly. Spread with cheese topping, then apple topping. Sprinkle with streusel. Bake at 375° for 20-25 minutes or until crust is golden brown. Serve warm or cold. **Yield:** 10-12 servings.

Ultimate Caramel Apples

(Pictured on page 134)

Prep: 45 min.   **Cook:** 25 min. + chilling

I have such a sweet tooth that I've been known to make a dessert just to satisfy my craving. One day, when I was in the mood for caramel, I came up with these fun treats.
— Clarissa Loyd, Mineral Wells, Texas

- 6 **medium Red Delicious apples**
- 6 **Popsicle sticks**
- 1 **cup sugar**
- 1 **cup water**
- 1/2 **cup heavy whipping cream**
- 1/2 **cup shelled pistachios, chopped, *divided***
- 3 **squares (1 ounce *each*) white baking chocolate, chopped**
- 3 **squares (1 ounce *each*) semisweet chocolate, chopped**
- 1 **tablespoon red-hot candies, optional**

Line a baking sheet with waxed paper and grease the paper; set aside. Wash and thoroughly dry apples. Insert a Popsicle stick into each; place on prepared pan. Chill.

In a large heavy saucepan, bring sugar and water to a boil over medium heat. Reduce heat; simmer, uncovered, without stirring for 20-25 minutes or until amber-colored. Remove from the heat; gradually stir in cream. Let stand for 10 minutes.

Place 1/4 cup pistachios in a shallow dish. Dip apples into caramel mixture until coated, then dip the bottom of each in pistachios. Return to baking sheet; chill.

In a small microwave-safe bowl, microwave white chocolate at 50% power for 1-2 minutes or until melted; stir until smooth. Transfer to a small heavy-duty resealable plastic bag; cut a small hole in a corner of bag. Drizzle over apples. Repeat with semisweet chocolate. Sprinkle tops with remaining pistachios and red-hots if desired. Chill until set. **Yield:** 6 servings.

Caramel Apple Crisp

(Pictured above)

Prep: 20 min.   **Bake:** 45 min.

When my children and I make this scrumptious, layered dessert at home, we use a variety of apples to give it a nice combination of flavors.
— Michelle Brooks
Clarkston, Michigan

- 3 **cups old-fashioned oats**
- 2 **cups all-purpose flour**
- 1-1/2 **cups packed brown sugar**
- 1 **teaspoon ground cinnamon**
- 1 **cup cold butter**
- 8 **cups thinly sliced peeled tart apples**
- 1 **package (14 ounces) caramels, halved**
- 1 **cup apple cider, *divided***

In a large bowl, combine the oats, flour, brown sugar and cinnamon; cut in butter until crumbly. Press half of the mixture into a greased 13-in. x 9-in. x 2-in. baking dish. Layer with half of the apples and caramels and 1 cup oat mixture; repeat layers. Pour 1/2 cup cider over top.

Bake, uncovered, at 350° for 30 minutes. Drizzle with remaining cider; bake 15-20 minutes longer or until apples are tender. **Yield:** 12-14 servings.

Almond-Topped Pumpkin Cheesecake

(Pictured below)

Prep: 30 min.   **Bake:** 70 min. + chilling

I won a blue ribbon when I entered this luscious, family-favorite cheesecake at the state fair a few years ago.
—*Carmel Mooney, Dobbins, California*

  1-1/2 cups graham cracker crumbs
    1/3 cup finely chopped almonds
      1 tablespoon sugar
    1/4 teaspoon pumpkin pie spice
    1/4 cup butter, melted
FILLING:
      3 packages (8 ounces *each*) cream cheese, softened
      1 cup canned pumpkin
    3/4 cup sugar
    1/4 cup eggnog
      3 tablespoons all-purpose flour
      2 tablespoons maple syrup
    1/2 teaspoon *each* ground ginger, cinnamon and nutmeg
      3 eggs, lightly beaten
TOPPING:
      1 cup (8 ounces) sour cream
      3 tablespoons sugar
    1/4 teaspoon vanilla extract
    1/4 cup sliced almonds

In a small bowl, combine graham cracker crumbs, almonds, sugar and pumpkin pie spice; stir in butter. Press onto the bottom of greased 9-in. springform pan. Place on a baking sheet. Bake at 325° for 10 minutes.

Cool on a wire rack.

In a large mixing bowl, beat cream cheese, pumpkin, sugar, eggnog, flour, syrup and spices until smooth. Add eggs; beat on low speed just until combined. Pour into crust. Place pan on a double thickness of heavy-duty foil (about 16 in. square); securely wrap foil around pan. Place in a large baking pan; add 1 in. of hot water to larger pan. Bake at 325° for 55-60 minutes or until center is just set.

In a small bowl, combine sour cream, sugar and vanilla. Spread over hot cheesecake. Sprinkle with almonds. Bake 15-18 minutes longer or until topping is set. Remove pan from water bath. Cool on a wire rack for 10 minutes. Carefully run a knife around edge of pan to loosen; cool 1 hour longer. Refrigerate overnight. Remove sides of pan. **Yield:** 12 servings.

Editor's Note: This recipe was tested with commercially prepared eggnog.

Berry Cheesecake Dessert

(Pictured on page 134)

Prep: 45 min.   **Bake:** 40 min. + chilling

My aunt tasted this classic dessert on a business trip at least 40 years ago and brought the recipe back to share with the family.   —*Jo Nunnally, Ripley, Mississippi*

  2-1/4 cups graham cracker crumbs
    1/2 cup butter, melted
      2 packages (8 ounces *each*) cream cheese, softened
      1 cup sugar
      3 eggs
      2 cups (16 ounces) sour cream
      1 package (3 ounces) strawberry gelatin
      1 cup boiling water
    3/4 cup cold water
      1 quart fresh strawberries, sliced

In a bowl, combine the cracker crumbs and butter. Press onto the bottom and 1 in. up the sides of a greased 13-in. x 9-in. x 2-in. baking dish. In a large mixing bowl, beat cream cheese and sugar until smooth. Add eggs; beat on low speed just until combined. Pour into the crust.

Bake at 350° for 30-35 minutes or until the center is almost set. Carefully spread sour cream over the top. Bake 10 minutes longer. Cool on a wire rack.

Meanwhile, in a small bowl, dissolve gelatin in boiling water. Stir in cold water. Refrigerate for 45 minutes or until thickened but not set.

Carefully pour a third of the gelatin over sour cream layer. Arrange strawberries over gelatin; pour remaining gelatin over berries. Cover and refrigerate for 4 hours or until set. **Yield:** 12-15 servings.

Chocolate Almond Ice Cream

Prep: 20 min. + chilling   **Freeze:** 30 min.

It wouldn't be the Fourth of July for our family without this special treat. Even though electric models make it easier, I still prefer to hand-crank ice cream.   —Alice Hicken
Heber City, Utah

- 2 **envelopes unflavored gelatin**
- 6 **tablespoons cold water**
- 3 **cups milk**
- 3 **cups sugar**
- 1/4 **teaspoon salt**
- 3 **eggs, lightly beaten**
- 6 to 7 **squares (1 ounce *each*) unsweetened chocolate, melted**
- 4 **cups heavy whipping cream**
- 2 **teaspoons vanilla extract**
- 1 **cup sliced *or* slivered almonds, toasted**

In a small bowl, sprinkle gelatin over cold water; let stand for at least 2 minutes. In a large heavy saucepan, heat milk to 175°; stir in sugar and salt. Cook and stir over medium heat until sugar is dissolved. Pour a small amount of hot mixture into eggs. Return all to the pan, whisking constantly. Cook and stir over medium-low heat until mixture reaches at least 160° and coats the back of a metal spoon.

Remove from the heat. Stir in gelatin mixture until dissolved; stir in chocolate until blended. Cool quickly by placing pan in a bowl of ice water; stir for 2 minutes. Stir in cream and vanilla. Press plastic wrap onto surface of custard. Refrigerate for several hours or overnight.

Fill cylinder of ice cream freezer two-thirds full with chilled custard; freeze according to manufacturer's directions. Stir in the toasted almonds.

Refrigerate remaining mixture until ready to freeze. Allow to ripen in refrigerator freezer for 2-4 hours before serving. **Yield:** 2-1/2 quarts.

Apple Turnovers

(Pictured above right)

Prep: 25 min.   **Bake:** 15 min.

I had a package of puff pastry in my freezer and mentioned to a friend that I'd like to make apple turnovers. She shared a recipe that I adapted for the puff pastry. The turnovers were a hit.   —Coleen Cavallaro, Oak Hill, New York

- 1/3 **cup sugar**
- 1 **tablespoon all-purpose flour**
- 1/2 **teaspoon ground cinnamon**
- 4 **cups chopped peeled apples**
- 1 **package (17.3 ounces) frozen puff pastry, thawed**

TOPPING:
- 3 **tablespoons butter, melted**
- 2 **tablespoons sugar**
- 1/4 **teaspoon ground cinnamon**

Vanilla ice cream, optional

In a large bowl, combine the sugar, flour and cinnamon; add apples and toss to coat. On a lightly floured surface, roll out each pastry sheet into a 12-in. square. Cut each into four squares. Spoon 1/2 cup apple mixture into the center of each square; fold diagonally in half and press edges to seal. Place on a parchment paper-lined baking sheet.

In a small bowl, combine the butter, sugar and cinnamon; brush over pastry. Bake at 400° for 12-16 minutes or until golden brown. Serve warm with ice cream if desired. **Yield:** 8 servings.

Simply Cinnamon

One of the oldest spices known to man, cinnamon is a common ingredient when it comes to baking. This fragrant spice gives pastries such as Apple Turnovers (recipe at left), as well as fruit pies, puddings, coffee cakes, rolls and other baked goods, a sweet-spicy flavor. A cinnamon quill, or stick, adds a woodsy touch to apple cider and other beverages.

Cinnamon also spruces up savory dishes, particularly ethnic fare such as Middle Eastern lamb and Indian curries. And it's found in many spice blends, including Chinese five-spice.

Try sprinkling cinnamon on your favorite fruit dish or chocolate dessert. Or, create a delicious pilaf by cooking rice in cinnamon and adding toasted nuts and dried fruit.

Potluck Pleasers

You're sure to bring home an empty dish, pan or bowl when you present one of these crowd-favorite main dishes, sides, salads, appetizers or desserts at your next get-together.

WOW THE CROWD. Clockwise from upper left: Meat 'n' Cheese Stromboli (p. 160), Walnut Corn Dip (p. 160), Olive Floret Salad (p. 160), Raisin Carrot Cake (p. 160), Creamed Potato Casseroles (p. 159), Friendship Coffee Cakes (p. 163), Summertime Barbecue Sauce (p. 169) and Roasted Asparagus Lasagna (p. 158).

onto a floured surface; knead until smooth and elastic, about 6-8 minutes. Place in a greased bowl; turn once to grease top. Cover and let rise in a warm place until doubled, about 45 minutes.

Punch dough down; roll into a 14-in. circle. Transfer to a well-greased 10-in. ovenproof skillet, letting dough drape over the side. Combine the mozzarella, Swiss and cheddar cheeses; sprinkle 1 cup over dough. Set remaining cheese mixture aside.

In a large skillet, saute green peppers, onions and herbs in oil until tender. Spoon half of vegetables over cheese. Layer with half of the Parmesan cheese and tomatoes. Sprinkle with 2 cups of the reserved cheese mixture. Layer with the remaining vegetables, Parmesan cheese and tomatoes.

Fold crust over filling toward center of skillet to form an edge. Bake at 400° for 30 minutes. Sprinkle with pepperoni and remaining cheese mixture. Bake 5 minutes longer or until crust is golden brown. Let stand for 10 minutes before slicing. **Yield:** 12 servings.

Deep-Dish Pizza

(Pictured above)

Prep: 20 min. + rising   **Bake:** 35 min. + standing

What's a party without pizza? This deep-dish delight is loaded with pepperoni, cheese and other favorite pizza toppings.   —Jane Shapton, Tustin, California

    1 **package (1/4 ounce) active dry yeast**
2/3 **cup warm water (110° to 115°)**
    1 **cup all-purpose flour**
1/4 **cup vegetable oil**
    1 **cup whole wheat flour**
    1 **tablespoon** *each* **minced fresh basil, oregano and marjoram**
    1 **teaspoon garlic powder**
    1 **teaspoon salt**
TOPPING:
    2 **cups (8 ounces) shredded part-skim mozzarella cheese**
    1 **cup (4 ounces) shredded Swiss cheese**
    1 **cup (4 ounces) shredded cheddar cheese**
    2 **large green peppers, chopped**
1-1/2 **cups chopped onions**
    1 **tablespoon** *each* **minced fresh basil, oregano and marjoram**
    1 **tablespoon vegetable oil**
    1 **cup (4 ounces) shredded Parmesan cheese**
    8 **plum tomatoes, seeded and chopped**
    1 **package (3 ounces) sliced pepperoni**

In a large mixing bowl, dissolve yeast in warm water. Add all-purpose flour and oil; beat until smooth. Add whole wheat flour, herbs, garlic powder and salt. Turn

Spicy Ranch Chicken Wings

(Pictured below)

Prep: 20 min. + marinating   **Bake:** 40 min.

My mother gave me this recipe more than 10 years ago. Since then, I've made these lip-smacking wings for all different occasions.   —Tracy Peters, Corinth, Mississippi

    4 **pounds whole chicken wings**
3/4 **cup hot pepper sauce**
1/4 **cup butter, melted**
    3 **tablespoons cider vinegar**
    1 **envelope ranch salad dressing mix**
1/2 **teaspoon paprika**

mallows. Bake 1-2 minutes longer or until marshmallows are soft but not browned. Sprinkle with cherries. Cool on a wire rack.

In a microwave-safe bowl, melt chocolate chips and cream; stir until smooth. Drizzle over brownies. Let stand until chocolate is set. **Yield:** 2 dozen.

Odds 'n' Ends Snack Mix

(Pictured below)

Prep: 10 min.   **Bake:** 1 hour + cooling

Cayenne pepper packs some punch in this crunchy blend of cereal, crackers, pretzels and nuts. Although it makes a big batch, you might end up having to make more!
　　　　　　　　　—*Terry Kuehn, Waunakee, Wisconsin*

> 4 cups Corn Chex
> 4 cups Rice Chex
> 4 cups Wheat Chex
> 1 package (10 ounces) pretzel sticks
> 2 cups dry roasted peanuts
> 1 package (6 ounces) miniature fish-shaped crackers
> 1 cup butter, melted
> 1/4 cup Worcestershire sauce
> 1 teaspoon seasoned salt
> 1/8 to 1/4 teaspoon cayenne pepper

In a large bowl, combine the first six ingredients. In a small bowl, combine the butter, Worcestershire sauce, seasoned salt and cayenne; pour over cereal mixture and stir to coat.

Spread into two greased 15-in. x 10-in. x 1-in. baking pans. Bake at 300° for 1 hour, stirring every 15 minutes. Spread on paper towels to cool. Store in airtight containers. **Yield:** about 4 quarts.

Cut the chicken wings into three sections; discard wing tip sections. In a gallon-size resealable plastic bag, combine the hot pepper sauce, butter and vinegar. Add chicken wings; seal bag and toss to coat evenly. Refrigerate for 4-8 hours.

Place chicken on racks in two greased 15-in. x 10-in. x 1-in. baking pans. Sprinkle with dressing mix and paprika. Bake, uncovered, at 350° for 40-50 minutes or until juices run clear. **Yield:** about 4 dozen.

Editor's Note: 3 pounds of uncooked chicken wing sections (wingettes) may be substituted for the whole chicken wings. Omit the first step.

Chocolate-Covered Cherry Brownies

(Pictured above)

Prep: 20 min.   **Bake:** 30 min. + cooling

Prefer sweet to salty? Top these chewy from-scratch brownies with mini marshmallows, maraschino cherries and a chocolate drizzle.　　　—*Susan Myers, Dublin, Ohio*

> 2 cups sugar
> 1 cup butter, melted
> 4 eggs
> 1 cup all-purpose flour
> 1 cup baking cocoa
> 2 teaspoons baking powder
> 1/2 teaspoon salt
> 2 cups miniature marshmallows
> 1 jar (10 ounces) maraschino cherries, chopped and well drained
> 1/2 cup semisweet chocolate chips
> 1 to 2 tablespoons heavy whipping cream

In a large mixing bowl, combine the sugar and butter. Beat in eggs. Combine the flour, cocoa, baking powder and salt; add to egg mixture and beat until smooth.

Pour into a greased 13-in. x 9-in. x 2-in. baking pan. Bake at 350° for 28 minutes. Sprinkle with marsh-

Peppery Roast Beef

(Pictured below)

Prep: 5 min. **Bake:** 2-1/2 hours + standing

With its spicy coating and creamy horseradish sauce, this tender roast is sure to be the star of any meal, whether it's a sit-down dinner or serve-yourself potluck.
—*Maureen Brand, Somers, Iowa*

- 1 tablespoon olive oil
- 1 tablespoon seasoned pepper
- 2 garlic cloves, minced
- 1/2 teaspoon dried thyme
- 1/4 teaspoon salt
- 1 boneless beef eye round roast (4 to 5 pounds)

HORSERADISH SAUCE:
- 1 cup (8 ounces) sour cream
- 2 tablespoons lemon juice
- 2 tablespoons milk
- 2 tablespoons prepared horseradish
- 1 tablespoon Dijon mustard
- 1/4 teaspoon salt
- 1/8 teaspoon pepper

In a small bowl, combine the oil, seasoned pepper, garlic, thyme and salt; rub over roast. Place fat side up on a rack in a shallow roasting pan. Bake, uncovered, at 325° for 2-1/2 to 3 hours or until meat reaches desired doneness (for medium-rare, a meat thermometer should read 145°; medium, 160°; well-done, 170°). Let stand for 10 minutes before slicing.

In a small bowl, combine the sauce ingredients. Serve with roast. **Yield:** 10-12 servings.

Onions Neptune

(Pictured above)

Prep: 20 min. **Bake:** 35 min.

I present this dish as an appetizer and often add whatever ingredients I have handy, such as mushrooms or sun-dried tomatoes. —*Todd Noon, Galloway, New Jersey*

- 5 to 6 medium sweet onions, sliced and separated into rings
- 1/2 cup butter, softened, *divided*
- 2 cans (6 ounces *each*) lump crabmeat, drained, *divided*
- 3 cups (12 ounces) shredded Swiss cheese
- 1 can (10-3/4 ounces) condensed cream of mushroom soup, undiluted
- 1/2 cup evaporated milk
- 1/2 teaspoon salt
- 1/4 teaspoon pepper
- 12 to 16 slices French bread (1/4 inch thick)

In a large skillet, saute onions in 1/4 cup butter until tender. Remove from the heat; gently stir in half of the crab. Spread into a greased 13-in. x 9-in. x 2-in. baking dish. Top with remaining crab. Combine the cheese, soup, milk, salt and pepper; spoon over crab.

Spread remaining butter over one side of each slice of bread; place buttered side up over casserole. Bake, uncovered, at 350° for 35-45 minutes or until golden brown. **Yield:** 12 servings.

Blue Cheese Spinach Salad

(Pictured below)

Prep/Total Time: 15 min.

A simple dressing made of currant jelly and balsamic vinegar coats this colorful salad, sprinkled with crunchy pine nuts. If you like blue cheese, you'll love this refreshing toss.
—*Grace Sandvigen, Rochester, New York*

- 1/2 **cup red currant jelly**
- 3 **tablespoons balsamic vinegar**
- 6 **cups fresh baby spinach**
- 2 **pints fresh strawberries, quartered**
- 1 **cup mandarin oranges, drained**
- 1/2 **medium red onion, thinly sliced**
- 1/2 **cup crumbled blue cheese**
- 1/2 **cup pine nuts, toasted**

For dressing, heat jelly in a small saucepan over low heat, stirring until smooth. Remove from the heat; stir in the vinegar. In a large bowl, combine the spinach, strawberries, oranges, onion and blue cheese. Drizzle with dressing and toss to coat. Sprinkle with pine nuts. Serve immediately. **Yield:** 12 servings.

Strawberry Tunnel Cake

(Pictured above)

Prep: 25 min. **Bake:** 45 min. + chilling

My son doesn't care for traditional birthday cakes and always asks for something with strawberries for the occasion. I hit the jackpot when I dreamed up this delicious cake with a "surprise" inside.
—*Janis Borstad Ponsford, Minnesota*

- 1 **package (16 ounces) angel food cake mix**
- 2 **packages (3 ounces *each*) cream cheese, softened**
- 1 **can (14 ounces) sweetened condensed milk**
- 1/3 **cup lemon juice**
- 1/4 **teaspoon almond extract, optional**
- 6 **drops red food coloring, optional**
- 1 **cup sliced fresh strawberries**
- 1 **carton (12 ounces) frozen whipped topping, thawed, *divided***

Prepare, bake and cool cake according to package directions. Slice the top fourth off the cake; set aside. To make tunnel, use a sharp knife to carefully hollow out bottom of cake, leaving a 1/2-in. shell. Tear removed cake into 1-in. cubes.

In a large mixing bowl, beat the cream cheese until fluffy. Beat in milk and lemon juice until smooth. Stir in extract and food coloring if desired. Stir in cake cubes and strawberries. Fold in 1 cup whipped topping. Spoon into tunnel; replace cake top. Spread remaining whipped topping over top and sides of cake. Refrigerate for 4 hours or overnight. **Yield:** 12-16 servings.

Antipasto Salad

(Pictured above)

Prep: 1 hour + marinating

This colorful salad is popular at any gathering. Guests like the homemade, from-scratch dressing, which is a nice change from bottled Italian. —Linda Harrington
Hudson, New Hampshire

- 2 **packages (1 pound** *each***) spiral pasta**
- 4 **cups chopped green peppers**
- 4 **cups chopped seeded tomatoes**
- 2 **cans (15 ounces** *each***) garbanzo beans** *or* **chickpeas, rinsed and drained**
- 3 **cups chopped onions**
- 1 **pound thinly sliced Genoa salami, julienned**
- 1 **pound sliced pepperoni, julienned**
- 1/2 **pound provolone cheese, cubed**
- 1 **cup pitted ripe olives, halved**
- 1-1/2 **cups olive oil**
- 1 **cup red wine vinegar**
- 1/2 **cup sugar**
- 2 **tablespoons dried oregano**
- 2 **teaspoons salt**
- 1 **teaspoon pepper**

Cook pasta according to package directions. Drain and rinse in cold water. In large bowls, combine the pasta, green peppers, tomatoes, beans, onions, salami, pepperoni, cheese and olives.

In a bowl, whisk the oil, vinegar, sugar, oregano, salt and pepper. Pour over pasta salad and toss to coat. Cover and refrigerate for 4 hours or overnight. **Yield:** 50 (3/4-cup) servings.

Lemon-Pecan Pork Chops

(Pictured below)

Prep/Total Time: 30 min.

Quick to prepare, this main dish also has an unforgettable taste. I accent the chops with a side of garlic mashed potatoes and sweet peas or a mix of vegetables.
—Katie Sloan, Charlotte, North Carolina

- 4 **boneless pork loin chops (7 ounces** *each***)**
- 1 **teaspoon lemon-pepper seasoning**
- 1/2 **teaspoon garlic salt**
- 1 **tablespoon butter**
- 1 **cup chopped pecans**
- 1/4 **cup lemon juice**

Sprinkle pork chops with lemon-pepper and garlic salt. In a large skillet over medium heat, cook chops in butter for 8-10 minutes on each side or until juices run clear. Remove and keep warm.

Add the pecans and lemon juice to the skillet; cook and stir for 1 minute or until heated through. Spoon over pork chops. **Yield:** 4 servings.

Sweet Potato Yeast Bread

(Pictured above right)

Prep: 25 min. + rising   **Bake:** 40 min. + cooling

I think this is the most delicious bread you can serve. Even sweet potato-haters love it. Don't expect leftovers!
—Mary Detweiler, West Farmington, Ohio

Cocoa for a Crowd

(Pictured below)

Prep/Total Time: 15 min.

Gather 'round the fireplace with this rich, satisfying cocoa. It's the perfect warm-you-up beverage for any winter get-together.   —*Julia Livingston, Frostproof, Florida*

> 5 **cups baking cocoa**
> 3 **cups sugar**
> 2 **teaspoons salt**
> 5 **quarts water,** *divided*
> 10 **quarts milk**
> 1 **quart heavy whipping cream**
> 2 **tablespoons vanilla extract**
> **Whipped cream and additional baking cocoa**

In each of two large stockpots, combine 2-1/2 cups cocoa, 1-1/2 cups sugar and 1 teaspoon salt. Gradually stir 5 cups water into each pot. Bring to a boil; reduce heat. Whisk in the milk, cream and remaining water; heat through. Remove from the heat; stir in vanilla. Garnish with whipped cream and additional cocoa. **Yield:** 65 (1-cup) servings.

> 2 **packages (1/4 ounce** *each*) **active dry yeast**
> 1-3/4 **cups warm water (110° to 115°)**
> 1 **cup mashed sweet potatoes (without added milk** *or* **butter)**
> 1/2 **cup plus 1 tablespoon butter, softened,** *divided*
> 1/2 **cup honey**
> 1 **egg**
> 2 **teaspoons salt**
> 3 **cups whole wheat flour**
> 3-1/4 **to 3-1/2 cups all-purpose flour**
> **CREAM CHEESE NUT SPREAD:**
> 1 **cup butter, softened**
> 1 **package (8 ounces) cream cheese, softened**
> 1/3 **cup finely chopped walnuts, toasted**

In a large mixing bowl, dissolve yeast in warm water. Add sweet potatoes, 1/2 cup butter, honey, egg, salt and whole wheat flour. Beat until smooth. Stir in enough all-purpose flour to form a soft dough.

Turn onto a floured surface; knead until smooth and elastic, about 6-8 minutes. Place in a greased bowl, turning once to grease top. Cover and let rise in a warm place until doubled, about 1 hour.

Punch dough down. Turn onto a lightly floured surface; divide in half. Shape into loaves. Place in two greased 9-in. x 5-in. x 3-in. loaf pans. Cover; let rise until doubled, about 25 minutes. Bake at 375° for 40-45 minutes or until golden brown (cover loosely with foil if top browns too quickly). Remove from pans to wire racks. Melt remaining butter; brush over warm bread. Cool.

In a small mixing bowl, beat butter and cream cheese until fluffy. Stir in walnuts. Serve with bread. **Yield:** 2 loaves.

Sausage-Mushroom Breakfast Bake

(Pictured below)

Prep: 25 min. **Bake:** 50 min. + standing

My mom shared this delicious recipe when I needed to bring a dish to a breakfast potluck. Everyone loved the flavorful sausage, mushrooms, cheese and tomatoes.
—*Diane Babbitt, Ludlow, Massachusetts*

- 1 pound bulk pork sausage
- 2 cups sliced fresh mushrooms
- 6 cups cubed bread
- 2 cups (8 ounces) shredded sharp cheddar cheese
- 1 cup chopped fresh tomatoes
- 10 eggs, lightly beaten
- 3 cups milk
- 2 teaspoons ground mustard
- 1/2 teaspoon salt
- 1/4 teaspoon pepper

In a large skillet, cook sausage and mushrooms over medium heat until meat is no longer pink; drain. Place half of the bread cubes in a greased 13-in. x 9-in. x 2-in. baking dish; top with 2 cups sausage mixture and half of the cheese and tomatoes. Repeat layers. In a large bowl, combine the eggs, milk, mustard, salt and pepper; pour over bread mixture.

Bake, uncovered, at 350° for 50-55 minutes or until a knife inserted near center comes out clean. Let stand for 10 minutes before serving. **Yield:** 12 servings.

Cheddar-Ham Oven Omelet

(Pictured above)

Prep: 15 min. **Bake:** 40 min. + standing

We had a family reunion for 50 relatives from the U.S. and Canada, and it took four pans of this hearty, five-ingredient omelet to feed the crowd. Fresh fruit and an assortment of muffins helped round out our brunch menu.
—*Betty Abrey, Imperial, Saskatchewan*

- 16 eggs
- 2 cups milk
- 2 cups (8 ounces) shredded cheddar cheese
- 3/4 cup cubed fully cooked ham
- 6 green onions, chopped

In a large bowl, beat eggs and milk. Stir in the cheese, ham and onions. Pour the egg mixture into a greased 13-in. x 9-in. x 2-in. baking dish.

Bake, uncovered, at 350° for 40-45 minutes or until a knife inserted near the center comes out clean. Let stand for 10 minutes before cutting. **Yield:** 12 servings.

Cherry Ribbon Salad

(Pictured below)

Prep: 10 min. + chilling

Filled with pineapple, pecans and cherry pie filling, this colorful salad mold brings fun, fruity flavor to any potluck menu. —Virginia Luke, Red Level, Alabama

- 1 package (3 ounces) cherry gelatin
- 2-1/4 cups boiling water, *divided*
- 1 can (21 ounces) cherry pie filling
- 1 package (3 ounces) orange gelatin
- 1 can (8 ounces) crushed pineapple, undrained
- 1 cup whipped topping
- 1/3 cup mayonnaise
- 1/4 cup chopped pecans, optional

In a bowl, dissolve cherry gelatin in 1-1/4 cups boiling water. Stir in pie filling. Pour into a 7-cup ring mold coated with nonstick cooking spray; refrigerate until set but not firm, about 1 hour.

Meanwhile, in a bowl, dissolve orange gelatin in remaining boiling water. Stir in pineapple. Chill until thickened but not set, about 1 hour.

Combine the whipped topping, mayonnaise and pecans if desired; fold into orange mixture. Spoon over cherry layer. Refrigerate for at least 1 hour or until firm. Unmold onto a serving plate. **Yield:** 12 servings.

Party Meatballs

(Pictured above)

Prep: 30 min. **Bake:** 1 hour

We served this scrumptious dish at our wedding. It went over so well that it's been served at other weddings and family functions, and the requests keep coming! —Stefany Blevins, Portsmouth, Ohio

- 2 eggs, beaten
- 1 can (12 ounces) evaporated milk
- 2 cups quick-cooking oats
- 1 cup finely chopped onion
- 2 teaspoons salt
- 2 teaspoons chili powder
- 1/2 teaspoon garlic powder
- 1/2 teaspoon pepper
- 3 pounds ground beef

SAUCE:
- 2 cups ketchup
- 1-1/2 cups packed brown sugar
- 1/2 cup chopped onion

In a large bowl, combine the first eight ingredients. Crumble beef over mixture and mix well. Shape into 1-in. balls. Place in three greased 13-in. x 9-in. x 2-in. baking dishes.

Combine the sauce ingredients; pour over meatballs. Bake, uncovered, at 325° for 1 hour or until meat is no longer pink. **Yield:** about 7 dozen.

1-1/4 teaspoons salt
1/2 teaspoon pepper
6 eggs, beaten

In a soup kettle, combine first seven ingredients. Bring to a boil. Reduce heat. Cover; simmer for 1-1/2 to 2 hours or until chicken is tender.

Remove chicken from broth. When cool enough to handle, remove meat from bones; dice and set aside. Strain broth and skim fat; discard onion, celery and bay leaf. Set aside 6 cups broth for sauce.

In a bowl, combine stuffing cubes, parsley and sage. Saute celery and onion in butter until tender. Add to stuffing mixture. Mix well; set aside.

In a large saucepan, melt butter. Whisk in flour, salt and pepper until smooth. Gradually add reserved broth; bring to a boil. Reduce heat; cook and stir for 2 minutes. Remove from the heat. Stir a small amount into eggs; return all to the pan, stirring constantly. Bring to a gentle boil; cook and stir 2 minutes longer.

In a greased 13-in. x 9-in. x 2-in. baking dish, layer half of the chicken, stuffing and sauce. Repeat layers. Cover; bake at 350° for 45 minutes. Uncover; bake 15-20 minutes longer or until a knife comes out clean. **Yield:** 12 servings.

Comforting Chicken Casserole

(Pictured above)

Prep: 1-3/4 hours + cooling **Bake:** 1 hour

If you're looking for a dish that's sure to satisfy a crowd, you can't beat this hearty casserole, with layers of chicken and stuffing. —Pat Price Cook, Mission Viejo, California

    1 broiler/fryer chicken (3 to 4 pounds)
    3 quarts water
    1 large onion, chopped
    2 celery ribs, coarsely chopped
    1 bay leaf
    1/2 teaspoon salt
    1/4 teaspoon pepper
STUFFING:
    6 cups unseasoned stuffing cubes
    1 tablespoon dried parsley flakes
    1/2 teaspoon rubbed sage
    1/2 cup chopped celery
    2 tablespoons chopped onion
    2 tablespoons butter
SAUCE:
    1/2 cup butter, cubed
    3/4 cup all-purpose flour

Roasted Asparagus Lasagna

(Pictured on page 148)

Prep: 20 min. **Bake:** 45 min. + standing

My husband is a "meat and potatoes" kind of guy, so the first time I made this meatless recipe, he was not thrilled. Once he tried it, he was hooked. Now he asks me to prepare it often.   —Cindy Macha, Richmond, Texas

    2 pounds fresh asparagus, trimmed and cut
        into 1-inch pieces
    1 cup sliced fresh mushrooms
    2 tablespoons olive oil, *divided*
    2 tablespoons butter
    3 tablespoons all-purpose flour
    1/4 teaspoon salt
    1/8 teaspoon white pepper
Dash ground cloves
 1-1/2 cups milk
    1 cup thinly sliced red onion
    2 garlic cloves, minced
    12 lasagna noodles, cooked and drained
 1-1/2 cups (6 ounces) shredded part-skim
        mozzarella cheese
    3/4 cup grated Parmesan cheese

Place asparagus and mushrooms in a shallow roasting pan. Drizzle with 1 tablespoon oil; toss to coat. Bake at 450° for 8-10 minutes or until the vegetables are browned; set aside. Reduce heat to 350°.

In a large saucepan, melt butter. Stir in flour, salt, pepper and cloves until smooth. Gradually stir in milk. Bring to a boil; cook and stir for 2 minutes or until thickened. Set aside. In a large skillet, saute onion and garlic in remaining oil until tender. Remove from heat; add roasted asparagus and mushrooms.

In a greased 13-in. x 9-in. x 2-in. baking dish, layer four noodles, a third of the asparagus mixture, a third of the white sauce, 1/2 cup mozzarella cheese and 1/4 cup Parmesan cheese. Repeat layers twice.

Cover and bake at 350° for 35 minutes. Uncover; bake 10-15 minutes longer or until heated through. Let stand for 15 minutes before cutting. **Yield:** 12 servings.

Creamed Potato Casseroles

(Pictured on page 148)

Prep: 1-1/4 hours **Bake:** 40 min.

This classic potato dish makes enough for 24 hungry people. Guests remark on its rich, creamy sauce and buttery crumb topping. —Norma Harder, Melfort, Saskatchewan

- 10 **pounds medium potatoes (about 30)**
- 2/3 **cup plus 3 tablespoons butter, *divided***
- 2/3 **cup all-purpose flour**
- 5 **cups chicken broth**
- 5 **cups half-and-half cream**
- 8 **egg yolks, lightly beaten**
- 1-1/2 **cups minced fresh parsley**
- 3 **teaspoons salt**
- 3/4 **teaspoon pepper**
- 1/4 **teaspoon cayenne pepper**
- 1 **cup seasoned bread crumbs**

Place potatoes in a large stockpot or soup kettle; cover with water. Bring to a boil. Reduce heat; cover and simmer for 20 minutes or until just tender. Drain and rinse in cold water. When cool enough to handle, peel potatoes and cut into 1/4-in. slices; set aside.

In a large saucepan, melt 2/3 cup butter. Stir in flour until smooth; gradually add broth and cream. Bring to a boil; cook and stir for 2 minutes or until thickened. Remove from the heat. Stir 1 cup hot cream mixture into egg yolks; return all to the pan, stirring constantly. Add the parsley, salt, pepper and cayenne. Bring to a gentle boil; cook and stir 2 minutes longer. Remove from the heat.

Spread 1 cup sauce into each of two 3-qt. baking dishes. Top with a third of the potato slices. Repeat layers twice. Spread with remaining sauce. Melt remaining butter; toss with bread crumbs. Sprinkle over casseroles. Bake, uncovered, at 375° for 40-45 minutes or until bubbly. **Yield:** 2 casseroles (12 servings each).

Family Picnic Salad

(Pictured below)

Prep/Total Time: 20 min.

The bountiful potluck at our annual family reunion includes favorites such as this salad. You can substitute Italian dressing or another type to give this dish a twist.
—Barb Hausey, Independence, Missouri

- 1 **can (16 ounces) kidney beans, rinsed and drained**
- 1 **can (15 ounces) white *or* shoepeg corn, drained**
- 1 **large zucchini, chopped**
- 1 **medium cucumber, chopped**
- 1 **large tomato, chopped**
- 1 **large green pepper, chopped**
- 1 **medium red onion, chopped**
- 6 **green onions, chopped**
- 1 **can (3.8 ounces) sliced ripe olives, drained**
- 1 **cup Catalina salad dressing**
- 1-1/2 **cups (6 ounces) shredded cheddar cheese**
- 1-1/2 **cups corn chips**

In a large salad bowl, combine the first nine ingredients. Drizzle with dressing and toss to coat evenly. Stir in cheese and corn chips. Serve immediately. **Yield:** 10 servings.

Meat 'n' Cheese Stromboli

(Pictured at far right and on page 148)

Prep: 25 min.   **Bake:** 15 min.

This Italian-style sandwich can be served warm or at room temperature, and it heats up nicely in the microwave.
—*Sue Shea, Defiance, Ohio*

- 1 medium onion, sliced and separated into rings
- 1 medium green pepper, sliced into rings
- 1 tablespoon butter
- 2 loaves (16 ounces *each*) frozen bread dough, thawed
- 1/2 pound thinly sliced hard salami
- 1/2 pound thinly sliced deli ham
- 1/2 pound sliced mozzarella cheese
- 1/2 pound sliced mild cheddar cheese
- 1/2 teaspoon Italian seasoning
- 1/4 teaspoon garlic powder
- 1/8 teaspoon pepper
- 1 egg, beaten
- 1 teaspoon poppy seeds

In a large skillet, saute onion and green pepper in butter until crisp-tender; set aside.

On two greased baking sheets, roll each loaf of dough into a 15-in. x 12-in. rectangle. Arrange the salami, ham and cheeses lengthwise over half of each rectangle to within 1/2 in. of edges. Top with onion mixture; sprinkle with Italian seasoning, garlic powder and pepper. Fold dough over filling; pinch edges to seal well.

Brush with the egg and sprinkle with poppy seeds. Bake at 400° for 15-20 minutes or until golden brown. Cool loaves for 5 minutes before slicing. **Yield:** 2 loaves (8 servings each).

Walnut Corn Dip

(Pictured at far right and on page 148)

Prep/Total Time: 15 min.

The walnuts in this recipe complement the Southwestern flavor of the creamy dip. It goes great with tortilla chips, crackers or carrot sticks.   —*Mavis Diment, Marcus, Iowa*

- 2 packages (8 ounces *each*) cream cheese, softened
- 1/4 cup lime juice
- 2 to 3 teaspoons ground cumin
- 1/2 to 1 teaspoon cayenne pepper
- 1/2 teaspoon salt
- Dash pepper
- 1 can (8-3/4 ounces) whole kernel corn, drained
- 1 cup chopped walnuts, toasted
- 1/3 cup finely chopped onion
- Tortilla chips

In a small mixing bowl, combine the cream cheese, lime juice, cumin, cayenne, salt and pepper. Stir in the corn, walnuts and onion. Refrigerate until serving. Serve with tortilla chips. **Yield:** 3 cups.

Olive Floret Salad

(Pictured at right and on page 148)

Prep: 20 min. + chilling

I'm retired from a large company but still work there when needed. When we have potlucks, everyone asks for this salad.   —*Joanne Flanigan, South Beloit, Illinois*

- 1 medium head cauliflower, cut into florets
- 1 bunch broccoli, cut into florets
- 2 cups cherry tomatoes
- 2 medium carrots, thinly sliced
- 1 can (6 ounces) pitted small ripe olives, drained
- 1 cup Italian salad dressing
- 1 envelope Italian salad dressing mix
- 1 cup (4 ounces) crumbled feta cheese

In a large bowl, combine the cauliflower, broccoli, tomatoes, carrots and olives. In a small bowl, combine the salad dressing and dressing mix; pour over vegetables and toss to coat. Cover and refrigerate overnight. Just before serving, toss again and sprinkle with feta cheese. **Yield:** 13 servings.

Raisin Carrot Cake

(Pictured at right and on page 148)

Prep: 15 min.   **Bake:** 55 min. + cooling

The room quiets down any time this scrumptious dessert is presented!   —*Ann Marie Vachon, London, Ontario*

- 1 cup raisins
- 2 cups all-purpose flour, *divided*
- 2 cups packed brown sugar
- 2 teaspoons baking powder
- 2 teaspoons ground cinnamon
- 1 teaspoon baking soda
- 1 teaspoon salt
- 3/4 cup vegetable oil
- 4 eggs
- 3 cups grated carrots
- FROSTING:
- 1 package (8 ounces) cream cheese, softened
- 1/2 cup butter, softened

A CROWD will gather fast when Raisin Carrot Cake, Walnut Corn Dip, Olive Floret Salad and Meat 'n' Cheese Stromboli (shown above) appear on the buffet table.

1 teaspoon orange juice
1 teaspoon vanilla extract
3-3/4 cups confectioners' sugar

Toss the raisins with 2 tablespoons flour; set aside. In a large mixing bowl, combine the brown sugar, baking powder, cinnamon, baking soda, salt and remaining flour. Add the oil and eggs; beat well. Stir in the carrots and reserved raisins.

Transfer to a greased 13-in. x 9-in. x 2-in. baking dish. Bake at 325° for 55-60 minutes or until a toothpick inserted near the center comes out clean. Cool on a wire rack.

For the frosting, in a large mixing bowl, beat the cream cheese and butter until smooth. Beat in orange juice and vanilla. Gradually add confectioners' sugar; beat until light and fluffy. Spread over cake. Store cake in the refrigerator. **Yield:** 12-16 servings.

Cover and bake at 350° for 1-1/4 hours. Uncover; bake 45 minutes longer or until meat is no longer pink and a meat thermometer reads 160°. Let stand for 10 minutes before slicing. **Yield:** 3 loaves.

Ed's Meat Loaves

(Pictured above)

Prep: 25 min.   **Bake:** 2 hours + standing

I've used this super recipe for years. Since it makes three loaves, I bake one and freeze the other two for later. That way, all I have to do is pull one out of the freezer, bake it and presto!...fresh meat loaf with no mixing.
        —*Edward Svercauski, San Diego, California*

>   5 **eggs, lightly beaten**
> 1-1/2 **cups water**
>   2 **tablespoons soy sauce**
>   2 **tablespoons steak sauce**
> 1-1/2 **cups seasoned bread crumbs**
>   1 **cup old-fashioned oats**
>   1 **jar (6 ounces) sliced mushrooms, drained**
>   1/4 **cup grated Parmesan cheese**
>   1 **envelope onion soup mix**
>   2 **tablespoons sweet pickle relish**
> 2-1/2 **teaspoons dried parsley flakes**
>   2 **teaspoons garlic powder**
>   2 **teaspoons pepper**
>   1 **teaspoon seasoned salt**
>   5 **pounds lean ground beef**

In a very large bowl, combine the first 14 ingredients. Crumble the ground beef over the mixture and mix well. Divide into thirds; shape into three loaves. Place on a rack in a large roasting pan.

Omelet Casseroles

(Pictured below)

Prep: 35 min.   **Bake:** 40 min.

Not only are these casseroles simple to make, but they're also perfect for a church breakfast or brunch for a crowd. You could substitute your favorite meat and cheese, if desired.   —*Renee Schwebach, Dumont, Minnesota*

>   1 **cup butter, melted**
>   100 **eggs**
> 2-1/2 **quarts milk**
> 1-1/4 **teaspoons white pepper**
> 7-1/2 **cups (30 ounces) shredded Swiss cheese**
> 7-1/2 **cups cubed fully cooked ham**

Divide the butter among five 13-in. x 9-in. x 2-in. baking dishes; set aside. In a large mixing bowl, beat 20 eggs, 2 cups milk and 1/4 teaspoon pepper until blended. Stir in 1-1/2 cups cheese and 1-1/2 cups ham; pour into one prepared dish. Repeat four times.

Bake, uncovered, at 350° for 40-45 minutes or until a knife inserted near the center comes out clean (cover with foil if the top browns too quickly). Let stand for 5 minutes before cutting. **Yield:** 60 servings.

Friendship Coffee Cakes

(Pictured at right and on page 148)

Prep: 35 min. + rising
Bake: 15 min. per batch + cooling

My family and friends always feel special when I bake this wreath-shaped bread for them. I even use the chocolate cream cheese filling as a surprise filling for cupcakes.
—*Marcia Sawatzky, Osgoode, Ontario*

14-1/2 to 15 cups all-purpose flour
    2 cups sugar
    1/4 cup active dry yeast
    4 teaspoons salt
    3 cups water
    1 cup orange juice
    1/2 cup vegetable oil
    4 eggs
    1/4 cup grated orange peel
    1 teaspoon orange extract
FILLING/ICING:
    1 package (8 ounces) cream cheese
    1/2 cup sugar
    1 cup semisweet chocolate chips, melted
      and cooled
    3 eggs
    1 teaspoon vanilla extract
    4 cups confectioners' sugar
    1 teaspoon orange extract
    6 tablespoons milk

In a very large mixing bowl, combine 8 cups flour, sugar, yeast and salt. In a large saucepan, heat water, orange juice and oil to 120°-130°. Add to dry ingredients; beat just until moistened. Beat in eggs, orange peel and extract. Stir in enough remaining flour to form a soft dough.

Turn onto a floured surface; knead until smooth and elastic. Place in a greased bowl, turning once to grease top. Cover and let rise in a warm place until doubled, about 1-1/2 hours.

In a small mixing bowl, beat cream cheese and sugar until smooth. Add chocolate chips, 1 egg and vanilla. Beat until blended; set aside.

Punch dough down. Turn onto a floured surface; divide into eight portions. Roll each into a 12-in. x 7-in. rectangle. Spread about 1/4 cup filling to within 1/2 in. of edges. Roll up each jelly-roll style, starting with a long side; pinch seams and tuck edges under. Place seam side down on greased baking sheets; pinch ends of each together to form a ring.

With scissors, cut from outside edge two-thirds of way toward center of ring at 2-in. intervals. Separate strips and twist so filling shows. Cover and let rise until doubled, about 30 minutes. Beat remaining eggs; brush over coffee cakes. Bake at 375° for 15-18 minutes or until golden. Remove from pans to wire racks;

cool. Combine remaining ingredients; drizzle over top.
Yield: 8 coffee cakes.

Hot Crab Hero

Prep: 15 min.　**Bake:** 20 min.

These cheesy sandwich slices make terrific appetizers, whether you're entertaining at home or taking a dish to a carry-in dinner.　—*Beverly Mix, Missoula, Montana*

    2 cans (6 ounces *each*) crabmeat, drained,
      flaked and cartilage removed
    1/2 cup mayonnaise
    1/4 cup minced fresh parsley
    1/4 cup sour cream
    1 tablespoon lemon juice
    1/2 teaspoon garlic powder
    1/8 teaspoon salt
    1 loaf (8 ounces) French bread
    2 tablespoons butter, softened
    4 slices Swiss cheese

In a large bowl, combine the first seven ingredients. Slice bread horizontally in half; spread cut sides with butter. Top with cheese; spread with crab mixture.

Place on an ungreased baking sheet. Bake at 350° for 20-25 minutes or until browned. **Yield:** 12-14 slices.

Romaine Salad with Avocado Dressing

(Pictured below)

Prep/Total Time: 25 min.

This colorful salad gets noticed quickly on a buffet table and doesn't disappoint. The crunchy corn chips are a nice change of pace from the usual salad croutons.
—*Sandra Forsyth, Edmonton, Alberta*

- 1 medium ripe avocado, peeled and cubed
- 1/2 cup mayonnaise
- 1/4 cup vegetable oil
- 3 tablespoons lemon juice
- 2 garlic cloves, peeled
- 1/2 teaspoon salt
- 1/4 teaspoon hot pepper sauce
- 1 bunch romaine, torn
- 3 medium tomatoes, cut into wedges
- 1 cup (4 ounces) shredded cheddar cheese
- 1 can (2-1/4 ounces) sliced ripe olives, drained
- 2 green onions, chopped

Corn chips

For the dressing, place the first seven ingredients in a blender or food processor; cover and process until blended.

In a large bowl, combine the romaine, tomatoes, cheddar cheese, olives and onions. Drizzle with the dressing and toss to coat. Sprinkle with the corn chips. **Yield:** 12 servings.

Vanilla Pudding Dessert

(Pictured above)

Prep/Total Time: 30 min.

So easy to prepare, this eye-catching dessert will go fast at potlucks...and everyone will want the recipe. If you like, try peaches, pineapple or bananas instead of the berries.
—*Betty Clemons, Hartselle, Alabama*

- 2-3/4 cups cold milk
- 1 package (5.1 ounces) instant vanilla pudding mix
- 1 can (14 ounces) sweetened condensed milk
- 1 carton (12 ounces) frozen whipped topping, thawed
- 4 cups crushed vanilla wafers
- 3 cups sliced fresh strawberries

In a large bowl, whisk milk and pudding mix for 2 minutes. Let stand for 15 minutes; fold in condensed milk. Set aside 1 tablespoon whipped topping and 2 tablespoons wafer crumbs. Fold remaining whipped topping into pudding.

In a 3-qt. serving bowl, layer a third of the strawberries, wafer crumbs and pudding mixture. Repeat layers twice. Sprinkle with reserved wafer crumbs; top with reserved whipped topping. Refrigerate until serving. **Yield:** 12-14 servings.

Mustard Coleslaw

(Pictured below)

Prep/Total Time: 25 min.

This is an outstanding coleslaw that gets a boost from cayenne and tastes great with just about any meal. I especially like serving it with barbecue pork sandwiches.
—*Janet Tigchelaar, Jerseyville, Ontario*

- 3/4 cup prepared mustard
- 3/4 cup cider vinegar
- 1/2 cup sour cream
- 1/2 cup ketchup
- 1/4 cup mayonnaise
- 1 tablespoon salt
- 1/2 teaspoon cayenne pepper
- 1-1/4 cups sugar
- 2 medium heads cabbage (about 4 pounds), shredded
- 1 medium onion, finely chopped
- 1 medium green pepper, chopped
- 1 large carrot, shredded
- 1 celery rib, finely chopped

For dressing, in a bowl, combine the mustard, vinegar, sour cream, ketchup, mayonnaise, salt and cayenne. Stir in the sugar.

In a large bowl, combine cabbage, onion, green pepper, carrot and celery. Add the desired amount of dressing and toss until well coated. Refrigerate until serving. Refrigerate any leftover dressing. Serve with a slotted spoon. **Yield:** 24 servings.

Salted Peanut Cookies

(Pictured above)

Prep: 25 min.   **Bake:** 10 min. per batch

Whenever I whip up a batch of these crunchy cookies, it seems my friends can smell the tempting aroma and they come running. —*Charleen Block, Hutchinson, Minnesota*

- 1-1/2 cups shortening
- 1 cup sugar
- 1 cup packed brown sugar
- 3 eggs
- 1 teaspoon vanilla extract
- 3-3/4 cups all-purpose flour
- 2 teaspoons baking soda
- 1 teaspoon salt
- 1-1/2 cups salted peanuts
- 1-1/2 cups semisweet chocolate chips

In a large mixing bowl, cream shortening and sugars. Add eggs, one at a time, beating well after each addition. Beat in vanilla. Combine the flour, baking soda and salt; gradually add to creamed mixture. Stir in peanuts and chocolate chips.

Drop by tablespoonfuls 2 in. apart onto greased baking sheets. Bake at 350° for 10-12 minutes or until lightly browned. Remove to wire racks. **Yield:** 10 dozen.

Drop Cookies

For even baking, Salted Peanut Cookies (recipe above) and other drop cookies should be made the same size. An ice cream scoop is a handy tool for making uniformly sized drop cookies. (A 1 tablespoon-size scoop will create a standard-size 2-in. cookie.) Just scoop the dough, then even off the top with a flat-edge metal spatula.

Cover and bake at 325° for 2-1/2 to 3 hours or until meat is tender. Remove roast; slice. Skim fat from cooking juices. Return meat to the pan; heat through. Serve on rolls. **Yield:** 12 servings.

Buttermilk Pancakes

(Pictured below)

Prep: 10 min.   **Cook:** 5 min. per batch

My mom's pancake recipe was a natural for the brunch we held at our family reunion. We made three batches and served the golden pancakes with a variety of toppings.
—*Betty Abrey, Imperial, Saskatchewan*

- 4 **cups all-purpose flour**
- 1/4 **cup sugar**
- 2 **teaspoons baking soda**
- 2 **teaspoons salt**
- 1-1/2 **teaspoons baking powder**
- 4 **eggs**
- 4 **cups buttermilk**

In a large bowl, combine the flour, sugar, baking soda, salt and baking powder. In another bowl, whisk the eggs and buttermilk until blended; stir into dry ingredients just until moistened.

Pour batter by 1/4 cupfuls onto a lightly greased hot griddle; turn when bubbles form on top. Cook until second side is golden brown. **Yield:** 2-1/2 dozen.

Barbecued Beef Sandwiches

(Pictured above)

Prep: 10 min.   **Bake:** 2-1/2 hours

I've been making this recipe for years, and it never fails to get big grins from family and guests. The meat is tender, and the sauce is tangy with a little kick.
—*Lynn Henderson, Powell, Ohio*

- 1 **boneless beef chuck roast (about 3 pounds)**
- 2 **teaspoons salt,** *divided*
- 1 **teaspoon pepper,** *divided*
- 2 **tablespoons vegetable oil**
- 2 **cups water**
- 1 **cup ketchup**
- 1 **large onion, chopped**
- 1/4 **cup cider vinegar**
- 1/4 **cup Worcestershire sauce**
- 1 **tablespoon chili powder**
- 1 **garlic clove, minced**
- 12 **kaiser rolls, split**

Sprinkle roast with 1 teaspoon salt and 1/2 teaspoon pepper. In a Dutch oven, brown roast in oil on both sides; drain. Combine the water, ketchup, onion, vinegar, Worcestershire sauce, chili powder, garlic and remaining salt and pepper; pour over meat.

Baked Spaghetti

(Pictured above)

Prep: 20 min.   **Bake:** 40 min.

This is the perfect casserole for potlucks. Wherever I take it, people enjoy it.   —*Pat Walter, Pine Island, Minnesota*

  1 package (16 ounces) spaghetti
1-1/2 pounds ground beef
  1 medium onion, chopped
1/2 cup chopped green pepper
  1 can (10-3/4 ounces) condensed cream of
    mushroom soup, undiluted
  1 can (10-3/4 ounces) condensed tomato
    soup, undiluted
  1 can (8 ounces) tomato sauce
  1 cup water
  2 tablespoons brown sugar
  1 teaspoon salt
  1 teaspoon dried basil
  1 teaspoon dried oregano
1/2 teaspoon dried marjoram
1/2 teaspoon dried rosemary, crushed
1/8 teaspoon garlic salt
  1 cup (4 ounces) shredded part-skim
    mozzarella cheese, *divided*

Break spaghetti in half; cook according to package directions. Meanwhile, in a Dutch oven, cook the beef, onion and green pepper over medium heat until meat is no longer pink; drain. Stir in the soups, tomato sauce, water, brown sugar and seasonings.

Drain spaghetti; stir into meat sauce. Add 1/2 cup of

the cheese. Transfer to a greased 13-in. x 9-in. x 2-in. baking dish. Cover and bake at 350° for 30 minutes. Uncover; sprinkle with remaining cheese. Bake 10-15 minutes longer or until the cheese is melted. **Yield:** 12 servings.

Apple 'n' Carrot Slaw

(Pictured below)

Prep/Total Time: 30 min.

The apples add color and a touch of sweetness to this crispy slaw.   —*Julia Livingston, Frostproof, Florida*

✓ **Uses less fat, sugar or salt. Includes Nutrition Facts and Diabetic Exchanges.**

  4 large heads cabbage, shredded
  1 pound carrots, shredded
  6 medium red apples, finely chopped
  3 cups mayonnaise
1/2 cup sugar
1/4 cup white vinegar
  3 teaspoons salt
  2 teaspoons pepper

In a very large bowl, combine the cabbage, carrots and apples. In a large bowl, combine the mayonnaise, sugar, vinegar, salt and pepper. Pour over the cabbage mixture and toss to coat. Cover and refrigerate until serving. **Yield:** 42 (3/4-cup) servings.

Nutrition Facts: 3/4 cup (prepared with fat-free mayonnaise) equals 68 calories, 1 g fat (trace saturated fat), 2 mg cholesterol, 331 mg sodium, 15 g carbohydrate, 4 g fiber, 2 g protein. **Diabetic Exchanges:** 1 fruit, 1/2 vegetable.

Bow Tie Seafood Salad

(Pictured above)

Prep: 25 min. + chilling

I served this satisfying pasta salad to a group of hospital volunteers, who were quick with compliments. It's brimming with shrimp, imitation crab and veggies.
—Lillian Julow, Gainesville, Florida

✓ **Uses less fat, sugar or salt. Includes Nutrition Facts and Diabetic Exchanges.**

   3 **pounds uncooked bow tie pasta**
1-1/2 **pounds imitation crabmeat, chopped**
   1 **pound frozen cooked salad shrimp, thawed**
   4 **celery ribs, chopped**
   1 **cup finely chopped green onions**
   1 **medium green pepper, diced**
   4 **cups mayonnaise**
 1/4 **cup dill pickle relish**
 1/4 **cup Dijon mustard**
   1 **tablespoon salt**
   1 **tablespoon dill weed**
 3/4 **teaspoon pepper**

Cook the pasta according to the package directions; drain and rinse in cold water. Place in a large bowl; add the crabmeat, salad shrimp, celery, onions and green pepper.

  In another bowl, whisk the mayonnaise, pickle relish, mustard, salt, dill and pepper. Pour over pasta mixture and toss to coat. Cover and refrigerate for at least

2 hours before serving. **Yield:** 32 (1-cup) servings.
  Nutrition Facts: 1 cup (prepared with fat-free mayonnaise) equals 217 calories, 2 g fat (trace saturated fat), 33 mg cholesterol, 686 mg sodium, 39 g carbohydrate, 2 g fiber, 11 g protein. **Diabetic Exchanges:** 2 starch, 2 vegetable, 1/2 very lean meat.

Caraway Rye Bread

(Pictured below)

Prep: 30 min. + rising   **Bake:** 30 min. + cooling

Feed the entire crowd with the four golden loaves this recipe produces. The bread's mild flavor and tender texture are outstanding.   —Denise Elder, Hanover, Ontario

✓ **Uses less fat, sugar or salt. Includes Nutrition Facts and Diabetic Exchanges.**

   4 **packages (1/4 ounce *each*) active dry yeast**
   4 **cups warm water (110° to 115°)**
   1 **cup warm milk (110° to 115°)**
   6 **tablespoons brown sugar**
 1/4 **cup sugar**
 1/4 **cup shortening**
 1/4 **cup molasses**
   2 **tablespoons salt**
   2 **cups rye flour**

10 to 11 cups all-purpose flour
1/4 cup caraway seeds

In a large mixing bowl, dissolve yeast in warm water. Add the milk, sugars, shortening, molasses and salt. Add rye flour and 4 cups all-purpose flour; beat until smooth. Stir in caraway seeds and enough remaining all-purpose flour to form a soft dough.

Turn onto a floured surface; knead until smooth and elastic, about 6-8 minutes. Place in a very large bowl coated with nonstick cooking spray, or divide between two large bowls coated with nonstick cooking spray, turning once to coat top. Cover and let rise in a warm place until doubled, about 1 hour.

Punch dough down. Turn onto a lightly floured surface; divide into four portions. Shape into four loaves. Place each loaf in a 9-in. x 5-in. x 3-in. loaf pan coated with nonstick cooking spray. Cover and let rise until doubled, about 30 minutes.

Bake at 375° for 30-35 minutes or until golden brown. Remove from pans to wire racks to cool. **Yield:** 4 loaves (16 slices each).

Nutrition Facts: 1 slice equals 105 calories, 1 g fat (trace saturated fat), 1 mg cholesterol, 225 mg sodium, 21 g carbohydrate, 1 g fiber, 3 g protein. **Diabetic Exchange:** 1-1/2 starch.

Summertime Barbecue Sauce

(Pictured on page 148)

Prep: 15 min. **Cook:** 25 min. + chilling

When my daughter was 7, she would come home from school and enjoy this sauce by the spoonfuls. Company loves it, too, on pork chops or ribs. Every time I make it, someone asks for the recipe!
—Diane Shipley
Painesville, Ohio

    4 cups finely chopped onion
    4 garlic cloves, minced
    1 cup vegetable oil
    4 cups water
    3 cups ketchup
1-1/3 cups lemon juice
    3/4 cup sugar
    1/2 cup Worcestershire sauce
    1/2 cup steak sauce
    1/4 cup prepared mustard
    2 tablespoons salt
    1/2 cup Liquid Smoke, optional
    1 teaspoon hot pepper sauce, optional

In a Dutch oven, saute the onion and garlic in oil for 8-10 minutes or until tender. Stir in the remaining ingredients. Bring to a boil. Reduce heat; simmer, uncovered, for 15 minutes. Cool. Transfer to storage containers; cover and refrigerate overnight. **Yield:** 3 quarts.

Caramel Chocolate Trifle

(Pictured above)

Prep: 20 min. **Bake:** 20 min. + cooling

A highlight of our annual family reunion is the dessert competition. The judges take their jobs very seriously! Last year's first-place winner was this tempting trifle.
—Barb Hausey, Independence, Missouri

    1 package (9 ounces) devil's food cake mix
    2 packages (3.9 ounces *each*) instant chocolate pudding mix
    1 carton (12 ounces) frozen whipped topping, thawed
    1 jar (12-1/4 ounces) caramel ice cream topping
    1 package (7-1/2 *or* 8 ounces) English toffee bits *or* almond brickle chips

Prepare and bake cake according to package directions for an 8-in. square baking pan. Cool on a wire rack. Prepare pudding according to package directions.

Cut cake into 1-1/2-in. cubes; place half of the cubes in a 3-qt. trifle bowl or large glass serving bowl; lightly press down to fill in gaps. Top with half of the whipped topping, pudding, caramel topping and toffee bits; repeat layers. Cover and refrigerate until serving. **Yield:** 16 servings.

Slow-Cooked Turkey Sandwiches

(Pictured below)

Prep: 15 min.   **Cook:** 3 hours

These sandwiches have been such a hit at office potlucks that I keep copies of the recipe in my desk to hand out.
—*Diane Twait Nelsen, Ringsted, Iowa*

- 6 **cups cubed cooked turkey**
- 2 **cups cubed process cheese (Velveeta)**
- 1 **can (10-3/4 ounces) condensed cream of chicken soup, undiluted**
- 1 **can (10-3/4 ounces) condensed cream of mushroom soup, undiluted**
- 1/2 **cup finely chopped onion**
- 1/2 **cup chopped celery**
- 22 **wheat sandwich buns, split**

In a 3-qt. slow cooker, combine the first six ingredients. Cover and cook on low for 3-4 hours or until celery and onion are tender and cheese is melted. Stir before spooning onto buns. **Yield:** 22 servings.

Make-Ahead Chicken Bake

(Pictured above)

Prep 25 min. + chilling   **Bake:** 30 min.

This crunchy, saucy dish is potluck-perfect! It's convenient because you can make the casserole the day before and bake it the day of the meal. If you like, substitute turkey for the chicken.   —*Joyce Wilson, Omaha, Nebraska*

- 5 **cups cubed cooked chicken**
- 2 **cups chopped celery**
- 5 **hard-cooked eggs, sliced**
- 1 **can (10-3/4 ounces) condensed cream of chicken soup, undiluted**
- 3/4 **cup mayonnaise**
- 2 **tablespoons lemon juice**
- 1 **tablespoon pimientos, optional**
- 1 **teaspoon finely chopped onion**
- 1 **cup (4 ounces) shredded cheddar cheese**
- 1 **can (3 ounces) chow mein noodles**
- 1/2 **cup slivered almonds, toasted**

In a large bowl, combine the first eight ingredients. Transfer to a greased 3-qt. baking dish; sprinkle with cheese, chow mein noodles and almonds. Cover and refrigerate overnight.

Remove the casserole from the refrigerator 30 minutes before baking. Bake, uncovered, at 350° for 30-35 minutes until lightly browned and cheese is bubbly. **Yield:** 12 servings.

Editor's Note: Reduced-fat or fat-free mayonnaise is not recommended for this recipe.

Pistachio Lettuce Salad

(Pictured below)

Prep/Total Time: 20 min.

Topped with a drizzle of delicious honey-and-ginger vinaigrette, this colorful salad always disappears fast.
—*Anna Minegar, Zolfo Springs, Florida*

- 10 **cups torn Bibb *or* Boston lettuce**
- 1 **can (11 ounces) mandarin oranges, drained**
- 1 **cup pistachios, coarsely chopped**
- 1 **cup raisins**

DRESSING:
- 1/4 **cup rice wine vinegar**
- 2 **tablespoons vegetable oil**
- 2 **teaspoons honey**
- 1/2 **teaspoon salt**
- 1/4 **teaspoon pepper**
- 1/4 **teaspoon ground ginger**

In a large salad bowl, combine the lettuce, oranges, pistachios and raisins. In a blender, combine the dressing ingredients; cover and process until blended. Drizzle over salad; toss to coat. **Yield:** 16 servings.

Lemon-Lime Poppy Seed Cake

(Pictured above)

Prep: 20 min.   **Bake:** 40 min. + cooling

There's enough lemon-lime flavor in this tender cake to please any citrus lover. Plus, it's a breeze to make.
—*Victoria Zmarzley-Hahn, Northampton, Pennsylvania*

- 1 **package (18-1/4 ounces) yellow cake mix**
- 1 **package (3.4 ounces) instant vanilla pudding mix**
- 1/4 **cup poppy seeds**
- 4 **eggs**
- 1/2 **cup water**
- 1/2 **cup vegetable oil**
- 1/4 **cup lemon juice**
- 1/4 **cup lime juice**

GLAZE:
- 1-3/4 **cups confectioners' sugar**
- 2 **tablespoons lemon juice**
- 2 **tablespoons lime juice**

In a large mixing bowl, combine the first eight ingredients. Beat on low speed for 30 seconds; beat on medium for 2 minutes. Pour into a greased and floured 10-in. fluted tube pan.

Bake at 350° for 40-45 minutes or until a toothpick inserted near the center comes out clean. Cool for 10 minutes before removing from the pan to a wire rack to cool completely. In a small bowl, combine the glaze ingredients until smooth; drizzle over the cake. **Yield:** 12 servings.

Remove meat; shred with two forks. Return to the pan; heat through. Use a slotted spoon to fill sandwich rolls. **Yield:** 30 servings.

Golden Potato Casserole

(Pictured below)

Prep: 20 min.   **Bake:** 40 min. + standing

The day after Thanksgiving, I prepare three of these golden brown bakes for our large family gathering. I complete the feast with an egg bake, banana nut bread and fruit.
—*Sally Durret, Palo Cedro, California*

      6 **large potatoes, peeled and cut into**
         1/2-inch cubes
      4 **cups (16 ounces) shredded cheddar**
         cheese
      1 **can (10-3/4 ounces) condensed cream of**
         chicken soup, undiluted
      1 **cup (8 ounces) sour cream**
   1/4 **cup butter, melted**
      8 **green onions, chopped**
Dash salt and pepper

Place potatoes in a large saucepan and cover with water. Bring to a boil. Reduce heat; cover and cook for 12-15 minutes or until tender. Drain.

   In a large bowl, combine the remaining ingredients; gently stir in the potatoes. Transfer to a greased 13-in. x 9-in. x 2-in. baking dish (the dish will be full).

Barbecued Pork Sandwiches

(Pictured above)

Prep: 15 min.   **Cook:** 2-3/4 hours

These moist and mouth-watering sandwiches will be gobbled up at your next get-together. The tender pork pieces, simmered in a unique and tangy sauce, make people come back for seconds—sometimes, even thirds.
—*Evelyn Brower, Holland, Michigan*

      1 **boneless pork shoulder roast (6 pounds)**
Dash pepper
      2 **cups reduced-sodium chicken broth**
   1/2 **cup sugar**
   1/2 **cup cider vinegar**
   1/2 **cup reduced-sodium soy sauce**
      2 **celery ribs, finely chopped**
      4 **teaspoons dried minced onion**
      4 **teaspoons ground mustard**
      4 **teaspoons paprika**
     30 **sandwich rolls, split**

Rub roast with pepper; place in a shallow roasting pan. Bake, uncovered, at 350° for 1 to 1-1/4 hours or until a meat thermometer reads 160°.

   Transfer roast to a Dutch oven. In a small bowl, combine the broth, sugar, vinegar, soy sauce, celery, onion, mustard and paprika; pour over roast. Bring to a boil. Reduce heat; cover and simmer for 1-1/2 hours or until meat is very tender.

Bake, uncovered, at 350° for 40-45 minutes or until bubbly. Let casserole stand for 10 minutes before serving. **Yield:** 12-14 servings.

Cran-Orange Relish

(Pictured at right)

Prep/Total Time: 25 min.

With its festive color and refreshing citrus-cranberry flavor, this lovely relish works well at big holiday dinners. It's also convenient because you can make it in advance.
—*Clara Honeyager, North Prairie, Wisconsin*

  8 packages (12 ounces *each*) fresh cranberries
  6 large unpeeled navel oranges, chopped
  4 cups sugar

In a food processor, process the cranberries and oranges in batches until finely chopped. Place in a large container; stir in sugar. Cover and refrigerate until serving. **Yield:** 4-1/2 quarts.

Buttercup Yeast Bread

Prep: 40 min. + rising   **Bake:** 35 min. + cooling

Just by tasting it, you'd never know there was squash in this delectable, fluffy bread. People rave about the colorful slices, even though they have a hard time guessing where the pretty orange tint comes from! —*Kelly Kirby Westville, Nova Scotia*

    3 packages (1/4 ounce *each*) active dry yeast
1/2 cup warm water (110° to 115°)
    2 tablespoons sugar
2-1/2 cups mashed cooked buttercup *or* butternut squash
    2 cups milk
2/3 cup packed brown sugar
2/3 cup butter, softened
    2 eggs, lightly beaten
    3 teaspoons salt
  13 cups all-purpose flour

In a very large mixing bowl, dissolve yeast in warm water. Add sugar; let stand for 5 minutes. Add the squash, milk, brown sugar, butter, eggs and salt; mix well. Add 6 cups flour. Beat on medium speed for 3 minutes. Stir in enough remaining flour to form a soft dough.

Turn onto a floured surface; knead until smooth and elastic, about 10 minutes. Place in a greased bowl, turning once to grease top. Cover and let rise in a warm place until doubled, about 1-1/4 hours.

Punch dough down. Divide into three portions; shape into loaves. Place in three greased 9-in. x 5-in.

x 3-in. loaf pans. Cover and let rise until doubled, about 45 minutes.

Bake at 350° for 35-40 minutes or until golden brown. Cool for 10 minutes before removing from pans to wire racks to cool completely. **Yield:** 3 loaves.

Chewy Apple Oatmeal Cookies

Prep: 20 min.   **Bake:** 10 min. per batch

My family has always loved oatmeal raisin cookies, but I wanted to try something new with that classic recipe. We enjoy apples, and I thought the dried fruit would be good in a cookie. —*Jan Marshall, Fenton, Missouri*

    1 cup butter, softened
    1 cup packed brown sugar
1/2 cup sugar
    2 eggs
    1 teaspoon vanilla extract
1-1/2 cups all-purpose flour
    2 teaspoons ground cinnamon
    1 teaspoon baking soda
    3 cups old-fashioned oats
1/2 cup chopped dried apples

In a large mixing bowl, cream butter and sugars. Beat in eggs and vanilla. Combine the flour, cinnamon and baking soda; gradually add to creamed mixture and mix well. Fold in oats and apples.

Drop by rounded tablespoonfuls 2 in. apart onto ungreased baking sheets. Bake at 350° for 10-12 minutes. Let stand for 1 minute before removing to wire racks. **Yield:** about 4 dozen.

Cooking for One or Two

Downsized dishes that yield enough for one or two can be every bit as special as foods that feed a group. Just try these tasty recipes and see!

LESS IS MORE. Clockwise from upper left: Summer Chicken Salad (p. 184), Sausage-Stuffed Squash (p. 185), Tomato Cheese Sandwiches (p. 185), Garlic Herb Rolls (p. 180), Sesame-Soy Broccoli Florets (p. 181), Skillet Lamb Chops (p. 180), Raspberry French Toast Cups (p. 178) and Almond-Lemon Pound Cake (p. 179).

PARED DOWN and delicious is this fast and easy dinner menu that features Salisbury Steak, Tomato Rice Pilaf and Baked Bananas in Orange Sauce (shown above).

Salisbury Steak

(Pictured above)

Prep/Total Time: 30 min.

Sometimes I forget about this ground beef recipe, so my husband will say, "How about Salisbury Steak for dinner?" He really likes it. —Toni Martin, Byron Center, Michigan

- **1 egg**
- **1/4 cup milk**
- **1/4 cup dry bread crumbs**
- **1 envelope brown gravy mix, *divided***
- **1 teaspoon dried minced onion**
- **1/2 pound lean ground beef**
- **1/2 cup water**
- **1 tablespoon prepared mustard**

In a bowl, whisk the egg and milk. Add bread crumbs, 1 tablespoon gravy mix and onion. Crumble beef over mixture and mix well. Shape into two patties about 3/4 in. thick. Broil 3-4 in. from the heat for 6-7 minutes on each side or until meat is no longer pink and a meat thermometer reads 160°.

Place the remaining gravy mix in a small saucepan; stir in the water and mustard. Bring to a boil; cook and stir until thickened. Serve the gravy over the beef patties. **Yield:** 2 servings.

Tomato Rice Pilaf

(Pictured above)

Prep/Total Time: 25 min.

Parsley, green onion and tomato add festive color to this mild rice dish. I serve this pilaf quite often as a change from potatoes. —Carole Fraser, Toronto, Ontario

- 2 teaspoons butter
- 1/2 cup uncooked long grain rice
- 1 small onion, sliced
- 1-1/4 cups chicken broth
- 2 tablespoons chopped green onion
- 2 tablespoons chopped tomato
- 2 tablespoons minced fresh parsley

In a 3-cup microwave-safe dish, melt butter. Stir in the rice and onion. Microwave, uncovered, on high for 2-3 minutes or until rice is lightly browned and onion is tender, stirring once. Add broth. Cover and cook on high for 13-15 minutes or until liquid is absorbed. Stir in the green onion, tomato and parsley. **Yield:** 2 servings.

Editor's Note: This recipe was tested in a 1,100-watt microwave.

Baked Bananas in Orange Sauce

(Pictured at left)

Prep/Total Time: 30 min.

This simply luscious dessert looks pretty enough to serve for a special occasion. The warm bananas are wonderful with ice cream. —*Gusty Crum, Dover, Ohio*

- 2 medium firm bananas
- 2 teaspoons butter, melted
- 1/4 cup orange juice
- 2 tablespoons brown sugar
- 2 teaspoons grated orange peel

Vanilla ice cream

Cut each banana in half lengthwise; place cut side down in a greased 8-in. square baking dish. Brush with butter. Bake, uncovered, at 350° for 10 minutes. Combine the orange juice, brown sugar and orange peel; pour over bananas. Bake 10 minutes longer. Serve with ice cream. **Yield:** 2 servings.

Chicken for One or Two

If you often cook for just a few people, you may find it handy to cook a larger amount of chicken than you need at once and then store the extras for use in future recipes, such as Chicken Veggie Salad Plate (recipe at right).

If you prefer, store cooked chicken in the refrigerator for use later in the week. The leftovers should be used within 3 to 4 days.

Or, freeze sliced or cubed chicken in an airtight container, a heavy-duty storage bag or heavy-duty foil. For maximum flavor and moistness, use the chicken within 2 to 3 months.

Chicken Veggie Salad Plate

(Pictured above)

Prep: 10 min. + chilling

When you'll be the only one eating, this single-serving main-dish salad is an ideal choice. It takes just minutes to assemble. —*Alanna Eaby, Paramount, California*

- 2 tablespoons mayonnaise
- 2 tablespoons plain yogurt
- 1/8 teaspoon salt
- 1/2 cup cubed cooked chicken
- 12 green grapes, halved
- 1 celery rib, chopped
- 2 whole fresh mushrooms, thinly sliced
- 1 fresh broccoli floret
- 2 slices cucumber
- 2 fresh sugar snap peas
- 2 to 3 lettuce leaves
- 3 pecan halves

In a small bowl, combine the mayonnaise, yogurt and salt. Stir in the chicken, grapes and celery. Cover and refrigerate for at least 1 hour.

Arrange the mushrooms, broccoli, cucumber and peas on a lettuce-lined plate. Top with chicken salad and pecans. **Yield:** 1 serving.

Raspberry French Toast Cups

(Pictured below and on page 174)

Prep: 20 min. + chilling **Bake:** 25 min.

These individual treats are a delightful twist on French toast and make any morning special. I prepared this for my mom last Mother's Day, and we both enjoyed it.
—*Sandi Tuttle, Hayward, Wisconsin*

> 2 slices Italian bread, cut into 1/2-inch cubes
> 1/2 cup fresh *or* frozen raspberries
> 2 ounces cream cheese, cut into 1/2-inch cubes
> 2 eggs
> 1/2 cup milk
> 1 tablespoon maple syrup
> **RASPBERRY SYRUP:**
> 2 teaspoons cornstarch
> 1/3 cup water
> 2 cups fresh *or* frozen raspberries, *divided*
> 1 tablespoon lemon juice
> 1 tablespoon maple syrup
> 1/2 teaspoon grated lemon peel
> **Ground cinnamon, optional**

Divide half of the bread cubes between two greased 8-oz. custard cups. Sprinkle with raspberries and cream cheese. Top with remaining bread. In a small bowl, whisk the eggs, milk and syrup; pour over bread. Cover and refrigerate for at least 1 hour.

Remove from the refrigerator 30 minutes before baking. Bake, uncovered, at 350° for 25-30 minutes or until golden brown.

Meanwhile, in a small saucepan, combine the cornstarch and water until smooth. Add 1-1/2 cups raspberries, lemon juice, syrup and lemon peel. Bring to a boil; reduce heat. Cook and stir 2 minutes or until thickened. Strain and discard seeds; cool slightly.

Gently stir the remaining berries into the syrup. Sprinkle the French toast cups with cinnamon if desired; serve with syrup. **Yield:** 2 servings.

Honey-Mustard Chicken

(Pictured at right)

Prep/Total Time: 30 min.

This entree combines my husband's love for mustard with my love for anything sweet. We like the curry, too!
—*Lisa Varner, Greenville, South Carolina*

> 1/4 cup honey
> 2 tablespoons butter, melted
> 2 tablespoons Dijon mustard
> 1 tablespoon orange juice
> 1/8 teaspoon curry powder
> 2 boneless skinless chicken breast halves
> 1 tablespoon vegetable oil
> 1/8 teaspoon salt
> 1/8 teaspoon pepper

In a small bowl, combine the honey, butter, mustard, orange juice and curry powder. Spoon half into a greased 8-in. baking dish.

In a skillet, brown chicken in oil. Sprinkle with salt and pepper. Place over sauce; turn to coat. Bake, uncovered, at 350° for 15 minutes. Drizzle with remaining sauce. Bake 5-10 minutes longer or until a meat thermometer reads 170°. **Yield:** 2 servings.

Sweet Herbed Carrots

(Pictured at right)

Prep/Total Time: 25 min.

Originally, this recipe called for two bunches of small carrots, so I had to guess the amount. I finally worked it out to my liking. —*Beverly Christofferson, Sioux City, Iowa*

> 2 tablespoons butter
> 1/4 teaspoon sugar
> 2 cups sliced fresh carrots
> 3 to 4 lettuce leaves
> 2 tablespoons water
> 2 tablespoons minced fresh parsley
> 2 tablespoons heavy whipping cream
> 1 tablespoon minced fresh tarragon
> *or* 1 teaspoon dried tarragon
> 1/4 teaspoon salt
> 1/8 teaspoon pepper

In a large skillet, cook and stir the butter and sugar over medium heat until butter is melted and sugar is dissolved. Stir in carrots; cover with lettuce leaves. Sprinkle with water. Cover and simmer for 15-20 minutes or until carrots are crisp-tender.

Discard lettuce. Stir in the parsley, cream, tarragon, salt and pepper. Bring to a boil. Reduce heat; simmer, uncovered, for 1-2 minutes or until heated through. Serve with a slotted spoon. **Yield:** 2 servings.

PERFECT FOR A PAIR is this mouth-watering menu featuring Honey-Mustard Chicken, Sweet Herbed Carrots and Almond-Lemon Pound Cake (shown above).

Almond-Lemon Pound Cake

(Pictured above and on page 174)

Prep: 15 min.   **Bake:** 40 min. + cooling

This is the first cake I ever made, and it's still a favorite of mine. You can freeze any leftover cake and topping.
—Michaela Rosenthal, Woodland Hills, California

> 1 **teaspoon plus 3/4 cup butter, softened,** *divided*
> 2 **teaspoons confectioners' sugar**
> 1 **cup slivered almonds**
> 1 **cup sugar**
> 2 **eggs**
> 1/3 **cup sour cream**
> 1 **tablespoon grated lemon peel**
> 1 **cup cake flour**
> 1 **teaspoon baking powder**
> 1/4 **cup lemon juice**
> **TOPPING:**
> 1 **cup** *each* **frozen unsweetened raspberries, strawberries and blueberries**
> 1/4 **cup sugar**
> 2 **tablespoons lemon juice**
> 2 **tablespoons confectioners' sugar**

Grease bottom and sides of a 9-in. round baking pan with 1 teaspoon butter. Sprinkle with confectioners' sugar; set aside. Place nuts and sugar in a blender or food processor; cover and process until finely ground.

In a small mixing bowl, cream remaining butter; beat in almond mixture until combined. Add eggs, one at a time, beating well after each addition. Stir in sour cream and lemon peel. Combine flour and baking powder; add to creamed mixture alternately with lemon juice. Pour into prepared pan.

Bake at 350° for 40-45 minutes or until a toothpick inserted near the center comes out clean. Cool on a wire rack for 10 minutes. Invert onto a wire rack to cool completely.

For topping, in a heavy saucepan, combine the berries, sugar and lemon juice. Cook and stir over medium-low heat for 10 minutes or until mixture begins to thicken. Sprinkle cake with confectioners' sugar. Serve with berry topping. **Yield:** 6 servings.

DINNER FOR TWO becomes an extra-special occasion when you serve Skillet Lamb Chops as the main course and add Garlic Herb Rolls and Sesame-Soy Broccoli Florets (shown above).

Skillet Lamb Chops

(Pictured above and on page 174)

Prep: 15 min.   **Cook:** 30 min.

These mildly seasoned chops are so satisfying. They're a great choice if you enjoy lamb for holiday dinners.
—*Alpha Wilson, Roswell, New Mexico*

> 2 **lamb shoulder blade chops (8 ounces *each*)**
> 2 **tablespoons vegetable oil**
> 1/2 **cup warm water**
> 1 **teaspoon lemon juice**
> 1 **teaspoon dried minced onion**
> 1/2 **teaspoon dried oregano**
> 1/4 **teaspoon salt**
> 1/8 **teaspoon pepper**

In a large skillet, brown lamb chops in oil. Add the remaining ingredients; bring to a boil. Reduce heat;
cover and simmer for 30-35 minutes or until meat juices run clear. **Yield:** 2 servings.

Garlic Herb Rolls

(Pictured above and on page 174)

Prep: 15 min. + rising   **Bake:** 10 min.

Baked in buttered muffin cups, these goodies are cute as a button. —*Virginia Lapierre, Greensboro Bend, Vermont*

> ✓ **Uses less fat, sugar or salt. Includes Nutrition Facts and Diabetic Exchanges.**

> 1 **teaspoon active dry yeast**
> 1/4 **teaspoon sugar**
> 1/4 **cup warm water (110° to 115°)**
> 1/2 **cup plus 2 tablespoons all-purpose flour**
> 1-1/2 **teaspoons canola oil**
> 1/4 **teaspoon salt**

1 tablespoon butter, softened
3/4 teaspoon garlic powder
3/4 teaspoon grated Parmesan cheese
1/4 teaspoon dried oregano
1/4 teaspoon dried basil

In a small mixing bowl, dissolve yeast and sugar in warm water. Beat in the flour, oil and salt until smooth. Turn onto a heavily floured surface; knead until smooth and elastic, about 6-8 minutes. Place in a bowl coated with nonstick cooking spray, turning once to coat top. Cover; let rise in a warm place until doubled, about 30 minutes.

Grease six muffin cups with the butter. Combine garlic powder, Parmesan cheese, oregano and basil; sprinkle into cups. Punch dough down; divide into six portions. Shape each into a ball; place in prepared cups, turning once to coat. Cover and let rise until doubled, about 30 minutes.

Bake at 425° for 10-15 minutes or until golden brown. Remove from pan to a wire rack. Serve warm. **Yield:** 6 servings.

Nutrition Facts: 1 roll equals 79 calories, 3 g fat (1 g saturated fat), 5 mg cholesterol, 122 mg sodium, 11 g carbohydrate, 1 g fiber, 2 g protein. **Diabetic Exchange:** 1 starch.

Sesame-Soy Broccoli Florets

(Pictured at left and on page 174)

Prep/Total Time 15 min.

This side dish has an Asian flair that's likely to please everyone. —*Marianne Bauman, Modesto, California*

✓ Uses less fat, sugar or salt. Includes Nutrition Facts and Diabetic Exchanges.

2 cups fresh *or* frozen broccoli florets
1 tablespoon sugar
1 tablespoon olive oil
1 tablespoon soy sauce
2 teaspoons rice wine vinegar
2 teaspoons sesame seeds, toasted

Place the broccoli in a steamer basket; place in a saucepan over 1 in. of water. Bring to a boil; cover and steam for 5-7 minutes or until crisp-tender.

Meanwhile, in a small saucepan, combine sugar, oil, soy sauce and vinegar. Cook and stir over medium heat until sugar is dissolved. Transfer the broccoli to a serving bowl. Drizzle with soy sauce mixture; sprinkle with sesame seeds. **Yield:** 2 servings.

Nutrition Facts: 3/4 cup (prepared with reduced-sodium soy sauce) equals 156 calories, 8 g fat (1 g saturated fat), 0 cholesterol, 358 mg sodium, 16 g carbohydrate, 4 g fiber, 5 g protein. **Diabetic Exchanges:** 3 vegetable, 1-1/2 fat.

Cucumber Shrimp Spread

(Pictured above)

Prep/Total Time: 10 min.

I like to serve this savory spread on rye bread slices, but it's just as satisfying on crackers or bagel chips.
—*Doris Heath, Franklin, North Carolina*

✓ Uses less fat, sugar or salt. Includes Nutrition Facts.

1 package (3 ounces) cream cheese, softened
2 tablespoons mayonnaise
1 tablespoon ketchup
1/2 to 3/4 teaspoon ground mustard
1/8 teaspoon garlic powder
1 can (4 ounces) tiny shrimp, rinsed and drained
1/4 cup chopped seeded peeled cucumber
1 teaspoon finely chopped onion
Assorted crackers

In a small mixing bowl, beat the cream cheese, mayonnaise, ketchup, mustard and garlic powder until smooth. Stir in the shrimp, cucumber and onion. Cover and refrigerate until serving. Serve with crackers. **Yield:** about 1 cup.

Nutrition Facts: 2 tablespoons spread (prepared with reduced-fat cream cheese and fat-free mayonnaise) equals 44 calories, 2 g fat (2 g saturated fat), 38 mg cholesterol, 265 mg sodium, 2 g carbohydrate, trace fiber, 4 g protein.

Pork Fried Rice

(Pictured above)

Prep/Total Time: 30 min.

We love pork roast, but we know there will be leftovers. I use them up in this quick stir-fry. —*Joyce Kramer Donalsonville, Georgia*

    1 tablespoon vegetable oil
    1 egg, beaten
  3/4 cup cubed cooked pork
  1/4 cup finely chopped onion
  1/4 cup canned bean sprouts
    2 cups cold cooked long grain rice
  1/4 cup chicken broth
    1 tablespoon soy sauce
    1 green onion, sliced
  1/4 teaspoon sugar
Dash pepper

In a skillet or wok, heat oil over medium-high heat; add egg. As egg sets, lift edges, letting uncooked portion flow underneath. When egg is completely cooked, remove to a plate and keep warm.

In the same pan, stir-fry the pork, onion and bean sprouts for 2-3 minutes or until onion is tender. Add rice and broth; cover and simmer for 1-2 minutes or until heated through. Chop egg into small pieces; add to rice mixture. Stir in the soy sauce, green onion, sugar and pepper. **Yield:** 2 servings.

Rib Eyes with Mushrooms

(Pictured at right)

Prep: 5 min. + marinating   **Cook:** 10 min.

This hearty steak is well seasoned with a robust marinade and topped with a fresh mushroom sauce.
—*Lissa Hutson, Phelan, California*

    8 green onions, sliced
    2 garlic cloves, minced
    1 cup beef broth
    2 tablespoons balsamic vinegar
  1/2 teaspoon dried thyme
  1/2 teaspoon pepper
    2 beef rib eye steaks (about 8 ounces *each*)
    1 cup sliced fresh mushrooms

In a bowl, combine the first six ingredients. Place the steaks in a large resealable plastic bag; add half of the marinade. Seal bag and turn to coat; refrigerate for 1-2 hours. Cover and refrigerate remaining marinade.

Drain and discard marinade. Broil steaks 4-6 in. from the heat for 5-6 minutes on each side or until meat reaches desired doneness (for medium-rare, a meat thermometer should read 145°; medium, 160°; well-done, 170°).

Meanwhile, place the remaining marinade in a small saucepan. Bring to a boil over medium heat; cook and stir for 1 minute. Stir in the mushrooms. Serve over steaks. **Yield:** 2 servings.

Zucchini Tomato Side Dish

(Pictured at right)

Prep/Total Time: 20 min.

Bacon bits add smoky flavor to this colorful combo. I've also prepared this as a lunch entree for one, served with a roll and fruit. —*Nancy Johnson, Laverne, Oklahoma*

    1 medium zucchini, sliced
    2 to 3 thin slices red onion, separated into rings
  1/8 teaspoon salt
    1 teaspoon olive oil
    1 can (5-1/2 ounces) spicy hot V8 juice
    1 medium tomato, cut into 8 wedges
  1/8 teaspoon dried basil
  1/8 teaspoon coarsely ground pepper
  1/2 cup shredded cheddar cheese
    1 tablespoon real bacon bits

In a large skillet, saute the zucchini, onion and salt in oil until vegetables are crisp-tender. Gently stir in the V8 juice, tomato, basil and pepper. Cook over medium heat for 2 minutes or until heated through. Sprinkle with cheese and bacon. **Yield:** 2 servings.

RIB EYES WITH MUSHROOMS, Zucchini Tomato Side Dish and Warm Pear Sundaes (shown above) make an inviting meal that's just the right size for a hungry twosome.

Warm Pear Sundaes

(Pictured above)

Prep/Total Time: 20 min.

This is a simple, attractive way to dress up fresh pears. You can easily double or triple the recipe for guests.
—*Janice Mitchell, Aurora, Colorado*

2 tablespoons brown sugar
2 teaspoons butter, melted
2 teaspoons heavy whipping cream
2 medium ripe pears, peeled and chopped
1-1/2 cups vanilla ice cream

In a bowl, combine the brown sugar, butter and cream. Add the pears; toss to coat. Spoon into a greased 1-qt. baking dish.

Cover and bake at 425° for 10-15 minutes or until the pears are tender. Serve the pears over vanilla ice cream. **Yield:** 2 servings.

Poppy Seed Muffins

(Pictured below)

Prep/Total Time: 30 min.

Sour cream brings a mild tang to these tender, golden poppy seed muffins. My daughter fell in love with these goodies when my sister made them. —Nancy Register
Raleigh, North Carolina

    3/4 **cup biscuit/baking mix**
    1/4 **cup sugar**
  1-1/2 **teaspoons poppy seeds**
      1 **egg**
    1/3 **cup sour cream**
    1/2 **teaspoon vanilla extract**

In a bowl, combine the biscuit mix, sugar and poppy seeds. In another bowl, whisk the egg, sour cream and vanilla; stir into dry ingredients just until moistened. Fill greased or paper-lined muffin cups two-thirds full.

Bake at 400° for 15-20 minutes or until a toothpick comes out clean. Cool for 5 minutes before removing from pan to a wire rack. Serve warm. **Yield:** 6 muffins.

Summer Chicken Salad

(Pictured above and on page 174)

Prep: 10 min. + chilling

Both men and women enjoy this version of chicken salad, whether served at lunch or for an evening meal.
—Marina Jines, Enid, Oklahoma

    2 **cups cubed cooked chicken**
    1 **cup halved green grapes**
    1 **can (8 ounces) pineapple chunks, drained
       and halved**
    1 **celery rib, chopped**
  1/3 **cup mayonnaise**
  1/4 **teaspoon salt**
  1/8 **teaspoon celery seed**
  1/8 **teaspoon pepper**
  1/4 **cup chopped pecans, toasted**
    1 **medium ripe avocado, peeled and sliced**
    6 **large slices cantaloupe**
Lettuce leaves

In a bowl, combine the chicken, grapes, pineapple and celery. In a small bowl, combine the mayonnaise, salt, celery seed and pepper. Stir into chicken mixture. Cover and refrigerate for at least 1 hour.

Just before serving, stir in pecans. Serve with avocado and cantaloupe slices on lettuce-lined plates. **Yield:** 2 servings.

Sausage-Stuffed Squash

(Pictured below and on page 174)

Prep: 30 min. **Bake:** 20 min.

Acorn squash makes a fitting bowl for the flavorful apple, pork and cheese stuffing in this recipe.
—*Carol Meyskens, Oregon, Wisconsin*

- 1 **medium acorn squash**
- 6 **ounces bulk pork sausage**
- 1/2 **cup chopped celery, optional**
- 2 **tablespoons chopped onion**
- 1/2 **cup chopped peeled tart apple**
- 1 **teaspoon all-purpose flour**
- 1 **egg, lightly beaten**
- 1/4 **cup sour cream**
- 1/8 **teaspoon salt**
- 1/3 **cup diced process cheese (Velveeta)**

Cut squash in half; remove seeds. Place cut side down in a greased 13-in. x 9-in. x 2-in. baking dish. Cover and bake at 350° for 25-30 minutes or until tender.

Meanwhile, in a small skillet, cook sausage, celery if desired and onion over medium heat until meat is no longer pink. Add apple; cook and stir for 3 minutes. Drain. In a bowl, combine the flour, egg and sour cream until smooth; stir into sausage mixture.

Turn squash over; sprinkle cut sides with salt. Stuff with sausage mixture. Bake, uncovered, for 15-20 minutes or until heated through. Sprinkle with cheese; bake 5 minutes longer or until cheese is melted. **Yield:** 2 servings.

Tomato Cheese Sandwiches

(Pictured below and on page 174)

Prep/Total Time: 20 min.

Couple this warm, cheesy bread with an entree, a salad or soup. —*Janet Watson, Crown Point, Indiana*

- 2 **tablespoons butter, softened**
- 4 **slices Vienna bread**
- 1/4 **cup tomato sauce**
- 1/8 **teaspoon garlic powder**
- 1/8 **teaspoon Italian seasoning**
- 1/8 **teaspoon fennel seed, crushed**
- 1/8 **teaspoon crushed red pepper flakes, optional**
- 1 **medium tomato, thinly sliced**
- 1 **cup (4 ounces) shredded part-skim mozzarella cheese**

Butter one side of bread slices; place buttered side up on a foil-lined baking sheet. In a small bowl, combine sauce, garlic powder, Italian seasoning, fennel seed and pepper flakes if desired. Spread over butter.

Top with tomato slices; sprinkle with cheese. Bake at 400° for 8-10 minutes or until cheese is melted. **Yield:** 2 servings.

WHEN THE WEATHER is cool, warm up with pared-down dishes that are hot from the oven—hearty Sausage-Stuffed Squash and open-faced Tomato Cheese Sandwiches (shown below).

'My Mom's Best Meal'

Six daughters reminisce about their mother's cooking...and share the recipes for their favorite made-by-mom feast.

MEMORABLE MENUS. Clockwise from upper left: Sensational Seafood Feast (p. 208), Special Spaghetti Dinner (p. 192), Ham and All the Fixings (p. 196) and Fare with French Flair (p. 204).

Her Italian mom's made-from-scratch dinners had mass appeal and left a legacy of love.

By Jodi Grable, Springfield, Missouri

COOKING for a crowd came naturally for my mom, Antoinette DeGear (above). She grew up in an Italian family in Iowa, the youngest of six kids. And she raised eight kids of her own (I'm the youngest).

With such a large family, huge gatherings were the norm. Mom loved to entertain, and we often had dinner parties for 30 people or more. Whether she was serving family or guests, she always set a beautiful table with crystal stemware and good china.

When I was a child, Mom always seemed to be cooking. My favorite days were when she was making homemade spaghetti sauce. I'd come home from school and eat a bowl of it like soup!

My mother has always cooked from scratch, and since she was a child of the Depression, she learned to be creative with garden produce and leftovers.

My favorite meal has to be her Hens with Apricot Rice Stuffing, Bacon Squash Saute, Orange 'n' Red Onion Salad and Banana Cream Pie.

We all love apricots, so Mom tried to work them into any recipe she could, including her tender stuffed hens. The sweet apricots and sauteed mushrooms make the wild rice stuffing so moist and flavorful.

Bacon Squash Saute is a delicious way to use up homegrown squash and zucchini. And Mom's pretty onion salad is a pleasing mix of sweet and tangy.

Cream pies are my mom's specialty, and Banana Cream Pie, with sliced almonds on top, is the best. My late husband requested this pie often.

Mom still cooks every day, but now for fewer people (her children, 27 grandchildren and 28 great-grandchildren are scattered across the country). She and my stepfather live near me and my son, Kirsch, and the four of us eat together on weekends.

For Mom's 75th birthday, I compiled a cookbook of her recipes and gave copies to her and my siblings. The cookbook wouldn't have been complete without the recipes I've shared with you. I hope everyone loves them as much as we do.

PICTURED AT LEFT: Hens with Apricot Rice Stuffing, Bacon Squash Saute, Orange 'n' Red Onion Salad and Banana Cream Pie (recipes are on the next page).

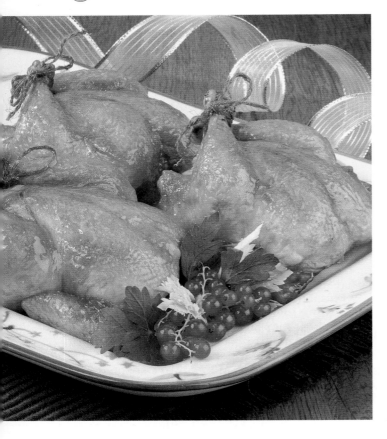

Hens with Apricot Rice Stuffing

Prep: 25 min.   **Bake:** 2 hours

    1 cup sliced fresh mushrooms
  3/4 cup chopped pecans
  1/2 cup chopped onion
    6 tablespoons butter, *divided*
    1 cup cooked wild rice
  1/2 cup chopped dried apricots
    1 tablespoon minced fresh parsley
  1/2 teaspoon salt
  1/4 teaspoon pepper
  1/8 teaspoon cayenne pepper
    4 Cornish game hens (24 ounces *each*)
  1/2 cup apricot preserves
    1 tablespoon white vinegar

In a large skillet, saute the mushrooms, pecans and onion in 4 tablespoons butter until tender. Stir in the rice, apricots, parsley, salt, pepper and cayenne.

Spoon about 3/4 cup rice mixture into each hen; tie legs together with kitchen string. Place hens, breast side up, on a rack in a shallow roasting pan. Melt remaining butter; brush over hens.

Bake, uncovered, at 350° for 1-3/4 to 2 hours or until a meat thermometer reads 180° for hens and 165° for stuffing. In a small saucepan, warm preserves and vinegar; spoon over hens. Bake 15 minutes longer. **Yield:** 4 servings.

Bacon Squash Saute

Prep/Total Time: 20 min.

    6 bacon strips, diced
    2 small zucchini, cut into 1/4-inch slices
    2 small yellow summer squash, cut into 1/4-inch slices
    1 medium onion, thinly sliced

In a large skillet, cook bacon over medium heat until crisp; remove to paper towels. Drain, reserving 2 tablespoons drippings. In the drippings, saute the zucchini, yellow squash and onion for 6-8 minutes or until crisp-tender. Sprinkle with bacon. **Yield:** 4 servings.

Orange 'n' Red Onion Salad

Prep/Total Time: 15 min.

    4 cups torn romaine
    2 medium navel oranges, peeled and sectioned
    1 small red onion, sliced and separated into rings
  1/4 cup olive oil
    3 tablespoons red wine vinegar
    1 teaspoon sugar
  1/4 teaspoon salt
  1/8 teaspoon pepper

turn all to the pan. Bring to a gentle boil; cook and stir 2 minutes longer.

Remove from the heat. Gently stir in butter and vanilla. Press plastic wrap onto surface of custard; cover and refrigerate for 30 minutes.

Slice the bananas into pastry shell; pour the custard over top. Spread with whipped cream; sprinkle with almonds. Chill for 6-8 hours or overnight. Refrigerate leftovers. **Yield:** 6-8 servings.

Banana Basics

The riper a banana becomes, the sweeter it will taste. That's because the starch in bananas turns to sugar as they ripen.

Green-tipped bananas are best for cooking, while yellow are great for salads, cereals or immediate eating. Fully ripe bananas with brown-speckled peels are perfect for baking in breads or mashing into fruit smoothies.

Cooler temperatures slow down the ripening process of bananas, while warmer temperatures speed it up. To make a banana ripen quickly, place it in a brown paper bag with either an apple or tomato and leave it overnight, keeping the bag out of direct sunlight.

On a serving platter, arrange the romaine, orange sections and onion. For the dressing, in a jar with a tight-fitting lid, combine the remaining ingredients; shake well. Drizzle the dressing over the salad; serve immediately. **Yield:** 4 servings.

Banana Cream Pie

Prep: 10 min.   **Cook:** 15 min. + chilling

- 1 cup sugar
- 1/4 cup cornstarch
- 1/2 teaspoon salt
- 3 cups milk
- 2 eggs, lightly beaten
- 3 tablespoons butter
- 1-1/2 teaspoons vanilla extract
- 2 large firm bananas
- 1 pastry shell (9 inches), baked
- 1 cup heavy whipping cream, whipped
- 1 tablespoon sliced almonds, toasted

In a large saucepan, combine the sugar, cornstarch, salt and milk until smooth. Cook and stir over medium-high heat until thickened and bubbly. Reduce heat; cook and stir 2 minutes longer. Remove from the heat. Stir a small amount of hot filling into eggs; re-

Family-pleasing and wholesome dishes were plentiful on her budget-minded mom's dinner menus.

By Anne Halfhill, Sunbury, Ohio

MY MOM, Myrtle Clarine Casey (above), learned a lot about cooking from my father, Paul, who was a cook in the Army, and from his mother.

Mom learned to cook healthy and delicious meals while stretching a dollar to feed our family of six. My dad often worked two jobs so Mom (who prefers to be called Billie) could stay home with my brother, two sisters and me. Now that I'm an adult, I really appreciate the effort and love it must have taken to prepare three meals a day on a budget.

The food was always satisfying and plentiful, and Dad, even when he worked two jobs, pitched in a lot—especially when Mom hosted her annual spaghetti dinner for family and friends.

My mother's spaghetti is the centerpiece of what I consider her best meal. Her Herbed Mushroom Spaghetti Sauce is thick, meaty and rich. When I visit her and Dad, who have retired to Florida, I always look forward to having spaghetti. I usually eat so much that I can't move!

As a before-dinner appetizer, Pineapple Cheese Ball hits the spot. I love the crunchiness of the green pepper and walnuts. It's great for a large crowd or during holidays.

Nine-Layer Salad is loaded with wonderful flavors. At family events, we tease my youngest sister, Chris, that she has a lifetime assignment to bring this salad. Although the recipe says to refrigerate overnight, I make it and toss it right before serving.

There's no better end to this mouth-watering meal than Lattice-Topped Apple Pie. It's so pretty that you hate to cut it. But the crust is soft and flaky, and the filling has just the right touch of spice. I told Mom that she's ruined me for any other pie.

I really enjoy preparing from-scratch dishes for my family, too. It's difficult to name one dish I make all the time, since I'm forever trying new recipes. But I always include some of Mom's recipes on my menus. I hope you'll try them, too!

PICTURED AT LEFT: Herbed Mushroom Spaghetti Sauce, Pineapple Cheese Ball, Nine-Layer Salad and Lattice-Topped Apple Pie (recipes are on the next page).

simmer for 45-60 minutes, stirring occasionally. Serve over spaghetti. **Yield:** 6 servings.

Nutrition Facts: 3/4 cup sauce with 1/2 cup spaghetti (calculated without salt) equals 330 calories, 11 g fat (3 g saturated fat), 37 mg cholesterol, 699 mg sodium, 36 g carbohydrate, 4 g fiber, 22 g protein. **Diabetic Exchanges:** 2 starch, 2 lean meat, 1 vegetable, 1 fat.

Pineapple Cheese Ball

Prep: 20 min. + chilling

> 2 packages (8 ounces *each*) cream cheese, softened
> 1 can (8 ounces) unsweetened crushed pineapple, drained
> 1/4 cup finely chopped green pepper
> 2 tablespoons finely chopped onion
> 2 teaspoons seasoned salt
> 1-1/2 cups finely chopped walnuts
> Assorted crackers

In a small mixing bowl, beat the cream cheese, pineapple, green pepper, onion and seasoned salt until blended. Cover and refrigerate 30 minutes. Shape into a ball; roll in walnuts. Cover and refrigerate overnight. Serve with crackers. **Yield:** 1 cheese ball (3 cups).

Herbed Mushroom Spaghetti Sauce

Prep: 15 min. **Cook:** 45 min.

✓ **Uses less fat, sugar or salt. Includes Nutrition Facts and Diabetic Exchanges.**

> 1 pound lean ground beef
> 1/2 pound sliced fresh mushrooms
> 1 large onion, chopped
> 1 small green pepper, chopped
> 4 garlic cloves, minced
> 2 tablespoons olive oil
> 2 cans (8 ounces *each*) tomato sauce
> 1 can (10-3/4 ounces) condensed tomato soup, undiluted
> 1 teaspoon dried basil
> 1/2 teaspoon salt, optional
> 1/2 teaspoon dried rosemary, crushed
> 1/2 teaspoon dried oregano
> 1/4 teaspoon pepper
> Hot cooked spaghetti

In a large skillet, cook beef, mushrooms, onion, green pepper and garlic in oil over medium heat until meat is no longer pink; drain. Stir in the tomato sauce, soup and seasonings. Bring to a boil; reduce heat. Cover and

Nine-Layer Salad

Prep: 30 min. + chilling

- 4 cups torn iceberg lettuce
- 4 cups fresh baby spinach
- 1 cup *each* chopped green pepper, celery and green onions
- 1 package (10 ounces) frozen peas, thawed and patted dry
- 1-1/2 cups mayonnaise
- 1/2 cup shredded Parmesan cheese
- 1/2 cup shredded Romano cheese
- 1 cup crumbled cooked bacon

In a large salad bowl, layer the lettuce, spinach, green pepper, celery, onions and peas. Spread with mayonnaise. Combine the cheeses; sprinkle cheeses and bacon over mayonnaise. Cover and refrigerate overnight. **Yield:** 6-8 servings.

Lattice-Topped Apple Pie

Prep: 25 min.   **Bake:** 55 min. + cooling

- 5-1/2 cups thinly sliced peeled apples (about 6 medium)
- 1 cup sugar
- 2 tablespoons water
- 4-1/2 teaspoons quick-cooking tapioca
- 1/2 teaspoon ground cinnamon
- 1/4 teaspoon ground nutmeg

PASTRY:
- 2 cups all-purpose flour
- 1/2 teaspoon baking powder
- 1/2 teaspoon salt
- 2/3 cup shortening
- 5 to 6 tablespoons cold water
- 3 tablespoons butter
- 2 tablespoons milk
- 1 tablespoon sugar

In a large bowl, combine the apples, sugar, water, tapioca, cinnamon and nutmeg; toss to coat. Let stand for 15 minutes.

In a large bowl, combine flour, baking powder and salt; cut in shortening until crumbly. Gradually add water, tossing with a fork until dough forms a ball. Divide in half; make one half slightly larger.

On a lightly floured surface, roll out larger portion of pastry to fit a 9-in. pie plate. Transfer pastry to plate; trim even with edge of plate. Add filling; dot with butter. Roll out remaining pastry; make a lattice crust. Trim, seal and flute edges. Brush with milk; sprinkle with sugar. Cover edges loosely with foil.

Bake at 400° for 15 minutes. Reduce heat to 350°; bake 40-50 minutes longer or until crust is golden brown and filling is bubbly. Cool on a wire rack. **Yield:** 6-8 servings.

Her mom's kitchen was overflowing with home-cooked, delicious dishes for family and friends.

By P. Lauren Fay-Neri, Syracuse, New York

IT DIDN'T MATTER if you were a relative, a neighbor or a friend. When you came to our house, my mother, Madeline Fay (above), would ask, "Did you eat? Sit down and have a bite!"

If you didn't eat at our house, she'd send you home with a container of food. Mom liked to take care of everyone.

When my four brothers and I were growing up, the house was always filled with delicious foods, from soups to desserts. We enjoyed Mom's great home-cooked meals as well as her delicious cookies and cakes. Everything was prepared from scratch; she never used packaged mixes.

One of our favorite meals featured beautiful Holiday Spiral Ham, Candied Carrots, Corn Pudding and Pineapple Sour Cream Pie for dessert.

Mom served the ham, with cranberry-apple relish and pineapple wedges, for holiday dinners. Although I preferred plain carrots to the Candied Carrots, everyone else enjoyed the sweet brown sugar glaze. Her Corn Pudding is delicious served warm. I also like the leftovers served cold.

Pineapple Sour Cream Pie is a refreshing alternative to traditional favorites like apple and pumpkin. Sometimes, instead of preparing meringue, I'll top the pie with fresh whipped cream. I make the pie a day ahead of time and add the whipped cream just before serving.

I'd call my mother a "natural" cook. She'd follow a recipe at first, but then substituted different ingredients. She memorized much of what she did.

I still have my mom's worn, wallpaper-covered cookbook. The envelopes inside are stuffed with recipes she gathered during her lifetime.

Because she didn't write down many of her own recipes, I don't often make a lot of Mom's dishes. But I think of her each night when I put together our meal. I hope you like this special menu.

PICTURED AT LEFT: Holiday Spiral Ham, Candied Carrots, Corn Pudding and Pineapple Sour Cream Pie (recipes are on the next page).

Candied Carrots

Prep/Total Time: 30 min.

2 pounds carrots, cut into sticks
1/4 cup butter
1/4 cup packed brown sugar
1/4 teaspoon salt
1/8 teaspoon white pepper

Place carrots in a large saucepan; add 1 in. of water. Bring to a boil. Reduce heat; cover and simmer for 8-10 minutes or until crisp-tender. Drain and set aside.

In the same pan, combine the butter, brown sugar, salt and pepper; cook and stir until butter is melted. Return carrots to the pan; cook and stir over medium heat for 5 minutes or until glazed. **Yield:** 8 servings.

Corn Pudding

Prep: 20 min.   **Bake:** 45 min.

1/2 cup butter, softened
1/2 cup sugar
 2 eggs
 1 cup (8 ounces) sour cream
 1 package (8-1/2 ounces) corn bread/muffin mix
1/2 cup milk
 1 can (15-1/4 ounces) whole kernel corn, drained
 1 can (14-3/4 ounces) cream-style corn

Holiday Spiral Ham

Prep: 30 min.   **Bake:** 1-1/2 hours + standing

 1 fully cooked spiral-sliced ham (8 pounds)
 1 fresh pineapple, peeled, cored and cut into four wedges
 1 package (12 ounces) fresh *or* frozen cranberries
 3 medium apples, peeled and cubed
1-1/4 cups sugar
 1 medium navel orange, peeled and cut into chunks
 3 tablespoons lemon juice

Place ham on a rack in a shallow roasting pan. Arrange pineapple wedges around the ham. Cover and bake at 325° for 1 to 1-1/2 hours.

Meanwhile, in a large saucepan, combine cranberries and apples. Cook over medium heat until the berries pop, about 15 minutes. Add the sugar, orange chunks and lemon juice. Cook and stir until sugar is dissolved. Remove from the heat.

Spoon half of the cranberry relish over ham. Bake 30 minutes longer or until a meat thermometer reads 140°. Let stand for 10 minutes before serving. Cut pineapple wedges into large chunks; serve with ham and remaining relish. **Yield:** 12-16 servings.

In a large mixing bowl, cream butter and sugar. Add eggs, one at a time, beating well after each addition. Beat in sour cream. Gradually add corn bread/muffin mix alternately with milk. Fold in the corn.

Pour into a greased 3-qt. baking dish. Bake, uncovered, at 325° for 45-50 minutes or until set and lightly browned. **Yield:** 8 servings.

Pineapple Sour Cream Pie

Prep: 35 min.   **Bake:** 15 min. + chilling

1/2 cup sugar
  2 tablespoons all-purpose flour
  1 can (20 ounces) crushed pineapple, undrained
  1 cup (8 ounces) sour cream
  3 egg yolks, beaten
  1 pastry shell (9 inches), baked
MERINGUE:
  3 egg whites
1/2 teaspoon vanilla extract
1/4 teaspoon cream of tartar
  6 tablespoons sugar

In a large saucepan, combine sugar and flour. Stir in pineapple and sour cream until combined. Cook and stir over medium-high heat until thickened and bubbly. Reduce heat; cook and stir 2 minutes longer.

Remove from the heat. Stir a small amount of the hot filling into the egg yolks; return all to the pan, stir-

ring constantly. Bring to a gentle boil; cook and stir 2 minutes longer. Remove from the heat. Pour into the pastry shell.

In a small mixing bowl, beat the egg whites, vanilla and cream of tartar on medium speed until soft peaks form. Gradually beat in sugar, 1 tablespoon at a time, on high until stiff glossy peaks form and sugar is dissolved. Spread evenly over hot filling, sealing edges to crust.

Bake at 350° for 15-18 minutes or until meringue is golden. Cool on a wire rack for 1 hour. Refrigerate for at least 3 hours before serving. Refrigerate leftovers. **Yield:** 8 servings.

Quick Ham Hints

- Purchase ham that has a rosy pink color. Also, the meat should be firm to the touch when pressed.
- Freezing deteriorates ham quality. But if you must freeze, wrap the ham tightly. It can be stored in the freezer for up to 2 months.
- If you're cooking more than one ham, make sure there is uniform space around the hams in the oven so they will cook evenly. They should not be touching.
- Leftover cooked ham should be wrapped tightly and put in the refrigerator within 1 to 2 hours after cooking. Ham may be stored this way for up to 4 days.

Saucy chicken dish takes center stage in her mother's Southern-style supper menu.

By Donna Sasser Hinds, Milwaukie, Oregon

DESPITE her German heritage and the fact that she raised her family in Oregon, my mother is a Southern belle at heart.

Hazel Bickel Sasser (my mom, above) grew up in Louisville, Kentucky. Her family owned a market, where Mother worked until she married my father, Merlyn, and moved to The Dalles, Oregon.

She took along the recipes she acquired from her German grandmother, her mother and the family's housekeeper, Mattie. Mattie greatly influenced my mother's taste for Southern fare.

So it's no surprise that my mom's best meal features Down-Home Chicken with Poached Corn, Freezer Coleslaw and Gingerbread Boy Cookies.

Down-Home Chicken evolved from a recipe my mother saw on a TV show in the 1950s. We lovingly called it Goopy Chicken because of its thick molasses sauce. Fresh, sweet Poached Corn and crispy Freezer Coleslaw were the perfect complements.

Mother excelled at baking treats, and her Gingerbread Boy Cookies were our favorites. My sister once asked for them instead of birthday cake. (My mom made a round cake and put the cookie boys hand to hand around it.)

My dad, who was a railroad conductor, seldom helped in the kitchen, but he was my mother's biggest fan. He often said he'd put her cooking up against anyone's.

Although my mother doesn't cook much anymore, she made her trademark mashed potatoes for Thanksgiving last year and supervised our family candy-making day before Christmas.

People always recall Mother's wonderful cooking. My 40-year high school reunion proved it. Former classmates came up to me and asked, "Does your mother still make…?"

I hope you and your family will enjoy my mother's Southern menu as much as we do.

PICTURED AT LEFT: Down-Home Chicken, Poached Corn, Freezer Coleslaw and Gingerbread Boy Cookies (recipes are on the next page).

Down-Home Chicken

Prep: 30 min.   **Cook:** 40 min.

1/2 cup all-purpose flour
  1 teaspoon salt
1/2 teaspoon pepper
  1 broiler/fryer chicken (3 to 4 pounds),
     cut up
1/4 cup vegetable oil
SAUCE:
2/3 cup lemon juice
2/3 cup ketchup
2/3 cup molasses
1/3 cup vegetable oil
1/4 cup Worcestershire sauce
  1 teaspoon ground cloves
1/2 teaspoon salt
1/4 teaspoon pepper
Hot cooked rice

In a large resealable plastic bag, combine the flour, salt and pepper. Add chicken, a few pieces at a time, and shake to coat. In a large skillet, heat oil. Brown chicken in oil on all sides; remove to paper towels. Drain drippings and return chicken to the pan.

In a bowl, combine the lemon juice, ketchup, molasses, oil, Worcestershire sauce, cloves, salt and pepper. Pour over chicken. Bring to a boil. Reduce heat; simmer, uncovered, for 35-40 minutes or until chicken juices run clear. Serve with rice. **Yield:** 6 servings.

Poached Corn

Prep/Total Time: 20 min.

5 cups fresh *or* frozen corn
2 cups milk
4 teaspoons sugar
1 tablespoon butter
3/4 teaspoon salt
1/2 teaspoon pepper

In a large saucepan, combine all ingredients. Cook over low heat for 10-12 minutes or until corn is tender, stirring frequently. Serve with a slotted spoon. **Yield:** 6 servings.

Sweet 'n' Spicy Cloves

Through the centuries, cloves have been used to freshen breath, relieve toothaches and even ward off the plague. Nowadays, many people rely on aromatic cloves to spice up ham, pumpkin pie or a hot holiday punch.

Cloves also flavor salad dressings, cookies, baked beans and chili as well as Indian, Chinese and German foods.

Whatever the dish, cloves add a fresh, sweet and spicy taste when used sparingly. Use too much, and the pungent flavor can easily overpower a recipe.

Reach for ground cloves to prepare terrific Down-Home Chicken (recipe at left).

1/2 cup molasses
2 teaspoons white vinegar
1 egg, beaten
3 cups all-purpose flour
1/2 teaspoon baking soda
1/2 teaspoon ground ginger
1/2 teaspoon ground cinnamon
1/4 teaspoon salt

In a saucepan, combine the butter, sugar, molasses and vinegar; bring to a boil, stirring constantly. Remove from the heat; cool to lukewarm. Stir in egg. Combine the flour, baking soda, ginger, cinnamon and salt; stir into molasses mixture to form a soft dough.

Divide dough into thirds. Shape each portion into a disk; wrap in plastic wrap. Refrigerate for at least 2 hours or until easy to handle.

On a lightly floured surface, roll dough to 1/4-in. thickness. Cut with a floured 3-in. gingerbread boy cookie cutter. Place on greased baking sheets. Bake at 375° for 7-9 minutes or until edges are firm. Remove to wire racks. **Yield:** 3-4 dozen.

Freezer Coleslaw

Prep: 25 min. + freezing

1 medium head cabbage (about 2 pounds), shredded
1 teaspoon salt
2 cups sugar
1 cup white vinegar
1/4 cup water
1 teaspoon celery seed
1 teaspoon mustard seed
1 large carrot, shredded
1/2 cup finely chopped green pepper

In a large bowl, combine cabbage and salt; let stand for 1 hour. In a saucepan, combine the sugar, vinegar, water, celery seed and mustard seed. Bring to a boil; boil for 1 minute. Remove from the heat; cool.

Drain cabbage. Add the carrot, green pepper and vinegar mixture. Transfer to freezer containers; cover and freeze. Remove from the freezer 2 hours before serving. Serve with a slotted spoon. **Yield:** 10 servings.

Gingerbread Boy Cookies

Prep: 1 hour + chilling   **Bake:** 10 min. per batch

1/2 cup butter, cubed
1/2 cup sugar

Turkey with a French accent is the highlight of her mother's best dinner menu...and gets the family reminiscing about the memorable flavors of France.

By Emma Rea, Hermann, Missouri

MY MOM, Diana Rea (above), never learned to cook while growing up. Her mother wasn't much into cooking, so she didn't pass on a love for it to her daughters. But through many experiments, some flops and hard work, my mom has become a fantastic cook!

After getting married, she and my dad, Tom, moved to France as missionaries. During the 12 years they lived and worked there—and raised a family—my mother developed a real appreciation for good, wholesome food.

She learned to prepare so many mouth-watering dishes from scratch that it was difficult to choose one meal I consider her best. But Turkey with Mushrooms and Cream has to be one of her best authentic French dishes.

The original turkey recipe, Dinde a la Crème et Champignons, uses white wine instead of apple juice, but either way, this main dish is absolutely scrumptious. Mom often serves it for Easter, Christmas and other celebrations.

As an accompaniment, crunchy Hazelnut Vegetable Salad can't be beat. Mom doesn't always add the asparagus spears, but I think the steamed spears make this colorful combination twice as good.

No one passes up Mom's golden brown Yummy Yeast Rolls, served warm with butter. To shape them, we cut them out of the rolled dough with a drinking glass, and they always turn out fine.

Layered Poppy Seed Torte, featuring a sweet nutty filling and creamy mocha frosting, makes an impressive finale for any occasion. It takes a little time to prepare, but everyone agrees that it's worth the effort!

While living in France, our family entertained almost weekly. Often on Sunday afternoons, we would have friends over for a five-course meal that lasted several hours. In true French style, Mom would serve an appetizer, salad, main dish, cheese and dessert... each as a separate course. Each course was accompanied by crusty baguettes from the bakery.

For birthdays, she'd serve a dish called raclette. It's a special melted cheese poured over potatoes,

served with pickled baby onions and tiny dill pickles.

Mom's style hasn't changed much since we moved back to the United States in 2000. She still cooks and bakes from scratch for our family, which now numbers 10. I'm the oldest of eight children; we're home-schooled by Mom and Dad, who's the pastor of a local church.

Every other week, Mom goes to the grocery store, which is 45 minutes away. We grind our own flour, so she buys 50 to 100 pounds of wheat berries at a time. She also buys 25 pounds of pasta and popcorn. (We love popcorn...in France, you sprinkle sugar on it.) We plant a huge garden in the summer with about 60 tomato plants.

My three sisters and I have always helped Mom in the kitchen, so we have a lot of cooking experience. Sometimes we'll make lunch or dinner by ourselves to give her a break. My brothers dry the dishes, take out the garbage and lick the spoons! They leave the cooking to us.

I am about to start college in South Carolina, and one of the first things I plan to do is join the university's kitchen club so I can continue making my mom's fantastic recipes.

I'm sure you'll like them, too. *Bon appetit!*

Rolls Like Mom Made

It's not difficult to treat your family to a batch of made-from-scratch, golden brown rolls like Yummy Yeast Rolls (recipe on page 207) for dinner. Want to know the keys to making successful yeast rolls? Follow these guidelines the next time you're in the kitchen:

• When mixing dough, always start with a minimum amount of flour until the dough reaches the desired consistency.

• Do not use light or whipped butter, diet spread or tub margarine in place of the butter, stick margarine (with at least 80% oil) or shortening that a recipe calls for.

• Knead dough only until it doesn't tear easily when stretched.

• Let dough rise in a warm (80° to 85°) draft-free area. Proper rising helps in the development of the texture.

PICTURED AT LEFT: Turkey with Mushrooms and Cream, Hazelnut Vegetable Salad, Yummy Yeast Rolls and Poppy Seed Torte (recipes are on the next page).

Turkey with Mushrooms And Cream

Prep/Total Time: 30 min.

☑ **Uses less fat, sugar or salt. Includes Nutrition Facts and Diabetic Exchanges.**

- 1 package (17.6 ounces) turkey breast slices
- 1 tablespoon canola oil
- 3 tablespoons butter, *divided*
- 3/4 cup water, *divided*
- 1/4 cup unsweetened apple juice
- 2 teaspoons chicken bouillon granules, *divided*
- 1/4 teaspoon pepper
- 1 cup (8 ounces) sour cream
- 1 pound fresh mushrooms, chopped

Hot cooked rice

In a large skillet over medium-high heat, cook turkey in oil and 2 tablespoons butter until golden brown and no pink remains. Remove and keep warm.

In the same skillet, combine 1/2 cup water, apple juice, 1 teaspoon bouillon and pepper; cook and stir over medium heat until bouillon is dissolved. Stir in sour cream; heat through.

Meanwhile, in another skillet, combine the remaining butter, water and bouillon; cook and stir over medium heat until bouillon is dissolved. Add mushrooms; cook for 10 minutes or until liquid has evaporated. Serve turkey over rice; top with cream sauce and mushrooms. **Yield:** 4 servings.

Nutrition Facts: 4 ounces (prepared with reduced-fat butter, reduced-sodium bouillon and reduced-fat sour cream; calculated without rice) equals 338 calories, 15 g fat (9 g saturated fat), 115 mg cholesterol, 249 mg sodium, 11 g carbohydrate, 1 g fiber, 39 g protein. **Diabetic Exchanges:** 4 lean meat, 1 reduced-fat milk.

Hazelnut Vegetable Salad

Prep/Total Time: 25 min.

☑ **Uses less fat, sugar or salt. Includes Nutrition Facts and Diabetic Exchanges.**

- 1/4 cup olive oil
- 2 tablespoons lemon juice
- 2 teaspoons cider vinegar
- 2 teaspoons honey
- 1/4 teaspoon salt
- 1/4 teaspoon coarsely ground pepper
- 1/2 pound sliced fresh mushrooms
- 1/2 medium sweet red pepper, julienned
- 2 celery ribs, julienned
- 3 tablespoons minced chives
- 4 lettuce leaves
- 8 asparagus spears, cooked and drained
- 2 tablespoons chopped hazelnuts

For dressing, in a small bowl, whisk the first six ingredients. In a large bowl, combine the mushrooms, red pepper, celery and chives. Drizzle with dressing and toss to coat. Refrigerate until serving.

Place lettuce on salad plates; top with asparagus and mushroom mixture. Sprinkle with hazelnuts. **Yield:** 4 servings.

Nutrition Facts: 1 cup equals 186 calories, 16 g fat

(2 g saturated fat), 0 cholesterol, 172 mg sodium, 10 g carbohydrate, 2 g fiber, 4 g protein. **Diabetic Exchanges:** 3 fat, 2 vegetable.

Yummy Yeast Rolls

Prep: 25 min. + rising   **Bake:** 15 min.

2 to 2-1/2 cups all-purpose flour
3 tablespoons sugar
1 package (1/4 ounce) quick-rise yeast
1/2 teaspoon salt
3/4 cup warm water (120° to 130°)
2 tablespoons butter, melted

In a large mixing bowl, combine 1-1/2 cups flour, sugar, yeast and salt. Add water and butter; beat on medium speed for 3 minutes or until smooth. Stir in enough remaining flour to form a soft dough.

Turn onto a well-floured surface; knead until smooth and elastic, about 4-6 minutes. Cover and let rest for 10 minutes. Roll dough to 3/8-in. thickness; cut with a floured 2-1/2-in. biscuit cutter.

Place 2 in. apart on a greased baking sheet. Cover and let rise in a warm place until doubled, about 30 minutes. Bake at 375° for 11-14 minutes or until lightly browned. Remove to a wire rack. **Yield:** about 1 dozen.

Poppy Seed Torte

Prep: 20 min. + standing   **Bake:** 15 min. + cooling

2/3 cup milk
1/2 cup poppy seeds
1/2 cup butter, softened
1 cup sugar
2 cups cake flour
2 teaspoons baking powder
1/4 teaspoon salt
3 egg whites

FILLING:
1 cup sugar
1 cup (8 ounces) sour cream
3 egg yolks
1 cup chopped walnuts
1 teaspoon vanilla extract
MOCHA FROSTING:
6 tablespoons butter, softened
3 cups confectioners' sugar
3 tablespoons baking cocoa
3 to 4 tablespoons hot strong brewed coffee

In a bowl, combine milk and poppy seeds; let stand for 1 hour. In a large mixing bowl, cream butter and sugar. Combine the flour, baking powder and salt; add to creamed mixture alternately with poppy seed mixture.

In another bowl with clean beaters, beat egg whites until soft peaks form; fold into batter. Pour into two greased and floured 9-in. round baking pans. Bake at 350° for 15-20 minutes or until a toothpick inserted near the center comes out clean. Cool for 10 minutes before removing from pans to wire racks.

For filling, in a heavy saucepan, combine the sugar, sour cream and egg yolks. Cook and stir over low heat just until mixture begins to simmer and reaches 160°. Remove from heat; add nuts and vanilla. Transfer to a bowl; cover with plastic wrap and refrigerate until completely cooled.

For frosting, in a small mixing bowl, beat butter, confectioners' sugar and cocoa until blended. Add coffee, 1 tablespoon at a time, until mixture achieves spreading consistency.

Place one cake layer on serving plate; spread with filling. Top with second layer; spread with frosting. Store in the refrigerator. **Yield:** 10-12 servings.

Featuring an elegant seafood entree as the main course, this special family-size spread delights everyone at weekly gatherings around her mother's dinner table.

By Kimberly Laabs, Hartford, Wisconsin

IT'S A TRADITION at our house to have dinner together each Sunday. Even now that my brother, sister and I are adults, we still gather at my parents' home in Erin, Wisconsin for one of Mom's incredible meals. It's a time that our family makes sure to reserve for each other.

My mom, Sharon Laabs (above), has always made mealtime special...and not just on Sundays. She puts plenty of thought, time and effort into each and every meal she prepares.

She loves to entertain, especially at Christmas. When company is coming, Mom will spend the whole day in the kitchen. She'll serve a four-course meal with appetizers, soup or salad, main course and dessert. Everything has to be perfect...right down to the presentation. The dining room table always looks beautiful with a tablecloth, centerpiece, candles and her good dishes.

When it's a special occasion—a birthday, graduation, anniversary, etc.—the person who is special that day can put in a menu request with Mom. If it's someone in the family, he or she also gets to eat off the "red plate," which says "You are special today." Last Christmas, Mom even gave each of us kids a red plate so we can carry on the tradition with our own families.

My mom's very best meal, I think, is the one my sister, Kristin, chose to have as her birthday dinner: Puff Pastry Salmon Bundles, Comforting Broccoli Casserole, Strawberry Spinach Salad and Ice Cream Cookie Dessert.

The Puff Pastry Salmon Bundles make any menu elegant. The crisp pastry and delicious cucumber sauce are a wonderful combination, and the salmon almost melts in your mouth.

Her Comforting Broccoli Casserole is not only flavorful but nutritious, too. And the Strawberry Spinach Salad is a refreshing, colorful toss with a raspberry vinaigrette.

Our entire family loves dessert and can't wait to see what Mom has prepared as a finishing touch to a meal. Her yummy Ice Cream Cookie Dessert is a real favorite...even during cold, winter months.

My mother grew up in Milwaukee and learned to cook from her mom, who was also a wonderful cook. She met my dad, Richard, when they were in the fourth grade! She was a stay-at-home mom when my sister, brother and I were young. Mom now teaches fourth grade and is assistant principal at an area elementary school. Dad's an executive director of three Lutheran schools.

When Mom cooked for our family of five, she always made too much food—and she still does. Now that our family is larger, though, she can send food home with each of her children.

My sister, Kristin, who's an attorney, is married, as is my brother, Bryan, who's a CPA. He and his wife have a daughter, Calla—my mom's only grandchild. I teach kindergarten at the same school where my mom teaches. It's a privilege to work with her each day and to share her career.

Everyone in our family gets along extremely well. The guys like to golf or attend football games together, while we girls like spending the day at the mall or in the spa. Of course, each week we make a point of joining together for Sunday dinner.

Dinner begins with a prayer and then a big toast to my mom for another wonderful meal. I know you'll enjoy this menu of hers as much as we do.

Sweet on Strawberries

Whether you're preparing Strawberry Spinach Salad (recipe on page 211), a fresh fruit platter or a classic layered shortcake, strawberries will make your dish a winner. After all, those little red gems have a sweet, refreshing flavor that folks of all ages love.

Peak season for strawberries occurs in April, May and June. When you're purchasing them fresh, look for berries that are shiny, firm and very fragrant. The berry should be almost completely red, although some whiteness near the cap is acceptable.

Refrigerate unwashed strawberries with the cap on until you're ready to use them. Just before using, wash and hull the berries.

PICTURED AT LEFT: Puff Pastry Salmon Bundles, Comforting Broccoli Casserole, Strawberry Spinach Salad and Ice Cream Cookie Dessert (recipes are on the next page).

Puff Pastry Salmon Bundles

Prep: 20 min.   **Bake:** 25 min.

- 2 **packages (17.3 ounces** *each***) frozen puff pastry, thawed**
- 8 **salmon fillets (6 ounces** *each***), skin removed**
- 1 **egg**
- 1 **tablespoon water**
- 2 **cups shredded cucumber**
- 1 **cup (8 ounces) sour cream**
- 1 **cup mayonnaise**
- 1 **teaspoon dill weed**
- 1/2 **teaspoon salt**

On a lightly floured surface, roll each pastry sheet into a 12-in. x 10-in. rectangle. Cut each into two 6-in. x 5-in. rectangles. Place a salmon fillet in the center of each rectangle.

Beat egg and water; lightly brush over pastry edges. Bring opposite corners of pastry over fillet; pinch seams to seal tightly. Place seam side down in a greased 15-in. x 10-in. x 1-in. baking pan; brush with remaining egg mixture.

Bake at 400° for 25-30 minutes or until pastry is golden brown. In a small bowl, combine the cucumber, sour cream, mayonnaise, dill and salt. Serve with bundles. **Yield:** 8 servings.

Comforting Broccoli Casserole

Prep: 20 min.   **Bake:** 30 min.

- 2 **eggs, lightly beaten**
- 1 **can (10-3/4 ounces) condensed cream of mushroom soup, undiluted**
- 1 **medium onion, chopped**
- 1 **cup (4 ounces) shredded cheddar cheese**
- 1 **cup (4 ounces) shredded Swiss cheese**
- 1/2 **cup mayonnaise**
- 2 **tablespoons butter, melted**
- 1 **package (16 ounces) frozen broccoli cuts, thawed**
- 1 **package (10 ounces) frozen chopped broccoli, thawed**
- 1/4 **cup dry bread crumbs**

In a large bowl, combine the first seven ingredients; fold in broccoli. Transfer to a greased 1-1/2-qt. baking dish. Sprinkle with bread crumbs. Cover and bake at 400° for 30-35 minutes or until heated through. **Yield:** 8 servings.

   Editor's Note: Reduced-fat or fat-free mayonnaise is not recommended for this recipe.

Purchasing Fish

When you need fresh fish fillets or steaks from the market, look for firm flesh that has a moist appearance. Don't buy fish that appears dried out. Fresh fish should have a mild smell, not a strong odor.

   When purchasing frozen fish, look for packages that are solidly frozen, tightly sealed and free of freezer burn and odor.

Ice Cream Cookie Dessert

Prep: 15 min. + freezing

- 1 package (18 ounces) cream-filled chocolate sandwich cookies, crushed, *divided*
- 1/4 cup butter, melted
- 1/2 gallon vanilla ice cream, softened
- 1 jar (16 ounces) hot fudge ice cream topping, warmed
- 1 carton (8 ounces) frozen whipped topping, thawed

In a bowl, combine 3-3/4 cups sandwich cookie crumbs and butter. Press into a greased 13-in. x 9-in. x 2-in. dish. Spread with the vanilla ice cream; cover and freeze until set.

Drizzle the fudge ice cream topping over the ice cream; cover and freeze until set. Spread with the whipped topping; sprinkle with the remaining cookie crumbs. Cover dessert and freeze for 2 hours or until firm. Remove from the freezer 10 minutes before serving. **Yield:** 12 servings.

Strawberry Spinach Salad

Prep: 20 min. + chilling

- 1/3 cup raspberry vinaigrette
- 1/2 cup sugar
- 1 teaspoon salt
- 1/4 teaspoon prepared mustard
- 1/2 cup vegetable oil
- 4-1/2 teaspoons poppy seeds
- 1 package (10 ounces) fresh baby spinach
- 1 pint fresh strawberries, sliced
- 1/2 cup coarsely chopped pecans, toasted

In a blender, combine the raspberry vinaigrette, sugar, salt and mustard. While processing, gradually add the oil in a steady stream. Stir in the poppy seeds. Transfer to a small pitcher or bowl. Refrigerate for 1 hour or until chilled.

Just before serving, toss the spinach, strawberries and pecans in a large salad bowl. Serve with dressing. **Yield:** 8 servings.

Editors' Meals

Taste of Home is edited by 1,000 cooks across North America. Here, you'll "meet" some of those cooks who share a family-favorite meal.

COOK'S CHOICE. Clockwise from upper left: Christmas Morning Menu (p. 214), Best Backyard Barbecue (p. 226), Savory Seafood Supper (p. 218) and Sunday Chicken with a Twist (p. 222).

Christmas Morning Menu

Holiday brunch is a highlight for one of our field editors and her family.

By Maryellen Hays, Wolcottville, Indiana

WE ALWAYS enjoy a buffet brunch after our morning church service on Christmas Day. It's so nice to have the family gathered around the table to celebrate this most beautiful of holidays.

Our simple but tasty menu has become an anticipated tradition. It includes Christmas Breakfast Casserole, Triple-Cheese Broccoli Puff, Hot Curried Fruit, Cider Wassail and Apple-Raisin Bundt Cake. This meal works so well for our schedule because much of the food can be prepared ahead of time.

Our celebration actually begins on Christmas Eve, when husband Ron and I host a family gathering with a gift exchange and potluck dinner at our home on Big Long Lake, about 45 miles north of Fort Wayne, Indiana. The property has been in my family since 1927, and my grandfather built our house.

We're joined by our daughters, Robin and Heather, and their families, including grandchildren Anthony, Samantha and Colton and great-granddaughter Gabi. After brunch on Christmas Day, they all move on to celebrate with the other side of their families.

My Christmas Breakfast Casserole is a convenient choice for busy mornings because it's assembled the day before. Light-textured and cheesy, this dish looks and tastes delicious. The bacon in it balances nicely with the other flavors.

Puffy and golden, Triple-Cheese Broccoli Puff is a lovely side-dish souffle. If you add some diced ham or poultry, it easily becomes an entree.

Hot Curried Fruit is a comforting, warm accompaniment that's so enjoyable in chilly weather. The recipe came from a cookbook I've had since my college days at Indiana State University.

I received the Cider Wassail recipe from a dear friend in Fort Wayne, where we lived for many years. Since it's warm, wonderful and nonalcoholic, we've even served it at church.

It's also perfect for a holiday open house, which we host every other year. Ron and I love to entertain, whether it be for a few friends, the family or our congregation after church service.

An old-fashioned holiday treat, Apple-Raisin Bundt Cake is very moist, pleasantly spicy and chock-full of raisins and nuts. This cake truly tastes better if you bake it several days ahead of time and let the flavors mellow.

I like to cook just about everything, but baking is my specialty. I've often said, "I'm a dump-and-pour cook. If you can't dump and pour it, I can't cook it." What I mean is that I'm not a gourmet cook at all. Plain old home cooking is my style.

I use lots of fresh garden produce in season. On almost any road around here, you'll find a fresh-produce stand.

My earliest memories of cooking are from when I was around 4. My grandmother, Fern Shannon, got me on the stool Grandpa made and guided me in making pancakes with her at the lake on Sundays.

Ron is the family's expert on the grill. He likes to do salmon and steaks as well as hamburgers and hot dogs. Now that we spend 2 months each winter in Green Valley, Arizona, he devotes more time to cooking outdoors.

Ron retired from a 34-year teaching career in 1994, and I recently retired from my job with an insurance company. These days, the two of us volunteer at a local county hospital, serve as house managers for the Fort Wayne Civic Theatre and are also active in our church.

Sharing my favorite recipes as a *Taste of Home* field editor is a lot of fun. I was also thrilled when another *Taste of Home* cook contacted me after I wrote about a Mardi Gras party we gave (Feb/Mar '99). It was fun to guide her through planning one of her own parties—from ordering the festive beads to planning the menu.

This Christmas, when I'm fixing our brunch, I'll be wondering if some of you readers might be preparing one or more of my recipes for your own celebration. I hope they please your family as much as they do mine.

Have a wonderful and joyous holiday season!

PICTURED AT LEFT: Christmas Breakfast Casserole, Triple-Cheese Broccoli Puff, Hot Curried Fruit, Cider Wassail and Apple-Raisin Bundt Cake (recipes are on the next page).

6 eggs
1 cup milk
3/4 cup biscuit/baking mix
1 package (10 ounces) frozen chopped broccoli, thawed
2 cups (8 ounces) shredded Monterey Jack cheese
1 cup (8 ounces) small-curd cottage cheese
1/4 teaspoon salt

In a small skillet, saute the mushrooms in butter until tender; set aside. In a large mixing bowl, beat the cream cheese, eggs, milk and biscuit/baking mix just until combined. Stir in the broccoli, cheeses, salt and mushrooms.

Pour into a greased round 2-1/2-qt. baking dish. Bake, uncovered, at 350° for 50-60 minutes or until a knife inserted near the center of the dish comes out clean. Let stand for 10 minutes before serving. **Yield:** 6-8 servings.

Christmas Breakfast Casserole

Prep: 10 min. + chilling   **Bake:** 50 min.

7 slices white bread, crusts removed and cubed
2 cups (8 ounces) shredded cheddar cheese
6 eggs
3 cups milk
1 teaspoon ground mustard
1/2 teaspoon salt
1/4 teaspoon pepper
6 bacon strips, cooked and crumbled

In a greased 11-in. x 7-in. x 2-in. baking dish, combine the bread cubes and cheese. In a large bowl, whisk the eggs, milk, mustard, salt and pepper; pour over bread and cheese. Top with bacon. Cover and refrigerate overnight.

Remove from the refrigerator 30 minutes before baking. Bake, uncovered, at 350° for 50-55 minutes or until a knife inserted near the center comes out clean. **Yield:** 6-8 servings.

Triple-Cheese Broccoli Puff

Prep: 15 min.   **Bake:** 50 min. + standing

1 cup sliced fresh mushrooms
1 tablespoon butter
1 package (3 ounces) cream cheese, softened

Hot Curried Fruit

Prep: 10 min.   **Bake:** 35 min.

1 can (20 ounces) unsweetened pineapple chunks
1 can (16 ounces) pitted dark sweet cherries, drained
1 can (15-1/4 ounces) pear halves, drained

Apple-Raisin Bundt Cake

Prep: 20 min.   **Bake:** 1 hour + cooling

3/4 cup butter, softened
1-1/2 cups sugar
1 cup plus 2 tablespoons strawberry jam
3-1/3 cups all-purpose flour
1-1/2 teaspoons baking soda
1-1/2 teaspoons ground nutmeg
3/4 teaspoon *each* ground allspice, cloves and cinnamon
1-1/2 cups buttermilk
1-3/4 cups raisins
3/4 cup chopped walnuts
3/4 cup chopped peeled apple
GLAZE:
1 cup confectioners' sugar
4 teaspoons milk

In a large mixing bowl, cream butter and sugar. Stir in jam. Combine the flour, baking soda and spices; beat into creamed mixture alternately with buttermilk. Add the raisins, walnuts and apple; mix well. Pour into a greased and floured 10-in. fluted tube pan.

Bake at 350° for 1 hour or until a toothpick inserted near the center comes out clean. Cool for 10 minutes before removing from pan to a wire rack to cool completely. Combine glaze ingredients; drizzle over cake. **Yield:** 12-16 servings.

1 can (15-1/4 ounces) peach halves, drained
3/4 cup packed brown sugar
1/4 cup butter, melted
1 teaspoon curry powder
1 teaspoon ground cinnamon
1/2 teaspoon ground nutmeg

Drain pineapple, reserving juice. In a greased 2-qt. baking dish, combine the pineapple, cherries, pears and peaches. Combine the brown sugar, butter, curry, cinnamon, nutmeg and reserved juice; pour over fruit. Cover and bake at 350° for 35-45 minutes or until heated through. **Yield:** 8 servings.

Cider Wassail

(Pictured on page 214)

Prep/Total Time: 30 min.

2 quarts apple cider
1-1/2 cups orange juice
3/4 cup pineapple juice
1 tablespoon brown sugar
1/2 teaspoon lemon juice
2 cinnamon sticks (3 inches)
Dash ground cinnamon
Dash ground cloves

In a large saucepan, combine all of the ingredients. Bring to a boil. Reduce heat; cover and simmer for 20-30 minutes. Discard cinnamon sticks. Serve hot in mugs. **Yield:** 10-12 servings (2-1/2 quarts).

Savory Seafood Supper

One of our field editors cooks up a fresh menu that's everyday-simple but company-special.

By Sundra Hauck, Bogalusa, Louisiana

WHEN THANKSGIVING, Christmas and New Year's are behind us for another year, my husband, Ron, and I are glad to change from traditional, rich seasonal favorites to basic menus and simple foods that are the signature "taste of our home."

We've entertained and been entertained...and now we really enjoy just sitting down together for a simple but delicious meal like Chunky Crawfish Spread, Citrus Quencher, Sunday Shrimp Pasta Bake, Olive-Cucumber Tossed Salad and No-Bake Chocolate Pie.

Crawfish are my favorite, and Chunky Crawfish Spread (pictured on page 220) is just the right touch for conversation and snacking while the main course is finishing up in the oven.

Complementing the food with a sweet-tart taste, my Citrus Quencher is sparkling and refreshing. It's so easy to mix up that I serve this sunny beverage year-round.

The Sunday Shrimp Pasta Bake isn't just for Sunday, but it is that good. This delicious dish also serves us well on a Saturday night before a big football game or even during the week, if time allows.

Seafood is plentiful here, so we enjoy it often. Shrimp (or "shrimps," as my 101-year-old mother-in-law, Bertha, calls them) are Ron's favorite.

We often enjoy shrimp and crawfish at the same meal. But if not, I make sure to rotate the two.

The Olive-Cucumber Tossed Salad can be prepped ahead of time and plated up at the last minute. I combine the dressing with the olives and sliced cucumbers in advance.

Sometimes dessert has to be served a bit later, as this is a filling meal. But when you bring out the No-Bake Chocolate Pie, no one will turn it down. It's a winner on any occasion.

Leftovers are not a problem when I prepare this meal for just the two of us. We appreciate these foods the second time around, or I'll take the leftovers to share with co-workers the next day. There's always plenty to go around because I cook "big." It's the way I learned.

I work full-time in a medical office, but I still look forward to preparing a nice supper for us. I go into the kitchen, turn on my favorite radio station and cook. It's very relaxing to me.

Since I work away from home full-time, friends have asked how I manage to find time to cook. I tell them...lists. That's my secret. Lists. It's actually a bit of a joke with those who know me well.

I organize a meal—the menu, the shopping list, even the seating arrangement for special occasions. The bonus for me is that Ron cleans up. Isn't that just the most wonderful thing of all? I think so!

We were married 7 years ago. Ron was born in New Orleans and spent most of his life there. He's retired from the U.S. Postal Service.

I'm a Bogalusa native and have a son, a daughter and son-in-law, and two young grandsons. My family loves Ron as if he has been with us always.

My personal cooking pleasures didn't begin until I was an adult. I have come a long way and now am even asked to prepare foods for weddings and showers on occasion. I must admit, however, that I much prefer the simple pleasures of cooking for my husband, family, friends and co-workers.

Ron enjoys his retirement and spending time outdoors. He has worked as a nature guide at a local boys' and girls' summer camp and is active in the Knights of Columbus.

I'm a member of the Secular Franciscans (a Roman Catholic fraternity), play in a Po-Ke-No group and enjoy "Eight Is Enough"—a group of ladies who get together several times a year.

Together, Ron and I like what we call "day-tripping," taking jaunts around Louisiana and nearby Mississippi. Often, our destination is Baton Rouge for a visit with our grandchildren. "The grands" are our hearts, so we visit for any occasion that comes up—from soccer games to birthday parties and "good grade" celebrations.

I hope you enjoy my recipes as much as we do.

PICTURED AT LEFT: Citrus Quencher, Sunday Shrimp Pasta Bake, Olive-Cucumber Tossed Salad and No-Bake Chocolate Pie (recipes are on the next page).

Chunky Crawfish Spread

Prep: 20 min. + chilling

☑ Uses less fat, sugar or salt. Includes Nutrition Facts and Diabetic Exchanges.

- 1 package (16 ounces) frozen cooked crawfish tails, thawed
- 1 package (8 ounces) cream cheese, softened
- 1 medium green pepper, finely chopped
- 1 medium sweet red pepper, finely chopped
- 1 small onion, finely chopped
- 6 garlic cloves, minced
- 1/2 to 1 teaspoon Creole seasoning
- 1/2 teaspoon salt
- 6 to 12 drops hot pepper sauce

Assorted crackers

Chop crawfish; pat dry. In a small mixing bowl, beat the cream cheese. Add the peppers, onion, garlic, Creole seasoning, salt and hot pepper sauce; stir in the crawfish. Cover and refrigerate for at least 2 hours. Serve with crackers. **Yield:** 3 cups.

Nutrition Facts: 1/4 cup (prepared with reduced-fat cream cheese) equals 88 calories, 5 g fat (3 g saturated fat), 65 mg cholesterol, 244 mg sodium, 3 g carbohydrate, trace fiber, 9 g protein. **Diabetic Exchanges:** 1 lean meat, 1/2 fat.

Citrus Quencher

(Pictured on page 218)

Prep/Total Time: 5 min.

- 2 liters lemon-lime soda, chilled
- 3/4 cup limeade concentrate
- 1/2 cup orange juice

In a large pitcher, combine all ingredients. Serve over ice. **Yield:** 8 servings (2-1/2 quarts).

Sunday Shrimp Pasta Bake

Prep: 30 min.   **Bake:** 25 min.

- 12 ounces uncooked vermicelli
- 1 medium green pepper, chopped
- 5 green onions, chopped
- 6 garlic cloves, minced
- 6 tablespoons butter, cubed
- 2 tablespoons all-purpose flour
- 2 pounds deveined peeled cooked medium shrimp
- 1 teaspoon celery salt
- 1/8 teaspoon pepper
- 1 pound process cheese (Velveeta), cubed
- 1 can (10 ounces) diced tomatoes and green chilies, drained
- 1 can (4 ounces) mushroom stems and pieces, drained
- 1 tablespoon grated Parmesan cheese

Cook vermicelli according to package directions. Meanwhile, in a large skillet, saute the green pepper, onions and garlic in butter until tender. Gradually stir in the flour until blended. Stir in the shrimp, celery salt and pepper; cook, uncovered, over medium heat for 5-6 minutes or until heated through.

In a microwave-safe bowl, combine the process cheese, tomatoes and mushrooms. Microwave, uncovered, on high for 3-4 minutes or until cheese is melted, stirring occasionally. Add to shrimp mixture. Drain vermicelli; stir into skillet.

Pour into a greased 13-in. x 9-in. x 2-in. baking dish. Sprinkle with the Parmesan cheese. Bake, uncovered, at 350° for 25-30 minutes or until heated through. **Yield:** 8 servings.

Editor's Note: This recipe was tested in a 1,100-watt microwave.

Olive-Cucumber Tossed Salad

Prep: 15 min. + marinating

1 cup Italian salad dressing
2 medium cucumbers, peeled, halved, seeded and sliced
1 cup pimiento-stuffed olives, halved
1 teaspoon Creole seasoning
2 packages (10 ounces *each*) ready-to-serve salad greens

In a large bowl, combine the salad dressing, cucumbers, olives and Creole seasoning. Cover and refrigerate for at least 30 minutes. Just before serving, place the salad greens in a large bowl; add cucumber mixture and toss to coat. **Yield:** 8 servings.

Editor's Note: The following spices may be substituted for the Creole seasoning: 1/2 teaspoon each paprika and garlic powder, and a pinch each cayenne pepper, dried thyme and ground cumin.

No-Bake Chocolate Pie

Prep: 15 min. + chilling

7 milk chocolate candy bars (1.55 ounces *each*), chopped
20 large marshmallows
1/2 cup milk
2 cups whipped topping
1 graham cracker crust (9 inches)
Additional whipped topping, optional

In a large heavy saucepan, combine the candy bars, marshmallows and milk. Cook and stir over low heat until smooth. Remove from the heat; cool. Fold in whipped topping; pour into crust. Cover and refrigerate for 4 hours or overnight. Garnish with additional whipped topping if desired. **Yield:** 8 servings.

Sunday Chicken with a Twist

This field editor's kitchen is full of cooks preparing the family's dinner.

By Arlene Butler, Ogden, Utah

SUNDAY is the one day when I can count on the family being together for a meal. And we all have a hand in cooking it!

This menu of Orange Chicken Kiev, Honey-Oat Pan Rolls, Sweet Spinach Salad and Frosted Chocolate Chip Cheesecake is one we think is outstanding.

Let me set the scene: We love to try new recipes, and on Sunday, I give each family member one to prepare. I'm lucky to have a big kitchen so the six of us can work comfortably.

Besides my husband, David, and me, the team of cooks includes Jared, Christy, Aaron and Laura. (Our oldest daughter is married and lives in France. She has three boys.)

When we sit down to eat, the conversation sounds like a bunch of food critics. We discuss what we do or don't like about each dish, what could be changed to make it better and whether or not the recipe is good enough to keep.

We all agreed that Orange Chicken Kiev is a delicious twist on the traditional dish. It has a lovely orange flavor without being overwhelming. Attractive and special enough to serve guests, this entree is impressive but easy to make.

Light-textured Honey-Oat Pan Rolls were another unanimous pick. They taste terrific, have a wonderful aroma while baking and are easy to make, according to Jared, who has become the family breads expert. The dough, after one rising, is simply rolled into balls and left to rise, then baked.

With a refreshing citrus dressing, Sweet Spinach Salad got all six votes, too. Its flavor nicely complements the Orange Chicken Kiev. Since none of us likes cooked spinach, this salad is a tasty way to add that nutritional vegetable to a meal.

Husband David (a mechanical engineer) specializes in meats, including grilling and Dutch-oven cooking. Aaron loves to make breakfast and brunch foods. For me, it's desserts. And Frosted Chocolate Chip

Cheesecake is the best of over 50 cheesecake recipes in my collection.

This dessert recipe was given to me by a friend when we lived in California. The chocolate crust, creamy cheesecake and fluffy frosting make the perfect balance of flavors.

I started trying new recipes as a newlywed. I now have a large collection of favorites, which I keep in binders. If I find several similar recipes that sound promising, I'll conduct a baking contest, and we'll decide which is the best.

Outside my kitchen, I work as an administrative assistant, and I've written food articles for area newspapers. I also enjoy needlework and gardening.

I took classes to become a certified Master Gardener. Having fresh and flavorful produce and herbs available outside my kitchen door is wonderful!

Perhaps I've planted a seed for you to try some new recipes and invite your family or a group of friends to help prepare them. Why not start with my favorite meal?

You're likely to find, as we have, that eating is definitely an adventure and can be a lot of fun from start to end!

Arlene's Tips for Cheesecake

HERE'S a handful of cheesecake secrets Arlene has learned over the years:

• To prevent a cheesecake from cracking, do not overbeat the batter. Mix the cream cheese and sugar well to eliminate lumps, but after the eggs are added, beat the mixture as little as possible. (The nice thing about a frosted cheesecake is that the frosting will cover any cracks!)

• Cheesecake will continue to bake after it is removed from the oven. Your cake is done when it is firm, even though the middle may still look moist.

• Run a knife around the outside of the cheesecake 10 minutes after it comes out of the oven. This allows the cake to pull away from the pan freely as it cools.

• Letting a cheesecake chill in the refrigerator overnight is a real key to its great flavor.

PICTURED AT LEFT: Orange Chicken Kiev, Honey-Oat Pan Rolls, Sweet Spinach Salad and Frosted Chocolate Chip Cheesecake (recipes are on the next page).

Orange Chicken Kiev

Prep: 50 min.   **Bake:** 35 min.

1/2 cup butter, softened
2 tablespoons minced chives
2 tablespoons minced fresh parsley
1/4 teaspoon salt
1/8 teaspoon pepper
6 boneless skinless chicken breast halves (6 ounces *each*)
1/4 cup all-purpose flour
1 egg
1/4 cup orange juice
1 cup dry bread crumbs
1/2 teaspoon grated orange peel

In a bowl, combine the butter, chives, parsley, salt and pepper. Shape into a 6-in. x 2-in. rectangle; place on waxed paper. Freeze until firm, about 30 minutes.

Flatten chicken to 1/4-in. thickness. Cut butter mixture into six strips; place one strip in the center of each chicken breast half. Roll up each and tuck in the ends; secure with a toothpick.

Place the flour in a shallow bowl. In another bowl, beat egg and orange juice. In a third bowl, combine bread crumbs and orange peel. Coat chicken with flour, dip in egg mixture, then roll in crumb mixture. Place seam side down in a greased 13-in. x 9-in. x 2-in. baking dish.

Bake, uncovered, at 375° for 35-40 minutes or until chicken juices run clear. Discard toothpicks before serving. **Yield:** 6 servings.

Honey-Oat Pan Rolls

(Also pictured on front cover)

Prep: 45 min. + rising   **Bake:** 20 min.

✓ **Uses less fat, sugar or salt. Includes Nutrition Facts and Diabetic Exchanges.**

2-1/2 to 2-3/4 cups all-purpose flour
3/4 cup whole wheat flour
1/2 cup old-fashioned oats
2 packages (1/4 ounce *each*) active dry yeast
1 teaspoon salt
1 cup water
1/4 cup honey
5 tablespoons butter, *divided*
1 egg

In a large mixing bowl, combine 1 cup all-purpose flour, whole wheat flour, oats, yeast and salt. In a small saucepan, heat the water, honey and 4 tablespoons butter to 120°-130°. Add to the dry ingredients; beat just until moistened. Add the egg; beat until well combined. Stir in enough remaining all-purpose flour to form a soft dough.

Turn onto a floured surface; knead until smooth and elastic, about 6-8 minutes. Place in a greased bowl, turning once to grease top. Cover and let rise in a warm place until doubled, about 1 hour.

Punch dough down. Turn onto a lightly floured surface; divide into 24 pieces. Shape each into a ball. Place in a greased 13-in. x 9-in. x 2-in. baking pan. Cover and let rise until doubled, about 30 minutes.

Bake at 375° for 20-22 minutes or until golden brown. Melt remaining butter; brush over the rolls. Remove from pan to a wire rack. **Yield:** 2 dozen.

Nutrition Facts: 1 roll equals 103 calories, 3 g fat (2 g saturated fat), 15 mg cholesterol, 126 mg sodium, 17 g carbohydrate, 1 g fiber, 3 g protein. **Diabetic Exchanges:** 1 starch, 1/2 fat.

Sweet Spinach Salad

Prep: 10 min. + chilling

    3 tablespoons orange juice concentrate
    2 tablespoons sugar
    2 tablespoons cider vinegar
1-1/2 teaspoons chopped onion
    1/4 teaspoon salt
    1/2 cup vegetable oil
1-1/2 teaspoons poppy seeds
    1 package (10 ounces) fresh baby spinach
    1 can (15 ounces) mandarin oranges, drained
    2/3 cup slivered almonds, toasted

In a blender, combine the orange juice concentrate, sugar, vinegar, onion and salt. While processing, gradually add oil in a steady stream. Stir in poppy seeds. Transfer to a small pitcher or bowl. Refrigerate for at least 1 hour or until chilled.

On salad plates, arrange the spinach, mandarin oranges and almonds. Drizzle with dressing. **Yield:** 6 servings.

Frosted Chocolate Chip Cheesecake

Prep: 40 min.   **Bake:** 55 min. + chilling

    2 cups chocolate wafer crumbs
    6 tablespoons butter, melted
    3 packages (8 ounces *each*) cream cheese, softened
    1 cup sugar
    1 teaspoon vanilla extract
    3 eggs, lightly beaten
    1 cup (6 ounces) miniature semisweet chocolate chips
    1 milk chocolate candy bar (4 ounces), chopped
    2 cups whipped topping
    1/4 cup sliced almonds, toasted

In a bowl, combine wafer crumbs and butter. Press onto the bottom and 1-1/2 in. up the sides of a greased 9-in. springform pan. Chill for 15 minutes or until set.

In a large mixing bowl, beat cream cheese, sugar and vanilla until smooth. Add eggs; beat on low speed just until combined. Stir in chocolate chips. Pour into crust.

Place pan on a baking sheet. Bake at 325° for 55-60 minutes or until center is almost set. Cool on a wire rack for 10 minutes. Carefully run a knife around edge of pan to loosen; cool 1 hour longer. Refrigerate overnight.

For frosting, in a microwave-safe bowl, melt candy bar; stir until smooth. Cool to room temperature. Gradually stir in the whipped topping. Remove sides of springform pan. Frost top of cheesecake; garnish with almonds. Refrigerate leftovers. **Yield:** 12 servings.

Best Backyard Barbecue

The sizzling summer fare this field editor serves has guests' mouths watering.

By Nancy Zimmerman, Cape May Court House, New Jersey

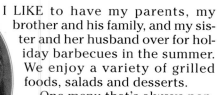

I LIKE to have my parents, my brother and his family, and my sister and her husband over for holiday barbecues in the summer. We enjoy a variety of grilled foods, salads and desserts.

One menu that's always popular is Tender 'n' Tasty Pork Chops, Grilled Corn in Husks, Stuffed Grilled Zucchini, Sunny Corn Bread Muffins and Hummingbird Cake.

My husband, Ken, loves to cook out and prefers using a traditional charcoal grill. He thinks it brings out the best flavor in the foods we prepare—and my family tends to agree.

Tender 'n' Tasty Pork Chops are wonderfully juicy, thanks to the flavorful marinade that is also used for basting. While the chops are grilling, the aroma seems to stir up everyone's appetite!

Seasoned with butter, Parmesan cheese and parsley, Grilled Corn in Husks is especially good. Be sure to give the ears a long soak before putting them on the grill. Hot off the grate, the kernels are moist and tender with a sweet flavor.

We always have plenty of zucchini in the garden, so it's only natural that we include it in summer meals. Stuffed Grilled Zucchini is one of the many ways we prepare it. The cheesy filling adds a special touch.

This stuffed zucchini also makes a great side dish for grilled beef, chicken or fish. It can be baked in the oven, too.

Sunny Corn Bread Muffins can be prepared with leftover cooked corn, canned whole kernel corn or frozen kernels that have been thawed. A great accompaniment to our barbecue, these tasty muffins are very moist and have an appealing golden yellow color. They're especially good warm, so if I bake them ahead of time, I warm them on the grill or in the microwave before serving.

Everyone always makes sure they leave room for a slice of Hummingbird Cake. I don't remember exactly where the recipe came from, but it is one of the most requested cakes I've made.

Family members often ask me to make this dessert for their birthday parties, and it's my dad's all-time favorite cake. I like the way it fills the whole house with a wonderful aroma while it bakes!

After our grilled meal, we like to play horseshoes or a game of Wiffle ball in the backyard. Our nieces play with our pet ducks. We have 11 of them, and they supply me with all the eggs that I use in my cooking and baking.

Ken and I live on 2-1/4 acres in the small community of Swainton, near Cape May Court House, and Ken is an excellent gardener. He grows a variety of vegetables, as well as plenty of berries, apples, pears and peaches.

As a result of the prolific produce from our garden, I have learned to can and freeze. Bread-and-butter pickles, jams, relishes and preserves line our pantry shelves. I give these foods as well as homemade candy and baked goods to friends and family for birthdays and special occasions.

Experimenting with recipes is fun for me. For example, I've altered my great-aunt's sour cream pound cake to create several variations. One of them, Triple Chocolate Sour Cream Pound Cake, won a *Taste of Home* Cooking Schools recipe contest a few years ago. Ken and I have enjoyed attending the Cooking Schools shows when they've come to our area.

Working part-time as a sales representative for a Christian radio station keeps me on the go. I'm also a committed runner and seldom miss an early morning run. It keeps me in shape, and I like to pray along the way. I have also come up with some creative baking ideas while out there!

Ken is an X-ray technician at a local hospital and an avid hunter. So I have learned to cook venison, rabbit, wild turkey, goose and duck.

Both of us play in volleyball leagues and, during the summer, like to play volleyball on the beach near our home.

I hope *Taste of Home* readers will enjoy these recipes as much as my family and I have. God bless!

PICTURED AT LEFT: Tender 'n' Tasty Pork Chops, Grilled Corn in Husks, Stuffed Grilled Zucchini, Sunny Corn Bread Muffins and Hummingbird Cake (recipes are on the next page).

Tender 'n' Tasty Pork Chops

Prep: 15 min. + marinating **Grill:** 20 min.

        1-2/3 cups unsweetened pineapple juice
          1/3 cup rice wine vinegar
          1/4 cup olive oil
            3 tablespoons soy sauce
            3 tablespoons chopped shallots
            4 garlic cloves, minced
        1-1/2 teaspoons salt
            1 teaspoon Louisiana-style hot sauce
          3/4 teaspoon ground cumin
          3/4 teaspoon pepper
            6 bone-in pork loin chops (3/4 inch thick)

In a large bowl, combine the first 10 ingredients. Place pork chops in a large resealable plastic bag; add half of the marinade. Seal bag and turn to coat; refrigerate for 4-5 hours, turning occasionally. Cover and refrigerate remaining marinade for basting.

Drain and discard marinade. Grill pork chops, covered, over medium heat for 8-10 minutes on each side or until a meat thermometer reads 160°, basting occasionally with reserved marinade. **Yield:** 6 servings.

Grilled Corn in Husks

(Pictured on page 226)

Prep: 20 min. + soaking **Grill:** 20 min.

☑ Uses less fat, sugar or salt. Includes Nutrition Facts and Diabetic Exchanges.

            4 large ears sweet corn in husks
          1/4 cup butter, softened
            2 tablespoons minced fresh parsley
          1/4 cup grated Parmesan cheese

Carefully peel back husk from each ear of corn to within 1 in. of bottom; remove silk. Combine the butter and pars-

ley; spread over corn. Rewrap corn in husks and secure with string. Soak in cold water for 20 minutes; drain.

Grill corn, covered, over medium heat for 20-25 minutes or until tender, turning often. Serve with Parmesan cheese. **Yield:** 4 servings.

Nutrition Facts: 1 ear of corn (prepared with reduced-fat butter) equals 196 calories, 9 g fat (5 g saturated fat), 24 mg cholesterol, 186 mg sodium, 28 g carbohydrate, 4 g fiber, 8 g protein. **Diabetic Exchanges:** 2 starch, 1 fat.

Stuffed Grilled Zucchini

Prep: 25 min. **Grill:** 10 min.

☑ Uses less fat, sugar or salt. Includes Nutrition Facts and Diabetic Exchanges.

            4 medium zucchini
            5 teaspoons olive oil, *divided*
            2 tablespoons finely chopped red onion
          1/4 teaspoon minced garlic
          1/2 cup dry bread crumbs
          1/2 cup shredded part-skim mozzarella cheese
            1 tablespoon minced fresh mint
          1/2 teaspoon salt
            3 tablespoons grated Parmesan cheese

Cut zucchini in half lengthwise; scoop out pulp, leaving 1/4-in. shells. Brush with 2 teaspoons oil; set aside. Chop pulp. In a large skillet, saute pulp and onion in remaining oil. Add garlic; cook 1 minute longer. Add bread crumbs; cook and stir for 2 minutes or until golden brown.

Remove from the heat. Stir in the mozzarella cheese, mint and salt. Spoon into the zucchini shells.

Sprinkle with Parmesan cheese. Grill, covered, over medium heat for 8-10 minutes or until zucchini is tender. **Yield:** 4 servings.

Nutrition Facts: 2 stuffed zucchini halves (prepared with part-skim mozzarella) equals 186 calories, 10 g fat (3 g saturated fat), 11 mg cholesterol, 553 mg sodium, 17 g carbohydrate, 3 g fiber, 9 g protein. **Diabetic Exchanges:** 1 lean meat, 1 vegetable, 1 fat, 1/2 starch.

Sunny Corn Bread Muffins

Prep/Total Time: 30 min.

3/4 cup all-purpose flour
3/4 cup yellow cornmeal
2 tablespoons sugar
1 teaspoon baking powder
1 teaspoon salt
1 egg
2/3 cup buttermilk
3 tablespoons canola oil
1 cup whole kernel corn

In a large bowl, combine the flour, cornmeal, sugar, baking powder and salt. In a small bowl, whisk the egg, buttermilk and oil. Stir into dry ingredients just until moistened. Fold in corn.

Fill greased muffin cups three-fourths full. Bake at 400° for 18-22 minutes or until a toothpick comes out clean. Cool for 5 minutes before removing from pan to a wire rack. Serve warm. **Yield:** 8 muffins.

Nutrition Facts: 1 muffin equals 187 calories, 6 g fat (1 g saturated fat), 27 mg cholesterol, 460 mg sodium, 27 g carbohydrate, 2 g fiber, 4 g protein. **Diabetic Exchanges:** 2 starch, 1 fat.

Hummingbird Cake

Prep: 40 min.   **Bake:** 25 min. + cooling

3 cups all-purpose flour
2 cups sugar

1 teaspoon salt
1 teaspoon baking soda
1 teaspoon ground cinnamon
3 eggs
2 cups mashed ripe bananas
1-1/2 cups vegetable oil
1 can (8 ounces) unsweetened crushed pineapple, undrained
1-1/2 teaspoons vanilla extract
1 cup chopped walnuts
PINEAPPLE FROSTING:
1/4 cup shortening
2 tablespoons butter, softened
1 teaspoon grated lemon peel
1/4 teaspoon salt
6 cups confectioners' sugar
1/2 cup unsweetened pineapple juice
2 teaspoons half-and-half cream
Chopped walnuts, optional

In a large mixing bowl, combine flour, sugar, salt, baking soda and cinnamon. Add eggs, bananas, oil, pineapple and vanilla; beat until combined. Stir in walnuts. Pour into three greased and floured 9-in. round baking pans.

Bake at 350° for 25-30 minutes or until a toothpick inserted near center comes out clean. Cool 10 minutes; then remove from the pans to wire racks. Cool completely.

For frosting, in a large mixing bowl, beat shortening, butter, lemon peel and salt until fluffy. Add confectioners' sugar alternately with pineapple juice. Beat in the cream. Spread between layers and over top and sides of cake. Sprinkle with walnuts if desired. **Yield:** 12-14 servings.

Special Meat 'n' Potatoes Meal

Little last-minute fuss makes this field editor's comforting supper easy on the cook.

By Gail Buss, Westminster, Maryland

COOKING for my family and friends has always been my way of saying, "I love you!"

They can taste my affection in this favorite meal of Italian Pinwheel Meat Loaf, Mashed Potato Bake, Mushroom Spinach Salad, Lemonade Iced Tea and Cherry Coffee Cake (pictured on page 233).

So much of this food can be made ahead of time that I can relax and enjoy the occasion when we entertain friends or when the whole family gets together. My husband, Joe, and I have four children—Lori, Darren, Ryan and David—and one grandchild, Kathryn. Our two youngest children still live at home.

I have been making the Italian Pinwheel Meat Loaf for at least 20 years. I assemble it, along with the Mashed Potato Bake, early in the day and just pop them in the oven when it's time.

Guests always think I went to a lot of trouble when they see this special-looking meat loaf. Layered on a platter, the spiral slices are very attractive and so delicious. But actually, it is easy to prepare in less than 30 minutes.

A co-worker gave me the Mashed Potato Bake recipe. Once Joe and the rest of the family tasted it, we all agreed it was a keeper! Speckled with ham and flavored with mozzarella and Parmesan cheeses, it's a little different.

I'm a firm believer that presentation really makes the meal. So I usually put some sprigs of parsley here and there over the potato bake and around the meat loaf platter before bringing them to the table. It's a simple way to add a finishing touch to these dishes.

The tangy dressing I always pour on Mushroom Spinach Salad can also be mixed up ahead of time. It's best if you wait to drizzle it on the salad until the very last minute.

I'd been using this herb vinaigrette for regular tossed salads. Then, one day, I decided to try it on spinach—I like to serve dark greens as often as I can since they are so nutritious and wholesome. The two went together beautifully. A glass bowl really shows off this pretty salad that includes plenty of red onion and fresh mushrooms.

I have always loved iced tea with lemon, and Lemonade Iced Tea—a great thirst-quencher—just takes it one step further. The lemonade gives this refreshing drink a nice color, too. I dress up each glass with a piece of lemon on the side.

Cherry Coffee Cake is the perfect casual dessert—and hopefully there is a piece left over to have with a cup of tea the next morning! The recipe calls for a cake mix and yeast, which is rather unusual, but the results are wonderful.

I first tasted this cake at a friend's party, and one piece wasn't enough. I kept taking another little sliver and then another little sliver! I asked her for the recipe so I could make it for my family any time we liked.

Originally from New York City, Joe and I have lived all over the East Coast but have now been in Westminster, Maryland for 18 years. Joe manages a senior retirement complex, and I'm an assistant to the principal at a local Catholic school.

When we were dating, I took a cooking class from nuns. Before that, I couldn't even boil water! It was a great way to learn the basics and what all the cooking terms meant. Once I got started, I knew I loved cooking and baking.

Now, the question is where to stop! I realize this as I'm trying to finish up a cookbook—in my own handwriting—containing our best-loved recipes for each of my children.

I also belong to a bunco group and spend time volunteering at church, crocheting, cross-stitching, sewing, reading and writing. But right now, my family cookbook is my labor of love.

The collection includes specialties such as my homemade pasta and ravioli. I also made sure to add the many kinds of Christmas cookies Joe and the children look forward to at holiday time.

Of course, the recipes for the favorite meal I'm sharing here will be in the cookbook, too. Hope you enjoy them!

PICTURED AT LEFT: Italian Pinwheel Meat Loaf, Mashed Potato Bake, Mushroom Spinach Salad and Lemonade Iced Tea (recipes are on the next page).

with remaining cheese; bake 5 minutes longer or until cheese is melted. Let stand for 10 minutes before slicing. Serve with additional spaghetti sauce if desired. **Yield:** 8 servings.

Mashed Potato Bake

Prep: 35 min.   **Bake:** 25 min.

- 3 pounds potatoes, peeled and quartered
- 2 eggs
- 1 cup diced fully cooked ham
- 1 cup (4 ounces) diced part-skim mozzarella cheese
- 1/4 cup grated Parmesan cheese
- 3 tablespoons minced fresh parsley, *divided*
- 3/4 teaspoon salt
- 1/4 teaspoon pepper
- 1/8 teaspoon garlic powder
- 1 tablespoon butter

Place potatoes in a Dutch oven and cover with water. Bring to a boil. Reduce heat; cover and cook for 20-25 minutes or until very tender. Drain well and mash.

In a large bowl, beat the eggs. Add ham, cheeses, 2 tablespoons parsley, salt, pepper and garlic powder. Stir in mashed potatoes.

Transfer to a greased shallow 2-qt. baking dish. Dot with butter. Bake, uncovered, at 350° for 25-30 minutes or until heated through. Sprinkle with remaining parsley. **Yield:** 8 servings.

Italian Pinwheel Meat Loaf

Prep: 25 min.   **Bake:** 1-1/4 hours + standing

- 2 eggs, beaten
- 3/4 cup seasoned bread crumbs
- 1/2 cup spaghetti sauce *or* ketchup
- 1 tablespoon minced fresh parsley
- 1 garlic clove, minced
- 1/2 teaspoon dried oregano
- 1/4 teaspoon onion powder
- 1/4 teaspoon salt
- 1/4 teaspoon pepper
- 2 pounds lean ground beef
- 16 slices part-skim mozzarella cheese, *divided*
- 4 ounces deli ham

Additional spaghetti sauce, warmed, optional

In a large bowl, combine the first nine ingredients. Crumble beef over mixture and mix well.

On a piece of heavy-duty foil, pat beef mixture into a 12-in. x 10-in. rectangle. Layer with six cheese slices, ham and six more cheese slices. Roll up jelly roll-style, starting with a short side and peeling foil away while rolling. Seal seam and ends. Place seam side down in a greased 13-in. x 9-in. x 2-in. baking dish.

Bake, uncovered, at 350° for 70 minutes or until no pink remains and a meat thermometer reads 160°. Top

Mushroom Spinach Salad

Prep/Total Time: 20 min.

✓ Uses less fat, sugar or salt. Includes Nutrition Facts and Diabetic Exchanges.

- 8 cups fresh baby spinach
- 2 cups sliced fresh mushrooms
- 1/2 cup sliced red *or* sweet onion
- 1/2 cup canola oil
- 2 tablespoons cider vinegar
- 1-1/2 teaspoons sugar
- 3/4 teaspoon salt
- 1/4 teaspoon garlic powder
- 1/4 teaspoon onion powder
- 1/4 teaspoon dried oregano
- 1/8 teaspoon pepper

In a large salad bowl, combine spinach, mushrooms and onion. In a jar with a tight-fitting lid, combine the remaining ingredients; shake well. Pour over salad and toss to coat. Serve immediately. **Yield:** 8 servings.

Nutrition Facts: 1-1/4 cups equals 138 calories, 14 g fat (2 g saturated fat), 0 cholesterol, 246 mg sodium, 4 g carbohydrate, 1 g fiber, 1 g protein. **Diabetic Exchanges:** 2 fat, 1 vegetable.

Lemonade Iced Tea

(Pictured on page 230)

Prep: 15 min. + chilling

- 3 quarts water
- 9 individual tea bags
- 3/4 to 1-1/4 cups sugar
- 1 can (12 ounces) frozen lemonade concentrate, thawed

In a Dutch oven, bring water to a boil. Remove from the heat; add tea bags. Cover and steep for 5 minutes. Discard tea bags. Stir in sugar and lemonade concentrate. Cover and refrigerate until chilled. Serve over ice. **Yield:** 12 servings (about 3 quarts).

Cherry Coffee Cake

Prep: 25 min.   Bake: 35 min. + cooling

- 1 package (18-1/4 ounces) yellow cake mix, *divided*
- 1 cup all-purpose flour
- 1 package (1/4 ounce) active dry yeast
- 2/3 cup warm water (120° to 130°)
- 2 eggs, lightly beaten
- 1 can (21 ounces) cherry pie filling
- 1/3 cup cold butter
GLAZE:
- 1 cup confectioners' sugar
- 1 tablespoon corn syrup
- 1 to 2 tablespoons water

In a large mixing bowl, combine 1-1/2 cups dry cake mix, flour, yeast and water until smooth. Stir in eggs until blended. Transfer to a greased 13-in. x 9-in. x 2-in. baking dish. Carefully spoon pie filling over top.

Place remaining cake mix in a bowl; cut in butter until crumbly. Sprinkle over filling. Bake at 350° for 35-40 minutes or until lightly browned. Cool on a wire rack. Combine glaze ingredients; drizzle over coffee cake. **Yield:** 12-16 servings.

Dinner After Turkey Day

Thanksgiving leftovers take on new life thanks to one of our field editors.

By Dixie Terry, Goreville, Illinois

THE DAY after Thanksgiving, not only is everyone full of turkey, but so is the refrigerator. Sound familiar at your house?

I've come up with a menu to utilize all those holiday extras that are left over. It's perfect for serving to company the weekend after the holiday!

Secondhand Turkey is a tasty, hearty casserole that I complement with Pretty Gelatin Molds, Cranberry Pumpkin Bread, Festive Cranberry Drink and Pumpkin Ice Cream Delight.

Leftover cranberry sauce can be used to prepare Pretty Gelatin Molds. This festive-looking salad is so easy—ideal for holiday entertaining or for toting to a potluck party.

I've taken this gelatin salad to several of the twice-monthly potluck suppers my husband, Jim, and I attend with our senior citizens group. There are always lots of *Taste of Home* recipes being passed around and tried at these gatherings!

For years, I baked regular pumpkin bread. Then I found the Cranberry Pumpkin Bread recipe in a local grocery ad and adopted this flavorful new twist.

Usually, I triple the pumpkin bread recipe, using my super-size mixing bowl, and bake six loaves at a time. A wrapped loaf makes a yummy gift to hand out to departing guests or to give a hostess when going to a holiday party.

Served hot or cold, Festive Cranberry Drink is delicious. I found the recipe in my late mother-in-law's collection, hand-written probably by one of her woman's club friends.

Besides working as a freelance writer and newspaper columnist, I cater tea luncheons and high teas in our home, which we've named "Teapot Cottage." I do all the food preparation, serving and cleanup myself—unless I can find an available daughter or granddaughter to help.

My tea party specialties—including Festive Cranberry Drink and Cranberry Pumpkin Bread—are lots of fun to put together. Other popular items are herbed crescent rolls, chicken Waldorf salad, pies, trifles, scones, crumpets and a variety of desserts.

Pumpkin Ice Cream Delight really appeals to those who might not like the traditional pie. You can make it ahead of time to have on hand when extra guests or unexpected ones arrive.

I often scoop this dessert into individual dishes and freeze them, tightly covered with foil. Take them out to soften on the counter for about 15 minutes before serving.

I don't consider myself a great cook—just a consistent one. I've been cooking since I was about 8. My mother, an excellent cook, worked at the post office and was too busy to show me how. I was always stirring up concoctions in the kitchen after school, before she got home.

I've written two cookbooks: *From My Kitchen Window* is a compilation of 10 years of cooking columns I wrote for *Springhouse* magazine, and *Serving Savory Shrimp* was created for our area's farm-pond shrimp industry.

When it's just Jim and me for meals, I like making homemade soup and a sandwich. But my favorite type of cooking is a hearty family meal, like the one I'm sharing here.

Put these five recipes together for a Thanksgiving weekend menu and create a memorable time, centered on wonderful food and family!

Spicy Substitute

Cranberry Pumpkin Bread (recipe on page 236) gets wonderful flavor from pumpkin pie spice. If you find that you're fresh out of this favorite spice blend, just use the following substitution (for 1 teaspoon pumpkin pie spice): Combine 1/2 teaspoon ground cinnamon, 1/4 teaspoon ground ginger and 1/4 teaspoon ground allspice, plus 1/8 teaspoon ground nutmeg or cloves.

PICTURED AT LEFT: Secondhand Turkey, Pretty Gelatin Molds, Cranberry Pumpkin Bread, Festive Cranberry Drink and Pumpkin Ice Cream Delight (recipes are on the next page).

Pretty Gelatin Molds

Prep: 15 min. + chilling

  1 **package (3 ounces) orange gelatin**
3/4 **cup boiling water**
3/4 **cup whole-berry cranberry sauce**
  1 **medium navel orange, peeled and finely
    chopped**
  4 **lettuce leaves**

In a bowl, dissolve gelatin in boiling water. Stir in cranberry sauce and orange. Pour into four 1/2-cup molds coated with nonstick cooking spray. Chill for 3-4 hours or until set. Unmold onto lettuce-lined plates. **Yield:** 4 servings.

Cranberry Pumpkin Bread

Prep: 20 min.   **Bake:** 70 min. + cooling

3-3/4 **cups all-purpose flour**
   3 **cups sugar**
   4 **teaspoons pumpkin pie spice**
   2 **teaspoons baking soda**
   1 **teaspoon salt**
   4 **eggs**
   1 **can (15 ounces) solid-pack pumpkin**
 1/2 **cup vegetable oil**
   2 **cups fresh *or* frozen cranberries, thawed**
   1 **cup chopped walnuts**

Secondhand Turkey

Prep: 30 min.   **Bake:** 20 min.

1/2 **pound sliced fresh mushrooms**
1/2 **cup chopped celery**
  5 **tablespoons butter, *divided***
  2 **tablespoons cornstarch**
  2 **cups milk**
  2 **cups cubed cooked turkey**
  2 **cups cooked egg noodles**
1/4 **cup chicken broth**
  1 **teaspoon salt**
1/2 **teaspoon dried thyme**
1/8 **teaspoon white pepper**
1/2 **cup dry bread crumbs**

In a large skillet, saute mushrooms and celery in 3 tablespoons butter until tender. Combine cornstarch and milk until smooth; stir into mushroom mixture. Bring to a boil over medium heat, stirring constantly. Cook for 1 minute or until thickened.

Stir in the turkey, noodles, broth, salt, thyme and pepper. Pour into a greased 2-qt. baking dish. Melt remaining butter; toss with bread crumbs. Sprinkle over casserole. Bake, uncovered, at 375° for 20-25 minutes or until heated through. **Yield:** 4 servings.

Stir in the sugar, juices, red-hots and remaining water. Place cloves on a double thickness of cheesecloth. Bring up corners of cloth and tie with kitchen string to form a bag; add to juice mixture. Bring to a boil; cook and stir until sugar and red-hots are dissolved.

Remove from the heat. Strain through a fine mesh sieve or cheesecloth. Discard spice bag. Serve drink warm or cold. **Yield:** 3 quarts.

Pumpkin Ice Cream Delight

Prep: 15 min. + freezing

>   1-1/2 **cups pumpkin pie filling**
>   1/3 **cup sugar**
>   1 **teaspoon vanilla extract**
>   1 **quart vanilla ice cream, softened**
>   1 **cup chopped pecans, toasted**

In a large bowl, combine the pumpkin pie filling, sugar and vanilla. Fold in ice cream. Transfer to a greased 8-in. square dish. Cover and freeze for 3-4 hours or until firm. Scoop into individual bowls. Sprinkle with pecans. **Yield:** 8 servings.

In a large bowl, combine the flour, sugar, pumpkin pie spice, baking soda and salt. In another bowl, beat the eggs, pumpkin and oil; stir into dry ingredients just until moistened. Fold in cranberries and walnuts.

Spoon into two greased 9-in. x 5-in. x 3-in. loaf pans. Bake at 350° for 70-80 minutes or until a toothpick inserted near the center comes out clean. Cool for 10 minutes before removing from pans to wire racks to cool completely. **Yield:** 2 loaves.

Festive Cranberry Drink

(Pictured on page 234)

Prep: 25 min.   **Cook:** 20 min.

>   4 **cups fresh *or* frozen cranberries**
>   3 **quarts water, *divided***
>   1-3/4 **cups sugar**
>   1 **cup orange juice**
>   2/3 **cup lemon juice**
>   1/2 **cup red-hot candies**
>   12 **whole cloves**

In a Dutch oven or large kettle, combine the cranberries and 1 qt. water. Cook over medium heat until the cranberries pop, about 15 minutes. Remove from the heat. Strain through a fine strainer, pressing the mixture with a spoon; discard the skins. Return the cranberry pulp and juice to the pan.

Meals in Minutes

Putting hot, home-cooked food on the table for you and your family doesn't have to be a time-consuming process. The 18 meals here are ready to eat in just 30 minutes...or less!

FEASTS IN A FLASH. Clockwise from upper left: Catch Fresh Fare for Spring (p. 258), Savor Flavors of the South (p. 254), Special Menu Has Fall Flair (p. 270) and Quick Lunch Dishes Are a Great Combination (p. 250).

Seafood Supper Will Catch Compliments

DURING the holiday season, everyone seems to be in a rush, so putting a pleasing meal on the dinner table for your family can be a challenge. The menu below—complete with a delectable dessert—can be ready in 30 minutes or less.

Onion and mustard complement tender Microwaved Orange Roughy. "We're trying to eat more fish these days, and this easy main dish is one of our favorites," writes Alice Keohane Feeney of Morristown, Pennsylvania.

"My husband, Doug, wowed me with Confetti Couscous while we were dating. It's still a regular part of our menus," relates Laurel Porterfield from Bristow, Virginia.

Field editor Tammy Logan of McComb, Ohio often makes her Pudding Pound Cake Dessert, a luscious, layered treat that relies on convenient instant pudding and store-bought pound cake.

Microwaved Orange Roughy

Prep/Total Time: 20 min.

✓ **Uses less fat, sugar or salt. Includes Nutrition Facts and Diabetic Exchanges.**

    1 small onion, sliced and separated into
      rings
    4 orange roughy fillets (5 ounces *each*)
  1/4 teaspoon salt
  1/4 teaspoon pepper
    4 tablespoons lemon juice, *divided*
    3 tablespoons butter, melted, *divided*
    2 teaspoons water, *divided*
    1 tablespoon Dijon mustard
  1/4 cup seasoned bread crumbs, toasted

Place the onion in an 11-in. x 7-in. x 2-in. microwave-safe dish coated with nonstick cooking spray. Top with orange roughy; sprinkle with salt and pepper. Combine 2 tablespoons lemon juice, 2 tablespoons butter and 1 teaspoon water; pour over fish. Cover and microwave on high for 4 minutes; drain.

Combine the mustard and remaining lemon juice and water; spoon over fish. Sprinkle with bread crumbs. Drizzle with remaining butter. Cook, uncovered, on high for 2 minutes or until fish flakes easily with a fork. **Yield:** 4 servings.

Nutrition Facts: 1 fillet (prepared with reduced-fat butter) equals 178 calories, 6 g fat (3 g saturated fat), 43 mg cholesterol, 492 mg sodium, 8 g carbohydrate, 1 g fiber, 23 g protein. **Diabetic Exchanges:** 3 very lean meat, 1 fat, 1/2 starch.

Editor's Note: This recipe was tested in a 1,100-watt microwave.

Confetti Couscous

Prep/Total Time: 20 min.

  2-1/4 cups chicken broth
      1 tablespoon butter
    1/2 teaspoon salt
  1-1/2 cups frozen corn
    3/4 cup dried cranberries
  1/4 to 1/2 teaspoon ground cinnamon
      1 package (10 ounces) couscous

In a large saucepan, bring the chicken broth, butter and salt to a boil. Stir in the corn, dried cranberries and cinnamon. Cover and return to a boil; cook for 2 minutes.

Stir in couscous. Remove from the heat; cover and let stand for 5 minutes or until broth is absorbed. Fluff with a fork. **Yield:** 4-6 servings.

Pudding Pound Cake Dessert

Prep/Total Time: 30 min.

    1 frozen pound cake (10-3/4 ounces), thawed
    3 cups cold milk
    2 packages (3.9 ounces *each*) instant
      chocolate pudding mix
    3 cups whipped topping
  1/2 cup chopped walnuts
  3/4 cup chopped cream-filled chocolate
      sandwich cookies

Cut cake horizontally into fourths; place two pieces side by side in an 8-in. square dish. In a bowl, whisk milk and pudding mixes for 2 minutes. Let stand for 2 minutes or until soft-set; fold in whipped topping. Spoon half over the cake; sprinkle with walnuts and 1/2 cup chopped cookies.

Layer with remaining cake, pudding mixture and cookies (dish will be full). Refrigerate until serving. **Yield:** 9 servings.

Special Ham Stars In Memorable Meal

ACTIVE LIFESTYLES don't always leave time for a sit-down dinner...much less time for preparing it. So you need quick fixes to satisfy your family.

This 30-minute menu, put together by our Test Kitchen, is made up of three reader favorites that are sure to be tops with your gang, too.

"A dear friend shared the recipe for Ham with Pineapple Salsa when she moved from Hawaii to Colorado. Now it's one of my favorite ways to eat ham," says Dawn Wilson of Buena Vista, Colorado. "I get lots of requests for the recipe when I make it for guests."

"Using frozen hash browns makes Easy Potato Pancakes a snap to fix," notes Marlene Harguth of Maynard, Minnesota. "I like to team them up with pork chops and applesauce."

Donna Jo Cuddy of Gainesville, Georgia dresses up ice cream with peaches, cinnamon and vanilla for a yummy Peach Freeze that's ready in no time.

Ham with Pineapple Salsa

Prep/Total Time: 25 min.

- 1 can (8 ounces) crushed pineapple, drained
- 2 tablespoons orange marmalade
- 1 tablespoon minced fresh cilantro
- 2 teaspoons lime juice
- 2 teaspoons chopped jalapeno pepper
- 1/4 teaspoon salt
- 1 bone-in fully cooked ham steak (1-1/2 pounds)

For salsa, combine the first six ingredients in a small bowl; set aside. Place the ham steak on an ungreased rack in a broiler pan. Broil 4-6 in. from the heat for 8-10 minutes or until a meat thermometer reads 140°, turning once. Cut into serving-size pieces; serve with salsa. **Yield:** 4 servings.

Editor's Note: When cutting or seeding hot peppers, use rubber or plastic gloves to protect your hands. Avoid touching your face.

Easy Potato Pancakes

Prep/Total Time: 20 min.

- 3 cups frozen shredded hash brown potatoes
- 2 tablespoons all-purpose flour
- 2 eggs, beaten
- 3 tablespoons butter, melted
- 1-1/2 teaspoons water
- 1/2 teaspoon salt
- 1 tablespoon vegetable oil

Place the hash brown potatoes in a strainer; rinse with cold water until thawed. Drain thoroughly; transfer to a large bowl. Add the flour, eggs, butter, water and salt; mix well.

Heat the oil in a large skillet over medium heat. Drop the batter by 1/3 cupfuls into oil; fry until golden brown on both sides. Drain the pancakes on paper towels. **Yield:** 4 servings.

Peach Freeze

Prep/Total Time: 30 min.

- 2 cups vanilla ice cream, softened
- 1-1/3 cups frozen unsweetened peach slices
- 1/8 teaspoon ground cinnamon
- 1/8 teaspoon vanilla extract

In a blender, combine the ice cream, peaches, cinnamon and vanilla; cover and process until smooth. Pour the mixture into small freezer-safe dessert dishes; cover and freeze desserts until serving. **Yield:** 4 servings.

Ham in a Hurry

No time to spare? Try one of these super-speedy ideas for ham steak:

If you can't take the time to make the salsa for Ham with Pineapple Salsa (recipe above left), just sprinkle a little brown sugar over the ham. Then top it with crushed pineapple with its juice before popping the ham in the oven.

You can also make an easy, delicious glaze by blending apricot preserves with some mustard, lemon juice and a dash of cinnamon. Simply heat the glaze in a pan and brush it on the ham during the final minutes of baking.

Soup, Slaw and Sandwich Make a Tasty Trio

THIS CASUAL MENU, consisting of three reader favorites, makes a delicious dinner or lunch that's ready to serve in 30 minutes or less. Your family will be munching this satisfying spread in no time!

"We like Swiss Tuna Melts served with homemade vegetable soup," writes field editor Karen Owen of Rising Sun, Indiana. "You'll love the crunch that celery gives to the creamy tuna filling."

The cool, refreshing taste of Pineapple Coleslaw makes it a welcome addition to many meals. The pineapple lends a sweet tang to this salad from field editor Shirley Glaab, Hattiesburg, Mississippi.

Marcia Orlando jots from Boyertown, Pennsylvania, "With colorful bits of veggies and a mild cheese flavor, Creamy Vegetable Soup really hits the spot on a brisk day."

Swiss Tuna Melts

Prep/Total Time: 20 min.

  1 can (6 ounces) light water-packed tuna, drained and flaked
3/4 cup shredded Swiss cheese
1/2 cup sour cream
1/2 cup mayonnaise
1/4 cup chopped onion
1/4 cup chopped celery
Pepper to taste
  8 slices bread
  2 to 3 tablespoons butter, softened

In a bowl, combine the first seven ingredients. Spread over four slices of bread, about 1/2 cup on each; top with remaining bread. Butter the outsides of sandwiches.

On a griddle or in a large skillet over medium heat, grill sandwiches for 4-5 minutes on each side or until lightly toasted. **Yield:** 4 servings.

Pineapple Coleslaw

Prep/Total Time: 10 min.

☑ Uses less fat, sugar or salt. Includes Nutrition Facts and Diabetic Exchanges.

  2 cups coleslaw mix
  1 cup unsweetened crushed pineapple, drained

1/3 cup shredded carrot
  3 medium radishes, shredded
1/4 teaspoon celery seed
1/3 cup mayonnaise

In a large bowl, combine the first five ingredients. Add mayonnaise and toss to coat. Cover and refrigerate until serving. **Yield:** 4 servings.

Nutrition Facts: 3/4 cup (prepared with fat-free mayonnaise) equals 66 calories, 1 g fat (trace saturated fat), 2 mg cholesterol, 173 mg sodium, 15 g carbohydrate, 2 g fiber, 1 g protein. **Diabetic Exchanges:** 1 vegetable, 1/2 fruit.

Creamy Vegetable Soup

Prep/Total Time: 30 min.

  2 cups chicken broth
1/4 cup diced carrot
1/4 cup diced celery
1/4 cup finely chopped onion
  2 tablespoons butter
1/4 cup all-purpose flour
Dash salt
  2 cups milk
1/2 cup cubed process cheese (Velveeta)

In a small saucepan, bring the chicken broth to a boil. Add the carrot and celery; simmer, uncovered, for 5 minutes or until tender.

In a large saucepan, saute onion in butter until tender. Stir in the flour and salt until blended. Gradually add milk. Bring to a boil over medium heat; cook and stir for 2 minutes or until thickened and bubbly. Stir in carrot mixture. Remove from the heat; add cheese and stir until melted. **Yield:** 4 servings.

Fast Finale

Want a delectable dessert to top off the mouthwatering menu on this page? Try this easy idea. Fill store-bought puff pastry shells with lemon yogurt and sprinkle them with berries or other fruit. Finish with a dollop of whipped cream.

Great Grilled Salmon Has The Taste of Summer

SUMMER FUN can leave little time for meal preparation...and who wants to be in the kitchen when the sun's shining, the weather's inviting and outdoor activities are beckoning?

Grilling allows you to be outside and put a great-tasting meal on the table for your family in a hurry. No wonder it's such a popular way to cook when the weather's warm.

This delicious menu, featuring an easy main dish and two terrific accompaniments, is ready to serve in only 30 minutes.

Grilled Salmon with Cheese Sauce, developed by our Test Kitchen home economists, uses just five ingredients. The creamy sauce complements the delicate flavor of the salmon, and the tomatoes make a colorful, nutritious side.

A delightfully simple sauce gives Sweet-and-Sour Zucchini its traditional Oriental flavor. This Test Kitchen recipe takes just 15 minutes to prepare...and it's a wonderful way to use up that excess zucchini from your garden.

Field editor Anna Minegar of Zolfo Springs, Florida mixes three refreshing citrus flavors with ginger ale for her pretty Fruity Punch. This thirst-quenching beverage is perfect any time of year.

Grilled Salmon with Cheese Sauce

Prep/Total Time: 30 min.

    2 cups cherry tomatoes
    4 teaspoons Greek seasoning
    4 salmon fillets (6 ounces *each*)
    1 carton (6-1/2 ounces) garden vegetable
       cheese spread
    2 tablespoons milk

Coat grill rack with nonstick cooking spray before starting the grill. Thread the cherry tomatoes onto metal or soaked wooden skewers; set aside.

Sprinkle Greek seasoning over salmon. Place on grill rack. Grill, covered, over medium heat for 5 minutes. Turn and grill 7-9 minutes longer or until fish flakes easily with a fork. Meanwhile, grill tomatoes for 5-8 minutes, turning frequently.

In a microwave-safe dish, combine the cheese spread and milk. Cook, uncovered, on high for 1 minute; stir until blended. Serve with salmon and tomatoes. **Yield:** 4 servings.

Sweet-and-Sour Zucchini

Prep/Total Time: 15 min.

✓ **Uses less fat, sugar or salt. Includes Nutrition Facts and Diabetic Exchanges.**

      2 large zucchini, cut into 1/4-inch slices
  1-1/2 teaspoons minced fresh gingerroot
      1 garlic clove, minced
      2 teaspoons canola oil
    1/4 cup sweet-and-sour sauce
    1/4 teaspoon salt

In a large skillet, saute the zucchini, ginger and garlic in oil for 5 minutes or until zucchini is crisp-tender. Stir in the sweet-and-sour sauce and salt; heat through. **Yield:** 4 servings.

Nutrition Facts: 3/4 cup equals 60 calories, 3 g fat (trace saturated fat), 0 cholesterol, 89 mg sodium, 9 g carbohydrate, 2 g fiber, 2 g protein. **Diabetic Exchanges:** 1 vegetable, 1/2 fat.

Fruity Punch

Prep/Total Time: 10 min.

    2 cups orange juice, chilled
    2 cups unsweetened pineapple juice, chilled
    2 cups sweetened pink grapefruit juice
       drink, chilled
    3 cans (12 ounces *each*) ginger ale, chilled

In a punch bowl or pitcher, combine the orange and pineapple juices and the pink grapefruit drink. Refrigerate until serving. Just before serving, stir in ginger ale. Serve over ice. **Yield:** about 2 quarts.

Soaking Skewers

If you choose to use wooden skewers when preparing Grilled Salmon with Cheese Sauce (recipe at left), make sure to soak the skewers first. This helps prevent them from burning or splinting during grilling.

Simply soak the skewers in water for 15-30 minutes. Then remove them from the water, thread on the cherry tomatoes and grill!

Present a Hearty Pasta Dinner, Pronto!

FAST AND FILLING, this easy-to-prepare menu makes feeding your family a breeze. The meaty entree, refreshing salad and light chocolaty dessert are ready to serve in 30 minutes or less.

Jean Komlos of Plymouth, Michigan sent the recipe for Fire-Roasted Ziti with Sausage. Her cheesy, Italian-style dish uses just six ingredients.

Nectarine and Beet Salad comes from Nicole Werner of Roseville, Minnesota. "The combination of ingredients may seem unlikely, but this colorful salad is delicious," she says.

Christy Hinrichs of Parkville, Missouri layers pudding with cookie crumbs and strawberries to make luscious Chocolate Hazelnut Parfaits.

Fire-Roasted Ziti with Sausage

Prep/Total Time: 30 min.

- 1 package (8 ounces) ziti *or* small tube pasta
- 1 can (28 ounces) Italian diced tomatoes, undrained
- 1 jar (26 ounces) fire-roasted tomato and garlic spaghetti sauce
- 1 package (16 ounces) smoked sausage, sliced
- 2 cups (8 ounces) shredded part-skim mozzarella cheese, *divided*
- 1 cup (8 ounces) small-curd cottage cheese

In a large saucepan or Dutch oven, cook pasta according to package directions; drain and return to the pan. Stir in the tomatoes, spaghetti sauce and sausage; heat through.

Stir in 1 cup mozzarella and cottage cheese. Top with remaining mozzarella cheese. Cover and heat over medium heat for 2-5 minutes or until mozzarella is melted. **Yield:** 8 servings.

Nectarine and Beet Salad

Prep/Total Time: 10 min.

☑ Uses less fat, sugar or salt. Includes Nutrition Facts and Diabetic Exchanges.

- 2 packages (5 ounces *each*) spring mix salad greens
- 2 cups sliced fresh nectarines
- 1 can (13-1/4 ounces) sliced beets, drained
- 1/2 cup balsamic vinaigrette
- 1/2 cup crumbled feta cheese

In a large salad bowl, combine the greens, nectarines and beets. Drizzle with dressing and toss gently to coat. Sprinkle with feta cheese. **Yield:** 8 servings.

Nutrition Facts: 1 cup equals 85 calories, 4 g fat (1 g saturated fat), 4 mg cholesterol, 293 mg sodium, 11 g carbohydrate, 2 g fiber, 3 g protein. **Diabetic Exchanges:** 2 vegetable, 1/2 fat.

Chocolate Hazelnut Parfaits

(Not pictured)

Prep: 10 min. + chilling

- 3 cups cold milk
- 1 cup refrigerated hazelnut nondairy creamer
- 2 packages (3.9 ounces *each*) instant chocolate pudding mix
- 1 cup crushed shortbread cookies
- 2 cups sliced fresh strawberries

Whipped cream, optional

In a large bowl, whisk the milk, creamer and pudding mixes for 2 minutes. Let stand for 2 minutes or until soft-set. Spoon 1/4 cup pudding into each of eight parfait glasses; sprinkle each with 1 tablespoon cookie crumbs. Top with strawberries and remaining pudding and crumbs. Refrigerate for 1 hour before serving. Garnish with whipped cream if desired. **Yield:** 8 servings.

Perfect Pasta

When cooking pasta for Fire-Roasted Ziti with Sausage (recipe above left) or for another dish, keep in mind the following guidelines:

- For 1 pound of dried pasta, bring 4 quarts of water to a full rolling boil. Add the pasta all at once and return the water to a boil, stirring occasionally.
- To test for doneness, remove a single piece of pasta from the boiling water with a fork, rinse it under cold water and taste. Pasta should be cooked until "al dente," or firm yet tender. Test pasta often to avoid overcooking.

Quick Lunch Dishes Are A Great Combination

WHAT goes together better than a hearty sandwich, hot soup and a salad? Your family will enjoy relaxing with this laid-back, 30-minute menu that works as a satisfying lunch or a light supper.

Chicken Florentine Panini, from Lee Bremson of Kansas City, Missouri, brings an Italian flair to this speedy meal. The grilled sandwich combines chicken with provolone cheese, spinach and red onion.

Why buy bottled dressing when you can make delicious, homemade Thousand Island Salad Dressing in a jiffy? This tangy version comes from Elizabeth Montgomery of Taylorville, Illinois.

"Ramen Corn Chowder tastes as good as if it simmered for hours, but it's ready in 15 minutes," writes field editor Darlene Brenden of Salem, Oregon. "I thought the original recipe was lacking in flavor, so I jazzed it up with extra corn and bacon bits."

Chicken Florentine Panini

Prep/Total Time: 25 min.

 1 package (6 ounces) fresh baby spinach
 2 teaspoons olive oil
 1/4 cup butter, softened
 8 slices sourdough bread
 1/4 cup creamy Italian salad dressing
 8 slices provolone cheese
 1/2 pound shaved deli chicken
 2 slices red onion, separated into rings

In a large skillet, saute spinach in oil for 2 minutes or until wilted. Butter one side of each slice of bread. Spread the unbuttered side of four slices with salad dressing; layer with a cheese slice, chicken, spinach, onion and another cheese slice. Top with remaining bread, buttered side up. Cook in a panini maker or on a griddle until golden brown on both sides. **Yield:** 4 servings.

Thousand Island Salad Dressing

Prep/Total Time: 15 min.

1-1/2 cups mayonnaise
 1/2 cup chili sauce
 1 hard-cooked egg, chopped
 2 tablespoons finely chopped celery
 2 tablespoons finely chopped green pepper
 2 tablespoons chopped pimiento-stuffed olives
 1 tablespoon grated onion

In a small bowl, combine all ingredients. Cover and refrigerate until serving. **Yield:** 2 cups.

Ramen Corn Chowder

Prep/Total Time: 15 min.

 2 cups water
 1 package (3 ounces) chicken ramen noodles
 1 can (15-1/4 ounces) whole kernel corn, drained
 1 can (14-3/4 ounces) cream-style corn
 1 cup milk
 1 teaspoon dried minced onion
 1/4 teaspoon curry powder
 3/4 cup shredded cheddar cheese
 1 tablespoon crumbled cooked bacon
 1 tablespoon minced fresh parsley

In a small saucepan, bring water to a boil. Break noodles into large pieces. Add noodles and contents of seasoning packet to water. Reduce heat to medium. Cook, uncovered, for 2-3 minutes or until noodles are tender.

Stir in the corn, cream corn, milk, onion and curry powder; heat through. Stir in the cheese, bacon and parsley until blended. **Yield:** 4 servings.

All Dressed Up

Sour cream- and mayonnaise-based salad dressings like Thousand Island Salad Dressing (recipe at left) go well with sturdy greens such as iceberg and romaine lettuce. Delicate greens such as Bibb or Boston lettuce are best with vinegar and oil dressings.

Toss greens with your dressing immediately before serving the salad or place the greens in a salad bowl and pass the dressing at the table. Keep in mind that putting too much dressing on the salad will make it soggy.

Warm Up with Comfort Food

NOTHING chases away winter chills quite like a hearty stew simmering on the stove. Chunky Beef Stew is packed with meat and vegetables, yet is quick to cook. Pair bowls of stew with Herbed Pita Chips and Peach-Filled Pastries, and you'll complete this winning dinner from our Test Kitchen staff.

Chunky Beef Stew

You don't need to simmer homemade stew for hours when you use a more tender cut of beef such as sirloin steak. This classic dish will fill you up after a day of sledding, skating or enjoying other wintertime activities.

      1 **pound boneless beef sirloin steak, cut into 1/2-inch cubes**
      3 **medium carrots, sliced**
      4 **celery ribs, sliced**
      1 **small onion, chopped**
      2 **tablespoons vegetable oil**
      2 **cans (14-1/2 ounces *each*) beef broth**
      2 **garlic cloves, minced**
      1 **teaspoon dried rosemary, crushed**
   3/4 **teaspoon pepper**
   1/4 **cup cornstarch**
   1/4 **cup cold water**
      1 **teaspoon browning sauce, optional**

In a Dutch oven, cook the beef, carrots, celery and onion in oil until beef is browned; drain. Add the broth, garlic, rosemary and pepper. Bring to a boil. Reduce heat; cover and simmer for 12-15 minutes or until beef and vegetables are tender.

   Combine the cornstarch and water until smooth; stir into beef mixture. Bring to a boil; cook and stir for 2 minutes or until thickened. Add browning sauce if desired. **Yield:** 6 servings.

Herbed Pita Chips

Instead of simply serving bread alongside stew, why not whip up a batch of these seasoned pita bread chips? They're a fun and flavorful addition to any meal.

      4 **pita breads (6 inches)**
      1 **tablespoon butter, melted**
   1/2 **teaspoon dried basil**
   1/2 **teaspoon dried thyme**

Place pita breads on an ungreased baking sheet; brush with butter. Combine the basil and thyme; sprinkle over pitas. Cut each into eight wedges. Bake at 400° for 8-10 minutes or until crisp. **Yield:** 6 servings.

Peach-Filled Pastries

When your family has a taste for pie but time is ticking away, make this fast and fruity dessert. For a yummy twist, use cherry pie filling instead of peach.

      1 **sheet frozen puff pastry, thawed**
      1 **egg white**
      1 **tablespoon water**
1-1/2 **teaspoons sugar**

1 can (21 ounces) peach *or* cherry pie filling
1/4 teaspoon almond extract
2 cups whipped topping

On a lightly floured surface, unfold the puff pastry and roll to 3/8-in. thickness. Cut along the fold seams into three pieces. Cut each piece in half widthwise; place on an ungreased baking sheet. Beat the egg white and water; brush over the pastry. Sprinkle with sugar. Bake at 400° for 9-11 minutes or until golden brown. Cool on a wire rack.

Split each pastry in half horizontally. Combine pie filling and extract; spoon over the bottom halves of pastries. Top with whipped topping and pastry tops. **Yield:** 6 servings.

Puff Pastry Pointers

Frozen puff pastry dough is available in sheets or individual shells. It has dozens of paper-thin layers of dough separated by butter. As the pastry bakes, steam created from water in the dough makes the layers rise up and pull apart, resulting in a crisp, flaky pastry.

Unbaked puff pastry dough may be wrapped tightly in plastic wrap and stored in the refrigerator for 2 or 3 days or frozen for up to 1 month. Baked pastries are best the day they are made and don't refrigerate well. Baked, unfilled pastry may be frozen for up to 6 weeks.

Savor Flavors Of the South

WHEN you have a taste for Cajun cooking, you don't need to travel to the Louisiana bayou. Just head to your kitchen and whip up this Test Kitchen menu featuring Jiffy Jambalaya, Cheesy Onion Breadsticks and creamy Chocolate Chip Mousse.

Jiffy Jambalaya

Smoked sausage gives this Cajun-style supper wonderful flavor. For those who like their foods a little spicier, add some more cayenne pepper.

- **1 pound fully cooked smoked sausage, halved lengthwise and cut into 1/2-inch slices**
- **1 medium green pepper, chopped**
- **1 medium onion, chopped**
- **1 tablespoon vegetable oil**
- **1 can (14-1/2 ounces) diced tomatoes, undrained**
- **1 teaspoon Worcestershire sauce**
- **2 garlic cloves, minced**
- **1 bay leaf**
- **1/8 teaspoon cayenne pepper**
- **1/8 teaspoon pepper**
- **1 cup cooked rice**

In a large saucepan, saute the sausage, green pepper and onion in oil until the vegetables are tender. Stir in the tomatoes, Worcestershire sauce, garlic, bay leaf, cayenne and pepper. Bring to a boil. Reduce heat; cover and simmer for 10-15 minutes or until the vegetables are tender. Discard the bay leaf. Stir in the rice. **Yield:** 4 servings.

Cheesy Onion Breadsticks

Here, basic biscuit mix gets a makeover with cheese, green onions and garlic powder. Brushing the breadsticks with melted butter when they come out of the oven adds to the eye appeal.

- **1 cup biscuit/baking mix**
- **1/4 cup milk**
- **1/2 cup shredded cheddar cheese**
- **2 green onions, finely chopped**
- **1/4 teaspoon garlic powder**
- **1 tablespoon butter, melted**

In a bowl, combine the biscuit mix, milk, cheese, onions and garlic powder. Turn onto a lightly floured surface; knead 8-10 times. Roll into an 8-in. x 6-in. rectangle. Cut lengthwise into eight strips.

Place on a greased baking sheet. Bake at 375° for 12-15 minutes or until golden brown. Brush with butter. **Yield:** 8 breadsticks.

Chocolate Chip Mousse

When a chocolate craving hits, reach for this recipe for rich and creamy mousse. The decadent treat will satisfy your sweet tooth in no time.

1 cup (6 ounces) semisweet chocolate chips
1 package (8 ounces) cream cheese, softened
1 teaspoon vanilla extract
1 carton (8 ounces) frozen whipped topping, thawed

In a microwave or heavy saucepan, melt chocolate chips; stir until smooth. Cool for 20 minutes. Meanwhile, in a small mixing bowl, beat cream cheese and vanilla until smooth; beat in melted chocolate. Fold in whipped topping. Spoon into dessert dishes. Refrigerate until serving. **Yield:** 4 servings.

Chicken Dinner Is a Delight

IF WINTER has made you blue, welcome spring with this colorful dinner from our home economists. Your hungry family will be nuts for Chicken Amandine and Gingered Baby Carrots. Have children help layer—then eat!—pretty Ice Blue Parfaits.

Chicken Amandine

These chicken breasts are coated with a tasty nut mixture. While they bake, you can fix the rest of your meal.

- **1-1/2 cups sliced almonds**
- **3/4 cup dry bread crumbs**
- **2 tablespoons dried parsley flakes**
- **1/2 teaspoon salt**
- **1/4 teaspoon pepper**
- **2 eggs**
- **1 tablespoon water**
- **4 boneless skinless chicken breast halves**

In a food processor or blender, process the almonds until finely chopped. Place in a shallow bowl. In another bowl, combine the bread crumbs, parsley, salt and pepper. In a third bowl, beat the eggs and water.

Coat chicken with crumb mixture, then dip in egg mixture and roll in almonds. Place on a greased baking sheet. Bake at 400° for 20-25 minutes or until juices run clear. **Yield:** 4 servings.

Gingered Baby Carrots

Ginger, salt and pepper team up to cover these tender carrots with an irresistible butter glaze.

- **4 cups fresh *or* frozen baby carrots (about 1-1/4 pounds)**
- **2 tablespoons water**
- **2 tablespoons butter**
- **1/2 teaspoon ground ginger**
- **1/4 teaspoon salt**
- **1/8 teaspoon pepper**

Place carrots and water in a microwave-safe dish. Cover and microwave on high for 9-11 minutes or until tender, stirring twice; drain. Stir in butter, ginger, salt and pepper. **Yield:** 4 servings.

Editor's Note: This recipe was tested in an 850-watt microwave.

Ice Blue Parfaits

Kids of all ages will get a kick out of this refreshing dessert. With cubes of bright blue gelatin, it adds a fun, colorful touch to a springtime table. If you like, substitute strawberries or other fruit for the blueberries.

- **1 package (3 ounces) cream cheese, softened**
- **1 carton (8 ounces) frozen whipped topping, thawed**
- **1 package (14 ounces) blue gelatin snack cups *or* 1-1/3 cups cubed blue gelatin**

1 cup fresh *or* frozen blueberries

In a small mixing bowl, beat the cream cheese until smooth; beat in the whipped topping. Unmold the gelatin from each snack cup; cut the gelatin into 1/2-in. cubes.

In four parfait glasses or dessert bowls, layer half of the cream cheese mixture, gelatin and blueberries. Repeat the layers. Refrigerate until serving. **Yield:** 4 servings.

Editor's Note: This recipe was tested with Kraft handi-snacks wacky gels. There are four snack cups in each package.

Baby Carrot Clues

Carrots are widely available in packages labeled "baby carrots." Despite what the name seems to imply, baby carrots are not young carrots harvested before they've grown to full size. They're actually large carrots that have been cut down to look like miniature ones.

Baby carrots have become popular not only for side dishes such as Gingered Baby Carrots (recipe at far left), but also as a healthy snack.

Catch Fresh Fare for Spring

WHEN you're looking for a new angle to your week-day menus, try Salmon with Dijon Mayonnaise! Coated with seasoned butter, Pecan Brussels Sprouts appeal to all palates. Top off this mouth-watering meal from our Test Kitchen by serving Rhubarb Cobbler.

Salmon with Dijon Mayonnaise

You won't need to fish for compliments when this eye-catching main course appears on the table. The dill and mustard topping pairs well with the salmon.

> 4 **salmon fillets (6 ounces** *each***)**
> 1/2 **cup mayonnaise**
> 2 **tablespoons grated Parmesan cheese**
> 1 **tablespoon Dijon mustard**
> 1/4 **teaspoon dill weed**

Place the salmon skin side down on a greased broiler pan. Broil 4 in. from the heat for 10-16 minutes or until fish flakes easily with a fork. Meanwhile, combine the remaining ingredients in a small bowl. Serve with the salmon. **Yield:** 4 servings.

Pecan Brussels Sprouts

Your family will eagerly eat their vegetables when you serve this dish. Crunchy pecans are a nice contrast to the tender brussels sprouts.

> 12 **ounces fresh** *or* **frozen brussels sprouts (3 cups)**
> 3 **tablespoons water**
> 1 **cup pecan halves**
> 2 **tablespoons butter, melted**
> 1/4 **teaspoon salt**
> 1/8 **teaspoon pepper**
> 1/8 **teaspoon ground nutmeg**

Place brussels sprouts and water in a microwave-safe dish. Cover and microwave on high for 4-6 minutes or until tender; drain. Add the pecan halves, butter, salt, pepper and nutmeg; toss to coat. **Yield:** 4 servings.

Editor's Note: This recipe was tested in an 850-watt microwave.

Rhubarb Cobbler

Crumbled macaroons are a unique addition to this cobbler's topping. Serve generous helpings alone or with scoops of vanilla ice cream.

> 4 **cups sliced fresh** *or* **frozen rhubarb (1-inch pieces)**
> 1 **large sweet apple, peeled and sliced**
> 1/2 **cup packed brown sugar**

1/2 teaspoon ground cinnamon, *divided*
1 tablespoon cornstarch
2 tablespoons cold water
8 macaroons, crumbled
1 tablespoon butter, melted
2 tablespoons sugar
Vanilla ice cream, optional

In a large skillet, combine the rhubarb, apple, brown sugar and 1/4 teaspoon cinnamon; bring to a boil. Reduce heat; cover and simmer for 10-13 minutes or until rhubarb is very tender. Combine cornstarch and water until smooth; add to the fruit mixture. Bring to a boil; cook and stir for 2 minutes or until thickened. Transfer to an ungreased 1-qt. baking dish.

In a bowl, combine the crumbled cookies, butter, sugar and remaining cinnamon. Sprinkle over fruit mixture. Broil 4 in. from the heat for 3-5 minutes or until lightly browned. Serve warm with ice cream if desired. **Yield:** 4 servings.

Fast Lunch Is Fun to Munch

LIVEN UP midday meals with these lunch-counter classics created by our home economists. Pepper Jack Melts feature chicken, cheese and salad dressing. For a dish you can make in a snap, rely on Veggie Macaroni Salad. And instead of serving soda, shake things up with Springtime Strawberry Malts.

Pepper Jack Melts

Peppercorn dressing and pepper Jack cheese jazz up every bite of these change-of-pace sandwiches.

- 8 bacon strips
- 4 tablespoons peppercorn ranch salad dressing
- 8 slices rye bread
- 3/4 pound thinly sliced deli chicken
- 4 slices pepper Jack cheese
- 2 tablespoons butter

Place four bacon strips at a time on a microwave-safe plate lined with microwave-safe paper towels. Cover with another paper towel; microwave on high for 5-7 minutes or until crisp.

Spread salad dressing on four slices of bread; top with the chicken, bacon, cheese and remaining bread.

In a large skillet or griddle, melt butter over medium heat. Cook sandwiches on both sides until bread is lightly toasted and cheese is melted. **Yield:** 4 servings.

Editor's Note: This recipe was tested in an 850-watt microwave.

Veggie Macaroni Salad

This recipe pleasantly proves that making pasta salad doesn't have to be a time-consuming task, thanks to the head start from bottled salad dressing.

- 1-1/2 cups uncooked elbow macaroni
- 1 pint cherry tomatoes, quartered
- 1/2 cup chopped green pepper
- 1 celery rib, chopped
- 2 green onions, chopped
- 1/2 cup Italian salad dressing
- 1 tablespoon mayonnaise
- 1/4 teaspoon pepper

Cook the macaroni according to package directions, then drain and rinse with cold water. In a large bowl,

combine the macaroni, tomatoes, green pepper, celery and onions. In a small bowl, whisk together the salad dressing, mayonnaise and pepper; drizzle over salad and toss to coat. Refrigerate salad until serving. **Yield:** 4 servings.

Springtime Strawberry Malts

Don't limit yourself to having a malt only when you're at a restaurant. This refreshing beverage makes mealtime fun

for the whole family. For variety, experiment with different fruits and flavors of ice cream.

- 1/4 cup milk
- 2 tablespoons strawberry syrup
- 1/2 cup malted milk powder
- 6 fresh *or* frozen strawberries
- 1 quart vanilla ice cream, softened

Place ingredients in a blender; cover and process until smooth. Pour into chilled glasses. **Yield:** 4 servings.

Makin' Bacon

Do your upcoming menu plans include a lunch or dinner recipe, such as Pepper Jack Melts (recipe at far left), that uses bacon? Give yourself a head start by preparing extra bacon for breakfast a day or two earlier. Store the leftovers in the refrigerator, and you'll have bacon slices that are cooked and ready to use later on.

Start Dad's Day Off Right

ON FATHER'S DAY, prepare a special breakfast for your top Pop! This morning meal from our Test Kitchen staff starts with Confetti Scrambled Eggs, loaded with peppers and cheese. Dad won't be able to resist the sweet glaze on hearty Ham 'n' Sausage Kabobs. And pastries are easy to prepare thanks to finger-lickin'-good Cinnamon Swirl Rolls.

Confetti Scrambled Eggs

There's nothing like a bright-eyed breakfast to get you going in the morning. Pretty red and green pepper pieces peek out from these extra-special scrambled eggs. They're so easy to fix, you'll want to make them regularly.

    12 eggs
     6 tablespoons half-and-half cream, milk *or* water
   1/2 teaspoon salt
   1/4 teaspoon pepper
   1/2 cup chopped sweet red pepper
   1/2 cup chopped green pepper
     2 green onions, chopped
     2 tablespoons butter
     1 cup (4 ounces) shredded cheddar cheese

In a bowl, beat the eggs, cream, salt and pepper until combined; set aside. In a large skillet, saute the peppers and onions in butter for 2 minutes.

Add the egg mixture; cook and stir over medium heat until the eggs are completely set. Remove from the heat; stir in the shredded cheese. Serve immediately. **Yield:** 4 servings.

Ham 'n' Sausage Kabobs

These meaty skewers will round out any breakfast menu. A glaze of honey, maple syrup and mustard pleasantly coats every bite-size piece.

     4 smoked sausage links, cut into 1/2-inch slices
   1/3 pound fully cooked ham (1 inch thick), cut into 1-inch cubes
     2 tablespoons honey
     2 tablespoons maple syrup
     1 teaspoon Dijon mustard

On metal or soaked wooden skewers, alternately thread sausage and ham. Place on a broiler pan coated with nonstick cooking spray. Combine the remaining ingredients; brush over kabobs. Bake at 375° for 10-15 minutes or until heated through. **Yield:** 4 servings.

Cinnamon Swirl Rolls

When you don't have time to make from-scratch rolls, rely on this recipe that begins with refrigerated breadsticks.

1/3 cup packed brown sugar
1/4 cup sugar
1 teaspoon ground cinnamon
1 tube (11 ounces) refrigerated breadsticks
3 tablespoons butter, melted
3/4 cup confectioners' sugar
4 teaspoons milk
1/4 teaspoon vanilla extract

In a shallow dish, combine the brown sugar, sugar and cinnamon. Separate breadsticks. Brush all sides with butter, then coat with sugar mixture.

On a greased baking sheet, form three breadsticks into a coil, overlapping ends slightly. Secure with toothpicks through the overlapped breadstick ends and at the end of the swirl. Repeat with remaining breadsticks. Pour remaining butter over rolls; sprinkle with remaining sugar mixture.

Bake at 375° for 15-17 minutes or until golden brown. Remove to a wire rack. Discard toothpicks. Combine the confectioners' sugar, milk and vanilla; drizzle over rolls. Serve warm. **Yield:** 4 servings.

Editor's Note: This recipe was tested with Pillsbury refrigerated breadsticks.

Meal Spices Up Summertime

IF YOU and your family savor the flavors of Mexican fare, you'll love this south-of-the-border spread from our Test Kitchen. Loaded with beef and beans, Taco Salad will satisfy the heartiest of appetites. Summer Squash Toss puts the season's finest produce to good use, while scoops of Nut-Coated Ice Cream are a fun twist on deep-fried ice cream.

Taco Salad

Instead of using fried salad shells, this recipe calls for baking flour tortillas in the microwave. Doing so keeps all the flavor and reduces the fat.

    1 pound ground beef
    1 envelope taco seasoning
  2/3 cup water
  1/2 teaspoon ground cumin
    4 flour tortillas (9 inches)
Refrigerated butter-flavored spray
    1 can (16 ounces) refried beans
  1/2 cup salsa
    2 cups (8 ounces) shredded cheddar cheese
Shredded lettuce, sliced ripe olives, chopped
  onions and sour cream

In a large skillet, cook beef over medium heat until no longer pink; drain. Stir in taco seasoning, water and cumin. Bring to a boil. Reduce heat; simmer, uncovered, for 5-7 minutes or until thickened.

Meanwhile, place each tortilla in a microwave-safe 7-in.-diameter shallow bowl, forming a shell. Spritz with butter spray. Microwave two at a time on high for 2 to 2-1/2 minutes or until crisp and lightly browned. Carefully remove from bowls to serving plates.

In a microwave-safe bowl, combine beans and salsa. Cover and microwave on high for 1-1/2 to 2 minutes or until heated through. Spoon into shells. Top with beef mixture and cheese. Serve with lettuce, olives, onions and sour cream. **Yield:** 4 servings.

Editor's Note: This recipe was tested with I Can't Believe It's Not Butter Spray in an 850-watt microwave.

Summer Squash Toss

Take advantage of summer's best produce with this nicely seasoned salad. The dependable oil-and-vinegar dressing stirs up in a jiffy and has fantastic flavor.

    1 medium yellow summer squash, julienned
    1 medium zucchini, julienned
    1 medium tomato, julienned
    3 tablespoons olive oil
    3 tablespoons cider vinegar
    4 teaspoons sugar
  1/2 teaspoon dried basil
  1/4 teaspoon dried thyme
  1/8 teaspoon salt
Dash pepper

In a serving bowl, combine the squash, zucchini and tomato. In a small bowl, combine the remaining ingredients. Drizzle over vegetables. **Yield:** 4 servings.

Nut-Coated Ice Cream

If you have the chance, make these nutty treats in advance and freeze them until dinnertime.

- **7 cream-filled chocolate sandwich cookies**
- **1/2 cup ground walnuts**
- **1 tablespoon brown sugar**
- **2 cups coffee ice cream, softened**

Break four cookies in half; set aside. Crush the remaining cookies and place in a small bowl; add the walnuts and brown sugar. Drop ice cream by 1/2 cupfuls into walnut mixture; roll into four balls. Place in serving bowls; garnish with halved cookies. **Yield:** 4 servings.

Savor Summer Squash

Members of the gourd family, summer squash are soft-skinned, tender and quick-cooking. Varieties include yellow crookneck, zucchini, sunburst and pattypan. All contain small, soft edible seeds and edible skins.

Buy summer squash that have smooth, glossy and firm but tender skins. Small squash are more tender and flavorful.

Keep unwashed summer squash in a sealed plastic bag in the refrigerator crisper drawer. It may be stored this way for up to 4 days.

Serve Italian Specialties

BRING a little bit of Italy to your table with this stand-out supper. You can serve Bruschetta as an appetizer or as a side dish. With a creamy garlic sauce and tender pasta, Shrimp Alfredo rivals any dish found in authentic Italian restaurants. And Frosty Lemon Drink is a refreshing addition to this irresistible, rich meal created by our home economists.

Shrimp Alfredo

Instead of buying a jar of Alfredo sauce, make it from scratch with this simple recipe. The garlic aroma is sure to draw your family to the table.

      4 **ounces uncooked spinach fettuccine**
      4 **ounces uncooked fettuccine**
    1/4 **cup butter**
  1-1/2 **cups heavy whipping cream**
      1 **pound cooked medium shrimp, peeled and deveined**
    3/4 **cup grated Parmesan cheese**
      1 **garlic clove, minced**
    1/4 **teaspoon pepper**
      1 **teaspoon minced fresh parsley**

Cook the fettuccine according to the package directions. Meanwhile, in a large saucepan, melt the butter over medium heat. Stir in the whipping cream. Bring to a gentle boil. Reduce heat; simmer, uncovered, for 3 minutes, stirring constantly.

Add the shrimp, Parmesan cheese, garlic and pepper; cook and stir until heated through. Drain the fettuccine; toss with the shrimp mixture. Sprinkle with the parsley. **Yield:** 4 servings.

Bruschetta

One of the best ways to showcase garden-fresh tomatoes is this satisfying bruschetta. When time allows, you can make the tomato mixture earlier in the day.

      6 **plum tomatoes, diced**
      2 **tablespoons olive oil, *divided***
    1/2 **teaspoon dried basil**
    1/4 **teaspoon dried rosemary, crushed**
    1/8 **teaspoon salt**
      8 **slices French bread (3/4 inch thick)**
    1/4 **teaspoon garlic powder**

In a bowl, combine the tomatoes, 1 teaspoon oil, basil, rosemary and salt; set aside. Brush bread with remaining oil and sprinkle with garlic powder. Place on an ungreased baking sheet. Broil 6 in. from the heat for 1-2 minutes or until lightly browned. Using a slotted spoon, top bread with tomato mixture. Serve immediately. **Yield:** 4 servings.

Frosty Lemon Drink

In the heat of summer, you'll find yourself making this refreshing beverage often. It's perfect as a light dessert, too.

3/4 cup lemonade concentrate
1/2 cup nonfat dry milk powder
1/3 cup sugar
3/4 cup cold water
1/8 teaspoon almond extract
16 to 18 ice cubes
3 drops yellow food coloring, optional

In a blender, combine the first five ingredients; cover and process on high until blended. Add ice cubes, a few at a time; cover and process until slushy. Add food coloring if desired. Pour into chilled glasses. Serve immediately. **Yield:** 4 servings.

Popular Parsley

Available in curly and flat-leaf varieties, fresh parsley adds refreshing flavor to main courses such as Shrimp Alfredo (recipe at far left), as well as soups, salads, salad dressings, sauces, stuffings and side dishes containing potatoes, grains and beans.

Flat-leaf, or Italian, parsley has a stronger flavor than the traditional curly variety. Dried parsley is mild in both flavor and color.

Casual Dinner Is a Winner

YOU'LL SCORE a touchdown during football season when you serve saucy Italian Meatball Sandwiches alongside fresh-tasting Broccoli Salad. (Plus, you won't need to work overtime to prepare them!) To complete this crowd-pleasing meal from our Test Kitchen, offer Toffee-Chip Sugar Cookies.

Italian Meatball Sandwiches

Frozen meatballs and store-bought spaghetti sauce are the time-saving secrets to these fast and filling sandwiches. Whip them up and watch them disappear!

> 2 packages (12 ounces *each*) frozen Italian meatballs
> 1 jar (28 ounces) spaghetti sauce
> 3/4 cup sliced fresh mushrooms
> 3/4 cup chopped green pepper
> 6 hoagie *or* submarine sandwich buns, split

Place the meatballs in a microwave-safe dish. Cover and microwave on high for 2-3 minutes or until slightly thawed.

Transfer meatballs to a large saucepan; add the spaghetti sauce, mushrooms and green pepper. Bring to a boil. Reduce heat; simmer, uncovered, for 4-7 minutes or until the meatballs are heated through. Serve on buns. **Yield:** 6 servings.

Editor's Note: This recipe was tested in an 850-watt microwave.

Broccoli Salad

After trying this crunchy salad, you'll likely rely on it for many meals and get-togethers. It's extra quick because it requires no cooking.

> 2-1/2 cups broccoli florets
> 1-3/4 cups cauliflowerets
> 1/2 cup chopped red onion
> 1/2 cup cubed cheddar cheese
> 1/4 cup crumbled cooked bacon
> 1/2 cup olive oil
> 1/4 cup cider vinegar
> 2 teaspoons sugar
> 1 teaspoon Worcestershire sauce
> 1/4 teaspoon pepper

In a large bowl, combine the broccoli, cauliflower, onion, cheese and bacon. In a small bowl, whisk the remaining ingredients. Pour over salad; toss to coat. Refrigerate until serving. **Yield:** 6 servings.

Toffee-Chip Sugar Cookies

When you taste these candy-topped cookies, you won't believe the recipe calls for only two ingredients!

1 **tube (18 ounces) refrigerated sugar cookie dough**
4 **Heath candy bars (1.4 ounces *each*), finely chopped**

Slice cookie dough into 1/4-in. slices. Place 2 in. apart on lightly greased baking sheets. Sprinkle each with 2 teaspoons chopped candy bars. Bake at 350° for 7-9 minutes or until edges are lightly browned. Remove to wire racks to cool. **Yield:** about 2-1/2 dozen.

Buying Broccoli

Broccoli bunches may no longer be your only choice at the supermarket. Many stores sell broccoli crowns, which give you the florets and little stem. Also, florets may be sold loose or in bags. When buying bagged florets, check the expiration date and for any discoloration.

Special Menu Has Fall Flair

SURPRISE your family with our Test Kitchen's easy yet elegant dinner in the middle of the week. Cran-Orange Pork Tenderloin tastes and looks impressive but requires little work. A few simple seasonings delightfully dress up Herbed Green Beans, while Bananas Foster is a fancy, fuss-free dessert.

Cran-Orange Pork Tenderloin

Cranberries and oranges are natural choices for flavoring pork in fall. Make someone's day with this tasty meal.

- 1/4 teaspoon garlic salt
- 1/4 teaspoon pepper
- 1/8 teaspoon ground mustard
- 1/8 teaspoon ground cinnamon
- 1 pork tenderloin (1 pound)

CRAN-ORANGE SAUCE:
- 1/2 cup dried cranberries
- 1/4 cup plus 1 tablespoon orange juice, *divided*
- 1/8 teaspoon ground ginger

Dash ground cloves
- 1 can (11 ounces) mandarin oranges
- 1 tablespoon cornstarch

In a small bowl, combine the first four ingredients; rub over pork. Place on a rack in a shallow roasting pan. Bake, uncovered, at 425° for 25-28 minutes or until a meat thermometer reads 160°.

Meanwhile, in a small saucepan, combine the cranberries, 1/4 cup orange juice, ginger and cloves. Drain oranges, reserving juice; set oranges aside.

Add reserved juice to cranberry mixture. Bring to a boil. Reduce heat; cover and simmer for 5 minutes. Combine cornstarch and remaining orange juice until smooth; stir into saucepan. Bring to a boil; cook and stir for 1 minute or until thickened. Fold in oranges. Serve over sliced pork. **Yield:** 3-4 servings.

Herbed Green Beans

Tarragon, garlic and onion bring fabulous flavor to these fresh green beans. The vibrant color of this side dish is an eye-catching addition to the table, too.

- 1/2 pound fresh green beans, trimmed
- 1 small onion, chopped
- 2 tablespoons water
- 1 garlic clove, minced
- 1/2 teaspoon white wine vinegar
- 1/8 teaspoon dried tarragon

Salt and pepper to taste

In a microwave-safe bowl, combine the green beans, onion, water and garlic. Cover and microwave on high for 5-7 minutes or until the beans are crisp-tender, stirring twice; drain. Stir in the vinegar, tarragon, salt and pepper.

Yield: 3-4 servings.

Editor's Note: This recipe was tested in an 850-watt microwave.

Bananas Foster

Dessert lovers of every kind will find this sweet treat very "apeeling!" It's an impressive ending to everyday meals.

1/4 **cup butter**
3/4 **cup packed brown sugar**
1/4 **teaspoon ground cinnamon**
1/8 **teaspoon ground nutmeg**
Dash ground cloves
1/4 **cup heavy whipping cream**
3 **medium firm bananas, halved lengthwise and cut into thirds**
1/4 **teaspoon rum extract**
Ice cream

In a large skillet, melt butter. Stir in the brown sugar, cinnamon, nutmeg and cloves. Cook and stir until sugar is dissolved. Stir in cream. Add bananas and extract. Serve warm over ice cream. **Yield:** 3-4 servings.

Soup Supper Is Quick to Fix

TURN leftover turkey from a holiday feast into a second-time-around delight with Basil Turkey Soup. For a full meal, our home economists combined it with slices of Red Onion Focaccia and rich Tiramisu. You can save time by preparing the dessert earlier in the day and refrigerating it until serving.

Basil Turkey Soup

After a busy day of Christmas shopping, it's easy to put together this soup with leftover turkey and frozen veggies.

      4 **cups beef broth**
2-1/2 **cups frozen mixed vegetables**
      1 **can (14-1/2 ounces) diced tomatoes, undrained**
   3/4 **cup uncooked small shell pasta**
   3/4 **teaspoon dried basil**
   3/4 **teaspoon pepper**
2-1/2 **cups cubed cooked turkey**
2-1/2 **teaspoons dried parsley flakes**

In a large saucepan, combine the first six ingredients. Bring to a boil. Reduce heat; cover and simmer for 7-10 minutes or until the pasta and vegetables are tender. Stir in the turkey and parsley; heat through. **Yield:** 6 servings.

Red Onion Focaccia

Sauteing the onions in oil before using them as a topping on this fast focaccia bread mellows their fantastic flavor…and a blend of cheeses tantalizes the taste buds!

2 **small red onions, sliced and separated into rings**
3 **tablespoons olive oil,** *divided*
1 **tube (10 ounces) refrigerated pizza crust**
2 **tablespoons grated Parmesan cheese**
2 **tablespoons grated Romano cheese**
1 **teaspoon dried rosemary, crushed**
1 **teaspoon garlic powder**

In a large skillet, saute onions in 1 tablespoon oil for 4 minutes; set aside. On a greased baking sheet, roll out pizza crust into a 12-in. x 8-in. rectangle. Brush with remaining oil. Sprinkle with cheeses, rosemary and garlic powder. Top with onions. Bake at 425° for 14-16 minutes or until lightly browned. **Yield:** 6 servings.

Tiramisu

No one can resist this classic, cool and creamy dessert. It's quick to prepare but can be made ahead of time for added mealtime convenience.

      2 **cups cold milk**
      1 **package (3.4 ounces) instant vanilla pudding mix**
      1 **cup heavy whipping cream**
      3 **tablespoons confectioners' sugar**
     18 **ladyfingers, split**
2-1/2 **teaspoons instant coffee granules**

1/2 cup boiling water
1 tablespoon baking cocoa

In a bowl, whisk milk and pudding mix for 2 minutes or until thickened. In a small mixing bowl, beat cream until it begins to thicken. Add confectioners' sugar; beat until soft peaks form. Fold into pudding; refrigerate.

Arrange half of the ladyfingers cut side up in an 11-in. x 7-in. x 2-in. dish. Dissolve coffee granules in boiling water; drizzle half over the ladyfingers. Spread with half of the pudding mixture. Repeat layers. Sprinkle with cocoa. Refrigerate until serving. **Yield:** 6 servings.

Tempting Tiramisu

An Italian classic that has become popular in the United States, tiramisu (pronounced tih-ruh-mee-SOO) is a layered dessert that includes ladyfingers or sponge cake infused with coffee. Translated from Italian, tiramisu means "pick me up." It's sometimes referred to as Italian trifle.

Traditional recipes for tiramisu can often be time-consuming. The simplified version at left is fast to fix but still makes a luscious treat.

Have a Festive Holiday Feast

YOUR FAMILY will be delighted to find the table decked out with this special Christmas dinner from our Test Kitchen. A mild rub nicely complements Bacon-Wrapped Beef Fillets. For a quick-cooking side dish, try Colorful Couscous. Chilled slices of White Chocolate Mint Pie make a refreshing finish.

Bacon-Wrapped Beef Fillets

Beef fillets add a bit of elegance to a casual holiday meal. Best of all, they are easy on the cook because they take mere minutes to prepare.

      12 bacon strips
       1 teaspoon rubbed sage
     1/2 teaspoon dried rosemary, crushed
     1/2 teaspoon dried savory
     1/2 teaspoon coarsely ground pepper
     1/4 teaspoon salt
       6 beef tenderloin fillets (1 to 1-1/2 inches
           thick)

Place six bacon strips at a time on a microwave-safe plate lined with microwave-safe paper towels. Cover with another paper towel; microwave on high for 3-4 minutes or until partially cooked. In a small bowl, combine the sage, rosemary, savory, pepper and salt; rub over steaks. Wrap two strips of bacon around sides of fillets and secure with toothpicks.

Broil 3-4 in. from the heat for 6-7 minutes on each side or until meat reaches desired doneness (for medium-rare, a meat thermometer should read 145°; medium, 160°; well-done, 170°). Discard toothpicks. **Yield:** 6 servings.

Editor's Note: This recipe was tested in an 850-watt microwave.

Colorful Couscous

Red and green peppers provide perfect Christmas color in this side dish. Light and fluffy couscous is a scrumptious switch from baked potatoes or rice.

     1/3 cup *each* finely chopped onion, green
           pepper and sweet red pepper
       2 garlic cloves, minced
       2 tablespoons olive oil
       1 can (14-1/2 ounces) chicken broth
     1/4 cup water
     1/2 teaspoon salt
     1/4 teaspoon pepper
       1 package (10 ounces) couscous

In a large saucepan, saute the onion, peppers and garlic in oil for 3 minutes. Stir in the broth, water, salt and pepper. Bring to a boil. Stir in the couscous. Cover and remove from the heat; let stand for 5 minutes. Fluff with a fork. Serve immediately. **Yield:** 6 servings.

White Chocolate Mint Pie

Two classic holiday flavors—chocolate and peppermint—combine in this creamy, festive-looking dessert.

1/3 cup hot fudge ice cream topping
  1 graham cracker crust (9 inches)
  1 package (8 ounces) cream cheese, softened
3/4 teaspoon peppermint extract
1-3/4 cups cold milk, *divided*
  1 package (3.3 ounces) instant white chocolate pudding mix
20 peppermint candies, crushed

In a microwave-safe bowl, heat fudge topping on high for 12-17 seconds or until spreadable. Spread over the bottom of crust; set aside.

In a small mixing bowl, beat cream cheese and peppermint extract until smooth. Gradually beat in 1/2 cup milk until smooth. Slowly add the remaining milk. Sprinkle with pudding mix; beat on low speed for 2-3 minutes or until slightly thickened. Pour into the crust. Chill for at least 25 minutes. Sprinkle with peppermints. **Yield:** 6-8 servings.

Meals on a Budget

Your family will never guess that these mouth-watering menus put together by our home economists are also easy on your wallet!

BUDGET-FRIENDLY FEASTS. Clockwise from upper left: Feed Your Family for $1.41 a Plate! (p. 284), Feed Your Family for $1.90 a Plate! (p. 286), Feed Your Family for $1.72 a Plate! (p. 282) and Feed Your Family for $1.99 a Plate! (p. 288).

Feed Your Family For $1.44 a Plate!

CELEBRATE the Chinese New Year—or enjoy Oriental food any time at all—with this budget meal that lets you feed the whole gang for just $1.44 a plate.

Our Test Kitchen put the menu together using tried-and-true recipes from three *Taste of Home* readers, so you know it's delicious!

Chinese New Year Skillet was inspired by a recipe on the back of a rice package in 1957, notes Sherilyn West of Lubbock, Texas. "If you like pork, I guarantee you'll love this recipe," she says. "It satisfies even the heartiest appetites."

Egg Drop Soup is the perfect way to start an Asian meal and requires just five ingredients. "If you want, you can add two minced water chestnuts," says Jenny Haen of Red Wing, Minnesota.

Beverly Preston of Fond du Lac, Wisconsin started making Almond Cookies after enjoying similar ones at her favorite Chinese restaurant. "These crisp cookies have wonderful almond flavor," she says. "They're a fitting end to a 'Far East' feast."

Chinese New Year Skillet

Prep: 15 min.   **Cook:** 25 min.

- 1 pound boneless pork butt roast, cut into 1/2-inch cubes
- 1 tablespoon vegetable oil
- 1 can (20 ounces) unsweetened pineapple tidbits
- 2 tablespoons white wine vinegar
- 1 tablespoon sugar
- 3/4 teaspoon salt
- 1/4 teaspoon garlic powder
- 1 cup uncooked long grain rice
- 1 tablespoon cornstarch
- 2 tablespoons water
- 1/2 cup coarsely chopped green pepper
- 1 medium tomato, cut into wedges
- 2 tablespoons Worcestershire sauce

In a large skillet, saute pork in oil. Drain pineapple, reserving juice in a 2-cup measuring cup; set pineapple aside. Add enough water to the juice to measure 1-1/4 cups; stir into pork. Add vinegar, sugar, salt and garlic powder.

Bring to a boil, stirring constantly. Reduce heat; cover and simmer for 20 minutes or until meat is tender. Meanwhile, cook rice according to package directions.

In a small bowl, combine the cornstarch and water until smooth; stir into the pork mixture. Bring to a boil; cook and stir for 2 minutes or until thickened. Stir in the green pepper, tomato wedges, Worcestershire sauce and reserved pineapple; heat through. Serve over rice. **Yield:** 4 servings.

Egg Drop Soup

Prep/Total Time: 10 min.

- 5 cups chicken broth
- 1/2 teaspoon sugar
- 1 egg, lightly beaten
- 1/3 cup sliced fresh spinach
- 2 green onions, sliced

In a large saucepan, bring the chicken broth and sugar to a boil over medium heat. Reduce heat to low. Drizzle the beaten egg into the hot broth. Remove from the heat; stir in the sliced spinach and green onions. **Yield:** 4 servings.

Almond Cookies

Prep: 10 min.   **Bake:** 10 min. per batch + cooling

- 1 cup shortening
- 1/2 cup plus 3 tablespoons sugar, *divided*
- 1/4 cup packed brown sugar
- 1 egg
- 1 teaspoon almond extract
- 2 cups all-purpose flour
- 1-1/2 teaspoons baking powder
- 1/8 teaspoon salt
- 3 tablespoons sliced almonds

In a small mixing bowl, cream the shortening, 1/2 cup sugar and brown sugar. Beat in egg and extract. Combine the flour, baking powder and salt; gradually add to creamed mixture and mix well. Shape into 1-in. balls. Roll in remaining sugar.

Place 2 in. apart on ungreased baking sheets. Flatten with the bottom of a glass. Press three almond slices into the center of each.

Bake at 350° for 9-11 minutes or until the edges are lightly browned. Cool for 2 minutes before removing from pans to wire racks. **Yield:** 3 dozen.

Feed Your Family For $1.52 a Plate!

FOR COMFORT FOOD that's low-cost, try this menu that features Caraway Pot Roast from Violet Beard of Marshall, Illinois. You'll also enjoy Mashed Potato Casserole from Margaret Lindberg of Richland, Washington and Meringue-Topped Pineapple Dessert from Donna Gaston, Coplay, Pennsylvania.

Caraway Pot Roast

Prep: 10 min.   **Cook:** 2-3/4 hours

- 1 boneless beef chuck roast (3 pounds)
- 2 tablespoons vegetable oil
- 2 medium onions, sliced
- 2 medium carrots, cut into large chunks
- 1 cup apple cider *or* apple juice
- 1 tablespoon caraway seeds
- 2 garlic cloves, minced
- 3/4 teaspoon salt, *divided*
- 1/2 teaspoon pepper, *divided*
- 2 tablespoons cornstarch
- 1/4 cup cold water
- 1/2 cup sour cream

In a Dutch oven, brown roast in oil on all sides over medium-high heat; drain. Combine the onions, carrots, cider, caraway seeds, garlic, 1/2 teaspoon salt and 1/4 teaspoon pepper; pour over roast. Bring to a boil. Reduce heat; cover and simmer for 2 to 2-1/2 hours or until meat is tender.

Remove roast and vegetables; keep warm. Strain pan juices into a 2-cup measuring cup. Skim fat; add enough water to measure 2 cups. Return to Dutch oven. Combine cornstarch and cold water until smooth; stir into pan juices. Bring to a boil; cook and stir for 2 minutes or until thickened. Remove from the heat; stir in the sour cream and remaining salt and pepper. Serve with roast and vegetables. **Yield:** 8 servings.

Mashed Potato Casserole

Prep: 30 min.   **Bake:** 30 min.

- 3 pounds potatoes, peeled and cubed
- 1 package (8 ounces) cream cheese, cubed
- 1 cup (8 ounces) sour cream
- 1/4 cup milk
- 1 small onion, chopped
- 1 teaspoon garlic salt
- 1/2 teaspoon salt
- 2 tablespoons butter, melted
- 1/4 teaspoon paprika

Place potatoes in a large saucepan and cover with water. Bring to a boil. Reduce heat; cover and simmer until tender. Drain; place potatoes in a large mixing bowl. Add cream cheese, sour cream, milk, onion, garlic salt and salt; beat until blended. Transfer to a greased 2-qt. baking dish. Drizzle with butter; sprinkle with paprika. Cover and bake at 350° for 30-35 minutes or until heated through. **Yield:** 8 servings.

Meringue-Topped Pineapple Dessert

Prep: 25 min.   **Bake:** 45 min. + cooling

- 1 cup butter, softened
- 1/2 cup sugar
- 3 egg yolks
- 1/2 cup sour cream
- 2-1/2 cups all-purpose flour
- 1 teaspoon baking powder

FILLING:
- 3 tablespoons all-purpose flour
- 2 egg yolks
- 2 cans (8 ounces *each*) crushed pineapple, undrained
- 1 teaspoon vanilla extract

TOPPING:
- 5 egg whites
- 1/2 cup confectioners' sugar
- 1 teaspoon vanilla extract
- 1/2 cup finely chopped walnuts

In a large mixing bowl, cream butter and sugar. Add egg yolks and sour cream; mix well. Combine flour and baking powder; gradually add to creamed mixture. Press into greased 13-in. x 9-in. x 2-in. baking pan.

In a small saucepan, combine the flour, egg yolks and pineapple. Cook and stir over medium heat until mixture reaches 160° and coats the back of a metal spoon. Remove from the heat; stir in vanilla. Pour over crust. Bake at 350° for 30 minutes.

In a small mixing bowl, beat egg whites until soft peaks form. Gradually add confectioners' sugar and vanilla, beating until stiff peaks form. Spread over hot filling, sealing edges to the pan. Sprinkle with walnuts. Bake 15 minutes longer or until golden brown. Cool on a wire rack for 1 hour. Store in the refrigerator. **Yield:** 16 servings.

Feed Your Family For $1.72 a Plate!

THERE'S NO NEED to scrimp on flavor when you're trying to cut back on grocery spending.

Take this scrumptious meal, for example. It consists of three reader favorites that cost just pennies to make but are so delicious that your family will ask for them again and again.

Field editor Doris Heath of Franklin, North Carolina shares her creamy Hot Chicken Salad. Topped with potato chips and almonds, the comforting casserole could be made with leftover cooked chicken.

"I received the recipe for Belgian-Style Carrot Coins years ago from a neighbor," notes Billye Crumlish of Dallas, Texas. "I've lost touch with the neighbor but not with this recipe. It's a family favorite."

Made in muffin tins, Peanut Butter Brownie Cups from Joyce Gibson of Rhinelander, Wisconsin are a year-round treat and especially nice for picnics.

Hot Chicken Salad

Prep: 10 min.   **Bake:** 30 min.

    2 cups diced cooked chicken
    1 can (10-3/4 ounces) condensed cream of
      chicken soup, undiluted
    2 celery ribs, finely chopped
  1/2 cup mayonnaise
    1 can (4 ounces) mushroom stems and
      pieces, drained
    2 tablespoons finely chopped onion
  1/2 cup crushed butter-flavored crackers
      (about 12 crackers)
  1/2 cup crushed potato chips
  1/2 cup sliced almonds, toasted

In a large bowl, combine the first six ingredients. Stir in cracker crumbs. Spoon into a greased 1-1/2-qt. baking dish. Bake, uncovered, at 375° for 15 minutes.

Sprinkle with potato chips and almonds. Bake 15 minutes longer or until bubbly and lightly browned. **Yield:** 4 servings.

Editor's Note: Reduced-fat or fat-free mayonnaise is not recommended for this recipe.

Belgian-Style Carrot Coins

Prep/Total Time: 20 min.

    3 tablespoons butter
    8 medium carrots, sliced
    2 tablespoons water
    2 teaspoons sugar
  1/8 teaspoon salt
  1/8 teaspoon pepper
  1/2 cup heavy whipping cream
    2 tablespoons minced fresh parsley
  1/4 teaspoon ground nutmeg

In a large saucepan, melt the butter over medium heat; add the sliced carrots, water, sugar, salt and pepper. Cover and cook for 8-10 minutes or until the carrots are tender.

Stir in the heavy whipping cream, parsley and nutmeg. Bring just to a boil; remove from the heat. **Yield:** 4 servings.

Peanut Butter Brownie Cups

Prep: 30 min.   **Bake:** 15 min. + cooling

  1/2 cup peanut butter
  1/4 cup packed brown sugar
    2 tablespoons plus 1-1/2 cups all-purpose
      flour, *divided*
    3 squares (1 ounce *each*) unsweetened
      chocolate
  1/2 cup butter, cubed
    3 eggs
1-1/2 cups sugar
    2 tablespoons water
    1 teaspoon vanilla extract
    1 teaspoon baking powder

In a small mixing bowl, beat the peanut butter, brown sugar and 2 tablespoons flour until blended; set aside.

In a microwave-safe bowl, melt chocolate and butter. Stir until smooth; cool slightly. In a large mixing bowl, beat the eggs, sugar and water; stir in the chocolate mixture and vanilla. Combine the baking powder and remaining flour; add to the chocolate mixture and mix well.

Fill paper-lined muffin cups one-fourth full. Top each with about 1 teaspoon of peanut butter mixture. Spoon remaining batter over the top. Bake at 350° for 13-15 minutes or until centers are set (do not overbake). Cool for 5 minutes before removing from pans to wire racks. **Yield:** 2 dozen.

Editor's Note: Reduced-fat or generic brands of peanut butter are not recommended for this recipe.

Feed Your Family For $1.41 a Plate!

YOU CAN'T BEAT meat loaf when you want to serve your family a satisfying, homey meal. From Gail Graham of Maple Ridge, British Columbia, Traditional Meat Loaf is both a flavorful and budget-friendly main dish everyone will love.

To round out a comforting and economical menu, serve Parmesan Potato Balls from Pat Habiger of Spearville, Kansas and Green Bean Salad shared by Mildred Sherrer of Fort Worth, Texas.

Traditional Meat Loaf

Prep: 15 min. **Bake:** 1 hour + standing

- 1 egg, beaten
- 2/3 cup milk
- 3 slices bread, crumbled
- 1 cup (4 ounces) shredded cheddar cheese
- 1 medium onion, chopped
- 1/2 cup finely shredded carrot
- 1 teaspoon salt
- 1/4 teaspoon pepper
- 1-1/2 pounds ground beef
- 1/4 cup packed brown sugar
- 1/4 cup ketchup
- 1 tablespoon prepared mustard

In a large bowl, combine the first eight ingredients. Crumble beef over mixture and mix well. Shape into a loaf. Place in a greased 9-in. x 5-in. x 3-in. loaf pan.

In a small bowl, combine the brown sugar, ketchup and mustard; spread over loaf. Bake at 350° for 60-75 minutes or until no pink remains and a meat thermometer reads 160°. Drain. Let stand for 10 minutes before slicing. **Yield:** 6 servings.

Parmesan Potato Balls

Prep: 45 min. **Bake:** 15 min.

- 3 large potatoes, peeled and cubed
- 2 ounces cream cheese, softened
- 2 tablespoons milk
- 1 tablespoon butter, softened
- 1/4 cup grated Parmesan cheese
- 1 tablespoon chopped green onion
- 2-1/2 teaspoons onion soup mix
- 1/2 teaspoon salt
- 1/8 teaspoon hot pepper sauce

Dash pepper
- 1 egg, beaten
- 1-1/2 cups crushed cornflakes

Place potatoes in a large saucepan and cover with water. Bring to a boil. Reduce heat; cover and cook for 15-20 minutes or until tender. Drain.

In a large mixing bowl, mash the potatoes. Beat in the cream cheese, milk and butter until smooth. Stir in the Parmesan cheese, onion, soup mix, salt, hot pepper sauce and pepper. Shape into 1-1/2-in. balls.

Place the egg and cornflakes in separate shallow bowls. Dip potato balls in egg, then roll in crumbs.

Place on ungreased baking sheets. Bake at 400° for 15-18 minutes or until crisp and golden brown. **Yield:** 3 dozen.

Green Bean Salad

Prep: 25 min. + chilling

✓ **Uses less fat, sugar or salt. Includes Nutrition Facts and Diabetic Exchanges.**

- 1 pound fresh green beans
- 3 tablespoons olive oil
- 2 tablespoons balsamic vinegar
- 1/2 teaspoon Dijon mustard
- 1/4 teaspoon salt
- 1/8 teaspoon pepper
- 1 medium tomato, seeded and chopped
- 1 small onion, chopped
- 2 tablespoons minced fresh parsley
- 2 teaspoons capers, drained
- 1 hard-cooked egg, chopped

Place beans in a large saucepan and cover with water. Bring to a boil; cook, uncovered, for 8-10 minutes or until crisp-tender. Drain and immediately place beans in ice water. Drain and pat dry. Place in a large bowl.

In a small bowl, whisk the oil, vinegar, mustard, salt and pepper. Pour over beans and toss to coat. Add the tomato, onion, parsley and capers; gently toss. Cover and refrigerate for at least 2 hours. Just before serving, sprinkle with egg. **Yield:** 6 servings.

Nutrition Facts: 3/4 cup equals 107 calories, 8 g fat (1 g saturated fat), 35 mg cholesterol, 156 mg sodium, 8 g carbohydrate, 3 g fiber, 3 g protein. **Diabetic Exchanges:** 2 vegetable, 1-1/2 fat.

Feed Your Family For $1.90 a Plate!

DON'T SAVE HAM for Sunday dinner. At this price, you can ham it up any night of the week!

In Chilliwack, British Columbia, Cornelia White-way serves Barbecued Ham 'n' Peaches for a main dish that's both economical and irresistible.

To complete a memorable meal, assemble pretty Three-Fruit Salad from Sue Gronholz of Beaver Dam, Wisconsin and delight everyone at the table with a special-looking dessert—glazed Pear-Filled Bundt Cake from Barbara Sievert of Yorktown, Virginia.

Barbecued Ham 'n' Peaches

Prep/Total Time: 20 min.

1/4 **cup ketchup**
1 **tablespoon brown sugar**
1 **tablespoon cider vinegar**
2 **teaspoons Worcestershire sauce**
1 **teaspoon vegetable oil**
1/4 **teaspoon pepper**
4 **boneless fully cooked ham slices (4 ounces** *each***)**
1 **can (8-1/2 ounces) sliced peaches, drained**

In a small bowl, combine the ketchup, brown sugar, vinegar, Worcestershire sauce, oil and pepper; brush some of the mixture over ham slices. Place each slice on a greased 12-in. square of heavy-duty foil. Top with peaches; drizzle with remaining ketchup mixture.

Fold foil over ham and peaches and seal tightly. Grill, covered, over medium heat for 10-12 minutes or until heated through, turning packets once. **Yield:** 4 servings.

Three-Fruit Salad

Prep: 10 min. **Cook:** 15 min. + cooling

1 **can (20 ounces) pineapple chunks**
1/3 **cup sugar**
1 **tablespoon cornstarch**
1 **tablespoon lemon juice**
1/8 **teaspoon salt**
2 **eggs, lightly beaten**
1 **to 2 small ripe bananas, sliced**
1 **cup halved seedless red grapes**
1 **cup miniature marshmallows**
6 **cups torn lettuce**

Drain pineapple, reserving juice; set pineapple aside. In a small saucepan, combine the sugar, cornstarch, lemon juice, salt and reserved juice until smooth. Bring to a boil over medium heat, stirring until sugar is dissolved.

Remove from the heat. Stir a small amount of hot juice mixture into eggs; return all to the pan, stirring constantly. Bring to a gentle boil; cook and stir for 2 minutes. Transfer to a small bowl; cool.

Just before serving, in a bowl, combine the bananas, grapes, marshmallows, pineapple and cooled dressing. Serve over lettuce. **Yield:** 4 servings.

Pear-Filled Bundt Cake

Prep: 25 min. **Bake:** 35 min. + cooling

1/2 **cup butter, softened**
1/2 **cup sugar**
3 **eggs**
1/2 **teaspoon vanilla extract**
2 **cups all-purpose flour**
1 **teaspoon baking powder**
1 **teaspoon baking soda**
1/3 **cup orange juice**
FILLING:
1/2 **cup packed brown sugar**
1/2 **cup diced peeled ripe pear**
1/2 **cup sliced almonds**
2 **tablespoons all-purpose flour**
4-1/2 **teaspoons butter, melted**
1/2 **teaspoon ground cinnamon**
GLAZE:
1/2 **cup confectioners' sugar**
2-1/4 **teaspoons orange juice**

In a large mixing bowl, cream butter and sugar. Add eggs, one at a time, beating well after each addition. Beat in vanilla. Combine flour, baking powder and baking soda; add to creamed mixture alternately with orange juice.

Pour half of the batter into a greased 10-in. fluted tube pan. Combine the filling ingredients; sprinkle over the batter. Top with the remaining batter. Smooth top with a spatula.

Bake at 350° for 35-40 minutes or until a toothpick inserted near the center comes out clean. Cool for 10 minutes before removing from pan to a wire rack. Combine glaze ingredients; drizzle over cake. **Yield:** 16-20 servings.

Feed Your Family For $1.99 a Plate!

THERE'S NO NEED to scrimp on flavor thanks to this scrumptious (and inexpensive) supper that features Sausage with Apple Sauerkraut.

Carolyn Schmeling of Brookfield, Wisconsin created this variation on classic sausage and sauerkraut. With a hint of fennel, the sauerkraut is wonderfully sweet. For extra tang, drizzle on some mustard.

"My mother used to serve Crispy Potato Cubes when I was growing up, and she included the recipe in a cookbook she made for me when I got married," writes Jenelle Piepmeier of Severna Park, Maryland. "They fill the kitchen with a heavenly aroma."

Barbara Carlucci of Orange Park, Florida developed Green Beans with Walnuts in her kitchen and has prepared it many times. "It requires just 15 minutes," she says. "The sauce is yummy not only on green beans but also on fresh or frozen broccoli."

Sausage with Apple Sauerkraut

Prep: 10 min.   **Cook:** 35 min.

- 1 medium sweet onion, sliced
- 3 tablespoons butter
- 2 medium apples, peeled and shredded
- 1 tablespoon lemon juice
- 1 can (8 ounces) sauerkraut, rinsed and well drained
- 1/2 cup unsweetened apple juice
- 1 teaspoon caraway seeds
- 1/2 teaspoon fennel seed, crushed
- 1 package (16 ounces) smoked Polish sausage

In a large skillet, saute onion in butter for 15 minutes or until lightly browned.

In a bowl, toss apples with lemon juice. Add the apples, sauerkraut, apple juice, caraway and fennel to the onion. Bring to a boil. Reduce heat; cover and simmer for 15 minutes. Meanwhile, heat sausage according to package directions; cut into slices. Serve with sauerkraut. **Yield:** 4 servings.

Crispy Potato Cubes

Prep: 10 min.   **Bake:** 35 min.

- 1/3 cup all-purpose flour
- 3/4 teaspoon salt
- 1/2 teaspoon dried thyme
- 1/2 teaspoon dried marjoram
- 1/8 teaspoon pepper
- 5 medium potatoes, peeled and cut into 1-inch cubes
- 1/4 cup butter, melted
- 1 garlic clove, minced
- 1 bay leaf

In a large resealable plastic bag, combine the flour, salt, thyme, marjoram and pepper. Add potatoes; seal bag and shake to coat. Pour butter into a 13-in. x 9-in. x 2-in. baking dish; stir in the garlic. Add potatoes and bay leaf.

Cover and bake at 450° for 20 minutes. Uncover and stir; bake 15-20 minutes longer or until potatoes are lightly browned and tender. Discard bay leaf. **Yield:** 4 servings.

Green Beans with Walnuts

Prep/Total Time: 15 min.

- 1 package (16 ounces) frozen cut green beans
- 1/4 cup chopped walnuts, *divided*
- 1/4 cup teriyaki sauce
- 2 tablespoons butter, cubed

In 1-1/2-qt. microwave-safe dish, combine the beans, 2 tablespoons walnuts, teriyaki sauce and butter. Cover and microwave on high for 3 minutes; stir. Cook 5-6 minutes longer or until beans are tender. Sprinkle with remaining walnuts. **Yield:** 4 servings.

Editor's Note: This recipe was tested in a 1,100-watt microwave.

Apple a Day

A common ingredient in dishes ranging from desserts to fruit salads, apples are also a nutritious and wholesome addition to meaty main dishes such as Sausage with Apple Sauerkraut (recipe above left).

This popular, versatile fruit is free of fat, sodium and cholesterol. It's also full of fiber—one medium apple contains 5 grams.

Getting in the Theme of Things

Fun-filled foods make special occasions even more enjoyable. These themed meals are sure to thrill your family and friends.

GET CREATIVE. Clockwise from upper left: Classic Books Inspire Dinner (p. 300), Party Harvests Food and Fun (p. 302), Brunch Is Fit for a Queen (p. 298) and Peppermint Flavors Party (p. 292).

Peppermint Flavors Party

By Pam Lancaster, Willis, Virginia

A MOTHER-DAUGHTER luncheon with a peppermint theme turned out to be one of the best Christmas parties I ever hosted!

Held at church, the luncheon was inspired by a study of Proverbs 31 in the Bible, which says a virtuous woman's worth is "far above rubies." I thought the ruby red and white colors of peppermint candy would be especially appropriate for the occasion.

On the day of the gathering, I decked out the tables in white lace and festive red ribbons, making them look like giant peppermints.

Shortly before the guests arrived, I prepared Angel Sandwiches to symbolize the announcement of Christ's birth and Star Sandwiches to reflect how the three wise men were guided to baby Jesus. Jeweled Fruit Salad, served in glass dishes, added bright color and fresh flavor to the festive spread.

Our dessert was Frozen Peppermint Delight, a minty ice cream torte drizzled with hot fudge. This yummy treat can be made ahead of time.

I set out red-and-white-striped candles and scattered candy canes prettily across the tables. Canning jars filled with blooming poinsettias and peppermint sticks added a nice touch.

Peppermint easels for place cards (shown at left) were a snap to put together—I turned three plastic-wrapped candy canes upside down and hot-glued their straight ends together.

By the end of the party, the ladies were beaming and light-spirited. Everyone truly enjoyed an afternoon that uplifted and pampered them in the midst of what can be a busy holiday season.

Angel Sandwiches

Prep/Total Time: 25 min.

2 packages (3 ounces *each*) cream cheese, softened
1/4 cup orange marmalade
16 slices white bread

In a small mixing bowl, beat the cream cheese and marmalade until blended. Using a 2-in. angel-shaped cookie cutter, cut out 16 angels from bread. Spread half with cream cheese mixture; top with remaining bread. **Yield:** 8 sandwiches.

Star Sandwiches

Prep/Total Time: 25 min.

4 hard-cooked eggs, diced
1/2 cup mayonnaise
1 teaspoon Dijon mustard
1/4 teaspoon dill weed
1/8 teaspoon salt
1/8 teaspoon pepper
16 slices egg bread *or* white bread

In a bowl, combine the eggs, mayonnaise, mustard, dill, salt and pepper. Using a large star-shaped cookie cutter, cut out 16 stars from bread. Spread half with egg salad; top with remaining bread. **Yield:** 8 sandwiches.

Jeweled Fruit Salad

Prep/Total Time: 30 min.

1 cup (8 ounces) vanilla yogurt
2 tablespoons orange juice

1 tablespoon mayonnaise
1/2 teaspoon grated orange peel
1 pint fresh strawberries, sliced
1-1/2 cups green grapes, halved
1 can (11 ounces) mandarin oranges, drained
1 cup fresh *or* frozen blueberries
1 cup fresh *or* frozen raspberries
1 medium kiwifruit, peeled and chopped
1/4 cup fresh *or* frozen cranberries, thawed and halved

In a small bowl, combine the yogurt, orange juice, mayonnaise and orange peel. In a large serving bowl, combine the fruit. Serve with dressing. **Yield:** 12 servings.

Frozen Peppermint Delight

Prep: 25 min. + freezing

1 package (14 ounces) cream-filled chocolate sandwich cookies, crushed
1/2 cup butter, melted
1 gallon peppermint ice cream, slightly softened
1 carton (12 ounces) frozen whipped topping, thawed
1 jar (11-3/4 ounces) hot fudge ice cream topping, warmed
Crushed peppermint candy

In a bowl, combine cookie crumbs and butter. Press into an ungreased 13-in. x 9-in. x 2-in. dish. Spread ice cream over crust; top with whipped topping. Cover and freeze until solid. May be frozen for up to 2 months. Just before serving, drizzle with hot fudge topping and sprinkle with peppermint candy. **Yield:** 12-15 servings.

Snowman Favors Are Fun

To add whimsy to her peppermint party, Pam assembled a sweet snowman favor for each place setting.

Want to roll out your own? Use icing to "glue" together Life Savers, peppermint candies and gumdrops to form the snowmen's bodies. Use a toothpick to dab on colored icing for the eyes and nose, then tie on a string of red licorice for the scarf. (Note: Corn syrup also works well for gluing.)

Food and Music Are in Harmony

By Alcy Thorne, Los Molinos, California

YEARS AGO, my girlfriends and I started a monthly gourmet group. As February's hostess, I wanted to come up with a really sweet theme. "That Lovin' Feeling" turned out to be perfect.

The party centered on nostalgic love songs and a savory menu that consisted of That's Amore Lettuce Wedges, Love Me Tender Chicken Bake, Golden Oldie Veggies, And the Beets Go On and Heart of My Heart Tarts.

My dining table, decked in a musical and valentine motif, was a melodic match to the food. My son-in-law's trumpet, not played in years, became the centerpiece and provided the finishing touch.

That's Amore Lettuce Wedges

Prep/Total Time: 15 min.

    6 garlic cloves, minced
    1 teaspoon vegetable oil
1-1/2 cups mayonnaise
  1/2 cup chopped Italian stewed tomatoes
  1/4 cup tomato puree
    3 tablespoons red wine vinegar
  1/4 teaspoon salt
  1/4 teaspoon cayenne pepper

1/4 teaspoon pepper
1 medium head iceberg lettuce
1 cup chopped walnuts, toasted

In a small skillet, saute garlic in oil until tender. In a bowl, combine the garlic, mayonnaise, tomatoes, tomato puree, vinegar, salt, cayenne and pepper. Cut lettuce into eight wedges; drizzle with desired amount of dressing. Sprinkle with walnuts. Refrigerate leftover dressing. **Yield:** 8 servings (2-1/2 cups dressing).

Love Me Tender Chicken Bake

Prep: 25 min. **Bake:** 20 min.

2 medium onions, chopped
6 celery ribs, chopped
1/2 cup butter, cubed
5 cups cubed cooked chicken
3/4 cup water
2 cans (10-3/4 ounces *each*) condensed
  cream of mushroom soup, undiluted
1 cup (8 ounces) sour cream
2 cans (8 ounces *each*) sliced water
  chestnuts, drained
1 cup sliced almonds, toasted
1 cup crushed butter-flavored crackers

In a large skillet, saute onions and celery in butter until tender. Add chicken and water; heat through. Remove from the heat. Stir in the soup, sour cream, water chestnuts and almonds.

Pour the chicken mixture into eight greased 1-1/2-cup baking dishes. Sprinkle with the cracker crumbs. Bake, uncovered, at 400° for 20-25 minutes or until bubbly. **Yield:** 8 servings.

Golden Oldie Veggies

Prep: 15 min. **Bake:** 25 min.

3 medium parsnips, peeled and sliced
5 medium carrots, cut into chunks
2 medium turnips, peeled and cubed
12 brussels sprouts, halved
8 small red potatoes, quartered
2 tablespoons minced fresh rosemary
1/2 teaspoon salt
1/4 teaspoon pepper
1/4 cup olive oil

In a large bowl, combine the first eight ingredients. Drizzle with oil; toss to coat. Transfer to two greased 15-in. x 10-in. x 1-in. baking pans.

Bake, uncovered, at 400° for 25-35 minutes or until the vegetables are tender. **Yield:** 8 servings.

And the Beets Go On

Prep/Total Time: 15 min.

2 cans (13-1/4 ounces *each*) sliced beets,
  drained
1 can (16 ounces) whole-berry cranberry
  sauce
1/4 cup orange juice concentrate

In a large saucepan, combine the beets, cranberry sauce and orange juice concentrate. Cook and stir over low heat until heated through. Serve with a slotted spoon. **Yield:** 8 servings.

Heart of My Heart Tarts

Prep: 15 min. + chilling **Bake:** 25 min. + cooling

1 package (3 ounces) cream cheese,
  softened
1/2 cup butter, softened
1 cup all-purpose flour
FILLING:
1 egg
3/4 cup packed brown sugar
1 teaspoon vanilla extract
2/3 cup chopped walnuts

In a small mixing bowl, beat cream cheese and butter until fluffy; beat in flour until blended. Cover and refrigerate for 1 hour or until easy to handle.

Shape dough into eight balls; press onto the bottom and up the sides of greased heart-shaped or regular muffin cups. In a small mixing bowl, beat egg. Beat in brown sugar and vanilla until blended. Stir in walnuts. Spoon into cups.

Bake at 325° for 25-30 minutes or until lightly browned. Cool for 10 minutes before carefully removing from pan to a wire rack. **Yield:** 8 servings.

Cooking Club 'Hangs Out'

By Sheila Bradshaw, Powell, Ohio

MY DAUGHTER AND I started a monthly cooking club with some of our friends a few years ago. Every time we meet, we enjoy a new food theme complete with coordinating decorations.

Not long ago, it was my turn to host, and I was having trouble coming up with an idea we hadn't already used. I wondered if we were all "washed up" in the theme department...and with that in mind, I decided to have a Laundry Day.

I thought of serving an appetizer that had been softened, a soup made with something dried, a main dish that had been folded, a bread made with unbleached flour and a fluffed dessert.

Following that idea, my party menu featured Shrimp Spread, Chicken Wild Rice Soup, Spanish Rice Empanadas, Grandma's Apple Bread and Frozen Pumpkin Mousse Pie.

My decorations put a fun spin on the task of laundry. Folded towels became place mats, and matching washcloths were the napkins. The centerpiece was a small laundry basket filled with new socks and dishcloths, which I used as party favors.

Shrimp Spread

Prep/Total Time: 10 min.

✓ **Uses less fat, sugar or salt. Includes Nutrition Facts and Diabetic Exchanges.**

    1 package (8 ounces) cream cheese, softened
1-1/2 teaspoons lemon juice
    1 teaspoon Worcestershire sauce
    1/8 teaspoon salt
Dash white pepper
    1 can (6 ounces) small shrimp, rinsed and drained
    1 tablespoon finely chopped onion
Assorted crackers

In a small mixing bowl, beat the cream cheese, lemon juice, Worcestershire sauce, salt and pepper until smooth. Fold in the shrimp and onion. Refrigerate until serving. Serve with crackers. **Yield:** 1-1/2 cups.

    Nutrition Facts: 2 tablespoons (prepared with

reduced-fat cream cheese) equals 59 calories, 4 g fat (3 g saturated fat), 43 mg cholesterol, 277 mg sodium, 1 g carbohydrate, trace fiber, 5 g protein. **Diabetic Exchanges:** 1/2 lean meat, 1/2 fat.

Chicken Wild Rice Soup

Prep: 25 min.   **Cook:** 15 min.

- 1 package (6 ounces) long grain and wild rice mix
- 1/2 pound boneless skinless chicken breasts, cubed
- 1/2 pound sliced fresh mushrooms
- 1-1/4 cups chopped onions
- 2 garlic cloves, minced
- 1 tablespoon vegetable oil
- 2 cans (14-1/2 ounces *each*) chicken broth
- 1/2 teaspoon dried tarragon
- 1/4 teaspoon dried thyme
- 1/8 teaspoon pepper
- 2 tablespoons cornstarch
- 1 can (12 ounces) evaporated milk
- 6 tablespoons sliced green onions

Prepare rice mix according to package directions, omitting butter. Meanwhile, in a large saucepan, saute chicken, mushrooms, onions and garlic in oil until chicken is no longer pink and vegetables are tender.

Add the prepared rice, broth, tarragon, thyme and pepper; bring to a boil. Combine cornstarch and evaporated milk until smooth; stir into rice mixture.

Return the mixture to a boil; cook for 1-2 minutes or until slightly thickened. Garnish with green onions. **Yield:** 10 servings (2-1/2 quarts).

Spanish Rice Empanadas

Prep: 25 min.   **Bake:** 20 min.

- 1 package (5.6 *or* 6.8 ounces) Spanish rice and vermicelli mix
- 1-1/2 cups cubed cooked chicken
- 1 cup (4 ounces) shredded cheddar cheese
- 1/2 cup sliced green onions
- 1/4 cup chopped ripe olives
- 2 packages (15 ounces *each*) refrigerated pie pastry
- 1 egg yolk
- 1 tablespoon water

Prepare rice mix according to package directions, omitting butter or oil. In a large bowl, combine the chicken, cheese, onions and olives. Stir in prepared rice.

Roll each sheet of pastry into a 12-in. circle; place on greased baking sheets. Spoon rice mixture over half of each circle; spread to within 1 in. of edges. Fold pastry over filling; crimp edges to seal. Beat egg yolk and water; brush over tops.

Bake at 400° for 20-25 minutes or until golden brown. Cut empanadas in half to serve. **Yield:** 8 servings.

Grandma's Apple Bread

Prep: 20 min.   **Bake:** 35 min. + cooling

- 1-1/3 cups all-purpose flour
- 2/3 cup rye flour
- 1/2 cup sugar
- 2 teaspoons baking powder
- 1-1/2 teaspoons ground cinnamon
- 1/2 teaspoon baking soda
- 1/2 teaspoon salt
- 1 egg
- 3/4 cup unsweetened apple juice
- 3/4 cup sweetened applesauce
- 1/3 cup vegetable oil
- 1/2 cup chopped pecans

In a large bowl, combine the flours, sugar, baking powder, cinnamon, baking soda and salt. In another bowl, whisk the egg, apple juice, applesauce and oil until smooth. Stir into dry ingredients just until moistened. Fold in pecans.

Pour into two greased 8-in. x 4-in. x 2-in. loaf pans. Bake at 350° for 35-40 minutes or until a toothpick inserted near the center comes out clean. Cool for 10 minutes before removing from pans to wire racks. **Yield:** 2 loaves.

Frozen Pumpkin Mousse Pie

Prep: 25 min.   **Bake:** 10 min. + freezing

- 1-1/2 cups graham cracker crumbs
- 1/4 cup packed brown sugar
- 6 tablespoons butter, melted

FILLING:
- 1 can (15 ounces) solid-pack pumpkin
- 1 jar (7 ounces) marshmallow creme
- 1/4 cup packed brown sugar
- 2 teaspoons pumpkin pie spice
- 1 carton (12 ounces) frozen whipped topping, thawed, *divided*

In a bowl, combine crumbs, brown sugar and butter. Press onto bottom and up the sides of a greased 9-in. deep-dish pie plate. Bake at 350° for 7-9 minutes or until lightly browned. Cool completely on a wire rack.

For filling, in a large bowl, whisk the pumpkin, marshmallow creme, brown sugar and pumpkin pie spice. Fold in 3-1/2 cups topping. Spoon into crust. Cover; freeze for at least 4 hours or until firm. Garnish with remaining topping. **Yield:** 8-10 servings.

Brunch Is Fit for a Queen

By Janice Hose, Hagerstown, Maryland

HOSTING a Victorian-themed brunch had been on my wish list for quite some time. The impetus to plan it came recently when I completed my Depression ware set. Inviting a great group of friends, I set out to make it an elegant and fun event.

My Victorian Friendship Brunch menu included a variety of dainty yet easy foods I knew we'd all enjoy. Among these was my Sausage Egg Casserole, which features subtle bursts of mustard and savory pork sausage. I like to refrigerate it overnight and pop it in the oven shortly before guests arrive.

A sweet treat was the Crumble-Top Coffee Cake. Thinly sliced apples (I use Golden Delicious) are baked right in the cake, providing luscious flavor and moisture. The nutty golden crumb topping only adds to the dessert's popularity.

Baked Mixed Fruit provides a delightful change from the traditional fresh fruit bowl. Stewed in a rich, cinnamon-clove butter sauce, this flavorful dish elicited many oohs and aahs.

And if you like pecan pie, you'll want to try the Pecan Goody Cups. These miniature tarts feature pecan halves, a caramel-like filling, and a butter and cream cheese crust that melts right in your mouth.

Complementing the food was my collection of pink hobnail and blue bubble Depression dishes. They looked beautiful with the matching china, crystal and polished silver placed at each setting.

I arranged linens, lace, miniature hats, Victorian figurines, pearls and lovely teapots across the table.

Attributes of each friend were inscribed on hand-made name tags, which we later read out loud, inducing laughter and a tear or two.

Adding to the fun, each of my friends donned elegant gloves and Victorian-style hats for the occasion. One or two of the ladies even wore blouses fashioned in 19th-century style.

Each lady received a hand-cut glove embellished with flowers, ribbons and a charm. The ornate favors resembled lovely Victorian valentines.

By the end of this fancy, fun afternoon, each of my friends said she'd been treated like a queen.

Sausage Egg Casserole

Prep: 20 min. + chilling **Bake:** 30 min. + standing

10 eggs
2-1/4 cups milk
1-1/2 teaspoons ground mustard
1/2 teaspoon salt
1 pound bulk pork sausage, cooked and drained
2 cups cubed white bread
1-1/2 cups (6 ounces) shredded cheddar cheese

In a large mixing bowl, beat the eggs, milk, mustard and salt for 1 minute or until combined. Stir in the sausage, bread cubes and cheese. Pour into a greased 13-in. x 9-in. x 2-in. baking dish. Cover and refrigerate overnight.

Remove from the refrigerator 30 minutes before baking. Bake, uncovered, at 350° for 30-40 minutes or until a knife inserted near the center comes out clean. Let stand for 10 minutes before serving. **Yield:** 12 servings.

Crumble-Top Coffee Cake

Prep: 25 min. **Bake:** 55 min.

1/3 cup butter, softened
1/3 cup shortening
2 cups sugar
2 eggs
3 cups all-purpose flour
2 teaspoons baking powder
1 teaspoon ground cinnamon
1/2 teaspoon baking soda
1/4 teaspoon salt
1-3/4 cups buttermilk
2 medium apples, peeled and sliced
TOPPING:
1/2 cup all-purpose flour
1/2 cup packed brown sugar
1-1/2 teaspoons ground cinnamon
3 tablespoons cold butter
1/2 cup chopped walnuts

In a large mixing bowl, beat butter, shortening and sugar until fluffy. Add eggs one at a time, beating well after each addition. Combine the flour, baking powder, cinnamon, baking soda and salt; add to creamed mixture alternately with buttermilk.

Spoon half of the batter into a greased 13-in. x 9-in. x 2-in. baking dish. Top with apple slices; spread with remaining batter.

In a small bowl, combine the flour, brown sugar and cinnamon; cut in butter until crumbly. Stir in walnuts. Sprinkle over batter. Bake at 350° for 55-60 minutes or

until a toothpick inserted near the center comes out clean. **Yield:** 12 servings.

Baked Mixed Fruit

Prep/Total Time: 30 min.

1 can (30 ounces) whole plums, drained, halved and pitted
1 can (29 ounces) peach halves, drained
1 can (16 ounces) pear halves, drained
1 can (16 ounces) apricot halves, drained
1 can (8 ounces) sliced pineapple
1/3 cup packed brown sugar
1 tablespoon butter
1/2 teaspoon ground cinnamon
1/4 teaspoon ground cloves

In a greased 3-qt. baking dish, layer the plums, peaches, pears and apricots. Drain pineapple, reserving 1/2 cup juice. Place pineapple over fruit.

In a small saucepan, combine the brown sugar, butter, cinnamon, cloves and reserved pineapple juice. Cook and stir over medium heat until sugar is dissolved and butter is melted. Pour over fruit. Bake, uncovered, at 350° for 20-25 minutes or until heated through. **Yield:** 12-16 servings.

Pecan Goody Cups

Prep: 35 min. + chilling **Bake:** 20 min. per batch

3/4 cup butter, softened
2 packages (3 ounces *each*) cream cheese, softened
2 cups all-purpose flour
FILLING:
1-1/2 cups packed brown sugar
2 eggs
1 tablespoon butter, melted
48 pecan halves

In a large mixing bowl, cream butter and cream cheese. Gradually add flour, beating until mixture forms a ball. Cover and refrigerate for 15 minutes.

For the filling, in a small bowl, combine the brown sugar, eggs and butter; set aside. Roll the dough into 48 balls. Press the balls onto the bottom and up the sides of greased miniature muffin cups. Spoon a scant teaspoon of the filling into each cup. Top each with a pecan half.

Bake at 350° for 20-25 minutes or until golden brown. Cool for 2-3 minutes before removing from pans to wire racks. **Yield:** 4 dozen.

Classic Books Inspire Dinner

By Sue Davis, Wausau, Wisconsin

LITTLE HOUSE on the Prairie was the perfect theme for my friend Sharon's 80th-birthday party. Sharon, who practically knows every *Little House* book by heart, arrived at the shindig dressed as Laura Ingalls Wilder, the famous author.

Also a *Little House* fan, I enjoyed paging through my old books and selecting recipes for the party.

My "pioneer" menu included a variety of authentic foods right from Ma Ingalls' kitchen—Old-Fashioned Chicken Potpie, Creamed Carrots, Fried Apples and Onions, and Blueberry Quick Bread.

All four recipes were adapted from *Farmer Boy*, the third book in the series. We had fun locating the recipes in the book and reading excerpts.

Old-Fashioned Chicken Potpie

Prep: 1-1/2 hours   **Bake:** 40 min. + standing

   3 **to 4 pounds bone-in chicken breast halves**
1-1/2 **quarts water**
   1 **small onion, peeled**
   1 **celery rib**
   1 **large carrot**
1-1/2 **teaspoons salt,** *divided*
Pastry for double-crust pie (9 inches)
  1/2 **cup all-purpose flour**
  1/2 **teaspoon onion salt**
  1/2 **teaspoon celery salt**
  1/4 **teaspoon pepper**

In a large kettle, bring the chicken, water, onion, celery, carrot and 1/2 teaspoon salt to a boil. Reduce heat; cover and simmer for 50-60 minutes or until chicken is tender.

Remove chicken and vegetables from broth. Set aside until cool enough to handle. Meanwhile, line a 9-in. deep-dish pie plate with bottom pastry; trim even with edge of plate. Set aside.

Remove chicken from bones; discard skin and bones and cut chicken into cubes. Set aside. Chop the onion, celery and carrot. Strain broth and skim fat; set broth aside.

In a small bowl, combine the flour, onion salt, celery salt, pepper and remaining salt. Add 1/2 cup broth; whisk until smooth. In a large saucepan, bring 3 cups of broth to a boil; whisk in the flour mixture. Cook and stir for 2 minutes or until thickened. Remove from the heat; add chicken and vegetables. Pour into crust.

Roll out remaining pastry to fit top of pie; place over filling. Trim, seal and flute edges. Cut slits in top. Cover edges loosely with foil. Bake at 400° for 40-45 minutes or until golden brown and filling is bubbly. Let stand for 15 minutes before cutting. **Yield:** 8 servings.

Creamed Carrots

Prep/Total Time: 20 min.

   3 **pounds fresh carrots, cut into 1/4-inch**
     slices
   1 **cup chicken broth**
   2 **tablespoons butter**
   2 **tablespoons all-purpose flour**
  1/4 **teaspoon salt**
  1/8 **teaspoon pepper**
1-1/4 **cups half-and-half cream**

In a large saucepan, bring carrots and broth to a boil. Reduce heat; cover and simmer for 8-10 minutes or until carrots are crisp-tender.

Meanwhile, in a small saucepan, melt butter. Stir in the flour, salt and pepper until smooth. Gradually add cream. Bring to a boil; cook and stir for 2 minutes or until thickened. Drain carrots. Drizzle with cream sauce and toss to coat. **Yield:** 8 servings.

Fried Apples and Onions

Prep/Total Time: 30 min.

   6 **medium onions, sliced and separated into**
     rings
   2 **tablespoons butter**
   6 **medium tart red apples, cut into 1/4-inch**
     wedges
   3 **tablespoons brown sugar**

In a large skillet, cook the onions in butter over medium heat for 3-5 minutes. Top with apples; sprinkle with brown sugar. Cover and cook for 15-20 minutes or until apples are tender. **Yield:** 8 servings.

Blueberry Quick Bread

Prep: 20 min.   **Bake:** 50 min. + cooling

   1 **egg**
   1 **cup milk**
   3 **tablespoons vegetable oil**
   2 **cups all-purpose flour**
   1 **cup sugar**
2-1/2 **teaspoons baking powder**
  1/2 **teaspoon salt**
   2 **cups fresh *or* frozen blueberries**
VANILLA SAUCE:
   1 **cup sugar**
   1 **tablespoon cornstarch**
   1 **cup heavy whipping cream**
  1/2 **cup butter, cubed**

In a large mixing bowl, beat the egg, milk and oil. Combine the flour, sugar, baking powder and salt; gradually add to egg mixture, beating just until combined. Fold in blueberries.

Pour the batter into a greased 9-in. x 5-in. x 3-in. loaf pan. Bake at 350° for 50-55 minutes or until a toothpick inserted near the center comes out clean. Cool for 10 minutes before removing from pan to a wire rack to cool completely.

For sauce, combine sugar and cornstarch in a saucepan. Stir in cream until smooth; add butter. Bring to a boil over medium heat; cook and stir for 2 minutes or until thickened. Serve with blueberry bread. **Yield:** 8 servings (2 cups sauce).

Editor's Note: If using frozen blueberries, do not thaw before adding to batter.

Party Harvests Food and Fun

By Sandra McKenzie, Braham, Minnesota

OUR FAMILY'S harvest party is always held in October, when the colorful trees here in Minnesota have hit their peak.

Every year, we meet at my parents' farm for a mouth-watering spread of seasonal foods, a bonfire and a tractor-drawn hayride through the woods. Because the fall celebration was my idea, I naturally became the menu planner.

The air can be brisk in October, so I always make Slow-Cooked Chili to warm us up. Packed with plenty of ground beef, beans, tomatoes and spices, this chili is hearty and filling.

The kids really love my Halloween Chocolate

Lollipops. The spooky ghost and jack-o'-lantern shapes are a hit, and the white and dark chocolate make a pretty pair. I purchased the chocolate molds from our local bakery.

Another recipe I make each year is my Pumpkin Sheet Cake. The cream cheese frosting complements the spice cake, and the pumpkin-shaped candies are so cute on top! We cozy up to the campfire with this dessert and mugs of hot Spiced Green Tea, a unique blend of tea, citrus juices and spices.

The fall season just wouldn't be the same if we didn't meet on the farm for our harvest party. It's truly my family's favorite time of year!

Slow-Cooked Chili

Prep: 25 min.   **Cook:** 6 hours

2 pounds ground beef
1/2 cup chopped onion
2 garlic cloves, minced
2 cans (16 ounces *each*) dark red kidney beans, rinsed and drained
2 cans (16 ounces *each*) light red kidney beans, rinsed and drained
2 cans (14-1/2 ounces *each*) stewed tomatoes, cut up
1 can (15 ounces) pizza sauce
1 can (4 ounces) chopped green chilies
4 teaspoons chili powder
1 teaspoon dried basil
1/2 teaspoon salt
1/8 teaspoon pepper

In a Dutch oven, cook the beef, onion and garlic over medium heat until meat is no longer pink; drain. Transfer to a 5-qt. slow cooker; stir in the remaining ingredients. Cover and cook on low for 6 hours. **Yield:** 14 servings.

Halloween Chocolate Lollipops

Prep: 30 min. + freezing

1-1/2 cups vanilla *or* white chips
1/8 teaspoon coconut extract
Ghost lollipop/candy molds
20 lollipop sticks
1-1/2 cups milk chocolate chips
1/8 teaspoon orange extract
Pumpkin lollipop/candy molds

In microwave-safe bowl, melt vanilla chips; stir until smooth. Stir in coconut extract. Cut a small hole in the corner of a pastry or plastic bag; insert #3 round pastry tip. Transfer melted vanilla chips to bag. Fill ghost molds three-fourths full. Press a lollipop stick into each ghost; top with a small amount of melted chips. Freeze until firm, about 15 minutes. Set remaining melted chips aside.

Melt milk chocolate chips; stir until smooth. Stir in orange extract. Prepare a second pastry or plastic bag; insert tip. Transfer melted chocolate to bag. Fill pumpkin molds three-fourths full. Press a lollipop stick into each pumpkin; top with a small amount of chocolate. Freeze until firm, about 15 minutes. Set remaining melted chocolate aside.

Remove lollipops from molds. Use reserved melted chips to add faces to ghosts and pumpkins. Refrigerate until serving. **Yield:** 20 lollipops.

Pumpkin Sheet Cake

Prep: 20 min.   **Bake:** 20 min. + cooling

1-1/2 cups sugar
1 can (15 ounces) solid-pack pumpkin
1 cup vegetable oil
4 eggs
2 cups all-purpose flour
2 teaspoons baking powder
2 teaspoons ground cinnamon
1 teaspoon baking soda
1/4 teaspoon salt
1/4 teaspoon ground cloves
CREAM CHEESE FROSTING:
2 packages (3 ounces *each*) cream cheese, softened
1/2 cup butter, softened
2 teaspoons vanilla extract
4-1/2 cups confectioners' sugar
24 candy pumpkins

In a large mixing bowl, beat the sugar, pumpkin, oil and eggs. Combine the flour, baking powder, cinnamon, baking soda, salt and cloves; gradually add to pumpkin mixture and mix well.

Pour batter into a greased 15-in. x 10-in. x 1-in. baking pan. Bake at 350° for 20-25 minutes or until a toothpick inserted near the center comes out clean. Cool on a wire rack.

For frosting, in a small mixing bowl, beat the cream cheese, butter and vanilla until smooth. Gradually beat in confectioners' sugar. Spread over cake; garnish with candy pumpkins. Cover and refrigerate until serving. **Yield:** 24 servings.

Spiced Green Tea

Prep/Total Time: 25 min.

5 cups boiling water
5 individual green tea bags
1/2 cup sugar
1/3 cup lemon juice
1/4 teaspoon pumpkin pie spice
5 cups unsweetened apple juice
2 cups cranberry juice

In a Dutch oven or large kettle, bring water to a boil. Remove from the heat; add tea bags. Cover and steep for 8 minutes. Discard tea bags.

Add sugar, lemon juice and pumpkin pie spice to tea; stir until sugar is dissolved. Stir in apple juice and cranberry juice. Serve warm or cold. **Yield:** 12 servings (3 quarts).

Halloween Scares Up Festive Fare

IT WAS a tricky job, but our Test Kitchen staff didn't get spooked! They put together this fun Halloween-theme meal using creepy recipes from readers.

"My annual Halloween bash wouldn't be the same without my Yummy Mummy Cheese Spread," says Rebecca Eremich of Barberton, Ohio. "When kids see the mummy, they just stare—totally amazed!"

Worms for Brains is a quick and easy main dish Julianna Tazzia serves her family each year on October 31. "I can get the kids ready for trick-or-treating, and I still have time to get this hot dish on the table," she shares from West Bloomfield, Michigan.

Jill Wright's Tombstone Treats can double as cute place cards. "My brother loves rice cereal bars, and my mom loves sugar cookies," says the Dixon, Illinois cook. "These goodies incorporate both."

With a little help from her sisters, Amy McCoy of Huntington Beach, California developed Trick-or-Treat Cake. It calls for a standard 9-in. x 13-in. pan, so you can easily conjure up this delightful dessert.

Yummy Mummy Cheese Spread

Prep/Total Time: 30 min.

- **2** port wine cheese logs (12 ounces *each*)
- **1** package (8 ounces) cream cheese, softened
- **1** tablespoon milk
- **2** whole peppercorns
- **1** pimiento strip

Cut the cheese logs into pieces for mummy's head, body, arms and legs; arrange the cheese pieces in a mummy shape on a serving plate.

In small mixing bowl, beat cream cheese and milk. Cut a small hole in the corner of a pastry or plastic bag; insert basket weave tip #47. Pipe rows across the mummy, creating bandages. Add peppercorns for eyes and a pimiento strip for mouth. Chill until serving. **Yield:** 1 cheese log.

Worms for Brains

Prep: 30 min.   **Cook:** 15 min.

**8 to 10 medium sweet orange peppers
1 package (16 ounces) spaghetti
1 pound ground beef
1 jar (26 ounces) spaghetti sauce**

Cut tops off peppers and set aside; remove seeds and membranes. Cut a jack-o'-lantern face on one side of each pepper; set aside.

Cook spaghetti according to package directions. Meanwhile, in a Dutch oven, cook beef over medium heat until no longer pink; drain.

Drain spaghetti and add to beef. Stir in spaghetti sauce; heat through. Spoon into peppers; replace tops. **Yield:** 8-10 servings.

Tombstone Treats

Prep: 45 min.   **Bake:** 10 min. + cooling

**3 tablespoons butter
4 cups miniature marshmallows
7-1/2 cups crisp rice cereal
1 tube (18 ounces) refrigerated sugar cookie dough
2/3 cup all-purpose flour
32 wooden toothpicks
1 teaspoon water
4 drops green food coloring
1-1/2 cups flaked coconut
Black decorating gel
Vanilla frosting
1 cup (6 ounces) semisweet chocolate chips, melted
Candy pumpkins**

In large saucepan over low heat, melt butter. Stir in marshmallows until completely melted. Remove from the heat. Stir in cereal until well coated. Press into a greased 13-in. x 9-in. x 2-in. pan with a buttered spatula. Cool.

In a large mixing bowl, beat cookie dough and flour until combined. On a lightly floured surface, roll dough to 1/4-in. thickness. Trace tombstone pattern onto waxed paper; cut out 16 tombstones from dough. Place 2 in. apart on ungreased baking sheets.

Along bottom edge of each cookie, insert two toothpicks halfway into dough, positioning them as shown on pattern. Bake at 350° for 8-10 minutes or until edges are golden brown. Remove to wire racks to cool.

In a large resealable plastic bag, combine water and green food coloring. Add coconut; seal bag and shake to coat. Toast coconut; set aside. Using black gel, tint frosting gray. Frost cookies; decorate with black gel.

Cut cereal bars into 3-in. x 2-in. rectangles; spread with melted chocolate. Using toothpicks, insert cookies into cereal bars. Decorate with coconut and candies as desired. **Yield:** 16 servings.

Trick-or-Treat Cake

Prep: 30 min.   **Bake:** 35 min. + cooling

**1 package (18-1/4 ounces) chocolate cake mix
2 cans (16 ounces *each*) vanilla frosting
1 tube *each* black, orange and green decorating gel
Assorted candies**

Prepare and bake cake according to package directions, using a greased 13-in. x 9-in. x 2-in. baking pan. Cool for 10 minutes before removing from pan to a wire rack to cool completely.

Transfer the cake to a 20-in. x 17-in. covered board. Create a zigzag pattern on one short end of cake to resemble the top of a treat bag. Frost top and sides of cake with frosting; decorate as desired with gels and candies. **Yield:** 12 servings.

Tombstone Pattern

To use the pattern below to shape the cookie tombstones for the Tombstone Treats (recipe at left), simply trace the pattern onto waxed paper and cut it out with a scissors.

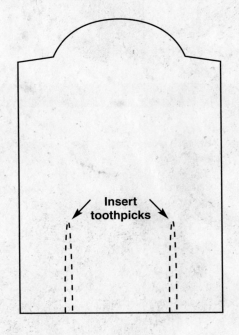

Insert toothpicks

Substitutions & Equivalents

Equivalent Measures

3 teaspoons	=	1 tablespoon	16 tablespoons	=	1 cup
4 tablespoons	=	1/4 cup	2 cups	=	1 pint
5-1/3 tablespoons	=	1/3 cup	4 cups	=	1 quart
8 tablespoons	=	1/2 cup	4 quarts	=	1 gallon

Food Equivalents

Grains

Macaroni	1 cup (3-1/2 ounces) uncooked	=	2-1/2 cups cooked
Noodles, Medium	3 cups (4 ounces) uncooked	=	4 cups cooked
Popcorn	1/3 to 1/2 cup unpopped	=	8 cups popped
Rice, Long Grain	1 cup uncooked	=	3 cups cooked
Rice, Quick-Cooking	1 cup uncooked	=	2 cups cooked
Spaghetti	8 ounces uncooked	=	4 cups cooked

Crumbs

Bread	1 slice	=	3/4 cup soft crumbs, 1/4 cup fine dry crumbs
Graham Crackers	7 squares	=	1/2 cup finely crushed
Buttery Round Crackers	12 crackers	=	1/2 cup finely crushed
Saltine Crackers	14 crackers	=	1/2 cup finely crushed

Fruits

Bananas	1 medium	=	1/3 cup mashed
Lemons	1 medium	=	3 tablespoons juice, 2 teaspoons grated peel
Limes	1 medium	=	2 tablespoons juice, 1-1/2 teaspoons grated peel
Oranges	1 medium	=	1/4 to 1/3 cup juice, 4 teaspoons grated peel

Vegetables

Cabbage	1 head	=	5 cups shredded	Green Pepper	1 large	=	1 cup chopped
Carrots	1 pound	=	3 cups shredded	Mushrooms	1/2 pound	=	3 cups sliced
Celery	1 rib	=	1/2 cup chopped	Onions	1 medium	=	1/2 cup chopped
Corn	1 ear fresh	=	2/3 cup kernels	Potatoes	3 medium	=	2 cups cubed

Nuts

Almonds	1 pound	=	3 cups chopped	Pecan Halves	1 pound	=	4-1/2 cups chopped
Ground Nuts	3-3/4 ounces	=	1 cup	Walnuts	1 pound	=	3-3/4 cups chopped

Easy Substitutions

When you need...		*Use...*
Baking Powder	1 teaspoon	1/2 teaspoon cream of tartar + 1/4 teaspoon baking soda
Buttermilk	1 cup	1 tablespoon lemon juice *or* vinegar + enough milk to measure 1 cup (let stand 5 minutes before using)
Cornstarch	1 tablespoon	2 tablespoons all-purpose flour
Honey	1 cup	1-1/4 cups sugar + 1/4 cup water
Half-and-Half Cream	1 cup	1 tablespoon melted butter + enough whole milk to measure 1 cup
Onion	1 small, chopped (1/3 cup)	1 teaspoon onion powder *or* 1 tablespoon dried minced onion
Tomato Juice	1 cup	1/2 cup tomato sauce + 1/2 cup water
Tomato Sauce	2 cups	3/4 cup tomato paste + 1 cup water
Unsweetened Chocolate	1 square (1 ounce)	3 tablespoons baking cocoa + 1 tablespoon shortening *or* oil
Whole Milk	1 cup	1/2 cup evaporated milk + 1/2 cup water

General Recipe Index

*This handy index lists every recipe by food category, major ingredient
and/or cooking method, so you can easily locate recipes to suit your needs.*

✓ Recipe includes Nutrition Facts and Diabetic Exchanges.

✓ *Recipe includes Nutrition Facts and Diabetic Exchanges.*

✓ Recipe includes Nutrition Facts and Diabetic Exchanges.

✓ Recipe includes Nutrition Facts and Diabetic Exchanges.

✓ Recipe includes Nutrition Facts and Diabetic Exchanges.

✓ *Recipe includes Nutrition Facts and Diabetic Exchanges.*

✓ *Recipe includes Nutrition Facts and Diabetic Exchanges.*

✓ Recipe includes Nutrition Facts and Diabetic Exchanges.

✓ *Recipe includes Nutrition Facts and Diabetic Exchanges.*

✓ Recipe includes Nutrition Facts and Diabetic Exchanges.

Alphabetical Recipe Index

This handy index lists every recipe in alphabetical order so you can easily find your favorites.

A

Almond-Butter Cookie Bouquet, 111
Almond Cookies, 279
Almond-Lemon Pound Cake, 179
Almond Pastry Puffs, 101
Almond-Topped Pumpkin Cheesecake, 146
And the Beets Go On, 295
Angel Sandwiches, 293
Antipasto Salad, 154
✓ Apple 'n' Carrot Slaw, 167
Apple 'n' Prosciutto Sandwiches, 37
Apple Pizza, 144
Apple-Raisin Bundt Cake, 217
Apple Streusel Muffins, 103
Apple-Stuffed French Toast, 84
Apple Turnovers, 147
Asparagus Cheese Triangles, 18
Asparagus Ham Crepes, 79
✓ Asparagus Tomato Salad, 25
Autumn Tossed Salad, 33
Avocado Eggs Benedict, 72

B

Bacon Honey Walleye, 65
Bacon Squash Saute, 190
Bacon-Wrapped Beef Fillets, 274
Bacon-Wrapped Cajun Jalapenos, 16
Baked Bananas in Orange Sauce, 177
Baked Mixed Fruit, 299
Baked Spaghetti, 167
Banana Cream Pie, 191
Bananas Foster, 271
Barbecued Beef Sandwiches, 166
Barbecued Ham 'n' Peaches, 287
Barbecued Pork Sandwiches, 172
✓ Basil-Cheese Bread Strips, 94
✓ Basil Cream Cheese Bruschetta, 14
Basil Turkey Soup, 272
✓ Beef Fajitas with Cilantro Sauce, 64
✓ Beef Gyros, 43
Beef Kabob Spinach Salad, 30
✓ Beef Stew with Dilly Dumplings, 88
Beef Stir-Fry on a Stick, 65
Belgian-Style Carrot Coins, 283

Berry-Almond Sandwich Cookies, 108
Berry Cheesecake Dessert, 146
Berry Cheesecake Muffins, 99
Berry-Patch Brownie Pizza, 143
✓ Black Bean Shrimp Salad, 31
BLT Dip, 7
Blue Cheese Bacon Dressing, 32
Blue Cheese Spinach Salad, 153
Blueberry Quick Bread, 301
Blueberry Sour Cream Coffee Cake, 102
✓ Bow Tie Seafood Salad, 168
✓ Broccoli Chowder, 38
Broccoli Salad, 268
Broccoli Scalloped Potatoes, 49
Broiled Buttery Shrimp, 11
Bruschetta, 266
Buttercup Yeast Bread, 173
Buttermilk Pancakes, 166
Butternut Squash Cake Roll, 132

C

Caesar Salad, 31
Cajun Shrimp Skewers, 81
Candied Carrots, 198
Candied Fruit Cranberry Chutney, 48
Caramel Apple Crisp, 145
Caramel Chocolate Trifle, 169
Caramel Pecan Candy, 114
Caramel Pecan Pie, 125
Caramel Pretzel Sticks, 10
Caraway Pot Roast, 281
✓ Caraway Rye Bread, 168
Cauliflower Ham Casserole, 70
Cheddar-Ham Oven Omelet, 156
Cheddar Ham Strata, 73
Cheesy Onion Breadsticks, 254
Cherry Cheesecake Mousse, 137
Cherry Coffee Cake, 233
Cherry Ribbon Salad, 157
Chewy Apple Oatmeal Cookies, 173
Chicago-Style Stuffed Pizza, 83
Chicken Amandine, 256
Chicken and Asparagus Kabobs, 61
Chicken Broccoli Calzones, 37
✓ Chicken Broccoli Toss, 24
✓ Chicken Fajita Pizza, 71

Chicken Florentine Panini, 251
✓ Chicken in Mushroom Sauce, 67
✓ Chicken Stew, 68
Chicken Veggie Salad Plate, 177
Chicken Wild Rice Soup, 297
Chinese New Year Skillet, 279
Chippy Peanut Butter Cookies, 113
Chocolate Almond Ice Cream, 147
Chocolate Chip Mousse, 255
Chocolate-Covered Cherry Brownies, 151
Chocolate-Covered Strawberries Cake, 126
Chocolate-Filled Meringue Shells, 141
Chocolate Hazelnut Parfaits, 249
Chocolate Pretzels, 110
Chocolate Zucchini Cake, 131
Christmas Breakfast Casserole, 216
Christmas Cutouts, 108
Chunky Apple Cake, 133
Chunky Beef Stew, 252
✓ Chunky Crawfish Spread, 220
Chunky Drop Cookies, 115
Cider Wassail, 217
Cinnamon Apple Cheesecake, 144
Cinnamon Chocolate Nachos, 11
✓ Cinnamon Mocha Coffee, 10
Cinnamon Raisin Strata, 90
Cinnamon-Sugar Rhubarb Cake, 131
Cinnamon Swirl Rolls, 262
Citrus Quencher, 220
Cloverleaf Bran Rolls, 96
Cocoa for a Crowd, 155
Coconut Chocolate Pie, 132
Colorful Chicken Fettuccine, 83
Colorful Couscous, 274
Comforting Broccoli Casserole, 210
Comforting Chicken Casserole, 158
Confetti Couscous, 241
Confetti Scrambled Eggs, 262
Corn Bread Pudding, 49
Corn Pudding, 198
Cornmeal Ham Cakes, 72
Crab 'n' Brie Strudel Slices, 20
Cran-Orange Pork Tenderloin, 270
Cran-Orange Relish, 173
Cranberry Almond Muffins, 94
✓ Cranberry Cheesecake Tart, 139
Cranberry Feta Cheesecake, 8
Cranberry Ham Loaf, 67
Cranberry Pumpkin Bread, 236

✓ Recipe includes Nutrition Facts and Diabetic Exchanges.

✓ *Recipe includes Nutrition Facts and Diabetic Exchanges.*

✓ Recipe includes Nutrition Facts and Diabetic Exchanges.

✓ Recipe includes Nutrition Facts and Diabetic Exchanges.